BROUGHT FORTH ON THIS CONTINENT

Authored, coauthored, edited, or coedited by Harold Holzer

BROUGHT FORTH ON THIS CONTINENT

ABRAHAM LINCOLN
AND AMERICAN IMMIGRATION

HAROLD HOLZER

DUTTON

DUTTON
An imprint of Penguin Random House LLC
penguinrandomhouse.com

LIBRARY OF CONGRESS CATALOGING-IN-PUBLICATION DATA
has been applied for.

ISBN 9780451489012 (hardcover)
ISBN 9780451489029 (ebook)

Printed in the United States of America

1st Printing

BOOK DESIGN BY ELKE SIGAL

While the author has made every effort to provide accurate telephone numbers, internet addresses, and other contact information at the time of publication, neither the publisher nor the author assumes any responsibility for errors or for changes that occur after publication. Further, the publisher does not have any control over and does not assume any responsibility for author or third-party websites or their content.

In loving memory of the immigrant grandparents
who made me American

Eva Goodman Holzer, Romania (ca. 1880–1965)

David Holzer, Austria, now Ukraine (1876–1952)

Fannie Eder Last, Galicia, now Poland (1874–1927)

Harry Last, Austria, now Ukraine (1873–1947)

CONTENTS

For the Encouragement of Immigration

I regard our emigrants as one of the principal replenishing streams appointed by Providence to repair the ravages of internal war, and its wastes of national strength and health.
—ABRAHAM LINCOLN, ANNUAL MESSAGE TO CONGRESS, DECEMBER 6, 1864[1]

Even under ideal circumstances, it would have been difficult for Abraham Lincoln to surpass his recent masterpiece at Gettysburg. And now, with a fresh rhetorical challenge awaiting him, he fell ill. Lincoln arrived back in Washington from Pennsylvania late on November 19, 1863, suffering from variola, a supposedly mild form of smallpox that proved severe enough to send the exhausted orator to his sickbed for weeks. By some accounts, Lincoln did not return to his White House desk until mid-December.[2] Tellingly, the valet who tended him during his convalescence, a Black man, caught smallpox, too—and died.

Debility notwithstanding, Lincoln faced an unavoidable deadline for not only a new manuscript but also a much lengthier one. With the thirty-eighth session of the House and Senate set to convene on December 7, the President was expected to present his Annual Message to Congress—the equivalent of today's State of the Union address—the following day. This would be his third such message, and the first to a Congress whose Republican strength had shriveled following setbacks in the most recent midterm elections.[3]

Nonetheless, Lincoln intended the message to include something dramatic: a historic proposal to encourage—and perhaps even financially underwrite—foreign immigration to the United States. By some accounts, Lincoln composed the entire message in bed.

The remarks for Gettysburg had been, in Lincoln's folksy description, "short, short, short": barely 270 words.[4] No such brevity ever satisfied Congress. By custom, the House and Senate anticipated a detailed summary on both foreign and domestic affairs. To be expected was a full accounting of federal spending as well as an update on the ongoing war against the Rebels. Congress would particularly desire reports on the enforcement of the President's Emancipation Proclamation ("I shall not attempt to retract or modify it," he would pledge) and on the first months of African American military recruitment (which, he would report, "gave to the future a new aspect").[5]

Tradition also called for the President to use this yearly opportunity to specify his legislative priorities. Here is where the bedridden Lincoln summoned what strength he could muster to craft a historically bold proposal. "I again submit to your consideration," he declared twenty paragraphs into his text, "the expediency of establishing a system for the encouragement of immigration."[6]

From 1830 through the outbreak of the American Civil War, nearly ten million Europeans had migrated to the United States, North as well as South, forever upending the demography, culture, and voting patterns of the nation, especially in its teeming urban centers. In the wake of such overwhelming change, resistance to immigration and immigrants metastasized until forces arose that were determined not only to restrict foreigners from entering the country but to disenfranchise, demonize, and, occasionally, terrorize those who had already arrived, settled, and earned citizenship here. And still the refugees poured across oceans and borders to reach our shores, their growing numbers inevitably challenging, and ultimately redefining, what it meant to be American.

Only when civil war broke out in 1861 did foreign migration to the United States slow significantly. Prospective immigrants understandably shrank from the notion of abandoning one troubled country to relocate to another. To some Americans, the reduction in new foreign arrivals came as an answered prayer. For decades, immigration, particularly by Catholics, had stirred resistance, resentment, and, in some cases, violence, destruction, and death. Politically, these tensions split and ultimately destroyed the old Whig Party, in which Lincoln had spent most of his political career, inspiring anti-immigration nativists to form a political organization of their own. The realignment had driven many immigrants into the ranks of the Democrats, who welcomed new arrivals with a warm embrace and a swift path to citizenship and voter registration. The issue roiled the country and exposed an ugly vein of bigotry in the American body politic. And its intractability deflected mainstream attention from the country's original sin: slavery.

Now President Lincoln looked beyond the longtime national divide over immigration to propose his revolutionary idea. Although he reported in his message that refugees were "again flowing with greater freedom" into America, their numbers had yet to reach their robust, if bitterly contested, prewar levels. And the reduction was causing what Lincoln called "a great deficiency of laborers in every field of industry, especially in agriculture and in our mines, as well of iron and coal as of the precious metals." In other words, America could no longer rely on American workers to fill American jobs. Employers needed to look elsewhere—namely overseas—for manpower.

True enough, the Lincoln administration had in a sense contributed to this crisis-level "deficiency." There were now as many as a million men enrolled in the Union armed forces to fight the Confederacy, and since spring, the newly introduced military draft had been wresting laborers from farms and factories and redeploying them into the army. As Lincoln saw matters, their necessary absence from the home front now threatened national productivity—of civilian goods as well as war matériel. Whether the situation might ease longtime hostility to foreign laborers would be left for another day. First, Lincoln urgently wanted robust immigration to resume—even if the government had to provide the means to accelerate it.

As Lincoln forcibly argued in his message, the time had come to regard immigrants not as interlopers but as assets; not as a drain on public resources but as a "source of national wealth and strength." He expressed it this way: "While the demand for labor is thus increased here, tens of thousands of persons, destitute of remunerative occupation, are thronging our foreign consulates, and offering to emigrate to the United States if essential, but very cheap, assistance can be afforded them. It is easy to see that, under the sharp discipline of civil war, the nation is beginning a new life. This noble effort demands the aid, and ought to receive the attention and support of the government."[7]

· · ·

Lincoln might not have realized it, but, in making his appeal, the sixteenth president echoed sentiments that the first president had expressed generations before. As George Washington once declared, "The bosom of America is open to receive not only the opulent & respectable Stranger, but the oppressed & persecuted of all Nations and Religions; whom we shall welcome to participation of all our rights & previleges, if by decency & propriety of conduct they appear to merit the enjoyment."[8]

Of course, Washington later backtracked and advised his successor, John Adams, that "with respect to emigration . . . except of useful mechanic's . . . there is no need of extra encouragement"—an emphasis not all that different from Lincoln's new focus on "laborers in every field of industry."[9] Washington's revised views reflected a growing discord over immigration, with some fearing that foreigners might flock here en masse and spread both revolutionary doctrine and Roman Catholic dogma to a people struggling to form a stable national identity. The rising xenophobia was given full voice by Washington's Federalist congressional ally Harrison Gray Otis of Massachusetts, who made clear that he did "not wish to invite hoards [*sic*] of wild Irishmen, nor the turbulent and disorderly of all parts of the world, [to] come here with a view to disturb our tranquility."[10]

President Adams went on to sign the notorious Alien and Sedition Acts, giving him power to deport unwelcome (or merely unsupportive) foreigners, and increasing from five to a discouraging fourteen years the residency required to qualify immigrants for naturalized American citizenship. In addition to its inflated concerns about foreign influence, the Adams administration worried that an influx of French and Irish immigrants would support and strengthen Jefferson's Democrats, reducing the voting power of the Federalists.[11] Only after Thomas Jefferson entered the White House did the citizenship threshold return to five years.

In other words, the immigration debate had been raging since the beginnings of the republic.[12] Lincoln's midcentury Whigs merely inherited the distrust of foreigners initially expressed by Adams's Federalists, while Andrew Jackson's Democrats emulated the Jeffersonians by welcoming the foreign-born and registering them as voters. The argument continued without consensus until secession and the outbreak of war put the age-old debate on hold. That is, until Lincoln made revived immigration a policy priority.

. . .

Summoning his full rhetorical power, Lincoln concluded his 1863 Annual Message with a resounding salute to the army and navy, "the gallant men, from commander to sentinel, who compose them"—many of them, he might have mentioned, foreign-born—"and to whom, more than to others, the world must stand indebted for the home of freedom disenthralled, regenerated, enlarged and perpetuated."[13] The key words were "regenerated" and "enlarged." At Gettysburg in November, Lincoln had spoken of the "fathers" who had "brought forth on this continent a new nation conceived in liberty." Now, addressing Congress in December, he proclaimed, more directly than had any previous chief magistrate, that a new generation conceived elsewhere might also enjoy a "new birth of freedom" in a land other than their birthplace.

It was a strong message, especially given Lincoln's reduced physical vitality. Still, the result evoked the usual partisan press response. To the pro-administration *New York Tribune*, the message showed "wide humanity and generous impulses." But to the hostile *Richmond Examiner*, its author remained a "Yankee monster of inhumanity and falsehood."[14] From whatever political viewpoint, nearly all the coverage focused on Lincoln's new plan for amnesty and reconstruction, a generous move to end the rebellion with the Emancipation Proclamation intact. Largely escaping notice was the landmark proposal on immigration, just as the entire subject of Lincoln and immigration policy has been largely overlooked by generations of historians and biographers.* Coming as it did less than a month after Lincoln's oratorical zenith at Gettysburg, Lincoln's message was quickly forgotten—and largely remains so.

Yet Lincoln's proposal did spur prompt and consequential action on what became the first piece of proactive federal legislation to encourage, rather than discourage, immigration to the United States. Congress made sure An Act to Encourage Immigration reached the President for his signature by a doubly symbolic date: July 4, 1864. It

---

*The major exception being Jason H. Silverman, whose brief but essential study *Lincoln and the Immigrant* ended decades of silence on the topic.

was not only Independence Day but the third anniversary of an earlier message Lincoln had sent to a special session of Congress at the start of the war in 1861. In words that would have fit well into his new argument for immigration reform, Lincoln had urged loyalty to the government, pledged, as he put it, "to clear the paths of laudable pursuit for all."[15] Now, for the first time, the government would openly encourage natives of the Old World to pursue such opportunity in the New.

. . .

It must be noted that Lincoln received no ovations from Congress the day he "delivered" his 1863 message, for the simple reason that he did not deliver it in person. Ever since Jefferson's day, and until Woodrow Wilson reintroduced the original tradition of declaiming Annual Messages in person, nineteenth-century presidents merely conveyed their yearly reports to Capitol Hill via messenger, there to be read aloud to legislators by Senate and House clerks.

Lincoln, still fatigued and now nursing a nasty facial rash— "something he can give them all," he joked to the office seekers still lining up for favors—could not have appeared on Capitol Hill that December had he wished to. Instead, he dispatched his private secretary, John George Nicolay, to Capitol Hill bearing copies of his manuscript.[16] After handing the document to the clerks, Nicolay took a seat in the chamber to bear witness to the recitation and response. Perhaps, when the senators and congressmen heard the opening words of Lincoln's immigration proposal that day, they craned their necks for a glance in Nicolay's direction, remembering that the presidential emissary was himself an immigrant—"German by birth," as Nicolay's daughter put it, "American by inclination and adoption."[17]

Born Johann Georg Nicolai in 1832 in the Bavarian village of Essingen, Nicolay had immigrated to the United States with his parents in 1838 and attended school in Cincinnati. Like Lincoln a former Whig, he went on to edit the *Pike County Free Press*, an Illinois newspaper friendly to the embryonic Republican Party, and became an early and enthusiastic supporter of Lincoln's candidacy for the White House. Reportedly, Nicolay still spoke English with a German accent. If nothing else, his wispy mustache and goatee made the slightly built chief of staff look vaguely European.

Now this foreign-born American—whom one journalist dubbed the "grim Cerberus of Teutonic descent who guards" the President's gate—had borne to Capitol Hill a bold presidential proposal to expand immigration rights to others.[18] What Congress—and perhaps Lincoln himself—did not know is that, for some unexplained reason, Nicolay had neglected to obtain his own American citizenship papers. Back in 1860, he had likely, even fraudulently, cast a vote for Lincoln for president, one hopes in the belief that his naturalization had been processed.[19] And now Nicolay proudly reported to Lincoln that legislators had cheered his message—one of the most consequential speeches Lincoln never gave—"as if the millennium had come."[20]

In his magisterial Second Inaugural Address fifteen months later, outside this same Capitol building, Lincoln would invoke God to sanctify the country's bloody war to destroy slavery. History has largely forgotten that in his recent Annual Message, he had invoked Providence to bless the overseas replenishment of the war-shattered American generation.

·   ·   ·

This is the story of the seismic political realignment, cultural upheaval, and personal growth that led Lincoln to introduce this remarkable immigration initiative. It is also the story of what contemporaries often referred to as the first American "civil war": the battle over ethnic and religious diversity that unfolded decades before the rebellion that erupted in 1861 over slavery. And it is the story of Lincoln's foreign-born contemporaries—some of whom became important friends (and foes) of the rising politician and then wartime president—and how they fought for acceptance and equal rights in the face of relentless discrimination.

As this book will endeavor to show, in dealing with the immigration issue for more than twenty years of his political career, Lincoln revealed himself as an increasingly progressive, sometimes inconsistent, but ultimately history-making leader. All too often maddeningly torn between welcoming the foreign-born and befriending those who despised them, he balanced a natural desire to expand the American dream and an understandable political reluctance to offend his less enlightened supporters. Ultimately—though the word has become a cliché too often deployed to excuse moral failure—Lincoln *evolved* on immigration, just as he would evolve on the issue of Black freedom and rights.

As a young, emerging leader, Lincoln raised no objections to immigrants, and the inveterate storyteller only occasionally made jokes at their expense. Yet for a long time, he found it difficult to condemn xenophobes if there was a chance they might help him reach his priority goals of funding vital infrastructure and, later, putting slavery "on the course of ultimate extinction."[21] Ever the strategic politician, Lincoln remained open to forging questionable alliances—to "fuse," as he often put it—with men who rejected foreigners and Catholics but also hated slavery. In much the same vein, he welcomed political support from those who believed liberated Black slaves could never be the equals of whites and, indeed, should be encouraged to become immigrants themselves—"back" to Africa.

Lincoln did not at first lead the movement to expand immigration, but he did not resist it, either. Just as he was neither an apologist for slavery nor a supporter of abolition bent on eradicating it immediately, he was initially neither as bigoted as the nativists of his era nor as devoted to broader diversity as those who worked actively to encourage it. Like most successful politicians then and now, Lincoln had aspirations that were too broad for some, and too narrow for others. Lincoln's vision of immigration always remained limited to those who sought refuge here from Europe—not Asia or the Spanish Americas. And he lacked sympathy for the claims of Native people who had dwelled on

American soil long before his own ancestors had arrived here. Yet Lincoln's powerful leadership in time proved critical to effecting change that widened the definition of American citizenship. Ultimately, Lincoln became an immigration champion.

In navigating early disputes over the foreign-born, Lincoln was compelled to confront and sometimes straddle a genuine xenophobic streak among even his own antislavery allies. Even as the rising Western political leader built a freedom coalition designed principally to restrict slavery and, we often forget, to broaden opportunity for free white men, Lincoln faced an alarming resistance to the notion of sharing the American dream with Americans from overseas. How he maneuvered both pro- and anti-immigration forces, not to mention immigrants themselves, into his own broad political tent tells us much about Lincoln's breathtaking political acumen while illumining the neglected story of poisonous ethnic politics in the years leading up to the Civil War.

While this book will fault Lincoln for too often, and for too long, dallying with deplorable nativists for political advantage, it will also acknowledge one of his signal moral achievements: maintaining and expressing consistent revulsion for the hatred of Catholics and foreigners, even those who did not support him politically. And it will recognize one of his most neglected but extraordinary policy accomplishments, moving a suspicious citizenry toward acceptance of meaningful immigration reform almost unimaginable today: wide-open borders that replenished an American population diminished by wartime death. Finally, it will endeavor to trace Lincoln's personal and political growth, not alone through statements and statutes but as seen through the eyes and words of some of the foreign-born contemporaries who interacted with him over the years: Germans like Carl Schurz, Gustave Koerner, and Franz Sigel; and Irishmen like James Shields, Archbishop John Hughes, and war hero Thomas Francis Meagher.

That Lincoln ultimately summoned the "better angels" of his nature when it came to so-called hyphenated Americans has long merited historical attention. As this book hopes to demonstrate, he deserves enormous credit for staving off the forces of fear and bigotry and envisioning a government of, by, and for the people, regardless of their national origin. Lincoln believed in borders, but he encouraged access. Yet it took him time to grow into an immigration advocate, just as it required time for him to refine his views on abolition and Black citizenship.

In the end, Lincoln not only won the Civil War fought over slavery, but he beat back the even longer rebellion against immigration, and it took significant political skill and enormous personal self-confidence to achieve both. Bravery would be shown not only by the commander in chief but by the thousands of immigrants who fought for the Union (and the Confederacy!) and made their own sacrifices, to paraphrase Lincoln, on the "altar of Freedom." The Civil War could not have been won without Lincoln's leadership, but it could not have been fought without the immigrant soldiers who served and, by the tens of thousands, died that the "nation might live."[22] This largely untold, deeply complicated American story of bias and bravery deserves to be better known.

In this accounting of Lincoln's part in this saga, readers may note startling parallels between the immigration debates of the nineteenth century and those of the twenty-first. That is because the still-frustrating, unendingly divisive issue remains with us even now. Thus, the book abounds with stories of religious prejudice, fear of refugees, riot and insurrection, controversies over government support for parochial schools, anxiety about the changing demographics in neighborhoods and cities, hostility to the speaking of foreign languages, competition (real and imagined) between domestic and foreign workers, and fevered complaints about partisan media coverage and election fraud.

Yet in pursuing the unfinished work of forging national consensus on immigration and citizenship, along with the other unfulfilled promises of the American dream, Abraham Lincoln emerged as a historical figure worthy of appreciation as well as a mythic one capable of inspiring new generations. After more than a century and a half, his life and leadership continue to provide insight into how best to explore issues and attitudes that characterized society in his own time while continuing to reverberate in our own. In a way, Lincoln was an architect of modernity—pro-freedom, pro-education, pro-infrastructure, and, perhaps least appreciated of all, pro-immigration—and willing to use the federal government to widen economic opportunity for all, regardless of national origin.

As the great Lincoln scholar Richard Nelson Current once observed, Lincoln's rare combination of effectiveness and eloquence made him both a symbol and exponent of the "Democratic dilemma and thus gives him a perpetual timeliness, an external relevance to the problems of popular government."[23]

That is why this complicated chapter of the Lincoln story—and the American story—needs to be fully explored, better understood, and more usefully remembered.

CHAPTER ONE

A World in Miniature

Like all Americans of European descent, Abraham Lincoln's ancestors were immigrants. Most of Lincoln's distant forebears are lost to history, with the notable exception of one great-great-great-great-grandfather: Samuel Lincoln. In 1637, the teenage weaver's apprentice left the East Anglian village of Hingham in the county of Norfolk, England, and headed across the sea to America.

We cannot know for certain why Samuel emigrated, but a number of his Puritan neighbors, as well as his brother Thomas, had preceded him to the New World earlier in the decade in search of economic opportunity or religious freedom, or both. Samuel's father had been disinherited, reducing the family's circumstances, so the young man most likely set out for the colonies to escape poverty.[1]

No hard evidence exists to support periodic speculation that earlier ancestors, perhaps named Linkhorn, may have been Melungeon Jews who had earlier fled thirteenth-century antisemitic persecution in the English village of Lincoln, in the East Midlands.[2] Yet, after Lincoln's death, the prominent Cincinnati rabbi Isaac Mayer Wise stoked this legend by claiming that the President "supposed himself to be a descendant of Hebrew parentage . . . bone from our bone and flesh from our flesh," adding, "He said so in my presence."[3] Other legends trace the family roots to *Lindum Colonia*, a Roman outpost established near the western coast of England in AD 58, or to a Thomas de Lingcole who lived in Norfolk in the thirteenth century during the reign of King Edward I.

We can be sure only that Samuel Lincoln, then barely fifteen years old, set sail from the port of Yarmouth aboard the ship *John & Dorothy*, along with the weaver to whom he was indentured, and arrived at Plymouth in the Massachusetts Bay Colony after a perilous three-thousand-mile journey that lasted more than two months.[4] Eventually, Samuel moved to a tiny Massachusetts village whose settlers had named it New Hingham after the English hamlet many of them had left behind.

It is worth noting that Samuel Lincoln's 1637 ocean crossing commenced only a few decades after the first slave ships from Africa deposited their abducted human cargo on North American soil. Unlike Samuel, these Black "immigrants" neither consented to their passage nor harbored hope for opportunity in the Western Hemisphere. They did not flee oppression at home; they found it here. They enjoyed no liberty of movement once in America, because slave traders sold them as property to white "owners" who kept their children in bondage, too, while Samuel Lincoln's descendants would migrate freely, south to Virginia, into Pennsylvania, then west to Kentucky.

Abraham Lincoln knew next to nothing about his origin story: only that he had come from a line of what he self-consciously termed "undistinguished families—second families, perhaps I should say."[5] In an autobiographical sketch submitted to the *Chicago Tribune* in 1860, he said little at all about his maternal ancestry, mapping his paternal side only as far as Berks County, Pennsylvania, a few generations earlier. "His lineage has been traced no farther back than this," he wrote (in the third person), even though several correspondents had recently alerted him to a "vague tradition" that earlier Lincolns might have lived elsewhere. "Further back than this," he nonetheless reiterated to a distant relative, "I have never heard any thing." He did admit that some of his forebears "were originally quakers," but hastened to add that "in later times they have fallen away from the peculiar habits of that people."[6]

He did know that in 1786, Native Americans had ambushed and killed his paternal grandfather and namesake, an earlier Abraham Lincoln, on the farm the pioneer was hewing out of the thick Kentucky forest. "The story of his death by the Indians," he later recalled, ". . . is the legend more strongly than all others imprinted upon my mind and memory."[7] The "stealth" murder left Lincoln's six-year-old father orphaned—"in poverty, and in a new country," Lincoln noted—and thus "he became a wholly uneducated man; which I suppose is the reason why I know so little of our family history."[8]

Of his mother's roots, Lincoln knew even less, and historians have learned little since. Nancy Hanks Lincoln, who gave birth to Abraham on February 12, 1809, died when the boy was nine, and the truth of her ancestry died with her. Rumors abounded—then and now—that she had been born to unmarried parents, complicating Lincoln's family history even more. The future president's law partner and biographer, William H. Herndon, claimed that Lincoln had revealed the alleged truth about his mother's background just once, during an 1850 buggy ride, supposedly confiding that Nancy's father was "a well-bred Virginia farmer or planter." He consoled himself by theorizing that "illegitimate children are oftentimes sturdier and brighter than those born in lawful wedlock; and in his case, he believed that his better nature and finer qualities came from" this "unknown" Virginian. Not that he did not credit the mother he had lost in early boyhood. According to Herndon, Lincoln believed that "all that I am or ever hope to be I owe to her."[9]

Of course, had he been more curious about his ancestry, Lincoln might have investigated his family tree more thoroughly, especially once various cousins began corresponding with him after he became a presidential contender. As a general rule, however, Lincoln preferred not to look back. From an early age, he focused exclusively on the future. "I don't know who my grandfather was," he once remarked, "and I am much more concerned to know what his grandson will be."[10]

It apparently never occurred to him that Grandfather Lincoln had died at the hands of Indigenous people whose own forebears had been forced away or killed off by settlers of European descent. The otherwise inspiring story of American immigration typically omits the parallel displacement and enslavement of nonwhites. European Americans of Lincoln's generation seldom viewed these phenomena as part of an interconnected ethnic and national realignment with ugly human consequences. The overlooked and inescapable impact of displacement, containment, and deportation deserves to be considered alongside European settlement in American history, even if Lincoln himself disregarded the ironies and inequities baked into the legacy of which he was a product.

. . .

Lincoln's own interactions with the foreign-born did not begin until he was nineteen years old, and only after a childhood spent in rural isolation on the prairies of Kentucky and Indiana. In his early youth, his closest exposure to this new breed of Americans came from his first teacher, an "old Irish schoolmaster" named Zachariah Riney.[11] The middle-aged settler, who actually hailed from Maryland, was described by Lincoln's future law associate Henry Clay Whitney as "a man of excellent character, deep piety, and a fair education. He had been born a Catholic," added Whitney, "but made no attempt to proselyte."[12] Apparently, Catholic educators of the day were all but expected to try to convert innocent students, and exceptions earned praise. (Riney would spend his final years of life as a Trappist monk at the Gethsemani monastery in Kentucky.)

Lincoln first came face-to-face with actual Europeans and other

Bird's-eye view of New Orleans—the first multicultural metropolis Abraham Lincoln ever saw—as the city appeared around 1830, the time of his visit.

foreigners during his now-fabled flatboat voyages down the Mississippi River to New Orleans in 1828 and 1831. There, in the most cosmopolitan of antebellum American cities, the wide-eyed visitor first heard the sounds of French and Spanish, two of the languages its diverse residents, tourists, and tradesmen routinely spoke on the streets and in the marketplaces. Visiting this "patch-work of peoples" at around the same time, even the more worldly Basil Hall of the British Royal Navy marveled, "my ears were struck with the curious mixture of languages."[13] As a recently issued multilingual city directory boasted: "The population is much mixed. [T]here is a great '*confusion of tongues*,' and on the Levée, during a busy day, can be seen people of every grade, colour, and condition: *in short it is a world in miniature*."[14] Lincoln's milestone experience vastly widened his horizons—New Orleans was as close as Lincoln would ever get to a foreign destination (except for a brief visit to Niagara Falls, Canada)—but unlike Captain Hall, he recorded no impressions of his exposure there to alien cultures and tongues.

Only in 1860 did he approve a description of the metropolis as he had seen it, as drafted by writer William Dean Howells for an authorized campaign biography. In Howells's ornate, un-Lincolnesque retelling, the young man had discovered in New Orleans a port "where the French voyageur and the rude hunter that trapped the beaver on the Osage and the Missouri, met the polished old-world exile, and the tongues of France, Spain, and England made babel in the streets."[15] In truth, what struck Lincoln most indelibly in the Crescent City was the repulsive omnipresence of slavery—"Negroes Chained—maltreated—whipt & scourged," remembered his cousin and traveling companion, John Hanks. "Lincoln Saw it—his heart bled."[16]

Lincoln also encountered free Blacks of Creole extraction on his visit to New Orleans. As historian Jason H. Silverman has speculated, that eye-opening experience likely laid the foundation for his future friendship with Springfield, Illinois, barber William Florville (originally de Fleurville), a Haitian immigrant who had lived in New Orleans for a time and had also observed slaves there "bought whipped, and sold."[17] Years later, Lincoln would become both a customer of and an attorney for the Black entrepreneur, and the two developed a cordial relationship. After Lincoln moved to the White House, "Billy the Barber" sent the President one of the few letters he ever received from his hometown unencumbered by pleas for money, favors, or government jobs. "May God grant you health, and strength," Florville wrote in late 1863 to the "truly great Man" who by then had broken the "Shackels" [*sic*] of slavery. "Tell Taddy"—Lincoln's youngest son—"that his (and Willys) Dog is alive and Kicking. . . . Your Residence here is Kept in good order. . . . Please accept my best wishes for yourself and family."[18]

. . .

Only after returning from his second journey to New Orleans did Lincoln strike out on his own in life. In July 1831, the twenty-two-year-old emigrated from his father's newly built log cabin in Coles County, Illinois, to a small mill town he had encountered on his most recent flatboat adventure: New Salem. To call New Salem a village amounted to a civic exaggeration; more accurately, it was a pioneer settlement, a cluster of two dozen small log buildings above a barely navigable stream known optimistically as the Sangamon River.

No one could have described the area as multicultural. Its residents or their parents had moved there from the South and the East, but not from other countries. Still, New Salem was more diverse than any place Lincoln had ever lived. The rowdy community included Baptists, Methodists, and a few freethinkers; the different religious beliefs led to many heated arguments about Sabbath observance and Bible reading, among other issues.[19] His neighbors later recalled that at one point Lincoln ventured into the religion debate by preparing "a pamphlet attacking the divinity of christ."[20] Admirers who quickly saw it as a threat to the already ambitious Lincoln's political future threw the text into a hot stove so that no one else would ever read it.

Standing out from the crowd in New Salem, Lincoln made friends, read books, honed his natural leadership skills, and cemented his Whig political leanings. Above all, he fervently embraced the party's core belief in "internal improvements"—infrastructure investments vital to transforming New Salem into an accessible destination. In his maiden political message to voters, the twenty-three-year-old enumerated these goals in terms any villager could understand: "good roads," "the clearing of navigable streams," and the introduction of the "rail road."[21]

Lincoln actually secured his first government position not from the Whigs but from the rival Democrats. He became town postmaster, a federal job so insignificant that no local Democrat asked the Jackson administration for the position. The assignment paid next to nothing but did afford Lincoln access to a regular flow of incoming newspapers from other regions. These he habitually perused before their subscribers came to call for them. On their pages he likely first read about the initial influx of Europeans seeking fortune and freedom, and stirring early resentments, in the still-young American nation.

A highlight of his New Salem years came in April 1832. Flush with war fever, Lincoln and several of his neighbors joined the Illinois Volunteers to fend off an Indian incursion led by the Sauk chief Black Hawk in violation of a harsh treaty banning the tribe from the state. Lincoln's company promptly elected him captain, and three decades later he asserted that "he has not since had any success in life which gave him so much satisfaction."[22] Lincoln would later make sport of his brief experience in uniform, declaring that the only blood he shed had been drawn by "musquetoes."[23] Whether he was accepting or shunning military glory, it apparently never struck Lincoln that Black Hawk and his followers regarded white soldiers as the real invaders, or at the very least as unwelcome "immigrants" occupying Native land.

Military service was considered a prerequisite for political success, but ironically, because he reenlisted (as a private) and remained largely unavailable to campaign for office, Lincoln lost his first bid for the Illinois state legislature in August 1832. Two years later, he did win a seat, after which he began to study law. By this time, he had outgrown his surroundings. Like the village dry goods store in which he had invested and lost money, New Salem itself seemed destined to "wink out," so Lincoln moved on.[24] In 1837, he packed his meager belongings into saddlebags and relocated to the newly minted state capital of Springfield—exactly two hundred years after his ancestor Samuel had abandoned England for America. In an even greater numerological coincidence, Lincoln arrived in Springfield on April 15; he was twenty-eight years old and had twenty-eight more years to live—to the day.

Foreign immigration was not quite yet a contentious issue in the American West. But enough foreign-born settlers had migrated to Illinois to fuel the newcomer's already renowned gift for storytelling. "Abraham Lincoln was the drollest man I ever saw," remembered his Illinois acquaintance Clark E. Carr. "He could make a cat laugh."[25] Lincoln's fellow Black Hawk War veteran Joseph Gillespie added, "No man could tell a story as well as he could[.] He never missed the nib on an anecdote."[26] By now the increasingly mesmerizing public speaker had armed himself with a seemingly endless supply of on-point stories. Although many of the yarns he spun to friends tended to the sexual or scatological, for a time he also told ethnic jokes in both public and private. No bigot, the Lincoln of this period can best be described as an equal-opportunity comedian. His jibes spared none and offended few.

Inevitably, recent immigrants—especially the Irish Catholics now beginning to flow into American cities in pursuit of paid work— became the occasional butt of Lincoln's ridicule. The jokes helped deflect from a serious political irony: Whig-supported public works projects were attracting hordes of foreign workers to build them, yet the Whigs remained at best wary of, and at times hostile to, foreigners. Not surprisingly, when these immigrant laborers became eligible for citizenship after the required five years' residency, they voted over- whelmingly Democratic.[27] And once the first naturalized Irish Americans found their political home with the opposition, Irish jokes became standard weapons in Lincoln's rhetorical arsenal. Lincoln unleashed one such barb in December 1839 when he squared off with another ambitious young politician, Democrat Stephen A. Douglas, on the seemingly arid subject of banking and currency—nineteen years before their storied senatorial debates.

In fact, banking, like infrastructure investment, was an emotional issue at the time. Illinois was just emerging from the economic Panic of 1837, along with the aftershocks of President Jackson's dissolution of the Second Bank of the United States. Democrats, including Douglas, believed that an independent sub-treasury, with branches in individual states, would restore public access to the cash and credit choked off by the financial downturn. Whigs like Lincoln insisted that full recovery would require the reestablishment of the federal bank and opposed the sub-treasury scheme. It became the burning topic of the day, and it grew even hotter when Illinois confronted a debt incurred in part by the public works spending long advocated by Lincoln and the Whigs. Without government intervention of some kind, Illinois seemed destined for bankruptcy.

For all its dry solemnity, the subject elicited flavorful oratory from both sides. In a particularly spirited stem-winder delivered at the newly built state capitol building on December 26, 1839, Lincoln opened by delving into complex economic theory.[28] Soon enough, he pivoted into stump-speech mode, taunting Democrats for exhibiting "a species of *'running itch'*" that sent them "scampering away with the public money to Texas, to Europe, and to every spot of the earth where a villain may hope to fund refuge from justice." Here he was referring to Democratic policies that allowed for tax revenues collected on Illinois land sales to be deposited in Missouri banks. Then Lincoln piled on with "an anecdote, which seems too strikingly in point to be omitted." It turned out to be his first recorded Irish joke.[29] In his telling:

"A witty Irish soldier, who was always boasting of his bravery, when no danger was near, but who invariably retreated without orders at the first charge of an engagement, being asked by his Captain why he did so, replied: 'Captain, I have as brave a *heart* as Julius Caesar ever had; but some how or other, whenever danger approaches, my *cowardly* legs will run away with it.'" So it was, Lincoln drawled, with Democrats committed to establishing a sub-treasury. "They take the public money *into* their hand for the most laudable purpose, that *wise heads* and *honest hearts* can dictate; but before they can possibly get it *out* again their rascally *'vulnerable heels'* will run away with them."[30]

The allusion might have strained for relevance to fiscal issues, but it deftly managed to land two political blows at once: Democrats were not to be trusted with public funds, and Irishmen, most of whom voted Democratic, were not to be relied on for much of anything. In telling the story, Lincoln probably assumed an Irish brogue for maximum effect. It was not only the initial Irish story he told in a public speech; it was the first recorded—that is, transcribed—funny story of any kind that he ever delivered anywhere.[31]

Making reference to clichéd Irish character flaws apparently proved even more irresistible when Lincoln rose at the local Second Presbyterian Church on Washington's birthday in 1842 to address the Springfield Washington Temperance Society.[32] To his credit, Lincoln handled the subject of the day in much the same way he hoped his contemporaries would approach drinking itself: in moderation. Notably, he resisted the impulse to link the Irish to their most notorious alleged weakness: what Lincoln called "the demon of Intemperance." Lincoln himself was by then a teetotaler, though not a reformer, and in his enlightened view, alcohol dependence did not represent "the *use* of a *bad thing*" but rather "the *abuse* of a *very good thing*." Chronic drunkenness should therefore be treated, he argued, "as a misfortune and not as a crime or even as a disgrace"—and never as a pathway to perdition.[33] Lincoln might have taken a different route and linked the pro-Democrat Irish to chronic alcohol abuse, but he did not. Besides, as he well knew, German Whigs liked their ale as much as Irish Democrats savored their whiskey, a point that critics of all kinds of immigration would make for years to come.

Yet Lincoln could not help himself from extracting one good Irish story from his repertoire, even if it lost much of its bite when his remarks appeared in print the following month in the pro-Whig *Sangamo Journal*. Judging from the absence of a setup introduction, Lincoln's audience must have known the gag well—an imaginary exchange of dialogue between an Irish thief and the onlooker who catches him in the act. "Better lay down that spade you're stealing, Paddy," declares the eyewitness, to which the robber replies: "By the powers, if ye'll credit me so long, I'll take another, jist." The oblique message, for those who did not get the joke, was that threats of punishment seldom reformed sinners; if they did not take a drink today, they would do so tomorrow when no one was watching. Since they had fallen from grace so often, they simply added new indiscretions to their bulging records of vice. "This system of consigning the habitual drunkard to hopeless ruin," Lincoln concluded his oration, ". . . should be replaced with 'a larger philanthropy'" focused on "present as well as future good." It was not Lincoln's fault if the audience went home still chuckling over his good-natured joke about the Irish recidivist burglar.[34]

What do we make of these early forays into ethnic humor? Of course, Lincoln was an inveterate yarn-spinner blessed with an indelibly strong memory for every funny story he had ever heard or read. For a man sorrowful by nature, comedy provided a tonic, and if anyone was addicted, it was Lincoln. "If it were not for these stories—jokes—jests I should die," he told William Herndon. "[T]hey are the vents of my mood & gloom."[35] Moreover, Lincoln's stories always scored points—"he wielded them as a weapon for satire and ridicule."[36] But the raconteur's early Irish jokes also reflected a genuine anxiety among Whigs that the Irish, if unchecked, or at least untaunted, might sooner or later permanently tilt the balance of power in American politics to the Democrats.

By the early 1840s, Irish refugees were streaming into the nation's Eastern ports, generally settling within the cities where they landed and taking immediate work in mills and factories. There they stirred competition, as well as resentment, by laboring for lower wages than natives did, though usually in menial jobs that locals did not really covet. Other newcomers found no employment at all, and their dependence on public assistance ignited hostility. In New York, the cost of hospital care for indigent immigrants rose to $800,000 a year, an expense that longtime, taxpaying residents begrudged the new arrivals. To the most bigoted of the native-born, these foreigners appeared unwashed, uneducated, cliquish, hard-drinking, and raucous. Both the Irish and the initial wave of German immigrants were also overwhelmingly Roman Catholic, and many Protestants worried that the new arrivals' fealty to the Church meant they could never be assimilated into civic life—that they would always consider the pope and their priests, and not the American president or their local aldermen, as their true leaders.

As noted, once these refugees satisfied the prevailing—and rather lenient—five-year residency requirement and gained citizenship and the right to vote, they invariably began casting ballots for the pro-immigration Democrats, rejecting the unwelcoming Whigs, whose very name evoked memories of a political party in despised England.

The outspoken *New York Tribune* editor Horace Greeley—who otherwise rejected "hatred to Foreigners"—complained that the "Foreign born . . . vote in a body for the side they are told is the Democratic, no matter what it proposes to do or leave undone. They contribute nothing to the aggregate of knowledge and wisdom with which our public affairs are directed, but are so much dead-weight in the scale." Along with others who were far less sympathetic, Greeley worried that these early immigrants—including "the Dutch" (Germans)—remained "unable to read or write . . . unable to speak our language," and ignorant of political issues. As Greeley warned, they "band together as Irishmen, Germans, or whatever they may be, to secure personal or clannish ends." Worst of all, they swelled the ranks of the opposition, threatening to create a "dynasty to be."[37] Lincoln, already a *Tribune* reader, knew that Greeley was among the most tolerant of Whig spokesmen. Others in their party harbored far more hostility toward immigrants.

. . .

Throughout his early career, Lincoln worked not only as a lawyer and politician but also unofficially as a pro-Whig freelance journalist—hardly as influential as Greeley but widely published in his home county. For years, he contributed pseudonymous, sharp-elbowed columns to the *Sangamo Journal*, the Whig-affiliated organ for which he became an official "agent" while still living in New Salem. That alliance broadened when Lincoln relocated to Springfield. As Herndon put it, "Whatever he wrote, or had written, went into the [*Journal*] editorial page without question."[38] Occasionally, Lincoln's contributions proved combative enough to set off political fireworks.

One example that got dangerously out of hand ensnared Irish-born Illinois Democrat James Shields and *Journal* editor Simeon Francis, along with an unexpected participant: Lincoln's former fiancée, Mary Todd.[39] At the time, their on-again, off-again courtship was on again. Previously engaged to wed, the couple had broken off their relationship on January 1, 1841—Lincoln might even have left Mary at the altar. Now, after a year of painful separation, they had reconciled.

In more ways than one, the local Whig paper brought them back together. When the couple resumed their friendship in 1842, Mary's sister, still smarting from the aborted wedding she had been set to host, refused to welcome Lincoln back to her home. So *Journal* editor Francis and his wife made their Springfield parlor available for the rekindled courtship. It was here that Abraham and Mary, who shared a love for reading, likely devised a scheme to compose a series of satires aimed principally at Shields, who served as the Illinois state auditor. These became known as the "Rebecca" letters, and all of them appeared in the *Journal*.

Shields made for a mouthwatering target. Born in 1806 in County Tyrone, Ireland, he had immigrated to Canada at the age of twenty, later settling in Kaskaskia, Illinois, where, like Lincoln, he studied law, fought in an Indian war, and won a seat in the state assembly. There the similarities ended. As a Democrat, Shields opposed all the pet Whig initiatives dear to Lincoln. In society, Shields perceived himself as a ladies' man—"a great '*beau*,'" in the words of a contemporary— though he stood but five feet nine inches and probably spoke with a brogue.[40] Lincoln, by now a master of irreverent stories and foreign accents, no doubt enjoyed telling jokes at Shields's expense—and behind his back—replete with mimicry. That Mary herself was partly of Irish stock did not seem to inhibit her own eagerness to join in the mockery.

In a more serious vein, the state auditor had recently angered Whigs by ordering state banknotes devalued, a blow to those who expected to redeem the paper at face value to pay their debts. Lincoln's response arrived in the latest installment of the *Journal*'s pseudonymous satires, like earlier ones crafted as a letter from the fictional pioneer widow "Rebecca," and lambasted Shields not only as a deceiver in affairs of politics but as a buffoon in affairs of the heart. "Shields is a fool as well as a liar," went the August 27, 1842, "letter," a ludicrous farce that bore hallmarks of Lincoln's style. "With him truth is out of the question, and as for getting a good bright passable lie out of him, you might as well try to strike fire from a cake of tallow."[41]

The farce went on to portray a malodorous Shields bursting into a fancy soiree and attempting to procure women with the type of worthless currency he had recently downgraded. One of these "galls" reports:

If I was deaf and blind I could tell him by the smell. . . . I seed him when I was down in Springfield last winter. . . . He was paying his money to this one and that one and tother one, and sufferin great loss because it wasn't silver instead of State paper. . . . [He] spoke audibly and distinctly, "Dear girls, *it is distressing*, but I cannot marry you all. Too well I know how much you suffer, but do, do *remember*, it is not my fault that I am *so* handsome and *so* interesting."[42]

The sarcasm proved too much for the "hot-blooded and impulsive" Shields.[43] His anger only intensified when this latest Rebecca letter was followed into the *Journal* by an inflammatory unsigned poem, probably the work of Mary and a female friend, asserting, with no shortage of anti-Irish contempt, that old Rebecca herself had fallen hard for the "soft-blarnied" Shields:

Ye jews-harps awake! The A[uditor]'s won—
Rebecca, the widow, has gained Erin's son.
The pride of the north from the emerald isle
Has been woo'd and won by a woman's sweet smile.[44]

His temper up, Shields called for the true author of the libels to identify himself, and Lincoln stepped forward to take sole responsibility. As Mary later boasted, her future husband "felt, he could do, no

About sun-set Gen. Whiteside called again, and received from Mr. Lincoln the following answer to Mr. Shields' note.

TREMONT, Sept. 17, 1842.

Jas. Shields, Esq.

Your note of to-day was handed me by Gen. Whiteside. In that note you say you have been informed, through the medium of the editor of the Journal, that I am the author of certain articles in that paper which you deem personally abusive of you : and without stopping to enquire whether I really am the author, or to point out what is offensive in them, you demand an unqualified retraction of all that is offensive ; and then proceed to hint at consequences.

Now, sir, there is in this so much assumption of facts, and so much of menace as to consequences, that I cannot submit to answer that note any farther than I have, and to add, that the consequence to which I suppose you allude, would be matter of as great regret to me as it possibly could to you. Respectfully,

A. LINCOLN.

Lincoln's icy, provocative 1842 reply to outraged Irish-born Democrat James Shields, as published in Springfield's pro-Whig newspaper.

less, than be my champion."[45] Lincoln's chivalry might have impressed the object of his affection, but it did not placate the target of his derision.

On September 17, Shields demanded that Lincoln apologize and issue "a full, positive and absolute retraction of all offensive allusions used by you" in the "articles . . . meant to degrade me" with "slander, vituperation and personal abuse."[46] Lincoln replied in irksome legalese, noting that "without stopping to enquire whether I really am the author, or to point out what is offensive . . . you demand an unqualified retraction." The arch response concluded, "Now, sir, there is in this so much assumption of facts, and so much of menace as to consequences, that I cannot submit to answer that note any farther than I have."[47] The exchange was hardly private; the entire correspondence appeared in the *Sangamo Journal.*

Unsatisfied, Shields challenged his adversary to a duel. Perhaps aware that his foe had once fought a duel to the death back in Ireland, an anxious Lincoln now made a feeble attempt to modify his position through an intermediary: "I had no intention of injuring your personal or private character or standing as a man or a gentleman." He had authored the Rebecca article, purely "for political effect."[48] Shields was neither convinced nor mollified. Lincoln was trapped.

Duels had become illegal in Illinois, so three days later, on September 22, the antagonists and their seconds headed to "Bloody Island," a towhead in the Mississippi River outside their home state's jurisdiction. Here, the principals actually came close to facing off in mortal combat. Lincoln saved the day—and perhaps his hide—by exercising a challenged party's right to choose weapons. To exploit his seven-inch height advantage, he had proposed "Cavalry broad swords of the largest size," hoping "his long arms would enable him to keep clear of his antagonist."[49] Some recalled that Lincoln even directed a few theatrical practice swings at the island's trees, effortlessly shearing off low-hanging branches as Shields looked on apprehensively. At the last minute, a truce was arranged. Whether Lincoln apologized is not known. But he later admitted that a fight would have been a "*degradation.*"[50]

The episode might at least have dissuaded him from further forays into published satire—especially of the ethnic variety. On the positive side, it bound Abraham and Mary closer together than ever. A few weeks after the incident, the coauthors of the Rebecca letter married. To Lincoln's embarrassment, however, his close encounter with an Irishman remained a hot topic in Springfield. Three weeks later, he told a friend, "You have heard of my duel with Shields, and I have now to inform you that the dueling business still rages in this city"—indeed, the duel-happy Shields had already challenged Lincoln's friend William Butler to yet another fight to the death.[51] As Lincoln later mused: "If all the good things I have ever done are remembered as long as my scrape with Shields, it is plain I shall not soon be forgotten."[52]

Years later, Mary rather ungratefully recalled that her husband "thought, he had some right, to assume to be *my* champion, even on frivolous occasions." She claimed that both of them were "always so ashamed" of the "foolish and uncalled for *rencontre*" with Shields that "Mr L & myself mutually agreed, never to refer to it & except in an

The near-duel with James Shields, as imagined by an illustrator decades later.

occasional light manner, between us." Otherwise, "it was never mentioned" again.[53]

Except twice. During the Civil War, a Union general called on the Lincolns at the White House and, as Mary remembered, "said, playfully, to my husband 'Mr. President, is it true, as I have heard that you, once went out, to fight a duel & all for the sake, of the lady by your side.' Mr. Lincoln, with a flushed face, replied, 'I do not deny it, but if you desire my friendship, you will never mention the circumstance again.'" On another occasion, one of the actual "participants of the affair" supposedly turned up in Washington and encouraged the President to "rehearse the particulars." A "sore" Lincoln complained, "That man is trying to revive his memory of a matter that I am trying to forget."[54]

One good reason to "forget" was that, by then, Shields was no longer the figure Abraham and Mary had tweaked two decades earlier. The Irish Democrat had gone on to serve as a brigadier general in the Mexican–American War, then as a U.S. senator from both Illinois and Minnesota. During the Civil War, he would see further action as a brigadier general, albeit without much distinction. No wonder Mary recalled of the close call on Bloody Island twenty years earlier: "This affair, always annoyed my husband's peaceful nerves."[55]

Perhaps the Shields "affair" also showed the future president that there were better ways for an ambitious politician to assail rivals than through stereotyping. Not that Lincoln or the Whig politicians and press ever lost their zeal for savaging Democrats. Nor did they ever exempt Democrats of Irish descent from their future assaults. If he retained any zeal to goad the sons of Erin after the Shields episode, however, Lincoln for the most part—but not always—kept such feelings out of the press. Storytelling, however, he could never resist. Nor would his rivalry with Shields end without a few more spats.

Coincidentally, twenty years to the day after his close call on Bloody Island, Abraham Lincoln issued his preliminary Emancipation Proclamation, ensuring that his name would indeed be remembered for something other than his near-affray with the state auditor. Thirty-one years after that, the state of Illinois presented a larger-than-life bronze likeness of James Shields to the U.S. Capitol to adorn Statuary Hall.

CHAPTER TWO

So Much Savage Feeling

Some duels Lincoln could not avoid, even if they occurred eight hundred miles from his hometown. Such proved the case in mid-1844, a momentous year for American immigration, when anti-Catholic violence erupted in the so-called City of Brotherly Love: Philadelphia. Although he had never even visited the birthplace of American independence, Lincoln was destined to involve himself in the ugly outbreak and its repercussions.

The stage for intolerance there had been set decades earlier, when Benjamin Franklin, revealing an ugly streak of bias, asked in an anti-immigrant screed, "Why should Pennsylvania, founded by the English, become a Colony of Aliens?"[1] Franklin aimed his wrath at "swarthy" German-born newcomers he feared would not only fail to assimilate but likely require the descendants of old England to adapt to *them*. Worse, as Franklin saw matters: "Those who come hither are generally of the most ignorant, Stupid Sort of their own Nation."[2] Notwithstanding Franklin's inhumane grumbling, Germans seeking affordable land trickled into Pennsylvania anyway, followed in the late

1830s by the first rush of immigrant Irish laborers seeking jobs at factories in the increasingly industrialized city. Franklin proved prescient in one regard: Catholic immigrants did further diversify Philadelphia and indeed altered its original Quaker character. And many local Protestants resented the transformation, warning that the newcomers drank and caroused too much and obeyed no laws but those handed down by their priests, their bishops, and the pope himself. America's tradition of open borders and unrestricted access, so the increasingly outspoken nativists argued, portended dangers that far outweighed the nation's commitments to growth and opportunity.

In May 1844, ninety-one years to the month after Franklin's tirade against "ignorant" newcomers, and ten years after the city witnessed an ugly uprising against free Blacks, rumors of papist interference in the Philadelphia public schools ignited a showdown.[3] Gossip had it that Irish Catholics in the working-class suburb of Kensington hoped to ban Bible reading from its classrooms, where instruction traditionally began each morning with a passage from Protestant scripture. In truth, the Dublin-born bishop of Philadelphia, Francis Patrick Kenrick, had asked only that Irish school districts be allowed to replace the King James Bible with the Douay–Rheims version translated from the Latin and used in most Catholic churches. (Similar requests had been made in New York.)

That proved enough of a sacrilege to outrage those who felt threatened, culturally as well as politically, by the growing Catholic presence among them. Papist immigrants, one Philadelphian complained, brandished "foreign emblems," wore "native costumes," and worshipped images.[4] Suspicious that Irish noncitizens were also committing voter fraud to increase their power, the angriest among the city's dwindling Protestant majority had recently founded anti-immigration newspapers and political clubs. The story was the same up and down the Atlantic Coast. In April, New Yorkers had elected a nativist mayor: publisher James Harper, who also happened to be the founder of that city's anti-immigrant Order of United Americans (OUA), now two thousand members strong. Harper's victory capped a ten-year-long anti-Catholic campaign by another notable yet bigoted New Yorker: Samuel F. B. Morse, the polymath artist and pioneer photographer who had only recently developed a working model for the telegraph. When not painting or tinkering, Morse regularly penned vitriolic newspaper columns arguing that "Popery" would lead to "despotism."[5] Forming his own American Protestant Union, Morse called on "every denomination of Christians"—except, of course, Catholics—to "secure to posterity the religious, civil and political principles . . . according to the spirit of our ancestors."[6]

Following suit, Philadelphia nativists demanded "An OPEN BIBLE and a PURE BALLOT BOX," adopting OUA's calls for an unprecedented twenty-one-year wait for naturalization along with a total ban on foreign-born officeholders.[7] Then the Philadelphians took their xenophobic message to the streets, even in Catholic communities. Striking back on May 3, a hundred Irish protestors stormed an outdoor nativist rally in the heart of Kensington, scattering the crowd and chasing the editor of the *Native American* newspaper from the speakers' platform.

After a series of street brawls, nativists escalated matters by setting fire to two Catholic churches and a seminary, burning down several dozen homes and a firehouse, and battling state militia dispatched by Pennsylvania's governor to quell what one Catholic called the "soul-sickening" melees.[8] More than a dozen combatants died in the riot. In the morning, dazed residents awoke to find gangs of Irish boys defacing the walls of charred houses and hauling down tottering chimneys so they could stockpile bricks as weapons for future battles. "These are the people who are deemed most worthy to be citizens," sneered one Protestant eyewitness, adding conspiratorially that "a popish priest was seen to leave the vicinity within an hour of the riot"—whether or not fleeing for his life the observer failed to say.[9]

Three days later, agitated afresh by reports that Irishmen had been spied trampling on an American flag, nativists called on their followers to resume resistance to "the bloody hand of the Pope."[10] This time a mob set upon a Catholic church in downtown Philadelphia, hurling brickbats, torching the interior, and ransacking its book collection. Again, it took the militia to scatter the rioters, though the presence of soldiers did not inhibit lusty cheers from onlookers when the church steeple collapsed in flames. "We have never heard of a transaction in our city," bemoaned one resident, "in which so much savage feeling and brutal ferocity were displayed."[11]

The 1844 anti-Irish riot in Philadelphia, as visualized by a period artist for one of the earliest depictions of the deadly outbreak.

Back in Lincoln's hometown, his by now official mouthpiece, the *Sangamo Journal*, reported on the "Dreadful Riots," concluding, "Humanity must weep at these scenes."[12] In New York City, at the urgent request of Catholic bishop John J. Hughes, who worried that the riots might spread northward, armed Irishmen took up positions in the churchyard to defend the original St. Patrick's Cathedral on Mott Street from rumored nativist attack.

To Democrats gaining strength with each new registered Irishborn voter, such threats presented an irresistible political opportunity:

blame the Whig opposition poisoned by anti-Catholic prejudice and willing to ignore, even tacitly encourage, violence aimed at diluting the Democrats' surging enrollment numbers. The conflict could not have erupted at a more fraught moment on the political calendar, with the 1844 presidential campaign just getting underway. Nationally, Whigs now faced a perilous challenge: they must repudiate mob violence and reject responsibility for arousing anti-Catholic animus, yet at the same time discourage Catholic turnout and woo nativist votes. Or, best of all, change the subject.

Inevitably, the political furor morphed west to the swing state of Illinois, where immigration was also on the rise even as Whigs like Lincoln scrambled to respond to the Philadelphia outbreak. To the state's own growing population of foreign-born residents, meanwhile, Illinois Democrats promoted themselves as "the protectors of the rights of aliens" while charging Whigs with discouraging the foreigners' presence and participation. Asserted one Illinois Democrat: "The strong, robust, able-bodied Irishman and German who enters this State, ploughs your prairies, fells our forests, opens our roads, and digs our canals"—all pursuits that reflected well-known Whig priorities—"is, according to this faction, unfit to enjoy the rights of the freeman." The charge was not far from the truth. As historian Kenneth J. Winkle has demonstrated, Springfield Whigs indeed hoped to stanch the flow of foreign incomers, lengthen the path to naturalization, and discourage the foreign-born from voting as long as they tended to vote Democrat. Despite their efforts, by the end of the decade a third of the residents of Lincoln's hometown would be foreign-born.[13]

By the 1840s, immigration—or, at least, immigrants—had already reached Lincoln's front door. Not long before the Philadelphia uprising, Abraham and Mary moved into their first—and only—home. As soon as they could afford help, Mary began hiring the young, indigent Irishwomen who had been routed westward by relief agencies specializing in finding domestic work for newly arrived migrants. Mary might have been expected to welcome them with open arms: her own great-grandfather had been born in County Longford, Ireland. Yet, according to later testimony by one of these servants, Margaret Ryan, Mary treated some of her maids abominably. She not only "struck" the "girls" who worked in the house but was allegedly observed by one of them bashing "L[incoln]. on head with [a] piece of wood while reading [a] paper in South Parlor—cut his nose."[14]

Outside the home, Lincoln stood up more effectively for immigrant rights. On June 12, 1844, a month after the Philadelphia riot, he and his fellow Springfield Whigs assembled at the statehouse for a public meeting on the issue. As a relatively new state capital, Springfield had emerged as a fertile staging ground for meetings, rallies, and lectures, most of them political in nature and many providing evening entertainment for townspeople hungry for civic engagement. The June 12 Whig gathering ostensibly aimed to "investigate" the recent Philadelphia riot, but more crucially to rebut charges that their party bore guilt for the outbreak.

Although the nod to deliver the principal oration went to another prominent local Whig—Edward D. Baker, who had recently outdistanced Lincoln to win the party's nomination for Congress—the tall, homely thirty-five-year-old did get the chance to address the meeting. No manuscript of his speech survives, but fragmentary newspaper summaries suggest he insisted that Whigs remained just as committed as Democrats to religious tolerance and fair-minded immigration policies. As for the Philadelphia outbreak, Lincoln argued that it needed to be "fairly discussed, and understood by the citizens of this State and country," but maintained "he had not yet seen an account of this affair which he could rely upon as *true*."[15]

Here Lincoln was being a bit disingenuous. After all, the pro-Whig *New York Tribune*, a newspaper Lincoln read whenever he could get his hands on it, had already published a raft of articles on the "outrages." True, the paper blamed Catholics and nativists alike for the "bloodshed, disgrace and destruction" in Philadelphia, but it assigned particular responsibility to "[news]papers that fondle Native Americans [anti-immigration nativists]."[16] Urged the *Tribune*'s noted editor, Horace Greeley: "Let us discriminate fairly . . . but hold none guiltless who has chosen to defy the laws and engage in murderous affrays in the streets and houses of a crowded City, to the great scandal of our Nation and the imminent peril of the innocent and helpless."[17] As Greeley well knew, but could not quite bring himself to write, not all Whigs were nativists, but nearly all nativists were Whigs.

The resolutions that passed in Springfield on June 12—all drafted by Lincoln—nonetheless held that "truth, and justice to ourselves, demand that we should repel the charge" of responsibility for the recent violence.[18] Otherwise, Lincoln's text labored to thread a political needle. It rejected hostility "to *foreigners and Catholics*." Yet it held that, "in admitting the foreigner to the rights of citizenship, he should be put to some reasonable test of his fidelity to our country and its institutions; and . . . should first dwell among us a reasonable time to become generally acquainted with the nature of those institutions." Precisely how long a waiting period remained unspecified. With some nativists now calling for quadrupling the five-year residency requirement, Lincoln's resolutions at least went on record liberally urging that the path to naturalization remain "as convenient, cheap, and expeditious as possible," reiterating that the founding documents made no distinction as to religion. Finally, the document took pains to "reprobate and condemn each and every thing in the Philadelphia riots, and the causes which led to them, from whatever quarter they may have come."[19]

Most important of all, Lincoln's resolutions forcefully condemned religious persecution, holding that "the rights of conscience, as found in our Constitution, is [*sic*] most sacred and inviolable, and one that belongs no less to the Catholic, than to the Protestant." The document pledged that "all attempts to abridge or interfere with these rights, either of Catholic or Protestant, directly or indirectly, have our decided disapprobation, and shall ever have our most effective opposition."[20] Here were Abraham Lincoln's first public words on immigration policy, even if, except to Springfield insiders, their authorship remained as un-acknowledged as that of the 1842 Rebecca letters. For modern readers, the text fully reflects Lincoln's already exceptional benevolence.

On June 20, the *Sangamo Journal* dutifully published the exculpatory but enlightened Springfield resolutions, leaving it to the Democratic *Illinois State Register* to react the following day. Springfield's party-affiliated newspapers could be relied on to portray newsworthy events from an entirely different perspective, and usually in the most acrimonious language. In typical fashion, the *Register* accused the Whig paper of "slanderous misrepresentations," taunting Lincoln to use his influence with the *Journal* to insist on a franker account of the riots. The *"Native Whigs* commenced the aggression in Philadelphia," charged the *Register*, and "Mr. Lincoln *cannot* doubt it." Moreover, the *Register* pointed out, Lincoln had been "incorrect" in advancing the canard that "the Catholics demanded the exclusion of the Bible from the public schools: this they *never* asked for; all they wanted was the privilege, as it was undoubtedly their right, of introducing and using their own translation."[21] This part of Lincoln's remarks had not made it into print. Evidently, Lincoln had swallowed the Bible-ban rumor as gullibly—or guilefully—as had the nativists in Philadelphia. False or not, the charge had become a Whig talking point.

Uncharacteristically, the *Register* added some laudatory comments about the ambitious Whig whom it customarily kept in its cross-hairs, albeit with a certain degree of respect. As *Register* editor William Walters reported of Lincoln's performance at the Springfield meeting, "Mr. Lincoln expressed the kindest, and most benevolent feelings towards foreigners; they were, I doubt not, the sincere and honest sentiments of *his heart*." Walters was quick to add that those sentiments "were not those of *his party*; Whiggery has never allowed them. Mr. Lincoln also alleged that the whigs were as much the friends of foreigners as democrats; but he failed to substantiate it in a manner satisfactory to the foreigners who heard him."[22] (Apparently, immigrants had attended the June 12 Springfield meeting.)

In issuing the backhanded compliment, Walters surely hoped to damn Lincoln with unexpected praise. For in complimenting him, the otherwise hostile *Register* managed by implication to paint the "benevolent" Lincoln as out of step with his own increasingly nativist base—perhaps even destined to become what might today be called a WINO (Whig in Name Only). If the *Register* could not halt Lincoln's political rise by arousing opposition from Democrats, perhaps it could derail him by implying that his egalitarian instincts ran counter to the rising anti-foreigner sentiment within his own party. After all, politicians had to be nominated before they could run for election. Edward Baker had just bested Lincoln for the Whig nomination for the House, and by previous agreement on rotation, Lincoln expected his own chance to come two years hence, in 1846.

As it turned out, neither Lincoln's personal empathy nor his party's public declarations of sympathy could forestall further ethnic violence in Philadelphia. In early July, its newly formed Native American Party provocatively announced an Independence Day parade through that city's still-smoldering streets. In anticipation, parishioners of the Roman Catholic Church of St. Philip Neri in suburban Southwark stocked muskets for its defense. Learning of the existence of this improvised arsenal, rioters subjected the church to rock throwing, interior desecration, and gunfire, again provoking a fierce response by the militia. In this latest wave of violence, another fifteen people died, with fifty more injured. An anti-immigrant pamphlet acknowledged that the situation in Philadelphia had deteriorated "from riot to civil war." Echoed another observer, "excitement" in "the infected districts" had provoked "anarchy . . . amounting almost to civil war."[23]

Although Lincoln fell silent on the latest outbreak, other Whigs around the country expressed horror at the seemingly uncontrollable violence. One was the young Wall Street lawyer George Templeton Strong. For forty years, this New York blueblood would commit trenchant daily observations to his personal diary, opening a valuable window onto nineteenth-century urban life among the elite. Earlier,

Strong had greeted James Harper's election as New York mayor by cheering, "Hurrah for the Natives!" But when word reached him of the Philadelphia church desecration, Strong declared that the perpetrators "richly deserve to be hanged." He could not help adding, "I shan't be caught voting a 'Native' ticket again in a hurry." Strong, too, worried about "civil war raging."[24]

In the opening battle of this pre–Civil War civil war, Abraham Lincoln displayed a combination of savvy and sympathy, defending his political party while evincing genuine solicitude for the embattled "foreigners," whom some of his fellow Whigs found objectionable and, worse, guilty for their own persecution. Six years earlier, Lincoln had forcefully condemned "the mobocratic spirit" that put antislavery abolitionists in physical danger; now he could not, and would not, excuse the "ravages of mob law" directed at Catholics.[25] Although more and more Whigs began embracing anti-Catholic monomania, Lincoln's instinct for fair play already set him apart.

. . .

Just one week after the Springfield public meeting, Illinois Whigs convened yet another gathering at Peoria, this time to endorse the party's recently nominated presidential candidate, Henry Clay. Delegates already knew that the platform adopted by the rival Democrats in May featured a plank affirming America's role as "the asylum of the oppressed of every nation." The Democrats' manifesto directed that "every attempt to abridge the present privilege of becoming citizens and the owners of soil among us, ought to be resisted with the same spirit which swept the alien and sedition laws from our statute books."* By contrast, save for a contrary allusion to the "protection of domestic labor," the Whig platform made no mention of immigration at all.[26]

---

*The same plank had appeared in the 1840 platform and would be readopted at every Democratic convention through 1860.

The disparity hardly mattered to Lincoln. Clay was not only the nominee of his party but also Lincoln's own "beau ideal of a Statesman." As Lincoln put it, "From my boyhood, the name of Henry Clay has been an inspiration to me."[27] Not surprisingly, the Peoria assemblage again called on Lincoln to draft the meeting's obligatory resolutions, this time meant to identify the policies Whigs planned to highlight in the coming campaign. In Lincoln's hands, the list of "foremost" discussion points covered protective tariffs, internal improvements, and sound currency, none of which was apt to trigger the kind of violence that had enveloped Philadelphia.[28] Immigration and nativism escaped the Illinois Whigs' attention just as it had on the national level.

Yet the issue would not die. Clay, who had once daringly attended a commencement ceremony at a Catholic college, had more recently attempted to appease his nativist supporters, casually admitting he was open to lengthening the residency requirements for naturalization.[29] Promptly accused of outright anti-foreigner bias, he hastened to assure voters he himself was not a nativist, even if some of his supporters were. In a public letter to James Watson Webb, editor of the pro-Whig *New York Courier and Enquirer*, the presidential candidate asserted, "I wish our Country, forever, to remain a sacred asylum for all unfortunate and oppressed men whether from religious or political causes."[30]* It was not enough.

In November, Clay did win healthy majorities in Lincoln's hometown and county but lost both Illinois and the nation. Dark-horse Democratic nominee James K. Polk prevailed nationally by a slim margin: thirty-nine thousand popular votes out of more than two million cast.[31] On the surface, Whigs foundered not because of immigration but over another increasingly divisive issue: slavery. In crucial New York, a third-party, antislavery candidate named James G. Birney siphoned off just enough support from Clay to throw the state's decisive

---

*A onetime Jacksonian, Webb had allegedly chosen the name "Whig" for the new anti-Jackson party and later became a Clay ally.

thirty-six electoral votes to Polk, clinching his victory nationwide. Among disappointed Whigs, the result triggered soul-searching, finger-pointing, and conspiracy theories. "Something *must* be done," one Maine Whig warned Clay after his defeat. "The naturalization laws must be modified somehow, or we must sink under the weight of the worst of all European influences." The angry writer insisted that an army of "*Irish* paupers . . . marshalled by their infernal priests" had swarmed across the Canadian border to vote en masse for Polk.[32] It was one of the first times, but certainly not the last, that opponents had accused Irish Democrats of massive voter fraud.

A quite different analysis came from New York's former Whig "boy governor," William H. Seward, who had fought alongside Bishop Hughes during his term to fund parochial schools ("to buy Catholic votes," opponents charged). Seward bluntly faulted nativist Whigs for the 1844 election loss. By courting anti-immigrant support for Clay, he argued, fellow Whigs had alienated voters offended by

Irish-born bishop John Hughes of New York, the highest-ranking Catholic prelate in America, as he looked around the time of the Philadelphia riots.

anti-Catholicism, driving them to Birney as the only alternative.[33] (Clay himself worried about the "tendency amongst the Whigs to unfurl the banner of the native American party."[34])

Neither man gave credence to the persistent reports that New York Democrats had granted last-minute ballot access to countless noncitizens, like those alleged to have voted illegally in Maine, in return for promises to vote the "right" ticket. Fake naturalization, one Democratic ward heeler indeed boasted, was "going on among our friends to an immense extent. On Saturday 200—*all* Democrats—received their papers."[35] All told, as many as five thousand *legally* naturalized Americans had registered to vote in New York in the weeks before Election Day, almost all of them pledged to the Democratic Party.

Indeed, George Templeton Strong had peeked into the citizenship registry office and, like many of his class, recoiled from the sight: "It was enough to turn a man's stomach to see the way they were naturalizing this morning. Wretched, filthy, bestial-looking Italians and Irish, the very scum and dregs of human nature filled the office so completely that I was almost afraid of being poisoned by going in." Yet Strong matured enough to attribute the 1844 result not to "wretched" immigrants but to "Native Americanism." As a result, he believed— prematurely, but not inaccurately—"the Whig Party is defunct, past all aid from warm blankets, galvanic batteries, and the Humane Society."[36] Lincoln still believed otherwise.

So did Horace Greeley's influential *New York Tribune*. It concurred that nativists and nativism had frightened off Clay voters while Catholic solidarity had benefited the Democrats. "The Naturalized Citizens have all been carried for Polk by appeals to their Religious and old-world feelings and prejudices," Greeley editorialized in an analysis Lincoln likely read when the edition reached Springfield. "They have been told that they would be deprived of their Political Rights and reduced to vassalage in the event of Mr. Clay's election, and this, with still more monstrous bugbears, has driven from us those who were formerly with us." Greeley could not resist heaping some of the blame for the Whig catastrophe on "an overwhelming Illegal Vote," insisting that the "Alien (unnaturalized) population" had been given "at least one ballot each, and many of them more than one." In short, he suggested, the Irish had indeed stolen the 1844 election. Still, Greeley urged Whigs to resist converting to any official nativist party. It would be fatally unwise, he cautioned, "to break our own ranks and fall into theirs."[37]

The finger-pointing would continue for years. New York nativist Thomas R. Whitney branded Seward a "scheming politician" who had "attempted to prostitute our system" and labeled the mercurial Greeley "a child of impulse, who lives in a dream-land, and knows no realities, no people, no country."[38] In Pennsylvania, where authorities were still prosecuting rioters and paying reparations to burned-out Catholic churches, unrepentant voters elected three "Native Americans" to Congress.

Whether Lincoln's fellow Whigs—East and West—would hereafter distance themselves from nativists or cultivate them to boost their chances for future success remained to be seen. Anti-Irish prejudice would prove more difficult to kill than the Whig Party.

. . .

Irish immigration was about to morph into a human tidal wave—propelled by widespread crop failure and famine on the other side of the ocean. The potato rot—a fungus technically known as *Phytophthora infestans*—first struck Ireland in 1845, the year of Polk's inauguration in America. For a land of farmers dependent on a single crop to feed its own population, and obligated under English rule to export healthy harvests to the mother country, the blight and resulting shortages proved catastrophic, especially when it recurred to blacken harvests for the next six years. With farmers and their families forced to eat whatever healthy potatoes survived, thus converting fewer and fewer to seed, future harvests grew smaller.

As many as a million Irish died of starvation or malnutrition in

Irish immigrants huddle dockside before boarding a ship bound for America. Until
the Lincoln administration called for new regulations, such transatlantic voyages
could be deadly for steerage passengers like those portrayed here.

what came to be called the Great Hunger, or *Drochshaol* (the "Bad
Times"). Some 1.5 million more fled to the United States, traveling
(and sometimes dying) aboard cramped, fetid ships in a desperate
transatlantic search for fresh food and a fresh chance.[39] The bitter
irony, as historian Roger Daniels has pointed out, is that the potato
itself was "an immigrant *from* the New World."[40]

The newest Irish arrivals to America faced surging resistance to
their residency—not to mention their citizenship. In Massachusetts,
fearful of bearing the cost of so-called pauper immigration, a legislative committee ominously suggested "that individual states can do
much towards checking this great evil, and that the government of the
United States can do the remainder."[41] In New York, a British visitor
witnessed Irish customers ignored by salesmen or outright "turned
out" of shops, judged "of so low and degraded a caste . . . that it would
be a waste of time, and utterly profitless, in attending to their inqui-
ries." The Englishman concluded that the "mere fact of being an Irishman" was "almost sufficient to warrant his conviction by an American

jury."[42] When another observer suggested that America's ongoing slavery dispute might be solved through a plan of compensated emancipation and the deportation of African Americans, a Bostonian "quaintly replied, he would rather get rid of the Irish."[43] In Maryland, nativists proclaimed that "foreign Jesuitism" had rendered *our Elections a curse rather than a blessing.*"[44]

Young, impoverished, and unwanted, but lacking the means to migrate once they reached American ports, Irish immigrants became this country's first "urban pioneers," accepting whatever work they could obtain, however menial, no matter how low the wage. As Kevin Kenny, an authority on the Irish diaspora, argues, "Here lie the origins of the familiar nativist refrain, 'they're taking away our jobs,' though in reality the immigrants were doing jobs—digging, demolishing, lifting, carrying, and cleaning—that most Americans refused to do."[45] A generation that one publication in Ireland had dubbed "the pride and the prime of our Nation" now found itself largely relegated to manual or domestic labor, dismissed by many here as intemperate rabble, and distrusted by Protestants for alleged fealty to the pope.[46] Meanwhile, the immigration wave produced a dramatic change in the hierarchy of the American Catholic Church, transforming it into a majority-Irish institution. In 1848, the wave of "Famine Irish" was augmented by the arrival of refugees from, and supporters of, the failed Young Ireland uprising in the small village of Farranrory.

By the next census, natives of Ireland would constitute 43 percent of all foreign-born American residents, with about 200,000 Irish-born crowded into New England alone, 151,000 in Pennsylvania, and 28,000 in Illinois.[47] In reaction, nativist societies renewed their vow, in Samuel Morse's toxic words, "to preserve for ourselves and secure to posterity the religious, civil and political principles of our country, according to the spirit of our ancestors."[48] It did not matter that such sentiments ran counter to the Whig Party's—and Lincoln's—oft-expressed belief in economic opportunity for all.

Fearing what amounted to an alien invasion, nativists launched new anti-Catholic journals with titles like *American Citizen, Spirit of '76,* and, most blatantly and clumsily of all, the *American Protestant Vindicator and Defender of Civil and Religious Liberty Against the Inroads of Popery.*[49] After Henry Clay's defeat, nativists formed new "brother-hoods" to "oppose foreign influence in our institutions or government in any shape in which it may be presented to us."[50]

Irish Catholics hewed to the Democratic Party in part out of self-preservation, while their class instincts warned them away from the Whig elite. American politics was in upheaval.

. . .

Meanwhile, Lincoln made plans of his own to emigrate—in his case, from Springfield to Washington. The system of congressional rotation previously adopted by Sangamon County's Whigs ensured that each of its ambitious political stars—most recently Edward Baker—would earn successive chances to run for the House of Representatives, then yield to a successor after a single term in office. In 1846, Lincoln's turn came. After securing the nomination, he went on to defeat his Democratic opponent in the general election. Then, in line with prevailing custom, he waited more than a year to begin serving, arriving in the nation's capital to take up his congressional duties in early December 1847.

Lincoln's one and only term in the House—he would yield (some-what reluctantly) to the next Whig nominee within months—is best remembered for his outspoken criticism of the Mexican–American War, even though the conflict had all but ended by the time he took his seat in Congress.[51] Lincoln's opposition did not reflect a particular sym-pathy for Mexico or Mexicans. Nor did Lincoln worry that any ceded territory might trap thousands of Spanish-speaking Mexican nationals within American borders. (In fact, the treaty ending the war gave all Mexicans in newly acquired territory the right to American citizenship.) Rather, he foresaw that any land acquired by the United States in the conflict would become fertile ground for the expansion of slavery, which he unequivocally opposed. Notably, the Illinois Whig also introduced a doomed bill to ban slavery in the District of Columbia.

The freshman was not reluctant to orate from the floor, and magnanimous as he remained about immigration and immigrants, he still could not resist the occasional temptation to tweak the prototypical Irishman for political effect. In a June 1848 speech on internal improvements, Lincoln once again took a humorous Hibernian detour to make a serious point. Democrats had insisted that harbor duties could be applied to improving only those harbors where the levies were collected. If that requirement stood unchallenged, Lincoln pointed out, then urgently needed infrastructure projects in harbors too deteriorated to amass fees would be stymied for want of funding: "How [to] make a road, a canal, or clear a greatly obstructed river?" he inquired. "The idea that we could involves the same absurdity of the irish bull about the new boots—'I shall niver git em on' says Patrick 'till I wear em a day or two, and stretch em a little.'" By that "irish bull" logic, he argued, "We shall never make a canal . . . until it shall already have been made for a while."[52] Once again, the barb was aimed not only at stubborn Democrats eager to deploy technicalities to inhibit public works projects but also at all the ignorant "Patricks" whose support perpetuated the Democratic Party's grip on power.

The expression "Irish bull," as audiences of Lincoln's day knew, was shorthand for a ludicrous, paradoxical absurdity—typified by the lament "If all the world were blind, what a melancholy *sight* it would be!" These garbled but somehow comprehensible expressions might arise from typographical and punctuation errors, misspellings, grammatical mistakes, or comical mispronunciation. The malaprops could be found in newspaper advertisements, street signs, product labels, Dr. Johnson's dictionary, even the Talmud—and were variously attributed to Germans, African Americans, Scots, or Welshmen (the French called it *construction bouche*—"squinting construction"). Most often, however, American storytellers relied on stereotypical "Hibernianisms." As the author of an 1893 compendium of "bulls and blunders"

Newly elected, slick-haired Illinois congressman Abraham Lincoln, his massive rail-splitter's hands undisguisable, photographed in Springfield by Nicholas H. Shepherd around 1846.

put it, most such illogical statements proceeded from "the superabundance of ideas, which crowd one another so fast in an Irishman's brain that they get joined together . . . in the doorway of his speech, and can only tumble out in their ordinary disorder." Fair or not, Lincoln saw nothing wrong in quoting and enjoying them. As he put it, "A good Irish bull is medicine for the blues."[53]

And no one was more prone to political melancholy than Lincoln. Already approaching lame-duck status because of the peculiarities of the election cycle, he prudently turned some of his attention in the last half of 1848 to electing Whig Zachary Taylor—a hero of the recent war he had opposed—to the presidency. With one eye on a postelection federal appointment, Lincoln at last visited strife-torn Philadelphia to attend the April convention that nominated General Taylor over the aging Henry Clay. If Lincoln was conscience-stricken about forsaking his longtime political hero, he never said so. That the emergent Taylor coalition included anti-Catholics did not concern Lincoln, either. He wanted the Whigs to win. Writing to William Herndon, he confidently predicted in June that "in my opinion we shall have a most overwhelming, glorious, triumph," explaining: "One unmistakable sign is, that all the odds and ends are with us—Barnburners, Native Americans, Tyler men, disappointed office seeking locofocos, and the Lord knows what. This is important, if nothing else, in showing which way the wind blows."[54]

Lincoln knew that Herndon would recognize all the code words packed into that message. "Barnburners" were New York antislavery zealots (so named because they were like farmers willing to burn down their barns to exterminate vermin). "Tyler men" were admirers of the former, "accidental" president John Tyler, a slave-owning Virginia Democrat who had served out William Henry Harrison's term when that unlucky Whig died only weeks after his 1841 inauguration. And "Locofocos" (so dubbed for the newfangled matches they lit whenever opponents doused the lights to break up their indoor rallies) were a faction of New York Democrats opposed to Tammany Hall and aligned with another former Democratic president, Martin Van Buren, now attempting a White House comeback. What is most notable is that Lincoln included "Native Americans" in his litany of "odds and ends" and "Lord knows what." By "Native Americans," he did not mean American Indians. He meant anti-Catholic nativists. Only four years after the Philadelphia riots, as this remark shows, Lincoln was prepared to tolerate nativists' bigotry if their support could now help blow the winds toward Whig victory. It was the first of many such attempts at what period politicians, Lincoln among them, benignly referred to as "fusion."

For some—both residents of Lincoln's hometown and scattered veterans of General Taylor's onetime army—Whig overtures to nativists evoked painful memories. During the recent Mexican–American War, members of Georgia's "Irish Greens" had gotten into a deadly brawl with the mostly Protestant Kennesaw Rangers. Lincoln's congressional predecessor, Edward Baker—an immigrant himself, but from Protestant England—broke up that fight, suffering a grievous gunshot wound during the melee, and then ordered that only the Irish regiment be arrested. Baker's hasty judgment had provoked enough notoriety since the encounter to remind voters of the unfair treatment to which some American soldiers were subjected on the basis of their religion. In response to unendurable harassment, a unit known as the Saint Patrick's Division had actually deserted, switched sides, and fought for Mexico—until American forces captured the "San Patricios" and had them hanged.[55]

In New York, Horace Greeley importuned immigrants from all nations to unite against the Democrats. "Irishmen and Germans do not leave the horrors of feudal aristocracy to spread a viler and meaner yoke over this free Continent," he argued in the *Tribune* a week before the election. "Yet so incessant, so successful, have been the exertions of the party to commend itself to the favor of [the foreign-born] as having a sort of patent-right to their votes," he wrote breathlessly that same day, "that we rejoice . . . [that] the time is at hand when our fellow-citizens of German, Irish, or other European birth will be united and blended with both the great parties as Native citizens are— each voter judging for himself and acting upon his own convictions of public duty."[56]

As it turned out, the 1848 presidential election once again tipped, precisely as it had four years earlier, on the antislavery vote in New York. This time, however, just as Greeley had hoped, Democrats, not Whigs, defected from their standard-bearer, with enough of them backing third-party Free-Soil candidate Van Buren to hand the state, and the country, to Zachary Taylor. Delighted at the outcome but now facing the end of his career in the House, Lincoln stepped up his efforts to secure a prime patronage reward: appointment as commissioner of the General Land Office, a post previously held by his Irish nemesis, James Shields. Such spoils ordinarily went to those who had done the most to elect the winners, and Lincoln had done his share, but the new Whig administration failed to award him the post he coveted. As a consolation, the administration offered the governorship of Oregon Territory. Mary Lincoln, unwilling to relocate to the Far West, reportedly prevailed on her husband to decline, thereby effectively changing the course of history by preventing Lincoln's exile. For the time being, the outgoing congressman retreated to Springfield, again unable to outdo Shields, and perhaps regretful about his party's growing tolerance of nativism.

Lincoln had not been the only Whig to welcome, or at least turn a blind eye to, nativists inside the organization's political tent in 1848, but the party would ultimately pay a price for tolerating intolerance. The growing power of nativism, combined with decreasing fealty to established political organizations, would give rise in the next decade to the Know-Nothing movement. And it would encourage creation of its entirely new, well-organized political arm: a new iteration of the anti-Catholic American Party. Precisely what constituted Americanism would become itself a major issue in the 1850s.

CHAPTER THREE

No Objection to Fuse with Any Body

William Herndon once expressed astonishment that his law partner Abraham Lincoln "had no prejudice against any class, preferring
the Germans to any foreign element, yet tolerating—as I never could—
even the Irish."[1] *Even the Irish*: here was the sort of bigoted remark
Lincoln never uttered. To be sure, he was a man of his times, susceptible
to the casual biases common to his era, though better able than most to
express them in relatively inoffensive, largely humorous ways. Snide
comments like Herndon's point to how far the tolerant Lincoln tilted
against the widespread Protestant revulsion for Irish Catholics—though
on occasion the Irish could rile even Lincoln to action, especially when
he suspected the Democrats among them of election interference.

"Once, in Springfield," Herndon recalled, "the Irish voters medi-
tated taking possession of the polls. News came down the street that
they would permit nobody to vote but those of their own party. Mr.
Lincoln seized an ax-handle from a hardware store, and went alone to
open a way to the ballot-box. His appearance intimidated them, and we
had neither threats nor collisions that day."[2] Doubtless, Herndon did

not realize that his recollection echoed a recent claim by New York nativist leader Thomas R. Whitney. Whitney claimed to have spotted "bands of foreign bullies" sent to voting places by an *"Irish alderman . . .* with a supply of bludgeons close at hand, for the purpose of preventing Americans from approaching the polls to exercise their birthright of the suffrage."[3]

The image of the imposing Lincoln wielding the iconic tool of his rail-splitting youth—the handle, if not the blade, of an ax—to clear a path into a blocked-off polling place seems almost too melodramatic to be believed. And Herndon was known to exaggerate. Yet Lincoln did fret about ballot integrity in Illinois and occasionally carped that Irish Democrats might be voting illegally—against Whigs. All the same, Herndon recalled that his partner consistently "advocated the policy of free immigration of foreigners and their right to vote," even "when Americanism here was popular and rampant."[4] This set him apart. Once, when Herndon took on a client pursuing a legal challenge to voting rights, Lincoln declined to participate in the case. "I am opposed to the limitation or lessening of the right of suffrage; if anything, I am in favor if its extension or enlargement," he explained. "I want to lift men up—to broaden rather than contract their privileges."[5]

A test was coming. By now, Lincoln's own Springfield neighborhood was growing more diverse. Dotting the town were the homes of immigrant residents hailing from not only Ireland but also Germany, Scotland, France, Switzerland, Norway, England, and even Portugal.[6] In the rosy view of James H. Matheny, a fellow lawyer who had served as a groomsman at Lincoln's wedding, "We have representatives of almost every nationality beneath the sun . . . with perhaps as little discord as any people throughout the world."[7] Matheny contributed these observations to a business-friendly Springfield city directory; hence he understandably glossed over any animus between the town's Protestants and Catholics and made no mention of the limited opportunities available—save for domestic servitude—to unmarried women from Springfield's immigrant households.

Among the first European immigrants to arrive in Illinois were the Swedes, including the so-called Janssonists—followers of pietist reformer Erik Jansson—who in their search of religious freedom established the Bishop Hill Colony near Peoria in 1846. A second Swedish settlement rose the following year in nearby Andover. "They are producers," the *Rock Island Republican* acknowledged admiringly. "We wish them success."[8] One of that community's spiritual leaders, Rev. Lars Paul Esbjörn, would later work as a teacher at Illinois State University, where Lincoln's eldest son, Robert, became one of his prep-school pupils.[9]

The Swedes were soon joined by other European refugees. From the remote island of Madeira in the North Atlantic came a sudden influx of some two hundred "Portuguese exiles . . . destitute of many things necessary for their comfort." Their 1849 arrival in Springfield inspired the *Sangamo Journal* to launch a charity drive for food and household goods to sustain them.[10]

German immigration to the American "promised land" cascaded around the same time, when brutally suppressed 1848 democratic revolutions on the Continent motivated thousands of liberals to flee oppression, sometimes one step ahead of capture and punishment. If Irish immigration had been economic in nature, and Swedish immigration mainly religious, the German exodus was largely political. "I heard many a man say," the recent German refugee Carl Schurz reminisced of the neighbors he left behind, "how happy he would be if he could go . . . to that great and free country, where . . . nobody need be poor, because everyone was free."[11]

At first, like the Swedes, the German "Forty-Eighters" (Achtundvierziger) clustered within separate and distinct communities—like Chicago's North Side and Cincinnati's Over-the-Rhine—effectively creating their own outposts of Kleinedeutschland (Little Germany) in America.[12] Reluctant to serve merely as "raw material for the construction of a Yankee nation," German immigrants remained "saturated with the feeling that their free qualities made them the best citizens" of their adopted republic."[13] Yet retaining old-country gemütlichkeit, they made clear that, as historian Carl Frederick Wittke colorfully put it, "they preferred sausage and sauerkraut to pie and pork and beans." The lure of freedom and opportunity remained paramount. In an "Ode to Emigrants on Their Journey to America," a German writer reminded homesick refugees that "in America's valleys abounding with flowers . . . the earth does not mock the sweat of its grower."[14] By 1860, the German-born would make up half the population of Cincinnati, Milwaukee, and St. Louis.

The American *Volk* did not escape the suspicions and resentments previously reserved for the Irish. Anton Hesing, later the first German-born political boss in Chicago, remembered "a time when Germans were persecuted by American mobs with as great a brutality, and as diabolic a cruelty, as that with which Europeans have ever been persecuted in China, Chinese in California, or Jews in Rumania." Hesing testified that "native Americans [nativists], drunk with the desire to kill," had "burned down churches of the 'damned Germans' . . . who are mocked and jeered at because they are not able to speak the English language as fluently as those whose mother tongue it is."[15] Only by founding their own vereins—organizations devoted to community building—did the Germans establish an impregnable foothold in America's towns and cities. Among these clubs were the turnvereins, where émigrés (sometimes called American Turners) nourished both mind and body through programs of physical exercise and cultural enrichment modeled on the gymnasia back in Germany.[16]

One of Lincoln's earliest German friends was Frankfort-born attorney and politician Gustave (sometimes Gustav or Gustavus) Philipp Koerner (or Körner), a future Illinois lieutenant governor who had arrived in the United States fifteen years before the 1848 immigration avalanche and initially affiliated with the Democrats. Soon after meeting the handsome, pale-eyed attorney, Lincoln undoubtedly learned of an amazing coincidence in their life stories. Back in the old country, Koerner had once fought a duel with broadswords, wounding a fellow law student named Friedrich Hecker—who would later immigrate to America and become a Lincoln confidant, too.[17]

Koerner was far from captivated by the Lincoln he first encountered at a political event at Belleville, Illinois, in 1840. "His appearance was not very prepossessing," the émigré remembered. "His exceedingly tall and very angular form made his movements rather awkward. . . . His complexion had no roseate hue of health, but was then rather bilious, and, when not speaking, his face seemed to be overshadowed by melancholy thoughts. . . . No one in the crowd would have dreamed that he was one day to be their President."[18] Lincoln was no doubt disappointed that Germans like Koerner did not rush to join the Whig Party. Not until 1854 would the political ground shift—and not before Lincoln worked hard to recruit to the antislavery movement the onetime German dissidents who made Springfield not only a state capital but a melting pot.

One ethnic group with whom Lincoln forged an early and easy bond was the Jews. To be sure, the Jewish presence in Illinois remained minuscule, though the synagogue Kehilath Anshe Magriv (or Ma'ariv)—Congregation of the Jewish Men of the West—opened its doors in Chicago as early as 1847. Around the same time, Lincoln began a long friendship with fellow lawyer Abraham Jonas, an immigrant from England and the first Jew to take up residence in the Illinois river town of Quincy. Lincoln and Jonas shared a commitment to the Whig Party, experience in the state legislature, and a reverence for Henry Clay. Gustave Koerner, a Christian, regarded Jonas—and not Lincoln!—as "perhaps the best debater and the best politician on the Whig side."[19] Over the years, the Lincoln–Jonas friendship would ripen, and Lincoln would develop political and business relationships with other foreign-born Jewish Illinoisans.

· · ·

The Lincoln of this or any subsequent period—even his presidency—rarely ventured into the realm of foreign policy. But in September

Immigrant Jewish attorney Abraham Jonas of Quincy, Illinois.
Fellow Whig Lincoln called him "one of my most valued friends."

1849, he enthusiastically joined "a large meeting of citizens" in Springfield and drafted resolutions expressing "admiration" for Hungarian
revolutionaries and their "present glorious struggle for liberty," an uprising destined to collapse along with the battle for democracy in Germany.[20] Then, in late 1851, Lincoln and his neighbors learned that the
deposed Hungarian reformer Lajos Kossuth, banished from the Continent and more recently from England, next planned a trip to America. Lincoln immediately saw in the visit an opportunity to reanimate
the argument for universal freedom and opportunity.

In exile, Kossuth had become a living martyr, and his December
arrival in New York City touched off an ecstatic welcome that featured
the playing of "Hail to the Chief."[21] The nobleman turned revolutionary drew huge, adoring throngs, inspired mass-produced merchandise
in his image, and earned an invitation to address Congress and meet
Henry Clay and President Millard Fillmore (who had succeeded Taylor when the general died in office). Kossuth, a spellbinding orator

fluent in English, mesmerized American crowds by wielding words, one contemporary marveled, "like burning arrows."[22]

When Kossuth's itinerary took him westward, and as tantalizingly close to Springfield as Columbus, Ohio, Lincoln, an enthusiastic victim of "Kossuth fever," helped organize a January 1852 public meeting in his hometown to salute the visitor in absentia. Surely a sincere initiative, the endeavor was also bound to reap political rewards among the progressive foreign-born. As usual, Lincoln wrote the resolutions adopted that evening, which hailed Kossuth as "the most worthy and distinguished representative of the cause of civil and religious liberty on the continent of Europe." In Lincoln's words, the "sacred" principle for which Kossuth had fought—"civil and religious liberty"—was "held dear by the friends of freedom everywhere, and more especially by the people of these United States." It remained "the right of any people, sufficiently numerous for national independence," Lincoln added, "to throw off, to revolutionize, their existing form of government, and to establish such other in its stead as they may choose"—an argument he would of course reject when slave states declared their independence from the United States.[23]

Lavish praise for the illustrious expatriate was to be expected, but Lincoln skillfully injected a few related causes into his Kossuth resolutions, some of them anathema to nativists, who feared an influx of political refugees from Europe. "Whilst we meet to do honor to Kossuth," went the eighth point in his nine-point statement, "we should not fail to pour out the tribute of our praise and approbation to the patriotic efforts of the Irish, the Germans and the French, who have unsuccessfully fought to establish in their several governments the supremacy of the people." Lincoln's sympathetic reference to the Irish was especially noteworthy in this pro-democracy context. He concluded with a condemnation of England for "her treatment of Ireland," specifically its persecution of insurgent nationalists William Smith O'Brien, John Mitchel, "and other worthy patriots."[24] Few politicians could combine savviness and sincerity as beguilingly as Lincoln.

Two weeks later, Lincoln joined yet another committee, this one assigned to lure Kossuth to Springfield after all, though there is no evidence that the peripatetic celebrity ever accepted.[25] Instead, shortly thereafter, Kossuth alarmed several audiences with calls for renewed revolution in Europe. Later that year, he endorsed Democratic presidential nominee Franklin Pierce, unleashing an outpouring of nativist criticism meant to reclassify Kossuth as an "unscrupulous agitator" and to accuse his admirers of "toadyism."[26] By the end of 1852, he departed America, again an outcast, with Kossuth fever in full remission. In navigating the Kossuth episode, Lincoln had again demonstrated both tolerance and political skill not only by publicly saluting a hero but also in embracing the spirit of his call for freedom throughout the world. Once again, he had firmly identified with the non-nativist element of the Whig Party, even though it was losing strength and influence.

By 1852, Lincoln had firmly established his bona fides on European immigration as well as on African emigration—and apparently saw no irony in his support for both. No one knows precisely when he began embracing the notion of voluntarily colonizing free Blacks to Africa. He offered his first public endorsement of the idea on July 6, toward the end of a eulogy in Springfield for the recently departed Henry Clay. The "Great Compromiser" had been leader of the American Colonization Society (ACS), an eleemosynary but undeniably racist movement viewed by many whites at the time as a philanthropic undertaking to atone for the evils of the slave trade. Lincoln had likely been on hand when Clay addressed the ACS in the House Chamber back in January 1848.[27]

Toward the end of his 1852 Clay eulogy, Lincoln made it clear he had come not only to bury Clay but to praise colonization: "This suggestion of the possible ultimate redemption of the African race and African continent, was made twenty-five years ago," he reminded his audience. "Every succeeding year has added strength to the hope of its realization. May it indeed be realized!" The future emancipator who would later be compared to Moses made clear he regarded colonization as a reward for African Americans, as well as a redemption for white Americans. "Pharaoh's country was cursed with plagues," Lincoln pointed out, "and his hosts were drowned in the Red Sea for striving to retain a captive people who had already served them more than four hundred years. May like disasters never befall us!"[28]

. . .

Although Lincoln's legal practice was now taking up much of his time, he continued to keep his hand in Whig Party affairs. Denied the chance to seek reelection to Congress and disappointed in his quest for a federal appointment, he slaked his thirst for political influence by running as a Whig presidential elector in 1852. President Taylor, like Harrison before him, had died in office, and to oppose Democratic nominee Franklin Pierce, the Whigs had nominated another Mexican War hero, General Winfield Scott, as vainglorious as Taylor had been "rough and ready." Lightning did not strike twice.

Before the campaign could even get underway, Scott unwisely stirred controversy on the immigration issue with his written acceptance of the nomination, usually a mere formality. Venturing beyond the Whig platform, the sententious warrior, known as "Old Fuss and Feathers," unexpectedly proposed "giving to all foreigners the right of citizenship" if they served "in time of war, one year on board our public ships or in our land forces, regular or volunteer."[29] Meant as a friendly gesture to veterans, the suggestion instead ignited a nativist outcry. In a lively example, crafted as a tongue-in-cheek ode to "Old Winfield Scott," one anonymous bard mockingly imagined the "proud, pompous" general degrading himself with a proposal blatantly advanced to attract Irish support. It was as if Mary Lincoln's 1842 anti-Shields poem had come back to life with a new cast of bromidic Irish characters:

"When I a soldier was and marched
Before the drum and fife,

To march exposed to rain and mud,
Was the pleasure of my life.

"To *be a citizen,* I think,
No less should be required,
Than that a man should see these lakes,
So lovely—so admired!"

Just here an Irishman sang out
"Y'er honor's welcome here,
Och darlint, bless y'er honor's heart,"
(The Irishmen they cheer.)

"Oh that rich brogue—I love it well,
It bringeth back to me,
The noble deeds of those I led
To glorious victory."[30]

On one level, the satire meant—like the *Illinois State Register*'s praise of Lincoln during the Philadelphia riot aftershocks—to remind nativist Whigs that some in their party were *too* generous to the foreign-born. Concurrently, Democrats worked to affirm their status as the true party of immigrant rights. Lincoln's old dueling rival, James Shields, now a U.S. senator, persuasively argued on August 5: "There seems to be no good reason why a man who flies from want and oppression in Europe, who selects this country in preference to all others as the future home of himself and his family, and who looks forward to the day when his ashes shall mingle peacefully with the soil of his adopted country . . . should not make as good as citizen, and take as deep an interest in the welfare of the government, as if he descended in a direct line from one of the pilgrim fathers."[31]

Two weeks later, another controversy roiled the Whigs when the pro-Democratic *Boston Pilot* suggested that their presidential candidate was actually *anti*-immigration, charging that "General Scott assuredly did once espouse the Native cause" himself. To contrast Scott's inconsistency with the purer record of the Democratic nominee, the *Pilot* included a letter from Pierce supporters in his native New Hampshire asserting that "Catholics . . . entertain for him the highest respect as a politician and a man." The tribute bore the signatures of men with surnames like Murphy, Leahy, Sullivan, and Lynch.[32]

In Springfield, the candidate for Whig elector responded on August 14 with a rather bilious address before the city's Scott Club. Taking the podium at the city courthouse, Lincoln denounced the recent "attempts to ridicule Gen. Scott's views on naturalization."[33] For this occasion, he directed much of his ire against his own political rival Stephen Douglas. The "Little Giant" was now an influential U.S. senator. Two years earlier, he had engineered the Compromise of 1850, complete with an odious new fugitive slave law, which mandated that runaways be returned to bondage even if they managed to reach states where slavery was banned. Like other Democrats, Douglas had recently mocked Scott's sudden penchant for immigration reform.

In rebuttal, Lincoln castigated Douglas for misrepresenting the Whig nominee's proposal in order "to base a charge of ignorance and stupidity against Gen. Scott." Lincoln countered that Douglas, who had sought his party's presidential nod for himself only weeks earlier, had clearly never studied the citizenship laws enacted in the early days of the republic. These unmistakably "provided that adult aliens should come in on one set of reasons; that their minor children should come in on another set; and that such particular foreigners as had been proscribed by any State, should come in, if at all, on still another set. . . . Is it possible," taunted Lincoln, "that this candidate for a nomination to the Presidency [Douglas] never read the naturalization laws?"[34] Foreign-born military veterans belonged to yet "another" class of applicants, Lincoln insisted, meaning that Douglas had been wrong to think that "the bulk" of civilian immigrants would, under Scott's proposal, "remain unnaturalized, and without rights of citizenship among us."[35]

This Lincoln followed with a gratuitous swipe at Douglas's own Irish admirers. "Even those adopted citizens, whose votes have given Judge Douglas all his consequence," Lincoln reminded his listeners, "came in under these very laws. Would not the Judge have considered the holding [of] those laws unconstitutional, and those particular votes illegal, as more deplorable, than even an army and navy, a million strong?"[36]*

Finally, Lincoln directed a volley of anti-Irish rancor at Democrat Edward Hannegan, a former U.S. senator from neighboring Indiana. Craftily, he conceded that in Congress, Hannegan "had done his state some credit, and gained some reputation for himself." But as Lincoln's audience also knew, the alcoholic Hannegan had recently gone berserk, stabbed his brother-in-law to death, and was "enduring the tortures of deepest mental agony." Lincoln went in for a kill of his own—a rhetorical one—reminding his audience: "He was the son of an Irishman, with a bit of the brogue still lingering on his tongue; and with a very large share of that sprightliness and generous feeling, which generally characterize Irishmen who have had anything of a fair chance in the world." Now Hannegan was "broken down politically and pecuniarily."[37]

Lincoln even got off a few barbs at his old foil James Shields, accusing him of exaggerating Pierce's Mexican War record (which indeed paled in comparison to Scott's), even as many Democrats were expressing an overall "horror of military records" in criticism of the Whigs' habit of nominating war heroes. The hypocritical effort by Shields, Lincoln suggested, "looks very much like a pertinacious purpose to

---

*Notwithstanding Douglas's growing stature, Lincoln continued calling Douglas "Judge," a none-too-subtle reminder that the Little Giant had once maneuvered himself into the job of associate justice of the Illinois Supreme Court, to be succeeded on the bench by Lincoln's other longtime nemesis, James Shields.

'pile up' the ridiculous" and "burlesque" Scott out of the military glory he had earned.[38]

This time, though Lincoln had again punctuated his remarks with borderline ethnic taunts, Shields did not take the bait. And despite Lincoln's best efforts to rouse both Whigs and the Irish against the Democrats, Scott went down to a nationwide defeat of landslide proportions in November, abandoned by Whigs who thought him a nativist and by nativists who thought he had gone soft on immigration. It was not the last hurrah for Old Fuss and Feathers, who would still be serving as general-in-chief of the army at the dawn of the Civil War. But Pierce's triumph did mark the beginning of the end for the incurably factionalized Whig Party.

One Whig star who remained favorably disposed toward immigration—without abandoning his bigoted views about immigrants— was the well-known orator Edward Everett. Nearing sixty, the Massachusetts statesman had already served as congressman, governor, minister to Great Britain, and president of Harvard—and was about to begin a stint as a U.S. senator. In 1853, he told British visitor Sir John Acton that he "rejoices at the influx of Irish," explaining that their "priests . . . keep them in order." The immigrants remained "easily satisfied, the American leaves the lowest work to them, and employs himself with higher occupations." The Germans, Everett added to this clichéd observation, "are better emigrants than the Irish. They are more thrifty, and settle farther west." Acton thought Everett's ideas "did not seem to me very clear or comprehensive."[39] (Ten years later, Everett, famous at that point mostly for being famous, would share the platform with Abraham Lincoln—and deliver a speech no one afterward remembered—at Gettysburg.)

By contrast, Lincoln, humane and loyal by nature and both tactical and tactful by design, had resisted the temptation to choose between embracing nativism or condemning his longtime political party. Unlike Everett, he avoided expressing overt preference for either Irish or German immigrants. Now, with the Whig coalition unraveling, and

a rising alternative movement openly advocating restrictions on immigration and naturalization, Lincoln faced the prospect of becoming
a politician without a party. He responded without much conviction
by insisting that he was out of politics anyway.

. . .

That situation changed dramatically in 1854, when Senator Douglas
championed, and engineered congressional passage, of the hotly disputed new Kansas–Nebraska Act, legislation that antislavery men
judged the worst assault on freedom since the Fugitive Slave Act.

On one level, Douglas meant his new measure to spur national
expansion by organizing the national territories acquired from the
Louisiana Purchase and Mexican Cession while maintaining the balance of power between slave and free states. As Douglas saw matters,
his legislation offered something for everyone, even Whigs. Its implicit
embrace of manifest destiny promised to open the way for the most
ambitious "internal improvement" yet: a long-desired transcontinental
railroad accompanied by coast-to-coast telegraph lines. (Douglas knew
such projects would require the kind of backbreaking manual labor
only democratically inclined immigrants were willing to perform.) As
a supposedly added benefit, Douglas promised that the new law would
eliminate "the savage barrier to the extension of our institutions"—
meaning American Indians—and hasten "the further progress of
[their] emigration."[40]

More seismically, as far as Lincoln was concerned, the Kansas–
Nebraska Act would mean the "extension" of one American institution
in particular: slavery. Douglas's legislative brainchild repealed the
long-standing Missouri Compromise, which since 1820 had outlawed
slavery north of the 36°30' parallel and kept the explosive issue from
dominating political discourse even as it condemned generations of
enslaved people to the horrors of further bondage. In its stead, Kansas–
Nebraska introduced the doctrine of "popular sovereignty," which offered white settlers in the new Western territories the right to vote on

whether to admit or prohibit slavery. Douglas saw the reform as inherently democratic—and as a tonic for his national ambitions. (He managed to dodge a possible political disaster when the House of Representatives eliminated a Senate amendment prohibiting new immigrants from either voting or holding political office in these same Western territories.) At once incensed and inspired, Lincoln viewed the new law as evidence of a pernicious scheme to make slavery national and perpetual.

"I was losing interest in politics," Lincoln later put it, "when the repeal of the Missouri Compromise aroused me again"—as he "had never been before."[41] At last, the frustrated politician had found his great cause. Reentering the fray with renewed vigor, he began focusing almost exclusively on the slavery expansion issue. Concern for immigrants receded into the background, though Lincoln would never exclude the foreign-born from the natural rights he believed America promised all its residents, Black and white, free and enslaved. "We proposed to give *all* a chance," he scribbled of the nation's founding in a fragment composed that year; "and we expected the weak to grow stronger, the ignorant, wiser; and all better, and happier together."[42] Even if not specifically stated, this credo extended to naturalized Americans. And yet, aware that many nativists opposed slavery as well as immigration, Lincoln took care to say nothing that might risk losing their sympathy for what now became known as the anti-Nebraska movement—especially with the Illinois legislature up for election in November 1854 and Lincoln himself standing for the first time in years as a candidate for the general assembly.

The unspoken question was whether the emerging anti-Nebraska coalition could welcome those who opposed immigration without tainting its crusade against slavery. The matter was complicated by the fact that Illinois was a geographically "vertical" state. Allegiances tilted according to the regional backgrounds of new arrivals and cemented consistent with proximity to either free or slave neighboring states. While southern Illinois remained sympathetic with slave inter ests, the northern part of the state became as hostile to slavery as it was resistant to foreigners.

Complicating matters further, die-hard nativists advanced an alluring alternative to further fusion with Whigs: a revitalized "American Party," the best-managed and most popular anti-Catholic political organization yet. The movement evolved from both New York's old Order of the Star Spangled Banner and the secretive anti-Catholic Know-Nothing society. The latter was reportedly so named (by Horace Greeley, some claimed) because each time an intruder knocked unannounced on the door during one of its lodge meetings and asked what was being discussed inside, the answer came back: "I know nothing." As one Chicagoan soon observed, even Lutheran Swedes "down on the Pope" were becoming "first-rate Know Nothings."[43]

While decrying its adherents as lacking in statesmanship and intelligence, the colorful Washington journalist Ben Perley Poore admitted that their "secretly held lodges, with their paraphernalia, pass-words, and degrees, grips and signs, tickled the popular fancy, and the new organization became formidable."[44] Greeley, who at first thought the movement was "confined to our great cities and their vicinage,"[45] now similarly conceded its epidemic-like spread. In the boastful but accurate words of one of the Know-Nothings' lead recruiters, "like a vast body of pent up waters when the floodgates have burst asunder, membership poured forth in torrents." By May 1854, just as Douglas's Nebraska bill was becoming law, "the order was planted" in Lincoln's Illinois.[46] Notably, Lincoln did not immediately try rooting it out.

Instead, sometime that summer, he agreed to sit down with a Know-Nothing delegation tasked with interviewing, vetting, and potentially endorsing major-party candidates for the state legislature. If we can believe the story told years later by one of that group, Richard Ballinger, Lincoln expressed absolutely no moral outrage toward his nativist visitors that day. Initially, he even bantered with his callers, telling them that "they might vote for him if they wanted to; so might the Democrats." This did not mean, he cautioned the Know-Nothings, that he was "in sentiment with this new party." Then Lincoln playfully postured that he was not even sure who Native Americans were. "Do they not wear breech-clout and carry tomahawk?" he jested, pretending he believed that the group was composed of American Indians. Finally growing serious—that is, about the original Native Americans—he added, "We pushed them from their homes and now turn upon others not fortunate enough to come over as early as our forefathers."[47] Whether Lincoln was alluding here to the old family stories about his own "forefather," killed decades earlier by Indians, is impossible to know.

Of course, Lincoln could not send the delegation on its way without at least one on-topic Irish joke. "When the Know-nothing party first came up," he drawled, "I had an Irishman, Patrick by name, hoeing in my garden. One morning I was there with him, and he said, 'Mr. Lincoln, what about the Know-nothings?' I explained to him that they would possibly carry a few elections and disappear, and I asked Pat why he was not born in this country. 'Faith, Mr. Lincoln,' he replied, 'I wanted to be, but my mother wouldn't let me.'" (Ballinger recalled that the cringe-evoking story made him wish he "had refused to serve on the committee."[48]) The recollection certainly has a ring of authenticity to it, particularly since Lincoln soon took to the stump to feign as much incredulity about the movement publicly as he had exhibited privately to his Know-Nothing visitors.

Appearing in front of a hometown crowd just before embarking on a speaking tour to assail the Kansas–Nebraska Act, Lincoln reiterated his incredible claim that the new anti-immigration party did not really exist. The Democratic *State Register* promptly mocked him, reporting: "He knew nothing of the secret institution . . . even 'doubted its existence.' Of course he did. He 'Knows Nothing' about it."[49] Instead of shifting his approach, however, Lincoln defiantly expanded it for more laughs at nearby Bloomington. As a Republican newspaper reported this time, the audience loved it:

Like many others he *Knew Nothing* in regard to the Know-Nothings, and he had serious doubts whether such an organization existed—if such was the case, he had been slighted, for no intimation thereof had been vouchsafed to him. But he would say in all seriousness, that if such an organization, secret or public, as Judge Douglas had described, really existed, and had for its object interference with the rights of foreigners, the Judge could not deprecate it more severely than himself. If there was an order styled the Know-Nothings, and there was any thing bad in it, he was unqualifiedly against it; and if there was anything good in it, why, he said God speed it! [Laughter and applause.] But he would like to be informed on one point: if such a society existed, and the members were bound by such horrid oaths as Judge Douglas told about, he would really like to know how the Judge found out his secrets? [Renewed laughter.][50]

Lincoln's finest—and longest—1854 campaign speech came on October 16 at Peoria. "Let no one be deceived," he proclaimed that day. "The spirit of seventy-six and the spirit of Nebraska, are utter antagonisms; and the former is being rapidly displaced by the latter." But he detoured from his message to observe that, owing to the illegal slave trade, Black population growth now outpaced that of white immigrants. He explained, "The African slave trade is not yet effectually suppressed; and if we make a reasonable deduction for the white people amongst us, who are foreigners, and the descendants of foreigners, arriving here since 1808, we shall find the increase of the black population out-running that of the white, to an extent unaccountable, except by supposing that some of them too, have been coming from Africa."[51] In an otherwise soaring address largely focused on the meaning of American democracy, the comparison between the slave trade and free immigration stands out as both clumsy and somewhat mischievous. Perhaps Lincoln injected it to remind foreign-born voters that the forced importation of Africans stood in stark contrast to their own volitional passages across the Atlantic. But some whites in the North already saw the rising free Black population as a threat to their job security and needed no reminders to stoke their resentment. Lincoln surely knew that as well. But he was still groping for a just and appealing policy on immigrants and immigration.[52]

Eleven days after his Peoria address, Lincoln spoke in Chicago at the invitation of George Schneider, a young immigrant ally born in the Rhineland.[53] Schneider now edited and co-owned the influential German-language newspaper *Illinois Staats-Zeitung*, one of the first presses in the growing city, in any tongue, to condemn the Kansas–Nebraska Act outright. At the time, nativist prejudice was on the ascent in Chicago. According to Hungarian immigrant Julian Kuné, the city "being under the dominion of the Knownothing party" was "not the most desirable place for a naturalized citizen."[54] Lincoln believed that even the *Chicago Tribune* had become "too much of a Know-Nothing sheet."[55] After Stephen Douglas publicly assailed nativism as "revolting to our sense of justice and right," the *Tribune* had responded by unapologetically labeling the senator's supporters "grog-house politicians" and "Irish rowdies."[56]

Following his speech at Chicago's North Market Hall, Lincoln strolled with Schneider and politician Isaac N. Arnold toward the *Staats-Zeitung's* Lake Street office, probably to cement a new alliance with the city's increasingly antislavery Germans. Before they could enter, Schneider importuned Lincoln into the photograph gallery next door operated by his friend and fellow immigrant Johan Carl Frederik Polycarpus von Schneidau, who traced his own roots (and polyglot name) to both Austria and Sweden. Inside, Lincoln posed for only his second-known photograph, his first in eight years, and his first by a foreign-born camera artist. Tellingly, von Schneidau posed his subject holding a copy of the *Staats-Zeitung* toward the camera as if advertising it. The daguerreotype does not show Lincoln at his best—his hair disordered, he is dressed in an ill-fitting velvet-lapelled coat and an

A garishly dressed Lincoln clutches a German-language newspaper
as he poses for Swedish-born photographer Polycarpus von Schneidau
after orating in Chicago, October 1854. The image was later retouched to
make it appear that Lincoln was holding the *Chicago Tribune*.

almost comically outsize bow tie—but the portrait seriously reflected the sitter's eagerness to promote a foreign-language paper he hoped would return the favor in the form of future editorial support and vote pulling.[57] With the Whig organization in shambles, Lincoln was likely pondering the creation of a fresh coalition that would welcome antislavery immigrants who, like Schneider, resented nativism.

Paradoxically, German and Irish immigration was now on the decline. Some attributed the downturn to the improved health of crops in Ireland, others to the fact that ships previously available to carry passengers from both nations to America were now increasingly diverted to Crimean War service. But news had also reached Europe that anti-foreigner violence had resurged in the United States—with new outbreaks in Cincinnati, Baltimore, St. Louis, and even multicultural New Orleans.[58] Such news did not exactly encourage new waves of immigration.

Privately, at least, Lincoln continued to make clear he had little tolerance for the growing Know-Nothing movement, or for Whigs who flirted with it openly. Campaigning at the end of October for the reelection of hard-drinking Illinois congressman Richard Yates, Lincoln learned Yates had come under criticism for seeking nativist support (including that of the same Ballinger committee with whom he himself had met). Writing to Yates from the town of Jacksonville a week before Election Day, Lincoln expressed alarm that "the English in Morgan county have become dissatisfied about No-Nothingism" [sic]. Although Yates dismissed a rumor that he had attended an actual Know-Nothing meeting, he seemed, much like Lincoln, reluctant to condemn the organization outright. In this case, Lincoln believed the congressman needed to respond more directly.[59]

Toward that end, he drafted a statement for Yates's signature that no doubt denied the charge explicitly—we do not know for certain because the enclosure has never come to light. "I think it would be well to make several copies," he instructed Yates with the specificity of a precinct captain distributing leaflets, "and have one placed in the hands of a safe friend, at each precinct where any considerable number of the foreign citizens, german as well as english—vote." (Lincoln made no mention of the Irish—as far as he was concerned, they had become a lost cause.) In a hectoring follow-up reminder to Yates two days later, Lincoln grew blunter: "On my way down I heard . . . a story which may harm you if not averted—namely, that you have been a Know-Nothing. I suggest that you get a denial." Lincoln's urgent recommendation apparently went unheeded.

Yates ended up losing his reelection bid by only two hundred votes, half of which, he later conceded, "would have voted for me but for a false and sworn to statement that I had been seen in a Know Nothing Lodge."[60] The Democrats had "the whiskey boys on their side," a friend from a nearby town told Lincoln. "Evry [sic] Irish man in the county that had not their papers are getting theirs if possible."[61] By contrast, without either rebuking or embracing the Know-Nothings publicly, Lincoln easily won his own campaign for the legislature. All but lost to history is the strange fact that Yates was defeated by Thomas L. Harris, the same Democrat who had succeeded to Lincoln's congressional seat back in 1849.*

. . .

A few weeks after Election Day 1854, Lincoln admitted, "I have got it into my head to try to be a U.S. Senator"—specifically, to win the expiring seat currently held by none other than his old antagonist James Shields.[62] Lincoln was widely admired and well-liked, and in his recent speeches he had emerged as the state's most passionate opponent of slavery expansion. Besides, it would have been sweet revenge if Lincoln could dislodge the vulnerable Irish Democrat who had once challenged him to mortal combat.

Stephen Douglas had other plans. "At all events our friends should

---

*Six years later, Yates would be elected governor of Illinois on the same 1860 Republican ticket headed by Abraham Lincoln as the party's candidate for president.

stand by Shields," the influential senator instructed fellow Democrats, "and throw the responsibility on the Whigs of beating him *because he was born in Ireland.*" As far as Douglas was concerned, Know-Nothingism had supplanted Nebraska "as the chief issue of the future," and if Shields faced defeat it would be clear "to the whole country that a gallant Soldier & a faithful public servant has been stricken down because of the place of his birth." The senator was convinced that nativism "will bring the Germans and all foreigners and Catholics to our side."[63]

At the time, U.S. senators were chosen by state legislatures, not by direct vote of the people, and Lincoln, dismissing the idea that ousting Shields would be seen as anti-Irish, calculated that the incoming class of lawmakers harbored enough anti-Nebraska sentiment to give his own candidacy a good chance of success. To conduct the race, he declined the legislative seat he had just won—because the state constitution barred state legislators from naming one of their own to the U.S. Senate.[64] Unexpectedly, his resignation irked potential supporters and threatened to upend his plan to assemble a winning coalition. Charles H. Ray, copublisher of the *Chicago Tribune*, complained that in declining to serve in the general assembly, the Senate aspirant had particularly offended "Know Nothings, who had supported Lincoln" and now resented "what they considered betrayal."[65] Indeed, in a special election held a few weeks later to fill the vacated seat, voters chose a Democrat to replace Lincoln—and to cast a potentially decisive vote against him in the upcoming legislative balloting for the Senate.

Amid further concerns that a majority of the new legislature might secretly identify as Know-Nothing—impossible to calculate accurately, since membership in its lodges remained secret—Lincoln maintained his usual public silence on nativism. This led another Chicago paper to suggest, without proof, that "Mr. Lincoln is a Know Nothing and expects the full vote . . . of the Know Nothings." In the run-up to the balloting, several of Lincoln's longtime Whig allies in the legislature came to the same conclusion and withdrew their support. One was married to a Catholic.[66]

Lincoln did demonstrate intolerance around this time—but to nativists who had long railed against immigration by citing the high cost of supporting indigent refugees. In mid-December, he was asked to mediate the case of an eighteen-year-old named John Fitzgerald—"ablebodied, but without pecuniary means," in Lincoln's description—who had come to Springfield directly from Ireland, sought employment, but after only three weeks "fell sick, and became a public charge." Was Springfield or was Sangamon County "by law to bear the charge"? In Lincoln's opinion, the obligation fell to the city. Paupers eligible for municipal support needed only be residents, Lincoln argued, not citizens.[67] Asked on this occasion only to choose between the city and the county to pay for Fitzgerald's support, Lincoln did not, in rendering a judgment, use the occasion to lambaste uncharitable nativists or ostracize impoverished immigrants. Not with the Senate contest coming to a head in the state legislature—and not under Lincoln's innate sense of sympathy and fair play.

The decisive legislative session took place at the state capitol on February 8, 1855, and saw Lincoln quickly jump to a first-ballot lead of 44–41 over Shields, just a few votes shy of an outright majority. That was as close as Lincoln got to the U.S. Senate that day. In subsequent roll calls, he initially clung to a slight advantage, then began faltering. Just before the tenth ballot, with his support now evaporating, he bowed out and threw his votes to antislavery ex-Democrat Lyman Trumbull in order to block the election of a pro-Nebraska Democrat named Joel Matteson. The two veterans of the Bloody Island affair, Lincoln and Shields, found themselves discarded.

"Shields was bitterly disappointed," recalled Lieutenant Governor Gustave Koerner. "He left the State almost immediately" and bought a farm near a Minnesota town "colonized largely by Irishmen."[68] As for Lincoln, he gamely told one supporter after the "agony" of the ordeal subsided, "I regret my defeat moderately, but I am not nervous about it."[69] Unlike Shields, he was not going anywhere.

. . .

By May 1855, even Lincoln's closest personal friend was wondering whether the recently defeated Senate aspirant remained a Whig or was drifting toward nativism.

Lincoln's "friend forever" Joshua Fry Speed, who inquired into his old roommate's rumored flirtation with nativism and received a now-famous reply.

Joshua Fry Speed, now a resident of Kentucky, had been Lincoln's roommate years earlier in Springfield. As anxious bachelors, they had once exchanged private letters about the potential joys and pitfalls of marriage. Now Speed had written his onetime confidant to inquire about his current political affiliation. Lincoln had been clear enough about his opposition to Kansas–Nebraska, but Speed doubtless noticed that his old friend had never openly denounced the nativist movement. Speed's original inquiry has never been located—Lincoln would not employ a secretary to organize his files for another five years—but we can surmise its contents (though not its tone) from Lincoln's reply, which took three months for the admittedly "poor correspondent" to compose and send. Perhaps he had difficulty framing his response, or even assessing his political situation. Finally he made abundantly clear, at least between old friends, that he opposed nativism and yet remained a Whig—that is, if the party still existed:

> I am not a Know-Nothing. That is certain. How could I be? How can any one who abhors the oppression of negroes, be in favor of degrading classes of white people? Our progress in degeneracy appears to me to be pretty rapid. As a nation, we began by declaring that "*all men are created equal.*" We now practically read it "all men are created equal, *except negroes.*" When the Know-Nothings get control, it will read "all men are created equal, except negroes, and *foreigners, and Catholics.*" When it comes to this I should prefer emigrating to some country where they make no pretence of loving liberty—to Russia, for instance, where despotism can be taken pure, and without the base alloy of hypocracy [*sic*].[70]

The letter has since been quoted in nearly every Lincoln biography. He had never been clearer about how revolted he was by any credo that diverged from the promise of equality animating the Declaration of Independence—never more perspicuous about America's standing as a refuge for the oppressed—and never more prescient about the kind of despotism to be found in totalitarian states like Russia.

Friend to friend, the message was unmistakable. But private letters seldom move public policy. And Lincoln had still not condemned the Know-Nothings outright before an audience of voters. Writing just a few days earlier to Illinois abolitionist Owen Lovejoy, Lincoln had at least been more candid about the political contortions he felt might be needed to lure nativists to the antislavery cause without offending naturalized citizens—and to attract the foreign-born to the antislavery

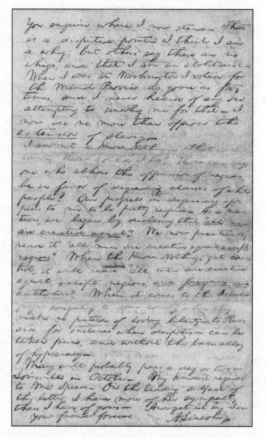

Speed preserved Lincoln's handwritten "I am not a Know-Nothing" letter, its most crucial sentence now blurred along the original fold crease.

movement without outraging the nativists. Revolted by Know-Nothing principles but reluctant to push their adherents toward the Democrats, a frustrated Lincoln found himself for once unable to navigate a politically advantageous course. As he agonized to Lovejoy, "I fear to do anything, lest I do wrong." In his view: "Know-nothingism has not yet entirely tumbled to pieces—nay, it is a little encouraged by the late elections," and "[u]ntil we can get the elements of this organization, there is not sufficient materials to successfully combat the Nebraska democracy with. We can not get them so long as they cling to a hope of success under their own organization; and I fear an open push by us now, may offend them, and tend to prevent our ever getting them." It is no wonder Lincoln's frank, tactical letter to Lovejoy has been cited far less frequently than his more idealistic one to Speed.

As Lincoln fretted bluntly to Lovejoy, Know-Nothing adherents now included his "old political and personal friends." He had "hoped their organization would die out without the painful necessity of my taking an open stand against them."[71] Such was not the case. The movement had instead grown large enough to embrace both "Sams"— steadfastly anti-Catholic and anti-immigration—and "Jonathans," who at least tempered their hostility to Catholicism and immigration with strong opposition to slavery. Lincoln was ready to disavow the former but not the latter. He still wanted to "get" them on his side.

To Lovejoy, whose elder brother Elijah had died at the hands of a pro-slavery mob nearly eighteen years earlier, Lincoln at least asserted his moral outrage toward bigoted nativists: "Of their principles I think little better than I do of those of the slavery extensionists," he avowed. Then he introduced the line of thought he would reiterate to Speed: "Indeed I do not perceive how any one professing to be sensitive to the wrongs of the negroes, can join in a league to degrade a class of white men."[72]

Then Lincoln turned his argument back to raw politics, for in the end he still believed that anti-Nebraska forces needed to expand, not reduce, their numbers, and he knew the Know-Nothing movement was still on the rise. "I have no objection to 'fuse' with any body," Lincoln made clear to Lovejoy, "provided I can fuse on ground which I think is right; and I believe the opponents of slavery extension could now do this, if it were not for this K.N.ism. In many speeches last summer I advised those who did me the honor of hearing to 'stand with any body who stands right'—and I am still quite willing to follow my own advice."[73] What precisely that advice was, however, remained a secret Lincoln did not share.

That same year, a new, anonymously authored book conceded that the Know-Nothings remained a secret association, but justified the movement's furtiveness by rationalizing that the Roman Catholic Church remained "the most secret and most formidable association that human ingenuity ever devised." It was papism, the screed insisted, not nativism, that remained "hostile to the principles of civil and religious liberty."[74]

How Lincoln planned to reconcile his own antislavery agenda with such abhorrent and intransigent bigotry remained unexplained.

CHAPTER FOUR

Our Equals in All Things

On February 22, 1856—not coincidentally Washington's birthday—
Lincoln braved a raging snowstorm to join a meeting of the state's
antislavery newspaper editors at Decatur, Illinois. The inclement
weather held the crowd down to a mere dozen, and Lincoln was the
only non-journalist to attend. His appearance stirred grateful talk of
another run for the Senate, or perhaps a campaign for governor.[1]

George Schneider, the pro-Lincoln editor of Chicago's *Staats-
Zeitung*, arrived at the gathering determined "to fight with all my
might" to make sure his fellow editors did not leave without officially
denouncing Know-Nothingism. Toward that end, he offered a resolution pledging to "welcome the exiles and migrants from the Old
World, to homes of enterprise and of freedom in the new . . . with
merit, not birthplace, the test."[2] To Schneider's "utter despair," the
proposal encountered a "storm of opposition" at the gathering. Lincoln
came to its rescue, arguing that "only through an unqualified proclamation can we count on support" from the foreign-born. "The citizens

who have adopted this country as their own," he argued, "have a right to demand this from us."[3] The resolution passed.

Most consequentially of all, the Decatur meeting heralded the imminent birth of the state's Republican Party and marked Lincoln's willingness to respond at last to the "tap of the fusion drum" and join up.[4] With the Whig Party moribund, Lincoln was finally ready to embrace the new coalition of ex-Whigs, Free-Soilers, anti-Nebraska Democrats, and foreign-born liberals. Two months later, a larger group met at Bloomington and formally organized the Illinois Republican Party, with Lincoln again in attendance and this time delivering a rousing speech.[5] There, Lincoln's friend and former state legislative colleague Orville Hickman Browning offered "a resolution intended to reconcile both Know nothings and German's to act with us" in the new coalition. As Browning proudly noted, the convention adopted it "without objection or amendment."[6]

In June, national Republicans nominated their first presidential candidate: former U.S. senator and fabled explorer John C. Frémont of California. At the party convention in Philadelphia, though not in attendance, Lincoln unexpectedly received 110 first-ballot votes for vice president before the delegates turned instead to former senator William L. Dayton of New Jersey to balance America's first coast-to-coast ticket. Nonetheless, the convention vote signaled an acknowledgment of Lincoln's growing prominence. Democrats, meeting in Cincinnati, awarded their own presidential nod to a "Doughface"—a Northerner with Southern sympathies—former secretary of state James Buchanan of Pennsylvania.

Had the contest offered these two alternatives alone, the embryonic Republicans might have stood an outside chance of success. To overcome the solidly Democratic South, the party needed only to solidify the newly assembled coalition, which included disaffected immigrants along with nativists who hated slavery more passionately than they disliked foreigners.[7] Illinois, again a bellwether state, was now home to thousands of liberal German-born voters infuriated by the

Kansas–Nebraska Act and invigorated when Frémont announced himself as antislavery. The standard-bearer's celebrity status promised to help him further: the "Pathfinder of the West" had earned Lewis and Clark–level renown.

Months before Democrats and Republicans met, however, retrograde Know-Nothings, along with the last remnants of the Whig organization, had gathered for a convention of the so-called American Party. Two years earlier, the upstart "Americans" had run seventy-six anti-immigration candidates for congressional seats—and won thirty-five of the races. Emboldened, they now nominated ex-president Millard Fillmore for the White House. Lincoln had once welcomed Fillmore to Springfield, looking on approvingly as admirers fired a "national salute" in his honor.[8] Now, running on a platform declaring that "Americans must rule America," Fillmore pledged "to preserve our political institutions in their original purity and vigor, and to keep them unadulterated by foreign influence." If the American Party prevailed, the foreign-born could never again hold elective office. Residency requirements for citizenship would be lengthened to as many as twenty-one years, and "all legal means . . . adopted to obstruct and prevent the immigration of the vicious and worthless, the criminal and pauper"—including imposition of a head tax to discourage the poor from seeking refuge here.[9] The Know-Nothings' "invisible, noiseless, mysterious" lodge meetings still remained closed to outsiders, but members made no secret of their overarching mission: to resist the supposedly "aggressive policy and corrupting tendencies of the Roman Catholic Church."[10] Here stood the most formidable challenge yet to national diversity and the two-party tradition. Indeed, the new copublisher of the ardently pro-Lincoln *Illinois State Journal* initially hoped Fillmore would win the presidency.[11]

As far as Lincoln was concerned, the rise of the American Party should have made it easier to lure antislavery immigrants, many of them longtime Democrats, to Republican ranks. It did not quite turn out as he predicted. At first "it was quite natural," Gustave Koerner

In this 1856 Currier & Ives campaign cartoon, Know-Nothing presidential nominee Fillmore is portrayed as "the right man" for the White House, holding off both rifle-toting Republican Frémont *(left)* and dagger-wielding Democrat Buchanan (the eventual winner).

tried explaining, that "voters of foreign birth, who had almost unanimously belonged to the Democratic party, should hesitate long before they joined a new party, among whom they recognized a great many people who had always been opposed to them." Yet, Koerner added, "the Germans were so much opposed to slavery that, with the exception of the Catholics amongst them, against whom the Know Nothings had more particularly directed their assaults . . . almost all marched to the polls under the Republican banner."[12] Nonetheless the Know-Nothings could point to significant inroads in the Northeast, notably in Massachusetts and New York.

Nor was Know-Nothing strength to be underestimated in the West. In Lincoln's Springfield, future Illinois governor Shelby M. Cullom helped finance a new Fillmore campaign paper opaquely called the *Conservative*.[13] Even Lincoln's most devoted press supporter, Simeon Francis of the *Sangamo Journal*—now rechristened the *Illinois*

State Journal—began expressing sympathy for the nativist movement before selling his interest in the paper. And in the upper part of the state, the editor of the Chicago *Native Citizen*, William W. Danenhower, embraced anti-Catholicism openly.[14] In a show of strength just after Lincoln's failed bid for the Senate, Chicago Know-Nothings had elected their first mayor, Dr. Levi Boone, who promptly ordered saloons closed on Sundays, provoking a deadly, German-led "Lager Beer Riot."

If all this were not concerning enough, an openly nativist paper called the *Springfield Capital* soon made its appearance in Lincoln's own hometown. Worse, its principal sponsor, Benjamin S. Edwards, was practically a member of the family: the brother-in-law of Mary Lincoln's sister. Speaking of Mary, had women enjoyed the right to vote in 1856, even she might have cast a ballot for the Know-Nothings. Fillmore "feels the *necessity* of keeping foreigners, within bounds," she confided to her Lexington-based half sister, perhaps only in jest, but more likely after another row with an immigrant maid. "If some of you Kentuckians, had to deal with the 'wild Irish,' as we housekeepers are sometimes called upon to do, the south would certainly elect Mr Fillmore next time."[15]

Hewing to tradition, none of the three 1856 presidential candidates campaigned directly for the office, but the race stimulated considerable activity from surrogates like Lincoln, who stumped for Frémont across Illinois. For their part, Know-Nothings aroused enthusiasm by promoting lurid anti-Catholic "convent literature" like *The Escaped Nun: or, Disclosures of Convent Life*, by a former "Sister of Charity," and the still-popular Maria Monk potboiler, *Awful Disclosures of the Hotel Nunnery in Montreal*.[16] Monk's 1836 book alone, a sordid tale of depraved priests and their sexual predation against innocent novitiates, sold three million copies before the Civil War, rivaling the reach of the sensational antislavery novel *Uncle Tom's Cabin*.

Joining these titles were nonfiction propaganda screeds like *A Defence of the American Policy, as Opposed to the Encroachments of Foreign*

Influence, and Especially to the Interference of the Papacy in the Political Interests and Affairs of the United States. The work of Thomas R. Whitney, founding architect of New York's nativist movement, it warned American-born workers that their labor was being "cheapened" and their "talent undermined by the ruinous competition" of foreigners.[17] Then there was the *Know Nothing Almanac*, which featured, alongside benign statistics about the phases of the moon, doomsday warnings to "ye who preach submission to the hordes of foreign immigrants swarming like vermin through the land."[18] From Philadelphia came *The Origin and Progress of the American Party in Politics*, a rehash that ascribed full blame for that city's infamous 1844 riots to the Irish.[19] And in Baltimore, Anna Ella Carroll, a pioneering female pamphleteer who would later supply polemics for hire to the Lincoln administration, contributed the equally splenetic *The Great American Battle; or, the Contest Between Christianity and Political Romanism*, which claimed America was "suffocating" under "the bloody code of Rome's Inquisition."[20] Such volumes abounded with hysterical conspiracy theories, including Jesuit plots to undermine the American military and papal schemes to rig popular sovereignty referenda in the West.

The avalanche of Know-Nothing publications overwhelmed the voices of advocates who argued that immigration was both true to the founders' intent and good for the modern economy. As one such writer put it, the "reckless" "and factious" warfare against the foreign-born was "against the principles on which our Revolution was started and . . . against the prosperity of the nation."[21]

Meanwhile, Democrats and Know-Nothings alike spread the potentially disqualifying rumor that Frémont himself was Catholic— plausible enough, since his father had been a French Canadian of that faith. (Although the Republican nominee had married his wife in a Catholic ceremony, Frémont regarded himself as an Episcopalian.[22]) By August, New York Republican boss Thurlow Weed was fretting that "the Catholic story is doing us much damage."[23] Against this tide, "Lincoln dared be just and stand bolt upright," William Herndon remembered admiringly. He "opposed Know Nothingism in all its phazes [*sic*], everywhere and at all times when it was sweeping over the land like wild fire." Still, Herndon admitted, Lincoln "did not say much" about it "in 1854 or 55."[24]

Nor in fact did he in 1856. Barnstorming for Frémont, Lincoln instead emphasized that votes for the American Party would siphon off antislavery support due the Republicans—and help elect pro-slavery Democrats. "The great difficulty," he told Senator Lyman Trumbull in August, was that voters supposed Fillmore was "as good as Fremont" against slavery extension.[25] In what Lincoln scholar Paul M. Angle indulgently judged an "ingenious" move, Lincoln composed a particularly "persuasive" warning that Buchanan could win Illinois, and with it the White House, "if men persist in throwing away votes upon Mr. Fillmore."[26] Lincoln ordered the missive printed up in quantity so he could personalize individual copies and mail them confidentially to undecided voters. The initiative ended up backfiring on Lincoln at a campaign rally at which several members of his audience produced their supposedly unique and confidential letters and shared a public laugh at their author's expense.[27]

Undaunted, Lincoln focused directly on turning out the immigrant vote. He arranged for wide distribution of what he called the "german Fremont paper"—the Chicago-based *Staats-Zeitung*—and then contributed $100 for the aid of Gustave Koerner's onetime dueling rival, Friedrich Hecker, who had lost his house to arson. Lincoln proposed raising ten times that amount in Hecker's behalf. "Such a sum no doubt would greatly relieve him," he told Charles Ray of the *Chicago Tribune*, "and enable him to take the field again . . . to address our german friends."[28]

Still, Lincoln could not—or would not—yet summon specific words to denounce the Know-Nothing movement outright.[29] Not with another potential battle for the U.S. Senate looming in just two years—this time for the seat held by Stephen A. Douglas himself. That tantalizing prospect alone made it crucial, as far as Lincoln was concerned, to expand, rather than contract, the Republicans' voter base—whatever concessions had been made to George Schneider back at Decatur. In this respect, with the notable exception of New York's William Seward, who still gave no quarter to nativists, Lincoln's hesitancy only mirrored the reluctance of Republicans around the country to condemn the American Party—or, for that matter, to speak up for immigration.

Back at June's nominating convention, delegate Henry J. Raymond, editor of the *New York Times*, had won applause when he proposed a platform plank acknowledging that "foreign immigration" had added "much to the wealth" of the nation and resolving that "the asylum of the oppressed of all nations should be fostered and encouraged by a liberal and just policy." Yet those words had not made it into the final document.[30] More recently, Republican Salmon P. Chase had won the Ohio governorship with Know-Nothing support—but without supporting the Know-Nothings. "My idea," Lincoln's future Treasury secretary confided to an ally, "is to fight nobody who does not fight us. We have enemies enough in the slaveholders and their aiders."[31]

In this regard, the two future political rivals shared a common strategy of silence. As Lincoln put it in July, the main obstacle to a "plan of union"—fusion between Republicans and Know-Nothings— lay "in the fact that of those germans which we now have with us, large numbers will fall away, so soon as it is seen that their votes, cast with us, may *possibly* be used to elevate Mr. Filmore [*sic*]." Lincoln remained convinced that quiet accommodation of the nativists remained "indispensable to our carrying the State against Buchanan."[32]

Around this time, in a courageous move largely overlooked by history, Lincoln did openly defy Know-Nothing sentiment on one key issue: he defended voting rights for immigrants who had yet to earn citizenship—albeit in an unsigned editorial for a small newspaper in Galena. Lincoln had earlier advocated for the privilege unnaturalized foreigners already held to cast ballots in Springfield's municipal elections, arguing that "the foreigner is taxed by the city and it is but justice that they should vote on all questions of city policy or inter-est.[33] Now he added a rationale meant to justify some noncitizen vot-ing in the presidential contest, too. Democrats, wary of the growing political might and Republican leanings of the Germans, had asserted that the unnaturalized could not participate in the upcoming White House contest at all. Lincoln disagreed when it came to foreign-born Illinoisans who had taken up residence before enactment of the state constitution. It was a distinction with a potential difference in a tight election. "Let not this class of foreigners be alarmed," Lincoln wrote. "Our Legislature has directed that they may vote for [presidential] Electors; and the U.S. Constitution has expressly authorized the Leg-islature to make that direction." That Lincoln was making this case to woo foreign-born Democrats became clear when he added: "But what's in the wind? Why are Mr. Buchanan's friends anxious to deprive for-eigners of their votes?"[34]

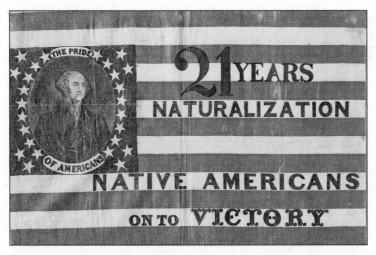

This political banner from the 1856 presidential race called for new restrictions on citizenship for the foreign-born, a position that appealed to nativists, appalled Democrats, and hurt indifferent Whigs.

That same month, Senator Stephen Douglas delivered a rousing Independence Day speech at Philadelphia—a city that had also elected a Know-Nothing as mayor—calculated to rally Irish voters around Buchanan and the Democrats. In an oration widely recirculated as a pamphlet, Douglas denounced the nativist movement as "subversive of all our ideas and principles of civil and religious freedom" and "revolting to our sense of justice and right." When it came to the open rebuke of Know-Nothingism, Democrats still marched where Republicans feared publicly to tread.[35]

What Lincoln possessed that no other orator of the day could match, however, was the ability to "reach the hearts of all his hearers"—immigrants included. In one of his final campaign speeches of 1856 to a largely German crowd at Belleville, Illinois, he declared that here, "as well in other places where he had spoken, he had found the Germans more enthusiastic for the cause of freedom than all other nationalities." Then, "almost with tears in his eyes," as Gustave Koerner remembered, he "broke out in words: 'God bless the Dutch!'" Democratic newspapers mocked Lincoln for deploying the slang term adapted a century earlier from the German *Deutsche*, but Koerner insisted: "Everybody felt that he said this in the simplicity of his heart, using the familiar Dutch as the Americans do when amongst themselves. A smart politician would not have failed to say, 'Germans.' But no one took offense."[36] Indeed, the episode further endeared Lincoln to this crucial ethnic group.

Yet only to his close friends did Lincoln make clear where his sympathies lay on nativists and nativism. As noted, when his fellow candidate for Republican elector-at-large, Friedrich Hecker, saw his home reduced to ashes in a suspicious fire—while he was out electioneering for Frémont—Lincoln advised the onetime German revolutionary to accept the charity his friends believed he deserved. "We cannot dispense with your services in this contest," Lincoln soothed him, "and we ought, in a pecuniary way, to give you some relief in the difficulty of having your house burnt. I have started a proposition for this, among our friends, with a prospect of some degree of success. It is but fair and just; and I hope you will not decline to accept what we may be able to

A cartoonist of the day views the 1856 election as a fight between Irish and German interests—whiskey versus lager "bier"—depicting stereotyped ethnics, encased in their respective barrels of liquid spirits, struggling for control of a ballot box.

do."[37] In this matter, Lincoln paid no heed to Koerner's warning (expressed in writing two years later) that among Catholics and even "orthodox Protestants," Hecker was "considered as the very Anti-Christ."[38]

Just before writing privately to Hecker, Lincoln did allow in a public speech that he "did not like the Know Nothings," though he hastened to assure his audience that theirs was "an ephemeral party, and would soon pass away."[39] But not soon enough to save the Republicans in 1856. On Election Day, although Buchanan failed to secure an outright popular majority nationwide, he outpolled Frémont by half a million votes and secured an electoral vote margin to spare. Fillmore won but a single state—Maryland—but attracted a sobering 875,000, or 22 percent, of the national popular vote. And in Illinois, the 16 percent cast for Fillmore proved more than enough to throw the state to the Democrats—just as Lincoln had feared. Yet if Republicans now expected from him a full-throated denunciation of nativism, they would remain disappointed. Only privately did Lincoln tell Herndon—"often

& often"—that in "advocating freedom for the slave . . . it was radically wrong to enslave the religious ideas and faiths of men."[40] When would he take that message public?

For now, he was content to tell a gathering of Republicans in Chicago merely that "in the late contest we were divided between Fremont and Fillmore." Then he importuned them: "Can we not come together, for the future . . . let bygones be bygones, let past differences as nothing be[?]"[41] In a strange footnote to history, around the same time Lincoln was sidestepping the nativist threat in Illinois, a newly elected U.S. senator from Mississippi forthrightly declared the Know-Nothing agenda "both saddening and sickening."[42] The author of that blunt comment was Democrat Jefferson Davis, destined not many years later to lead the Confederate States of America and wage war against Abraham Lincoln and the Union.

After the off-year elections of 1857, the *Chicago Tribune*, as usual, accused the Irish of "knocking down, throttling, clubbing, and stabbing" Republicans trying to make their way to the polls.[43] But not until the spring of 1858 did Lincoln at last begin viewing Know-Nothingism as an impediment, not a pathway, to Republican success. "I think our prospects gradually, and steadily, grow better," he told his friend Illinois congressman Elihu Washburne that May, "though we are not yet clear out of the woods by a great deal. There is still some effort to make trouble out of 'Americanism.' If that were out of the way, for all the rest, I believe we should be 'out of the woods.'"[44]

. . .

"I do not pretend that I would not like to go the United States Senate," Lincoln admitted, tortured syntax and all, to a crowd in 1858.[45] What he did not want to do was risk another bout of wrangling for the seat in the state legislature. Douglas was seeking a third term and would surely enjoy the support of every Democratic legislator. So Lincoln let it be known he would challenge the incumbent only if Illinois

Republicans united at the outset and named him their "first and only choice." Convening at Springfield in June, they did exactly that. Serving as convention chairman, in marked deference to German voting power, was Gustave Koerner.[46]

Rising inside the statehouse to accept the nomination on the sixteenth, Lincoln made his campaign theme clear in one of his most famous declarations yet—by deploying a portentous quote from the New Testament that advisors begged him to delete lest it strike his audience as too radical. Ethnic diversity was far from his mind that evening, or Lincoln might have turned to the gospel of John 14—"In my father's house there are many mansions." Instead, he intoned Jesus's apocalyptic warning from Luke: "A house divided against itself cannot stand."[47] With that particular slice of scripture, Lincoln announced to the party, the public, and the press that he would devote his campaign exclusively to the national schism over slavery. And except for rare tributary arguments, that is exactly what he did.

Just a few weeks after his "House Divided" address, Lincoln in fact declined a tempting invitation from Chicago's Anton Hesing to join German Republicans there on Independence Day.[48] Though he would need a strong Chicago—and German—turnout to compete for the Senate, the nominee pleaded scheduling conflicts and forwarded a "sentiment" by mail. Really more of a fragment, it did at least heap praise on Hesing's constituency. "*Our German Fellow-Citizens*," it began. "Ever true to *Liberty*, the *Union*, and the Constitution—true to Liberty, not *selfishly*, but upon *principle*—not for special *classes* of men, but for *all* men; true to the Union and the Constitution, as the best means to advance that liberty."[49] Lincoln was not about to ignore such an important voting bloc, even if he missed the "Pic-Nic and Festival" that, Lincoln later learned, attracted "the largest number of people," politicians included, of any of the city's Independence Day events.[50]

Only days later, Lincoln made it to Chicago after all, and there, during a lengthy antislavery speech delivered from the Tremont House, provided an unanticipated, and eloquent, defense of immigration. Though the oration was not officially part of the Lincoln–Douglas debates—those would come later—Douglas had spoken from the same spot the night before, and Lincoln had vowed to respond. Appearing on the hotel's balcony on July 10 before a crowd "about three-fourths as large as that of the previous evening . . . and in point of enthusiasm, about four times as great," Lincoln lit into popular sovereignty, the 1857 Dred Scott decision, and Douglas himself.[51] No doubt remembering that he had disappointed Hesing and his German committee on the Fourth, he now noticed the taller-than-average Chicago politician among the crowd at the Tremont House. Coincidence or not, Lincoln directed some of his most suggestive observations that night to the "mighty" American nation made mightier by the foreign-born.[52]

Granting particular honor to the "race of men living in that day" of revolution—and to their descendants—Lincoln attributed the magnitude of current American prosperity in part to "something else": the immigrants who had more recently populated and enhanced the nation. For its time, this was an extraordinarily inclusive sentiment. As Lincoln expressed it:

We have besides these men—descended by blood from our ancestors—among us perhaps half our people . . . who have come from Europe—Germans, Irish, French, and Scandinavian—men that have come from Europe themselves, or whose ancestors have come hither and settled here, finding themselves our equals in all things. If they look back through this history to trace their connection with those days by blood, they find they have none, they cannot carry themselves back into that glorious epoch and make themselves feel that they are part of us, but when they look through that old Declaration of Independence they find that those old men say that "We hold these truths to be self-evident, that all men are created equal," and then they feel that moral sentiment taught in that day evidences their relation to those men, that it is the father of all moral principle in them, and that they have a right to claim it as though they were blood of the blood, and flesh of the flesh of the men who wrote that Declaration, (loud and long continued applause) and so they are.

"That," Lincoln said, concluding the gorgeous passage to more applause, "is the electric cord . . . that links the hearts of patriotic and liberty-loving men together, that will link those patriotic hearts as long as the love of freedom exists in the minds of men throughout the world."[53] Arguably, nothing Lincoln would say during the seven three-hour-long debates with Douglas later that year would match this offering in benevolence or eloquence.

Political realities on the ground called for less inspiration and more latitude. Within days of his enlightened Chicago remarks, still focused primarily on cobbling together a winning Republican coalition, Lincoln launched one more behind-the-scenes attempt to woo nativists to his cause. His latest plea went to Edwardsville politician Joseph Gillespie, a onetime Know-Nothing now running for re-election to the Illinois State Senate as a Republican. If Gillespie won his race, Lincoln could count on his vote in the forthcoming legislative confrontation for Douglas's U.S. Senate seat. So, in a letter he did not even bother to mark "private," Lincoln stressed to Gillespie the crucial importance of "carrying the Fillmore men of 1856"—the Know-Nothings.[54]

Gillespie responded with alarming political news. He believed that Democrats would "carry off at least one half of the American party vote if not more" on Election Day. Worse, the prospect of voter intimidation against Lincoln supporters loomed large: "The German Republican vote here will go to the polls with the intention of voting their ticket but will be cheated or their views changed so that in my opinion more than half of them will not cast their votes in the way they expect to do when they leave home."[55] Refusing to accept Gillespie's "doleful" prediction, Lincoln instructed him: "Lay hold of the proper agencies and secure all the Americans [Know-Nothings] you can, at once. . . . Don't fail to check the stampede." No doubt, Gillespie knew what "agencies" the candidate was referring to, and if not, Lincoln assured him, "We will set other agencies to work, which shall compensate for the loss of a good many Americans." Specifically, Lincoln urged Gillespie to track down the poll books from the last election, identify the first hundred voters who had cast ballots for the Know-Nothings, and then "quietly" inquire about their preferences in the current senate contest. Political polling had yet to be introduced into American politics, but Abraham Lincoln had already devised an early form of that sampling technique.[56]

That very day, Lincoln urged another scheme on Gustave Koerner: to turn out supporters and prevent voter fraud. "It is said half the Americans are going for Douglas," he blithely alerted the German leader, "and that slam will ruin us if not counteracted. . . . Every edge must be made to cut." To gain that "edge," the master strategist urged Koerner "and some other influential Germans" to "set a plan on foot that shall gain us accession from the Germans, and see that, at the election, none are cheated in their ballots." As Lincoln emphasized: "Others of us must find the way to save as many Americans as possible. Still others must do other things. Nothing must be left undone."[57] Whether or not Lincoln's answer to cheating was more cheating remained unsaid. But how else should we interpret his dark suggestion to deploy all "agencies" and leave nothing "undone"? Anything and everything—including the insensitive demand that a well-respected German immigrant court anti-immigrant "American" voters—were worth undertaking in the name of antislavery (and his own candidacy). In any event, Lincoln soon had no choice but to leave on-the-ground organizing to surrogates. Douglas had accepted his challenge to "divide time, and address the same audiences," and it was time to prepare for the all-important debates.[58]

But not before Lincoln asked Koerner to enlist Friedrich Hecker to "visit this region, and address the germans" in his behalf.[59]

. . .

Throughout the ensuing "joint meetings," still among the most famous political debates in American history, Lincoln worked to keep the focus fixed on the moral outrage of slavery and the legal objections to its expansion. Douglas, in turn, labored to identify Lincoln as a dangerous radical abolitionist who covertly favored race mixing and equal rights for African Americans.[60] The encounters caused a sensation. Spectators from all over Illinois, and from neighboring states as well, packed fairgrounds and village squares, in towns from the state's cool northern reaches near Wisconsin to the steamy river towns bordering the slaveholding South, to listen as the Democratic incumbent and the Republican challenger argued the issue of slavery. Those who could not attend in person followed the debates in print. Before long, a New York newspaperman reported, "The prairies are on fire."[61]

With Germans and Irishmen thronging the events, too, a bit of back-and-forth ethnic sniping found its way into the proceedings— and the press coverage. When, for example, a Democratic newspaper reported that Douglas had been greeted at the first debate by "a dense mass" of appreciative supporters, a Republican daily sneered that the turnout was "plentifully interspersed with the Hibernian element."[62] Douglas's arrival for the sixth encounter at Quincy attracted what a Democratic reporter called another "extensive" crowd, reduced in a Republican journalist's description to "a small sized Irish mob."[63] In turn, a Democratic sheet warned that Lincoln's party "would grant the negro rights that foreign born white citizens would be deprived of," advising, "Let no foreigner vote for a party that would place a negro above the white man."[64]

At both Jonesboro on September 15 and Charleston three days later, Douglas charged that Lincoln had allied himself directly with nativists. "The Whigs, Abolitionists, Know Nothings, and renegade

Democrats," he asserted, had "made a solemn contract" back in 1855 to fuse together to elect Lincoln to the Senate. According to the report published by the pro-Democrat *Chicago Times* (one of whose on-site stenographers was an immigrant), the Douglas onslaught at Jonesboro left Lincoln "looking very miserable" until Herman Kreismann, a German Republican seated alongside him on the speakers' platform, "whispered 'never mind' into his ear." For his part, Douglas remained ardent in defense of immigration. The "stream of intelligence, which is constantly flowing from the Old World to the New," he argued at the Quincy debate, was "filling up our prairies, clearing our wildernesses and building cities, towns, railroads and other internal improvements," making America "the asylum of the oppressed of the whole earth." Lincoln's antislavery position, he implied, would fill the nation's new territories instead with newly freed Blacks.[65]

There are no photographs of the actual Lincoln–Douglas debates. This later painting by Robert Marshall Root imagined how Lincoln might have looked speaking at Charleston on September 18, 1858, with opponent Douglas seated to his right.

Rather pleased to witness Lincoln's discomfiture, German American reporter Henry Villard smirked, "It really is a pity that Douglas and Lincoln do not participate jointly in debates in every county of Illinois . . . the cure for the Republican fever would come surprisingly swift."[66] The twenty-three-year-old Villard—born Ferdinand Heinrich Gustav Hilgard in Bavaria—had been in the United States only since the autumn of 1853, and if he enjoyed the right to vote here, he had only just met the five-year residency requirement. A devoted Douglas enthusiast, Villard had been hired to file debate dispatches for the pro-Democrat *New-Yorker Staats Zeitung*, the nation's oldest and largest German-language paper. Villard also delivered at least thirteen speeches in Douglas's behalf and exchanged correspondence with the senator regarding tactics, assuring him that he remained "as enthusiastic and faithful supporter of your political claims as any can be found anywhere in the state of Illinois."[67] Then, one "hot, sultry evening," Villard unexpectedly found himself sharing private time alone with Lincoln when, while waiting for a train, a severe thunderstorm drove both men to seek shelter inside an idle freight car.

Villard seemed delighted when the candidate "expressed some surprise at my fluent use of English after so short a residence in the United States." Wisely making no mention of their political differences, Lincoln instead wondered "whether it was true that most of the educated people in Germany were 'infidels.'" Villard replied that many were "not church-goers." "I do not wonder at that," Lincoln responded, "my own inclination is that way." Before the downpour eased, Lincoln allegedly confided that Mary expected him to be elected senator, then president. "These last words," Villard remembered, "he followed with a roar of laughter . . . his arms around his knees, and shaking all over with mirth at his wife's ambition."[68]

The "accidental rencontre" did nothing to convert the young correspondent to the Republicans. Villard soon resumed his Douglas advocacy, lingering at Quincy after the sixth debate to offer a cash reward for any local witnesses who would swear that Lincoln had once frequented Know-Nothing lodges there. As Villard later admitted, his antipathy toward Lincoln went beyond politics. "I could not take a real personal liking to the the man," he said. He was simply "too fond of jokes," the "coarser" the better.[69] Villard would change his mind later.

Other German observers proved more sympathetic. Gustave Koerner, for one, conceding that the Little Giant proved himself "eminently talented" during the debates, thought "even the most obtuse hearer could see at once that Douglas spoke for himself, and Lincoln for his cause."[70] Koerner campaigned for Lincoln and attended several of his encounters with Douglas. Not until the eve of the sixth debate at Quincy (which Lincoln's Jewish friend Abraham Jonas also witnessed) would Lincoln meet another German American destined to play an even more significant role in his political future: Carl Schurz.

Born in Prussia in 1829, Schurz had been an active member of the pro-revolution fraternity Deutsche Burschenschaft before fleeing for his life to France, then England, after the suppression of the 1848 uprisings. Then he dramatically returned from exile to rescue his fellow revolutionary Gottfried Kinkel from Spandau prison. It took Schurz four more years to reach the United States. Eventually making his way to Wisconsin, he became an attorney and joined the Republicans. Schurz had already campaigned on Lincoln's behalf in 1858—in both German and English—before finding himself traveling to Quincy one day aboard the same railroad car as the Senate candidate. "I must confess that I was somewhat startled by his appearance," Schurz admitted. ". . . I had seen, in Washington and in the West, several public men of rough appearance; but none whose looks seemed quite so uncouth, not to say grotesque, as Lincoln's."

Schurz was no less odd-looking. Tall and thin, with piercing, almost demonic-looking dark eyes framed by wire-rimmed spectacles, he sported wild, wavy hair and a handlebar mustache (later adding a square-shaped beard), giving him the overall appearance of a comic nobleman in a German opera. "There he stood," Schurz marveled of Lincoln at their first meeting, "overtopping by several inches all those surrounding him. Although measuring something over six feet myself,

German-born antislavery Republican Carl Schurz (seen here with his schoolteacher wife, Margarethe) met Lincoln for the first time during the 1858 senatorial debate season.

I had, standing quite near to him, to throw my head backward in order to look into his eyes. . . . His lank, ungainly body was clad in a rusty black dress coat with sleeves that should have been longer; but his arms appeared so long that the sleeves of a 'store' coat could hardly be expected to cover them all the way down to the wrists." Yet, in debate, Schurz admitted, the ungainly Lincoln exhibited "a tone of earnest truthfulness, of elevated, noble sentiment, and of kindly sympathy, which added greatly to the strength of his argument."[71] The two men would remain associated for the rest of Lincoln's life.

· · ·

One of the most misunderstood moments of the debate season occurred at Galesburg on October 7, after Lincoln charged that Douglas and the Democrats harbored designs on Mexico, Central America, and the Caribbean islands in hopes of expanding America's "slave field" beyond even the disputed West. This was a legitimate concern, but Lincoln took it further by sarcastically pointing out that such territorial acquisitions might require popular sovereignty referendums open to that region's mixed-blood inhabitants. Lincoln made the point by deploying seemingly insensitive language. "When we get Mexico, I don't know that the Judge will have a desire to let them settle that question for themselves," Lincoln teased, "for the Judge has a great horror of mongrels, and I understand that the people of Mexico are most decidedly a race of mongrels—not more than one out of eight are white. I don't know, but I don't suppose he is in favor of these mongrels settling this question, which would bring him somewhat in collision with this inferior race." According to the Republican press, the crowd punctuated the sardonic interlude with "repeated laughter."[72]

No wonder. Most listeners and readers undoubtedly recalled that in a widely reported speech at Bloomington three months earlier—a performance Lincoln himself had witnessed—Douglas had introduced the unseemly term "mongrels" to demean non-whites. In arguing that the signers of the Declaration of Independence did not expect its "all men are created equal" promise to extend "to the Chinese or Coolies, the Indians, the Japanese, or any other inferior race," Douglas had insisted, "They were speaking of the white race, the European race in this continent, and their descendants, and emigrants who should come here." Lincoln maintained the Declaration of Independence spoke "alike to the down trodden of all nations—Germans, French, Spanish, etc." Deriding Lincoln for tilting toward racial equality, Douglas countered that the founders never "supposed it possible that their language would be used in an attempt to make this nation a mixed nation of Indians, negroes, whites and mongrels."[73] Without this context in mind, Lincoln's 1858 reference to "mongrels" sounds callously racist. At the time, however, listeners would have interpreted it as a reminder of Douglas's overt racism, not Lincoln's.

The final campaign debate took place on October 15 at Alton, where Lincoln elevated the discourse by summoning "the two principles that have stood face to face from the beginning of time; and will ever continue to struggle. The one is the common right of humanity and the other the divine right of kings. . . . No matter in what shape it comes, whether from the mouth of a king who seeks to bestride the people of his own nation and live by the fruit of their labor, or from one race of men as an apology for enslaving another race, it is the same tyrannical principle." Here was a closing argument aimed squarely at foreign-born voters who had fled royal tyranny in Europe. Gustave Koerner, who witnessed the debate from the speakers' platform, thought Lincoln's closing remarks "contained . . . some of the finest passages of all the speeches he ever made."[74]

Not for the first time, however, Lincoln also made clear at Alton that his vision for the American West did not include African Americans; he hoped that "white men may find a home" in "our new Territories." But he again included immigrants within this utopian vision, deploying quaint nicknames to drive home his notion of Eurocentric inclusiveness. "I am in favor of this not merely . . . for our own people who are born amongst us," he stressed, "but as an outlet for *free white people everywhere*, the world over—in which Hans and Baptiste and Patrick, and all other men from all the world, may find new homes and better their conditions in life."[75]

In the wake of this unexpectedly broad appeal to Germans, Frenchmen, and even the Irish, Democrats searched for any opportunity to reintroduce the nativism charge against Lincoln before the campaign ended. Three days after the Alton debate, in the town of Meredosia, they found one. There, Lincoln reportedly insisted that "the negro was born with rights equal with the whites" while simultaneously questioning the right of Irish Americans to cast ballots on Election Day. Democrats pounced on the remarks to charge that Lincoln favored voting rights for Blacks but not for foreign-born whites. This undoubtedly surprised Lincoln, who had argued against "making voters . . . of negroes" at the fourth debate at Charleston.[76]

The Meredosia speech survives only as a summary in a local pro-Douglas paper, which linked two distinct passages to make Lincoln's arguments sound more provocative. It is easier to accept another part of the *Jackson Sentinel*'s account in which Lincoln remarked that "the preceding day he had noticed about a dozen Irishmen on the levee, and it had occurred to him that those Irishmen had been imported expressly to vote him down." Lincoln was growing increasingly worried about potential voter fraud in the fast-approaching election, although the *Sentinel*'s next comments surely exaggerated both Lincoln's anxiety and the newspaper's righteous indignation about Lincoln's remarks at Meredosia:

Doubtless Mr. Lincoln entertains a holy horror of all Irishmen and other adopted citizens who have sufficient self-respect to believe themselves superior to the negro. What right have adopted citizens to vote Mr. Lincoln and his negro equality doctrines down? He would doubtless disenfranchise every one of them if he had the power. His reference to the danger of his being voted down by foreigners, was a cue to his followers . . . that under the pretext of protecting their rights, they [Republicans] should keep adopted citizens from the polls. We hope no adopted citizen will attempt to put in an illegal vote; yet every adopted citizen, be [he] a democrat or republican, should have his vote. And every foreigner . . . who is a legal voter, *will have his vote* in spite of Mr. Lincoln.[77]

Supposedly, Lincoln added insult to injury that day by confronting an individual foreign-born audience member. "The effect produced by Mr. Lincoln's significant reference to the danger he apprehended from the foreign vote," the *Sentinel* insisted, came to the surface "before the close of the meeting" when the candidate responded to Dr. W. J. Wackerle, a "highly respectable" local merchant of German extraction who had "expressed the opinion that Mr. Lincoln was a know-nothing." In one more volley of character assassination, the paper charged that Lincoln had "retorted on to the Dr. in severe, personal manner."[78]

Here was an example of partisan coverage at its most blatantly selective, yet the report made an impact. Two weeks later, Lincoln was still on the defensive about the Meredosia incident, enough to take time to reassure a sole voter there, farmer Edward Lusk, that Dr. Wackerle had been misinformed. "I understand the story is still being told, and insisted upon," wrote Lincoln, "that I have been a Know-Nothing. I repeat, what I stated in a public speech at Meredosia, that I am not, nor ever have been, connected with the party called the Know-Nothing party, or party calling themselves the American party. *Certainly* no man of truth, and I *believe*, no man [of] good character for truth can be found to say on his own knowledge that I ever was connected with that party."[79] For good measure, Lincoln had his friend Illinois secretary of state and onetime Meredosia resident Ozias M. Hatch add a postscript to the note corroborating his declaration. That Hatch had once been a Know-Nothing himself went unmentioned.

Lincoln's reassurances did not mean that he ended his campaign unconcerned about potential voting irregularities from the Irish. With the election less than two weeks away, he expressed "a high degree of confidence that we shall succeed," but only "if we are not over-run with fraudulent votes to a greater extent than usual." In a blunt note to supporter Norman Judd, Lincoln let paranoia get the better of him: "On alighting from the cars and walking three squares at Naples [Illinois] on Monday, I met about fifteen Celtic gentlemen, with black carpet-sacks in their hands . . . and [they] were still hanging about when I left. . . . What I most dread is that they will introduce into the doubtful districts numbers of men who . . . will swear to residence and thus put it beyond our power to exclude them." What, Lincoln wondered, could be done "to head this thing off"?

"I have a bare suggestion," he answered his own question. "When there is a known body of these voters, could not a true man, of the '*detective*' class, be introduced among them in disguise, who could, at the nick of time, control their votes? Think this over. It would be a great thing, when this trick is attempted upon us, to have the saddle come up on the other horse."[80]

Lincoln was not the only Republican imagining "Celtic" loiterers intent on casting illegal ballots. Judge David Davis, a respected jurist and longtime friend, accused Douglas of "colonizing Irish voters." The *Missouri Democrat*—a Republican paper despite its name—claimed that swarms of Irishman were being hired in St. Louis and sent into Illinois, "ostensibly to work on the Railroads, but really to vote for the Democrats."[81] In a series of exposés in late October, the *Chicago Tribune* reported Irishmen "daily pouring into Illinois by the hundred" to be "dumped by the road side" and "scattered out among the Douglas men" until they resurfaced on "election day."[82] More likely, the Irishmen had come west to install tracks—not tilt elections.

The ever-volatile William Herndon, who might usefully have tamped down Lincoln's pre-vote jitters, instead claimed that he, too, had spied "the wandering roving robbing Irish who have flooded over the State." Herndon went well beyond the idea of hiring detectives by ruminating: "Shall we tamely submit to the Irish, or shall we arise and cut their throats? If blood is shed . . . to maintain the purity of the ballot box, and the rights of the popular will, do not be at all surprised."[83] When a drunken spectator heckled him at a pro-Lincoln rally in Springfield, Herndon "brutally hauled him down the stairs, yelling 'God damn the Irish.'"[84]

No hard evidence exists to suggest that the 1858 campaign ended with the harvesting of Irish vote or the blocking of German ones. In the assessment of Pittsfield lawyer William A. Grimshaw—a rarity in Pike County politics as an Irish-born Republican—the "Irish overwhelmed us," but not necessarily through fraud. So he told Lincoln a few days after the election.[85]

As it turned out, Republicans won a slight popular-vote majority in statewide races that November, but not enough to overcome existing gerrymandering that overrepresented the southern, conservative part of Illinois and ensured a continued Democratic majority in the state legislature. Whatever the cause, when the new session convened in early 1859, Lincoln already knew that Douglas would be returned to the Senate. Depressed but magnanimous in defeat, Lincoln concluded that the incumbent had won the race through "ingenuity," not irregularity, by managing to present himself "both as the best means to *break down*, and to *uphold* the Slave interest." With a touch of self-pity, Lincoln prophesied that he would "now sink out of view" to "be forgotten," consoling himself, "I have made some marks which will tell for the cause of civil liberty long after I am gone."[86]

But William Herndon remained convinced the election had been stolen, insisting that "thousands of . . . bloated pock-marked Catholic Irish" had been "imported upon us from Phila[delphia]—St Louis and other cities."[87]

. . .

In May 1859, the Senate contest behind them, Springfield residents called one of those periodic mass meetings they loved to organize when issues arose that invited discussion, debate, and socializing. Just as the town's Whigs had assembled fifteen years earlier to lament the 1844 Philadelphia riots, this time its Young Men's Republican Association rallied to express outrage over a newly approved, retrograde amendment to the Massachusetts state convention curtailing immigrant voting rights.[88]

Initiated by its Know-Nothing governor Henry L. Gardner in 1855, the Massachusetts amendment withheld the elective franchise to foreign-born residents until seven years after their arrival in America and two years after their naturalization.[89] The regulation upended the five-year citizenship benchmark in place since the days of Jefferson. Almost immediately, the *New York Tribune* warned that it "would work enormous mischief, especially throughout the Free West," likely inspiring copycat legislation specifically designed to "defeat the election of a Republican President in 1860."[90] Meant as a roadblocking response to Irish voting power, the amendment ended up inflaming the Germans. German-language papers in Illinois, Indiana, and Iowa echoed Greeley's alarm, portraying the Massachusetts initiative as a cynical effort to reduce voting rights for increasingly German—and devotedly antislavery—immigrants.

In response, Carl Schurz had rushed to Boston to insist in a speech at Faneuil Hall that "the banner of liberty" must apply not only to "the natives of the soil, but an innumerable host of Germans, Scandinavians, Scotchmen, French and a goodly number of Irishmen also." Schurz's vision of American liberty already required a commitment to immigration and against slavery.[91]

Gustave Koerner was among the first to alert Lincoln to the political danger. "The Pro Slavery papers from Maine to Georgia are making capital of this unjust and injudicious move," he warned, "and what is (though to be expected) much more damaging, the entire Republican German press is very much exercised about it, and some leading papers have declared, that unless this step is disavowed by the Republicans in other states, they will leave the party. . . . I deem it necessary for our future success, that we should speak out on this subject. It is time that we should quit the absurd hope of gaining converts from the Knownothings by a tenderfooted course."[92] If nothing else, Koerner's advice suggests that Lincoln was still flirting with Know-Nothing support as late as the spring of 1859.

Indeed, when Springfield's Young Republicans assembled at Klein's Hall on May 4 to decry the amendment, Lincoln stuck to the "tenderfooted" course and remained conspicuous by his absence. Instead, the event featured an oration by his law partner, William Herndon, who delivered a fiery denunciation of anti-foreigner "despotism." Lincoln's stand-in usually supported immigration when the immigrants were not Irish Democrats. Now calling for equal rights for "foreign born people, Protestant and Catholic, 'Jew and Gentile,'" Herndon proclaimed: "Once an American citizen, always so."[93]

Three days later, with the issue still a burning topic in town, and the political pressure for a personal response building, Lincoln wisely did an about-face and issued a belated statement of his own. It came in the form of a written reply to Dr. Theodore Canisius, the editor of a struggling downstate German-language Republican paper who invited Lincoln to address not only the Massachusetts case but also the controversy over Republican fusion with former Know-Nothings. It was Canisius who had rallied local Germans to participate in the Springfield meeting of the Young Men's Republican Association.

Lincoln would by no means be the first prominent Illinois Republican to go on record condemning the Massachusetts amendment. Senator Lyman Trumbull, Congressman Owen Lovejoy, state chairman Norman Judd, and others had already spoken out.[94] Yet Lincoln's May 17 statement felt like a milestone. After cautioning that Massachusetts remained "a sovereign and independent state," and that he lacked the "privilege . . . to scold her for what she does," Lincoln made clear that, regarding the controversial amendment, "I am against it's [*sic*] adoption in Illinois, or in any other place, where I have a right to oppose it."

With those characteristically Lincolnian caveats on record, he proceeded to offer one of his most fervent public endorsements of immigration to date. At last taking public the argument he had introduced in his private letters to Joshua Speed and Owen Lovejoy four years earlier, Lincoln now declared: "Understanding the spirit of our institutions to aim at the *elevation* of men, I am opposed to whatever tends to *degrade* them. I have some little notoriety for commiserating the oppressed condition of the negro; and I should be strangely inconsistent if I could favor any project for curtailing the existing rights of *white men*, even though born in different lands, and speaking different languages from myself." As to fusion, Lincoln added: "I am for it, if it can be had on republican grounds; and I am not for it on any other terms. A fusion on any other terms, would be as foolish as unprincipled."[95]

While one Democratic paper argued that the message showed Republicans to be "panic stricken" over the Massachusetts amendment, Lincoln's letter proved pitch-perfect to the Germans.[96] The text appeared in print the following day in the *State Journal*, augmented by commentary from Canisius hailing Lincoln as "one of the gallant champions of the Republican party of our State." As Canisius made clear, Lincoln's statement was fully "in accordance with the views of the whole German population, supporting the Republican party, and also with the views of the entire German Republican press." At Canisius's urging, translations enjoyed further circulation in German-language papers. And within days, Lincoln's statement made it onto the pages of the *Chicago Tribune*.[97]

His eye on the future, Lincoln had accomplished his mission without denouncing either immigrants or nativists, and without pitting his own region against New England.[98] Alone among the leading Republicans who issued statements condemning the amendment, Lincoln had even kept the door of fusion ajar for former Know-Nothings. At all costs, as Lincoln lectured Indiana congressman Schuyler Colfax (whom he had yet to meet), Republicans hoping to elect a president in 1860 must avoid "the temptation in different localities to '*platform*' for something which will be popular just there, but which, nevertheless, will be a firebrand elsewhere, and especially in a National convention"— case in point, "the movement against foreigners in Massachusetts." Putting aside moral objections to tampering with citizenship law, Lincoln felt, "Massachusetts republicans should have looked beyond their noses; and then they could not have failed to see that tilting against foreigners would ruin us in the whole North-West."[99]

Beyond the significance of his message, Lincoln's Massachusetts declaration also demonstrated mastery of a new medium. The statement ranks as one of the earliest examples of a genre that Lincoln would later turn into an art form as president: the public letter—a communication ostensibly written to an individual but crafted as a statement meant for public release through in the press.[100] In this case, the individual was a prominent German immigrant. Born Heinrich Theodore Canisius in Westphalia, the doctor turned publisher of the Alton *Freie Presse* had fled Europe in 1848, become an antislavery activist in America, joined the Republicans, and supported Lincoln for

Theodore Canisius, the pro-Republican journalist who edited the German-language newspaper secretly owned by Lincoln from 1859 through 1860.

senator in 1858. When Lincoln sent Canisius his statement on Massachusetts, the doctor had been an American citizen for just four years, and a resident of Springfield for only two months. He could not yet vote in the United States.

Canisius enjoyed little time to savor his elevated prominence. Even as he was procuring Lincoln's newsworthy letter, his Alton paper was hemorrhaging both subscribers and advertising. Canisius had come to Springfield primarily to save the enterprise, initially hoping to publish a Springfield edition. Earlier in the year, he had asked Senator Trumbull to give him "a recommendation to some influential men in that city" who might serve as investors. Now Canisius opted to shut down the Alton paper altogether and launch an entirely new German weekly in the friendlier Illinois capital.[101] He would call it the *Illinois Staats-Anzeiger* (the "State Gazette," or "Advertiser").

Credulously, Canisius then shipped his printing press and German typeface to Springfield, where German-born creditor John M. Burkhardt promptly repossessed the equipment and held it until the editor could satisfy debts, which now totaled close to $500. Again it was Lincoln to the rescue, though he spoke and read no German himself. Aspiring to address German-born audiences in their own tongue, Lincoln had once joined a group taking lessons from a language instructor from Philadelphia. But according to a fellow pupil, "Lincoln told so many funny stories" in class "that we laughed at them instead of studying the lesson. . . . I don't think he made a very apt scholar."[102] Yet he turned out to be an adept newspaperman.

At first, Lincoln expected that the Republican state committee might supply funding for a Canisius bailout, but chairman Judd adamantly refused. "Canisius is a leech," he warned Lincoln. ". . . You can get no guarantee that if you make the first expenditure there will not be afterwards continued calls."[103] Eager to embrace the prevailing tradition of mixing politics with the press, Lincoln disregarded the caution. After all, other important Republicans—among them Simon Cameron of Pennsylvania and Schuyler Colfax of Indiana—had long owned and operated newspapers while pursuing public office. And New York publishers Horace Greeley of the *Tribune* and Henry Raymond of the *Times* had each run for office while managing their newspapers—the latter, successfully. Here was Lincoln's chance to join that elite group of message managers, even if he lacked the personal resources. To invest, he might simply have appropriated a recent $500 legal fee and handed it over to the doctor, even though he customarily split such income fifty-fifty with his law partner. In "the coolest way," Lincoln told Herndon, "I gave the Germans $250 of yours the other day."[104]

Disappointingly, not a single issue of the resulting newspaper has ever been located, though the search for surviving copies has gone on for more than a century and a half.[105] The original Lincoln–Canisius business contracts, however, for which Lincoln served as his own lawyer, endure. The deal called for Lincoln to rescue Canisius's printing press and "german types" and then hand the supplies back to the editor at no cost.[106] Canisius would run the paper, finance its subsequent operations, and retain whatever "incomes and profits" it yielded. The *Staats-Anzeiger* was to publish each week and remain headquartered in Springfield. It would appear "chiefly in the german language," but could be supplemented by "occasional translations into English."[107]

Lincoln required only that Canisius remain faithful to state and national "Republican platforms."[108] Should he publish "any thing opposed to, or designed to injure the Republican party," the contract stipulated, Lincoln could "at once take possession of said press, types &c, and deal with them as his own."[109] As long as the editor conformed to party principles until after the presidential election of 1860—a due date that implied Lincoln's already percolating ambitions for the White House—then the equipment and the enterprise would revert to Canisius. Until then, Lincoln became the de facto publisher of a German-language newspaper.

In late June, the *Illinois State Journal* began advertising the new paper "published at the home of Abraham Lincoln . . . devoted to the advancement of the Republican Party and its standard bearer," and available in bulk to party organizations at twenty-five dollars for fifty copies—a slight discount over the hefty seventy-five-cent cover price per copy.[110] Lincoln's co-ownership remained unacknowledged. Pride in the product, however, soon got the better of the silent investor. Within weeks, Lincoln commenced mailing what he called "specimen" copies of "the new german paper started here" to leading German American Republicans in nearby towns, urging them to engage friends to sign up. "I think you could not do a more efficient service than to get it a few subscribers, if possible," he cajoled Frederick C. W. Koehnle, a circuit clerk from neighboring Logan County.[111] Lincoln did not expect to recoup his underwriting. He expected his reward purely in political capital: editorial backing from Canisius, enthusiastic allegiance from his readers, and political support from Illinois Germans like Koehnle. In the modern sense, he was self-financing his own presidential exploratory committee.

The ethnic dimensions of the approaching 1860 political battle had already revealed themselves. A few weeks later, clearly fearful about rising German voting power, a Democratic paper in Iowa labeled German immigrants "busy-bodies and mischief-makers," charging, "They aim at anarchy in politics, morals, and religion, and are a curse to any country or community."[112] Yet that very same month, the Black abolitionist leader Frederick Douglass gratefully noted: "A German has only to be a German to be utterly opposed to slavery. In feeling, as well as in conviction and principle, they are antislavery." Douglass had yet to take notice of the growing popularity of Abraham Lincoln among Germans and all manner of Republicans.[113] That attention would soon follow. For now Democrats continued to remind Irish voters that Lincoln's party still remained cozy with anti-foreigner nativists.

Indeed, unabashedly punctuating his own limited sympathy for the non-Republican foreign-born, Lincoln took pains to reveal, in an arch and clumsy February 1859 lecture, exactly whom he still excluded from his Eurocentric vision of the American future. In his estimation, those yet unworthy of contributing to "Young America" were "indians and Mexican greasers" too ignorant to have noticed the abundance of gold awaiting discovery under their feet in California. To these he added the people of Asia, whom, "in civilization, and the arts," he judged, "entirely behind those of Europe." Clearly, it was Lincoln himself who still remained woefully ignorant of the ancient glories of Chinese and Japanese painting, calligraphy, and ceramics, not to mention the dazzling beauty of Native American masks and bowls or the Aztec gold fashioned centuries earlier in Mexico.[114]

. . .

Eight months later, in October 1859, buoyed by German American votes, the Republicans won key off-year election contests in Pennsylvania, Minnesota, Iowa, Ohio, Indiana, and Wisconsin.[115] Even in Kansas, Republicans held on despite the alleged "importation of Irish votes . . . sent from Washington, funded by the Democrats."[116] Lincoln had campaigned personally in four of these states and now deservedly shared credit for the party's noteworthy victories. Back home in Springfield, he began to foresee a path to Republican victory in the presidential election the following year. Perhaps he allowed himself to ponder how he himself might redeem the goodwill he had generated among Republicans outside Illinois. He soon headed off to Kansas for yet another speaking tour. But not until the following April would he first reveal his presidential ambitions, confiding to a supporter, "The taste *is* in my mouth a little."[117]

At the very least, Lincoln could now confidently remind a crowd that while "in '56 a middle party (the American) was in existence, but now that organization was absorbed into both the other great parties, and that *now*, and only *now*, we could rejoice over a true and genuine Republican triumph." The Know-Nothings had dispersed and reaffiliated, fusion had somehow succeeded, and German support for the antislavery movement had solidified as its voting population swelled. These developments had combined to generate what Lincoln proudly called "glorious Republican victories . . . East and West."[118] And the contest for the biggest political prize of all was fast approaching.

First, another young men's Republican association wrote to invite Lincoln to deliver a lecture in a spot where he had never before appeared in public: Henry Ward Beecher's renowned Plymouth Church in Brooklyn, just across the river from newspaper-rich New York City. The effort would require an arduous journey, a brand-new suit of clothes, and an entirely fresh speech, but it would at last introduce the Western orator to the East. And it paid an honorarium of $200 plus expenses. Lincoln decided to accept the invitation.[119]

CHAPTER FIVE

A Vital Part of Freedom

Lincoln chose to take up temporary residence at Manhattan's sprawling Astor House during his 1860 visit to the East. He had occupied a suite there when he and Mary visited New York on a pleasure trip three years earlier, and he likely took further comfort knowing that his late idol, Henry Clay, had once given a speech from the hotel's public rooms. Arriving on February 25, Lincoln discovered that he had made a more fortuitous choice than he imagined. For the first time, he learned that his upcoming lecture would take place not across the river in Brooklyn but at the Cooper Union, a recently opened college two miles north of the hotel.

Although he now needed time to modify the seven-thousand-word manuscript he had composed for delivery at a church, the change of venue encouraged Lincoln to explore the city, and his hosts obliged by taking him on a walking tour up Broadway the morning of his scheduled address. The crowded metropolis had expanded rapidly since Lincoln's last visit. During the 1850s, its population had swelled from 515,547 to 814,254, meaning it was now home to more people than in all but four of the nation's thirty-three states. Around 300,000 of its inhabitants hailed from overseas, more than half of them from Ireland; as a result, New York leaned heavily Democratic. Yet it was said that only three cities in the world—Vienna, Berlin, and Hamburg— boasted "more German inhabitants than New York," signifying that Republicans had a major presence there, too.[1]

The city was also home to an astonishing 174 newspapers: not just powerhouse dailies like the *Tribune* and *Times*, but also a babel of foreign-language and religious weeklies that together made New York the nation's multicultural media center. These included *L'Eco d'Italia*, the German-language *New-Yorker Abend Zeitung* and *Staats Zeitung* (for which Henry Villard had written), and the *Jewish Messenger*. For Catholic readers, there was the *Irish News*, introduced four years earlier by Thomas Francis Meagher, leader of the Young Ireland movement and passionate advocate for Irish independence; and the *Freeman's Journal*, an anti-abolitionist diocesan organ founded, during the days when "broken heads were not uncommon at church doors," by James A. McMaster, who regarded Stephen A. Douglas as his political hero.[2]

Among the daily papers, the most widely circulated was the sensationalist *New York Herald*, published since 1835 by an immigrant from Scotland, James Gordon Bennett. Although Catholic-born, Bennett malevolently stirred anti-Catholic prejudice by railing against the pope as "a decrepit, licentious, stupid, Italian blockhead" and by feuding publicly with the Irish-born prince of the church John Hughes, now archbishop of New York.[3] Critics dubbed Bennett "His Satanic Majesty," and caricaturists often depicted him garbed in a plaid kilt, tartan sash, and tam-o'-shanter, a continuing reminder of the disputatious editor's own "foreignness."[4]

Within the same downtown neighborhood where the *Herald*'s presses rolled, foreign-born engravers created the woodcuts that graced widely read periodicals like *Harper's Weekly* and *Frank Leslie's Illustrated Newspaper*. Nearby, at the print-publishing houses clustered just south of city hall (and Lincoln's hotel), talented foreign-born lithographers

Lincoln poses at Mathew B. Brady's Manhattan gallery, February 27, 1860. A year later, or so Brady claimed, Lincoln told him this widely reproduced image, along with his Cooper Union address—delivered later that day— "made me President."

designed popular prints for home display (delineating their work on special stones imported from Bavaria). This roster of artists included the gifted Thomas Nast, an immigrant from Germany, and Frank Bellew, born in India to British parents, both of whom produced woodcuts for the picture weeklies. Two mainstays at the thriving lithography firm of Currier & Ives had also come to America from overseas: illustrators Louis Maurer of Biebrich, Germany, and Frances Flora Bond "Fanny" Palmer, a native of Leicester, England. All these artists, at some point during the tumultuous year of 1860, would portray Abraham Lincoln as well as his opponents.[5]

On the unseasonably warm winter morning of February 27, only hours before his appearance at Cooper Union, Lincoln's hosts took him as far uptown as Bleecker Street, where the celebrated photographer Mathew Brady had recently moved his Gallery of Photographs and Ambrotypes to temporary but opulent new headquarters.[6] Urged on by his admirers, the lanky visitor entered the establishment to have his picture taken, just as Clay, Douglas, and numerous other leading politicians had done before him.

With his spectacles and devilish goatee, Brady was already the most recognizable—and acclaimed—photographer in America. Specializing in celebrities, and considering himself one of them, he promoted his work as lavishly as he furnished his newest studio. For some reason, he proved less than forthcoming about his origins. Although the 1860 census recorded his birthplace as Ireland, Brady subsequently insisted that he had been born near Lake George in upstate New York, albeit to Irish-born parents.[7] Why Brady disguised his nativity remains a mystery, but it is possible the motive was commercial: by the 1850s, his clientele included the city's elite, whose antipathy toward the Irish, never entirely concealed, had bubbled to the surface along with the rise of the Know-Nothing movement. Brady's heritage would not have concerned Lincoln, who had already posed for two immigrant photographers: Chicago's Polycarpus von Schneidau and the German Jewish Samuel Alschuler. The latter had been so mortified by Lincoln's attire the day he visited his Urbana, Illinois, gallery that he had lent him his own skimpy overcoat for the sitting, taking care to aim his camera away from the gangling arms jutting past its sleeves.[8]

Notwithstanding recent improvements in technology, photographers could not yet reproduce their works in quantity; engravers and lithographers were still needed to copy and mass-produce adaptations. By the time Lincoln reached Brady's gallery on February 27, 1860, not one of the politician's sixteen previous camera portraits had been duplicated or widely circulated. But perhaps Lincoln sensed that anything by Mathew Brady might be copied by the New York picture press or perhaps even for a new edition of the photographer's 1850 book, *The Gallery of Illustrious Americans*. Although Lincoln lacked, say, Frederick Douglass's instinct for immortalizing himself before the cameras each time he delivered a speech, there can be little doubt that at this key career moment, here in America's image-making capital, Lincoln agreed to pose for Brady with the potential for publicity very much in mind.[9]

Beyond even Lincoln's expectations, the result would become iconic. Unlike most of Lincoln's previous photographers, Brady decided against a close-up of his subject's weathered face. Instead, he positioned his camera at some distance to emphasize Lincoln's formidable stature. To add grandeur, Brady introduced symbolic props: to one side, a pillar representing statecraft, and on the other, a stack of books suggesting wisdom. Still, Brady admitted, "I had great trouble in making a natural picture." Lincoln still looked too rustic. "When I got him before the camera," the photographer remembered, "I asked him if I might not arrange his collar and with that he began to pull it up."

"Ah," said Lincoln, "I see you want to shorten my neck." To which the photographer replied, "That's just it, and we both laughed."[10]

The dignified result was destined to take its place as the standard Lincoln likeness of the 1860 campaign, copied for display prints, book illustrations, election broadsides, cartoons, and pins. But not immediately. Five weeks after he posed, even Lincoln remained uncertain of what had become of the original. When an admirer wrote in April to request his most recent photograph, Lincoln drawled: "I have not a single one now at my control; but I think you can easily get one at New-York. While I was there I was taken to one of the places where they get up such things, and I suppose they got my shaddow [*sic*], and can multiply copies indefinitely."[11] The "shaddow" would make almost as huge an impact as the speech Lincoln delivered later that day; but only when printmakers, responding to swelling public demand for Lincoln images, began adapting it in late May. According to the photographer, Lincoln later claimed, "Brady and the Cooper Institute made me President."[12] More accurately, engraved and lithographed copies, not the photo itself, served to introduce Lincoln to voters dubious about whether he possessed the dignity to occupy the nation's highest office.

Lincoln delivers the speech that elevated him into a presidential contender, standing in the Great Hall of New York's Cooper Union, February 27, 1860— an artist's re-creation produced years later.

The "right makes might" Cooper Union address itself proved a more immediate triumph, both in person and in print. Expanding its reach exponentially only hours after its delivery before an elite audience of 1,500 men and women, newspapers in New York and other Northern cities quickly published the full text, often adding praiseworthy editorial comment. Pamphlet editions soon followed.[13] Foreign-language versions appeared for non-English-speaking readers, particularly those likeliest to lean Republican: the Germans. The *New-Yorker Demokrat* issued one such edition, *Rede von Abraham Lincoln, von New-York. Gehalten im Cooper Institut.* This was followed by a Dutch translation, *De Republikeinsche Party verdedigd enz. Redevoering von Abraham Lincoln, in het Cooper Institut.*

Lincoln's "toil," as he wearily described his New York endeavor, was not yet over. Following his Cooper Union success, he headed north for what he termed "a little speech-making tour" through New England. Just before an appearance at Providence, Rhode Island, the local Democratic newspaper disapprovingly reminded readers that Lincoln favored "allowing foreigners to vote, even before they are naturalized."[14]

He returned to Manhattan by rail on Sunday, March 11, for a final day of worship and leisure before heading home to Springfield, having made a huge success in the East.[15] There were still sights to see. A mile or so east of his hotel sat the infamous neighborhood known as the Five Points, whose squalid streets and overcrowded tenements housed impoverished immigrants side by side with destitute African Americans, along with thieves, gangs, and prostitutes. The *New York Times* had only recently cautioned that here "murder and lust, drunkenness and theft, the most abject poverty and the most beastly sensuality, joined hands."[16] Despite such warnings, the wretched quarter had long served as a must-see tourist destination, luring celebrated visitors like Charles Dickens, who shuddered at its "wretchedness, and vice"— from which the author was guarded by two policemen.[17]

Like other visiting dignitaries, Lincoln desired to see the Five

Points for himself, especially after learning that the slum had become a laboratory for charity work. Reformers there now operated a rescue mission, the Five Points House of Industry, at the ironically named Paradise Square. It sheltered 150 abandoned and abused boys, almost all of them Irish, offering them free accommodations in exchange for "honest toil."

After detouring back to Brooklyn for a Sabbath service at the Plymouth Church, Lincoln ferried back across the river to Manhattan and rendezvoused there with one of his Cooper Union hosts, attorney Hiram Barney, to pay his visit to the Five Points. Guided by Barney, who served as a House of Industry trustee, and Rev. Samuel B. Halliday, one of its founders, Lincoln explored all of the facility's six floors. At one point, he took in a religion class, where a teacher could not help noticing the "tall, and remarkable-looking man enter the room, and take a seat among us." The instructor failed to recognize the visitor, but recalled:

He listened with fixed attention to our exercises, and his countenance manifested such genuine interest, that I approached him and suggested that he might be willing to say something to the children. He accepted the invitation with evident pleasure, and coming forward began a simple address, which at once fascinated every little hearer, and hushed the room into silence.

His language was strikingly beautiful, and his tones musical with intensest feeling. The little faces around would drop into sad conviction as he uttered sentences of warning, and would brighten into sunshine as he spoke cheerful words of promise. Once or twice he attempted to close his remarks, but the imperative shout of "Go on!" "Oh, do go on!" would compel him to resume. As I looked upon the gaunt and sinewy frame of the stranger, now touched into softness by the impressions of the moment, I felt an irrepressible curiosity to learn something more about him, and when he was quietly leaving the room, I begged to know his name. He courteously replied, "It is Abra'm Lincoln, from Illinois!"[18]

The Five Points House of Industry—a beacon of hope within Manhattan's worst slum. Lincoln visited this all-boys facility on March 11, 1860, impressing its young Irish residents.

Before Lincoln took his leave, his hosts gushed that the stories he had related of his own childhood deprivations had truly inspired the House of Industry boys. "No, they are the ones who have inspired me, given me courage," Lincoln insisted. ". . . I shall never forget this as long as I live." As a keepsake, Rev. Halliday presented him with his recent book, *The Lost and Found; or Life Among the Poor.* The volume made the case for federal support for immigrants, pointing out that "while the whole country shares in the benefits growing out of . . . immigration, the city of New York is called alone to carry its burdens"— a harbinger of generations of future policy debate.[19] Lincoln took the volume back to Springfield, where his wife, Mary, read it "with much interest" and lent it to friends. Her husband, she told Halliday a month later, harbored "a lively recollection, of his visit to the Inst[it]ution, whilst in New York."[20] The volume might have influenced Lincoln more than she realized; as it turned out, he would eventually take its recommendations for federal intervention on immigration to heart—and to Congress.

Lincoln arrived back home in Springfield on March 14 "in excellent health and in his usual spirits."[21] Three days later, his mood changed when he visited the rapidly fading Illinois governor William Bissell on his deathbed. Yet, on the streets just outside, a far jollier scene unfolded, one that served to remind residents how diverse their town had become. It was March 17, a rousing ethnic holiday. The city's Irish, "dressed in their best bib and tucker," paraded to the tune of "Saint Patrick's Day in the Morning." As one resident cheerfully observed, "The streets were overwhelmed."[22] There was life in Springfield's Irish community yet.

. . .

In mid-May, less than a year after Theodore Canisius had entered into the secret partnership with Abraham Lincoln to establish the *Illinois Staats-Anzeiger*, the editor joined other locals and headed from Springfield to the Republican National Convention in Chicago to advocate Lincoln's nomination for president. In a city overflowing with far more experienced kingmakers, Canisius quickly discovered that he faced an uphill battle enlisting fellow German Americans to the Lincoln banner. Most of them preferred other candidates.

One such delegate was the highly influential Carl Schurz, who had pledged his support to the convention favorite: Senator William Seward of New York. Though harboring "no real antagonism" to Lincoln, Schurz made clear before heading to Chicago: "We were for Seward, 'first, last, and all the time.'"[23] Cincinnati Republican Richard M. Corwine tried warning Schurz in vain that "he was running the Repub. party on a Rock by pressing Mr. Seward," arguing that "leading German Republican papers would not" support him in the West—not after he had provocatively declared the slavery divide an "irrepressible conflict."[24] Onetime Douglas enthusiast Henry Villard sided with Schurz: "I was enthusiastically for the nomination of William H. Seward. . . . It seemed to me incomprehensible and outrageous that the uncouth, common Illinois politician . . . should carry the day over the eminent and tried statesman."[25]

Wilhelm Rapp, editor of the *Turn-Zeitung*, official organ of the German Turner movement, favored the New Yorker as well, yet reluctantly added, "If they want to take Seward out of the running, then Lincoln is the logical choice."[26] Yet Seward seemed unbeatable. Even Illinois delegate-at-large Gustave Koerner admitted after canvassing "German localities" in the days leading up to the convention, he was "almost the only one who advocated the claims of Lincoln."[27]

Arriving in Chicago just before the proceedings were set to begin, Koerner took the temperature of attendees and found to his chagrin that "nearly all the German delegates, with the exception of those from Ohio, Missouri, and Illinois, considered Lincoln only as a possible candidate, and preferred Seward to Chase, Cameron, or [Edward] Bates." Koerner found it especially "strange" that antislavery Germans outside Bates's home state of Missouri could be "very enthusiastic" for the conservative sixty-six-year-old, a onetime slave owner who had supported the nativist American Party in 1856. Yet the aged judge enjoyed the backing of *New York Tribune* editor Horace Greeley, who saw him as the best vehicle to stop Seward, whom he loathed. German Republicans in Iowa grew so alarmed that they forwarded a stop-Bates resolution to the convention; in Indianapolis, the editor of the *Freie Presse*, Theodore Hielscher, urged that the convention accept no candidate who had not voted Republican four years earlier—a demand clearly aimed at stopping the Missourian.[28]

Presidential aspirant Simon Cameron of Pennsylvania, who had also flirted with the Know-Nothings before joining the Republicans, had his own share of detractors.[29] As Mary Lincoln's brother-in-law Edward C. Wallace warned, Cameron's onetime affiliation with the American Party would "be a serious difficulty with the German voters" in the fall.[30] The situation remained fluid. Kansas judge Mark W. Delahay, a Lincoln backer, reported that his own state's "German" at-large delegate might yet come around for the Illinoisan. Determined to remain everyone's second choice, Lincoln instructed Delahay to "give no offence, and keep cool under all circumstances."[31]

A few days before the convention gaveled to order, hundreds of prominent German leaders—among them a number of voting delegates— assembled in advance at Chicago's Deutsches Haus, built four years earlier as a meeting hall for lodges, bunds, and vereins.[32] For three consecutive days, attendees sought to coalesce around key issues and, optimally, a preferred candidate for president. Press reports suggested that their true goal was to stop Bates and promote Seward, but the mini-convention focused much of its attention on policy issues it wanted stressed in the party platform: strong condemnation of slavery expansion and a clear repudiation of the Massachusetts amendment. Only then did an additional resolution reiterate that Germans preferred nominees who had supported the party in 1856 and had opposed the recent change in Massachusetts—a clear rebuke of both Bates and another possibility, the Bay State's Republican governor, Nathaniel P. Banks, who had promised to enforce the hated anti-immigration amendment.[33]

On May 17, the real convention officially got underway at the vast, temporary Lake Street arena called the Wigwam, where attention turned immediately to platform language. Schurz and Koerner, though still at odds over their commitments to rival nominees, joined two other German members of the Platform Committee to recommend a plank condemning the Massachusetts amendment outright.[34] "The Republican party is opposed," the draft asserted, "to any change in our national laws, or any State legislation, by which the rights of individual citizenship heretofore accorded to immigrants from foreign lands shall be abridged or impaired." The wording of the resolution called for "giving a full and sufficient protection to all classes of citizens, native or naturalized, both at home and abroad."[35]

More than one Republican worried aloud that this "Dutch plank" might offend former Know-Nothings at the cost of their votes in the November election. Among them were Lincoln supporters who wanted nothing less than an ongoing fracas between nativists and immigrants. In the end, the convention adopted the draft as platform plank 14 but shunned mentioning, much less condemning, the Know-Nothings by name.[36] As the German delegates hoped, the platform also featured strong antislavery language and a homestead plank advocating the free distribution of Western land. (Many Germans opposed popular sovereignty because it threatened to open the territories to slave labor rather than immigrant enterprise.) A onetime Know-Nothing decried the result as "the complete *Dutchifi*cation of the Republican Party . . . progress with a vengeance."[37] (Enthusiastically, those "Dutch" Republicans would soon publish the final *Republikanische Platform und Candidaten* as a German-language broadside.[38])

With the platform debate behind them, German delegates from Pennsylvania and Indiana converged that night for another lively caucus, this time at the Chicago courthouse, with Koerner on hand to counter any potential stampede to Bates. The Missourian's candidacy, Koerner believed more strongly than ever, "would drive off . . . the German element" in November. Koerner listened uneasily as Missouri delegate Friedrich Muensch, a native of the Hesse region, and Bavarian-born Judge Arnold Krekel argued forcibly in Bates's behalf. "I now asked leave to speak for Lincoln," Koerner proudly recalled. ". . . The moment I named Lincoln the cheers almost shook the court house." Koerner concluded his impassioned talk by warning "that if Bates was nominated, the German Republicans in the other States would never vote for him; I for one would not, and I would advise my countrymen to the same effect." There and then, the Bates boomlet evaporated.[39]

None of the presidential aspirants was on hand when the convention returned to business on May 18 to choose its ticket. Lincoln awaited word in Springfield and Seward remained at his home in

Harper's Weekly depicted the eleven Republican presidential hopefuls days before the 1860 convention. A crude woodcut of dark-horse Lincoln was relegated to the bottom row.

Auburn. To no one's surprise, the New York senator led the pack on the convention's first ballot, but with Lincoln a surprisingly strong second. On the next roll call, Lincoln pulled within two and a half votes of the front-runner, and then, on the decisive third ballot, a significant number of delegates, including Germans, abandoned their original choices and defected to Lincoln, securing him the nomination. Even Seward supporters agreed that "the German element" had emerged from the convention "a vital part of freedom and progress . . . for all time."[40] But Schurz and the rest of the Wisconsin delegation remained unified for Seward to the end, though as Schurz conceded when a cannon salute erupted from the Wigwam's rooftop, "not only the great convention hall, but . . . the whole City of Chicago shook with triumphant cheers" for the ultimate nominee.[41]

For his part, Koerner complained that Schurz failed to mask his "regret" at the defeat of his "favorite." (Not for decades would Schurz concede that a Seward candidacy would have been "too hazardous an experiment" for the Republicans of 1860.[42]) Arriving later that day at a local gathering spot favored by "German delegates and German visitors from other States," Koerner "found them generally very despondent," believing "Lincoln's nomination would not meet with half the enthusiasm that Seward's would have." In this attitude, Koerner told them, "they were very much mistaken."[43]

The day after the convention adjourned, Schurz joined the committee of delegates chosen to journey to Springfield on a special train for the traditional ceremony organized to notify the candidate in person of what he had already learned by telegraph: that he had won the nomination. Eager to get there ahead of them, Koerner had boarded an earlier train and arrived at Springfield in time to give the freshly anointed nominee "a good many particulars about the convention."[44] Koerner also noticed to his dismay that Mary Lincoln had set out "a decanter or two of brandy" to serve her guests. She explained that she thought it would be appropriate to supply refreshments to the committee, and that neighbors had supplied the spirits because they kept none of their own in the house. Koerner gently advised her that such an offering might be "misconstrued"; the notification ceremony would be "solemn" and several members of the committee were "strictly temperance." Mary grew angry and "remonstrated in her very lively manner" until, with Lincoln's approval, Koerner ordered a servant to remove the bottles and glasses. Committee members, the nominee said, could have "a good time" later.[45]

Schurz and the official delegation reached town early that evening. "Mr. Lincoln received us in the parlor of his modest frame house," Schurz reported, "served ice-water," and offered the committee his "profoundest thanks for the high honor done me." Staring at the candidate through his small wire-rimmed spectacles, the stiffly formal Schurz remained troubled by Lincoln's unconventional appearance and inelegant attire. "There the Republican candidate stood," the austere Schurz observed, "tall and ungainly, in his black suit of apparently new but ill-fitting clothes . . . his melancholy eyes sunken deep in his haggard face."[46]

Whatever his misgivings, Schurz assured Lincoln he harbored "no feeling of disappointment" at Seward's convention defeat, vowing "to do the work of a hundred men" for the winning candidate's election. Following up with a long letter, Schurz proposed assembling "a complete list of all the Germans, Norwegians, Hollanders, &c who can serve our cause in the way of public speaking" and sending them "in little squads" to swing states, undertaking "the heavy work myself." Outlining these plans, Schurz could not resist calling it "my campaign."[47] Lincoln replied—although it took a full month, along with a reminder from Koerner, to prompt him to write—that Schurz's plan seemed "excellent." Indeed, it was. Promising never again to neglect his correspondence, Lincoln closed by assuring Schurz "that your having supported Gov. Seward, in preference to myself in the convention, is not even remembered by me for any practical purpose . . . and, to the extent of our limited acquaintance, no man stands nearer my heart than yourself."[48]

True to his word, Schurz hit the campaign trail energetically, heading first to his home state, then stumping across Illinois, Ohio, Missouri, Pennsylvania, Indiana, and New York (where he spoke at Cooper Union—never more "brilliantly," he saluted himself).[49] Assuming leadership of the Republican National Committee's new "foreign department," he deployed additional speakers to reach Germans, Norwegians, and Swedes throughout the Northwest.[50] To cover expenses, and perhaps a bit of extra cash to enlist campaign workers, Schurz received "$500 for Indiana" alone, a quarter of the total the National Committee appropriated to underwrite both German orators and newspapers in the entire state.[51]

Finding himself in Springfield one sweltering July evening, Schurz joined the Lincolns for dinner at their home, then accompanied the nominee to the nearby state capitol grounds for an "open-air" rally hosted by local German- and English-speaking Wide Awakes, a newly organized marching club of boisterous young torch-bearing Republicans. Lincoln wore a summer-style white linen duster, "the back of which," Schurz observed disapprovingly, "had been marked by repeated perspirations and looked somewhat like a rough map of the two hemispheres." Lincoln seemed "utterly unconscious of his grotesque appearance," but Schurz overcame his shock and delivered yet another enthusiastic campaign speech—in German.[52] Lincoln stayed to listen, though he could not understand a word. Afterward, he enveloped Schurz's palm in his own giant hand to thank him. "Ouch," Schurz reported to his wife.[53]

Resuming his travels, Schurz stormed through "large cities" and "small country towns alike . . . addressing meetings of German-born voters in their and my native language." The rallies occasionally triggered "noisy conduct" from opposition Democrats, but Schurz persevered, maintaining a grave, humorless tone (unlike that of the man for whom he was stumping) because he believed Germans did not want to be "amusingly entertained" at campaign events. Perhaps he understood his audiences. Whether he was in schoolhouses, "roomy" barns, or open fields, his message resonated with fellow immigrants, "who remembered the same old Fatherland . . . the cradle of us all," and who, like him, "had come from afar to find new homes for themselves and their children in this new land of freedom and betterment."[54] Together they now forged common purpose in the election of Abraham Lincoln.

"The jubilation is almost oppressive," Schurz once again congratulated himself. "The Germans are coming over in masses. . . . I was almost cheered, drummed and trumpeted to deafness."[55] Following a rally in late August, he told Lincoln, "I wish I could multiply myself by ten over the next two months," assuring the candidate that "at all events I shall do as much as one man is able to do."[56] (Not for years did Schurz concede that his efforts had been "superfluous.")

Each time one of his speeches generated publicity, Schurz received further entreaties to speak in Lincoln's behalf. A Young Men's Lincoln

Club in Missouri wrote to insist there was "no place where you can do more good for the Cause than here in St. Louis." And from Ohio came the report of "an earnest desire on the part of the people and particularly the Germans in this section of Ohio, to see and hear you."[57] Privately, Schurz worked to assuage progressive leaders still chafing over Seward's defeat. To antislavery icon Charles Sumner, he wrote: "I know Mr. Lincoln and I am sure his administration will very favorably disappoint those, who look upon him as a 'conservative' man. His impulses are in the right direction, and I think he has courage enough to follow them."[58]

Gustave Koerner did his own good work for the campaign, advocating for Lincoln among German newspaper editors, appearing at dozens of rallies, and on occasion campaigning alongside his rival Schurz, sometimes speaking in German while Schurz orated in English. "Amongst all the friends and admirers of Lincoln," Koerner came to believe, "none were more ardent and eager than the German Republicans. The name of Lincoln seemed to have a charm in it."[59] In Koerner's rosy view, "Lincoln had always opposed Native Americanism," and this, he predicted, "would secure him the foreign Republican vote all over the country."[60]

Joining the cadre of German-speaking surrogates fanning out across the North to promote Lincoln were, among others: Theodore Hielscher of Indiana; Kansas convention delegate John P. Hatterscheidt; August Thieme, editor of the Cleveland *Wächter am Erie* ("Erie Sentinel"); and Vienna-born lawyer and journalist Friedrich Hassaurek of Ohio. At one contentious event, Hassaurek brandished a pistol to hold off a stone-pelting crowd of hostile Democrats. Fearlessly, he even stumped for Lincoln in the slave state of Kentucky.[61] In central New York, the heart of Seward country, Abram Jesse Dittenhoefer, the Jewish son of German immigrants, delivered up to three speeches a day.[62] Then there was Reinhold Solger, a Polish-born, German-educated historian and lecturer who had held American citizenship for only a year. According to Massachusetts's Republican gubernatorial candidate John A. Andrew, Solger did "as much to secure the support of the Eastern Germans" for Lincoln as "his friend and fellow patriot . . . Carl Schurz did for the Western."[63]

The liberal foreign-language press did its own campaigning in newsprint, feeding readers a regular diet of pro-Lincoln coverage. By July, a German paper in Minnesota proudly counted seventy-three German newspapers now on board the Lincoln bandwagon. The Madison, Wisconsin, *Emigranten*, a Norwegian paper, and Chicago's *Hemlandet*, published in Swedish, joined the crusade as well. Of course, not all the nation's press celebrated Lincoln's rising popularity with the foreign-born. Some of the desperate criticism from Democrats now echoed the inflammatory charges of voter fraud once leveled against them by Republicans. The *Charleston Mercury*, for one, reported trains "freighted with Germans and their plunder" bound for the Northwest "in numbers sufficient to control the elections."[64]

. . .

Lincoln squared off against three opponents that fall: Southern Democrat John C. Breckinridge, Northern Democrat Stephen A. Douglas, and Constitutional Union Party nominee John Bell (the closest of the candidates to "Know-Nothingism," in Lincoln's opinion).[65] With the Democratic Party split into geographic factions, Lincoln seemed from the start a favorite to prevail in November, but even as Republicans campaigned to turn out the crucial German vote in the Northwest, Douglas forces worked tenaciously to rally the Irish immigrant vote in the East, leaving electoral vote-rich strongholds like New York and Pennsylvania very much in play.

Living proof that not all Germans rallied to Lincoln in 1860 came in the person of the financier born August Schönberg to Jewish parents in the Hessian city of Alzey and educated at a Jewish school in Frankfurt. Before joining the banking firm of Rothschild & Sons as an apprentice, the precocious young man changed his name in honor of the Portuguese town where his ancestors once lived. He became "August Belmont."

At the age of only twenty-four, Belmont had taken charge of Rothschild interests in Cuba, then founded his own successful firm and later served as Austrian consul general to New York. He cemented his ties to American society by marrying the daughter of the naval hero Commodore Matthew Perry and converting to the Episcopalian faith. By 1850, disgusted by Austria's ill treatment of Louis Kossuth, Belmont resigned from the consulate and decided to establish himself permanently in New York City, where he took American citizenship, raked in money, and became a generous contributor to the Democratic Party. President Pierce rewarded Belmont by making him minister to the Netherlands. Then, in 1860, Stephen Douglas chose him as chairman of the Democratic National Committee, an honorific that Belmont quickly transformed into a position of real power and influence.

At first, the new party chair predicted to Douglas that the nomination of the antislavery Lincoln would "open the eyes of the South to the necessity of adhering to you."[66] That did not happen. After two months of frustration, Belmont admitted that he could not overcome the "apathy" that descended on the New York party after the Democrats split in two. "I fear that it will be impossible to raise the necessary funds for our campaign," a dispirited Belmont advised Douglas in late July. ". . . [T]he opinion has gained ground, that nothing can prevent the election of Lincoln and that it is consequently useless to spend any money in a hopeless cause."[67]

In the West, no one labored harder for Douglas than Irish American newspaper editor James W. Sheahan, whose *Chicago Times* resumed the virulent anti-Lincoln "reporting" it had featured during the 1858 senatorial debates. Sheahan also produced *The Life of Stephen A. Douglas*, a flattering account for which the senator provided suggestions and emendations.[68] The volume forcefully reminded voters that both Old Whigs and nascent Republicans had held their silence during the rise of the "political monster" of Know-Nothingism while Douglas had spoken out with "condemnation and defiance" against its "proscriptive principles."[69] The pro-Republican *Chicago Tribune* responded in much the same way that Democrats had libeled Frémont four years earlier: advancing the false rumor that Douglas had converted to Catholicism after marrying his Catholic second wife.[70] Writing to Lincoln, A. Morton Braley of Peoria—who claimed he had yet to find an "Irish catholic who will vote republican"—insisted the contest had boiled down to "Slavery & Catholicism vs. Liberty & Protestantism."[71] But in Ohio, the wife of William T. Sherman told the future Civil War general: "Now that the Know Nothing element has left the party I am for Lincoln in spite of slavery clauses."[72]

. . .

In a race in which three of the quartet of candidates remained home— Douglas alone took to the stump in his own behalf—campaign biographies, print portraits, and cartoons kept the nominees before the public. Douglas, long a Senate lion; Breckinridge, the sitting vice president; and Bell, a former senator and Speaker of the House, were already familiar to voters. Lincoln, the least known of the four, required the most introduction—both biographically and pictorially. Among the slew of new Lincoln books produced in response was the authorized work of future "Dean of American Letters" William Dean Howells, the assignment for which German-born former newspaper editor John G. Nicolay, now assistant to the Illinois secretary of state, had yearned to secure for himself.[73]

As a kind of consolation, Nicolay became Lincoln's private secretary—a post some had anticipated would instead go to Lincoln's longtime law partner, William Herndon.[74] In fact, Lincoln's former legal colleague Henry Clay Whitney told Herndon that "he should have insisted on you as his private secretary. . . . [It] is astonishing that he took Nicolay—a mere clerk."[75] But Lincoln wanted an aide, not a "mentor" or "*alter Ego*" at his side, as Whitney ultimately concluded.

Hired in 1860, John (formerly Johann) Nicolay—Lincoln's first and only private secretary—provided the candidate the clerical help he had long needed.

Moreover, Nicolay's loyalty was absolute. As editor of the Pike County, Illinois, *Free Press*, he had endorsed Lincoln's presidential candidacy two weeks *before* the Cooper Union address.

No evidence exists to suggest that Lincoln selected Nicolay to appeal further to the German vote, though Nicolay did begin brushing up on his native tongue in order to communicate better with foreign-born correspondents and callers. A thin, serious man with a drooping mustache and wispy beard, the twenty-eight-year-old assumed efficient supervision of Lincoln's mail, files, and schedule, operating from new, temporary quarters in the governor's suite on the second floor of the Illinois statehouse—just steps from the spot where, two years earlier, Lincoln had delivered his "House Divided" address. Lincoln even entrusted Nicolay to carry his personally assembled scrapbook of Lincoln–Douglas debate clippings from Springfield to Columbus, Ohio, where the firm of Follett, Foster and Company published the newspaper transcripts (lightly edited by Lincoln himself) in time for distribution during the presidential campaign. The book became a bestseller.

Nicolay might not have secured the commission to pen a Lincoln campaign life, but other writers flooded the market with titles aimed specifically at the crucial German audience. These included: *Das Leben von Abraham Lincoln, nebst auszu[um]gen aus seinen Reden*, a translation of James Quay Howard's *The Life of Abraham Lincoln*, also published in Columbus; and *Leben, Wirken und Reden des republicanischen Präsidentschafts-Candidaten Abraham Lincoln*, a translation of Ruben Vose's *The Life and Speeches of Abraham Lincoln*, issued in New York.[76] Testifying further to the robust demand for such works, two entirely original German-language Lincoln biographies appeared as well. From Chicago came *Das Leben von Abraham Lincoln, nebst einer kurzen Skizze des Lebens* [along with a brief life sketch] *von Hannibal Hamlin*. (Hamlin, of Maine, was Lincoln's vice presidential running mate). And in New York, the Young Men's Republican Union—the same group that had invited Lincoln to Cooper Union earlier in the year— issued its own, illustrated *Das Leben von Abraham Lincoln*, published by the *New-Yorker Demokrat* and offered for five cents per copy, and fifteen dollars for bulk orders of a thousand. In total, nearly a dozen German-language Lincoln books went on sale in 1860 alone.[77]

For Germans loyal to the Democrats, the Douglas campaign produced a German-language campaign biography of its own and supplied financial underwriting to German newspapers that offered editorial support to the Little Giant.[78] But their efforts paled before those undertaken by German Republicans.

Some of the innumerable 1860 Lincoln campaign portraits also reflected a distinctive foreign accent—though only a few patrons would have recognized their multinational origins. In New York, for example, the German-born Currier & Ives lithographer Louis Maurer adapted Irishman Mathew Brady's Cooper Union photograph for both flattering likenesses and amusing caricatures, while the French-born

One of many 1860 Lincoln campaign biographies, this German-language example featured illustrations highlighting the candidate's inspiring rise from rural poverty to national prominence.

New York engraver Thomas Doney issued a mezzotint version of a three-year-old Lincoln photograph by Montreal-born, Chicago-based Alexander Hesler. In Chicago, Belgian American lithographer Dominique Fabronius adapted a Lincoln photograph taken in 1859 by Canadian native Samuel M. Fassett for a print issued just a few weeks after the convention by German American printmaker Edward Mendel. Sent a copy of the Fabronius–Mendel collaboration for his personal inspection in June, Lincoln ranked the image "a truthful Lithograph portrait of myself."[79]

That same month, Lincoln posed in his office at the Illinois state-house for artist Thomas Hicks, the first time he had ever sat for a painting. Though a New Yorker by birth, Hicks had been commissioned by German-born print publisher William Schaus, who arranged for the finished canvas to be copied by French-born lithographer Leopold Grozelier. (Pausing in Chicago between trains, Hicks made hurried sketches of newly arrived, still-homeless Swedish immigrants washing their clothes on the shore of Lake Michigan.) To make sure he captured Lincoln accurately—the sitter seldom sat still while any artist painted him—Hicks commissioned new photographs by Hesler, born, as noted, in Canada.[80]

In Boston, another Lincoln portrait from life, the work of artist Thomas M. Johnston, appeared in a lithograph by French-born Francis D'Avignon, who a decade earlier had crafted the portraits for Brady's book *Gallery of Illustrious Americans*. As for the original Brady photograph that had launched this entire cottage industry, the Cooper Union pose reappeared in woodcut adaptations for *Harper's Weekly* on May 26 and in *Frank Leslie's Illustrated Newspaper* on October 20. By Election Day, thanks to this "multiplicity of photographs and engravings," Lincoln's once-unknown face—the "homeliest I ever saw," according to Ohio journalist Donn Piatt—became in Piatt's words "familiar to the public," in fact, nearly as recognizable as George Washington's.[81]

Understandably, Republicans hoped the entire 1860 campaign might remain focused on Lincoln's common-man, "Honest Abe" image and his inspiring pioneer-to-hero life story—with volatile issues like slavery and immigration relegated to the background. However, unexpected and uncomfortable matters occasionally arose to threaten the equilibrium of the contest, and they periodically involved nativism. Opponents who did not accuse Lincoln of encouraging immigration charged that he opposed it.

As rumors of his secret fidelity to Know-Nothingism circulated, Lincoln felt obliged in June to assure Samuel Haycraft of Elizabeth-

town, Kentucky, "I never belonged to the American party organization."[82] A month later, Lincoln's Quincy, Illinois, friend Abraham
Jonas apprehensively reported that a local Democratic congressman
was at work in town soliciting affidavits from "certain Irish men" who
reportedly had once seen Lincoln "come out of a Know Nothing
Lodge" there—the same charge that Henry Villard had investigated
without success two years earlier. Now the pro-Douglas congressman
Isaac N. Morris was threatening "to send the affidavits to Washington for publication." Jonas fretted that "the object is to work on the
Germans"—who, just a day earlier, had cheered a Carl Schurz oration
at Quincy. Lincoln's Jewish ally needed guidance. "I do not know if
there is any truth in the matter, neither do I care," Jonas wrote, but "if
it [be] all false, let me know."[83]

"I suppose as good, or even better, men than I may have been in
American, or Know-Nothing lodges; but in point of fact, I never was
in one, at Quincy, or elsewhere," Lincoln nonchalantly responded in a
confidential letter to Jonas the following day. "I was never in Quincy
but one day and two nights, while Know-Nothing lodges were in existence, and you were with me that day and both those nights. . . . That
I never was in a Knownothing lodge in Quincy, I should expect, could
be easily proved, by respectable men, who were always in the lodges
and never saw me there. An affidavit of one or two such would put the
matter at rest."[84]

Whether or not a war of affidavits might ensue, Lincoln wanted to
be certain that any denials would not imperil the delicate fusion he had
worked so long to assemble. Toward that end, his reply to Jonas suggested that men who actually frequented Know-Nothing lodges were
not only as "respectable" as Lincoln but perhaps even "better." He still
wanted to avoid irritating both Germans who despised nativists and
nativists who now tilted Republican out of antipathy toward the slave
power. Therefore, Lincoln concluded his defense with "a word of caution," advising Jonas: "Our adversaries think they can gain a point, if
they could force me to openly deny this charge, by which some degree

of offence would be given to the Americans. For this reason, it must not publicly appear that I am paying any attention to the charge."[85] Even on the cusp of national victory, Lincoln would not explicitly denounce or even risk affronting the Know-Nothings. He still believed he could woo both nativists and Germans united in their opposition to slavery.

At the last minute, the old fears of Irish cheating resurfaced, too, further poisoning an already bitter campaign. As voting began on November 6, an explosive *Chicago Tribune* report alerted "Republicans of Know Nothing proclivities" that "500 Irish *Deputy Sheriffs*" were allegedly "swaggering about polling places . . . under the pretense of preserving 'order,' screening their countrymen in ballot box stuffing operations."[86] For noncitizens inclined to vote for Lincoln, the paper had quite different advice: "Get Naturalized," adding: "If you know of any Republican foreigners prepared to take out his final papers, take him to see the Republican Committee at the Wigwam, who will aid him in perfecting his naturalization."[87] The suggestion reminded anxious voters not only of the constant (if overstated) fear of voter fraud but also of the relative ease with which newcomers of that era could legitimately obtain both citizenship and the right to cast ballots in American elections.

When all the 1860 votes were counted, Lincoln amassed only 39 percent of the popular tally nationwide, but swept the North to amass more than enough electoral support to win the White House. Voting records for the contest are nearly impossible to categorize reliably by ethnic group, but by some period accounts, Lincoln won the Northwestern states of Illinois, Ohio, Wisconsin, Indiana, and Iowa by amassing lopsided majorities in predominately German districts.[88] Scandinavian votes added to the Republican totals: in Chicago, the Swedish Republican Club had marched under the banner "Liberty and Right Forever. Extended Thralldom Never." In nearby Rockford, Swedes had held an Election Day rally at their church and then marched off to vote en masse for Lincoln.[89] "Hail to the Swedish

Republicans," exulted the *Chicago Tribune*. They had done "their whole duty."[90]

German support also made a difference in the East. Although the "Ould Ward" Irish as usual voted overwhelmingly Democratic in New York City, Lincoln substantially outpaced Frémont's 1856 numbers in the *Kleinedeutschland* districts of Manhattan and Brooklyn. Buoyed by "Dutch" enthusiasm for Lincoln, Republicans did just well enough downstate and raked in such large majorities north of the Bronx that New York State fell easily into Lincoln's column.[91]

So Henry Villard acknowledged. He credited Lincoln's triumph to the Germans' "ablest journals, their best speakers, their most prominent and popular men." They had "worked with the peculiar zeal, earnestness and indefatigableness with which the German mind is wont to make propaganda for its convictions; and hence the result—namely, an overwhelming majority among their compatriots for Lincoln."[92] Charles Sumner put it more succinctly: Lincoln and the Republicans, the Massachusetts senator asserted, "would not have triumphed" in 1860 without "our German fellow citizens."[93]

In turn, ordinary German voters had found in Lincoln a model citizen worthy of their esteem. "The Republicans have elected Abraham Lincoln president," cheered one such immigrant, Otto Albrecht, a Braunschweig-born draftsman living in Philadelphia. "This man shows how far you can get here: his father was a farmer and he himself worked on his father's farm until he was twenty, splitting logs . . . which is why he now has the nickname *rail splitter*, used either in honor or mockery, depending on the party . . . and now he's arrived at the position of the greatest honor here or anywhere else in the whole world."

Albrecht could not help adding that the candidate's only-in-America success had come despite one obvious handicap: "Lincoln is supposed to have the ugliest physiognomy to be found in the entire United States."[94]

CHAPTER SIX

Teutonic Expectants

To the victor—and his supporters—now belonged the spoils, and among the first to line up for the loaves and fishes were the German Americans whose support had proved so crucial to Lincoln's sectional victory.[1]

Quizzed about the German "party campaigners" to whom he owed tangible gratitude, Lincoln "named Carl Schurz as foremost of all," at least according to the *New York Tribune*. The paper did not mean the appraisal as a compliment: after all, Schurz had once backed William Seward, who remained editor Horace Greeley's enemy. "You see now," Schurz nonetheless exultantly wrote to his wife after reading the report, "that Old Abe remembers me." Schurz expected to be remembered further, and tangibly. By now he had developed an extravagant opinion of his value to the late campaign. "I have scored triumph after triumph and achieved almost superhuman results," he boasted, ". . . become as much the subject of newspaper discussion as if I were myself a presidential candidate."[2] He would soon learn if the official candidate shared his generous self-evaluation. For the time being,

Schurz came away with from his initial effort at self-promotion with nothing more than an inscribed copy of the Lincoln–Douglas debates.

Undaunted, Schurz returned home to Wisconsin and launched himself into a new campaign—this one to fend off talk of Southern secession in the wake of the Republican triumph. He argued that Lincoln had been "elected by overwhelming majorities" (not quite true judging alone by popular vote totals) and warned that any plot to block his swearing-in "would be as foolish as it would be treasonable." Schurz no doubt meant this expression of loyalty as much for Lincoln's ears as for disaffected Southerners'.[3]

Two weeks after his election victory, Lincoln traveled to Chicago to confer with incoming vice president Hamlin about cabinet selections and other matters. An effort to squeeze in a meeting with Schurz fizzled—Lincoln claimed he had no time to spare, but conceivably did not yet want to engage with him again on the subject of high-level patronage.[4] Image making proved a higher priority. On Sunday, November 25, following worship services at a local Episcopal church, Lincoln did visit another German American: the onetime Urbana photographer Samuel Alschuler, for whom he had posed so awkwardly in a borrowed coat in 1858. Alschuler now ran his business out of Chicago, occupying the onetime von Schneidau studio where Lincoln had posed back in 1854 in yet another ill-chosen suit. This time, Alschuler did not need to supply appropriate clothing for Lincoln to wear for the sitting. His subject looked almost elegant. Something else was different. Lincoln's chin now featured what Villard called an "unusual adornment": an emergent stubble of whiskers. As the newspapers jocularly put it, "Lincoln is putting on (h)airs."[5] Perhaps to convey gravitas, the first Republican president had decided to become the first president to wear a beard, and the first to change his appearance between his election and his inauguration. Now a Jewish photographer from Bavaria became the first to record the transfiguration from "Honest Old Abe" to "Uncle Abraham."[6]

Back home in the state capital, another German native awaited

The first photograph of President-elect Lincoln wearing
his soon-familiar whiskers, Chicago, November 25, 1860—
the work of German-born Samuel Alschuler.

word from Lincoln, in this case regarding the future of their jointly owned newspaper—and perhaps its editor's next career move as well. Throughout the campaign, as agreed, Springfield's *Staats-Anzeiger* had remained "devoted to the advancement of the Republican Party" and to the presidential standard-bearer who also happened to be the paper's shadow owner. Shortly after Election Day, Lincoln's English-language mouthpiece, the *Illinois State Journal*, acknowledged Theodore Canisius's good work by declaring, "The Republicans of Sangamon [County] are greatly indebted for their victory to the gallantry of the service of the Anzeiger, the German Republican organ of this city."[7] Still no mention was made of the Lincoln–Canisius business relationship.[8]

None ever was—not even in the German-language Lincoln biography Canisius published seven years later.[9] A month after the election, Lincoln fulfilled the bargain crafted the previous May, scrawling this addendum to their original contract: "Dr. Theodore Canisius having faithfully published a newspaper according to the within, I now relinquish to him the press, types, &c . . . without any further claim of ownership on my part."[10] The *Staats-Anzeiger* continued to appear for a few months more but, without a clear new political mission, soon ceased publication.

Lincoln's "kindness and attention" to the editor he judged as "a true and worthy man," however, would continue, although to Canisius's frustration the President-elect delayed further recognition for months.[11] Determined to replace long-serving Democrats with Republicans, Lincoln began naming other Germans, but not Canisius, to coveted diplomatic posts abroad, among them some of Canisius's fellow newspaper editors.[12] The St. Louis–based journalist, Hesse-Darmstadt native, and onetime Bates supporter, Charles L. Bernays, for example, secured the post of consul to Zurich, while his Hamburg-born *Anzeiger des Westens* associate, Henry Boernstein (né Heinrich Börnstein), was promised the consulate at Bremen. Ohio newspaperman Friedrich Hassaurek (in Lincoln's view, "one of our best german Republican workers in America") got the job of minister to Ecuador. This was the "highest position the administration had the power to give," Hassaurek quipped, since the Ecuadorian capital city of Quito reached an elevation of almost ten thousand feet. Lincoln reportedly appreciated the witticism so much he later repeated it to his cabinet.[13]

Patronage appointments were no laughing matter to Gustave Koerner, who now intervened directly on behalf of the neglected Canisius. Praising him as "an original Republican" who "worked hard in the cause," Koerner reminded Lincoln that the editor had "been honestly at work for your success" while others, "whom Doctor Canisius had to fight to the very death at Chicago, when they used every effort to defeat you"—namely Bates supporters—had received "high and distinguished offices." Koerner noted that "this does seem strange, and it ought to be remedied. . . . May I not hope that Dr. Canisius will succeed?"[14]

Eventually, Canisius did. After a few more weeks of delay, Lincoln finally named him American consul to Vienna, explaining that his hesitancy had arisen only at the prospect of appointing a fellow Illinoisan to a plum post when so many other states harbored compelling patronage claims of their own. "The place is but $1000 [annual salary], and not much sought," Lincoln explained to the State Department in ordering the Vienna appointment, "and I must relieve myself of the Dr.[,] Illinoisan, tho, he be."[15] Before Lincoln left for Washington, he also quietly saw to it that the state legislature appropriated $504 to acquire and distribute the remaining—though outdated—copies of the *Staats-Anzeiger*. The buyback netted Canisius four dollars more than Lincoln had invested in the paper back in 1859, providing the new consul a handsome cushion to defray future expenses in Austria. The transaction might also help explain why remaining copies of the paper vanished, a result Lincoln might actually have desired to safeguard the secret of his involvement.

For all of Gustave Koerner's own efforts during the Lincoln campaign, he would not be so fortunate, at least not during the first burst of presidential appointments. Like Canisius, Koerner was one of the surfeit of Illinois residents vying for patronage even as Lincoln determined to limit awards to his home state. Koerner later claimed that he never spoke directly to Lincoln about "having a wish to hold an office," but he surely knew that incoming governor Richard Yates and lieutenant governor–elect Francis A. Hoffmann, a native of Prussia, had both lobbied the President-elect in his behalf.[16]

Journalist Henry Villard championed Koerner's aspirations publicly, writing of him in the *New York Herald*: "He is German by birth . . . an intimate friend and ardent supporter of the President-elect, did yeoman's service for the cause during the last campaign, and hence may well expect a substantial reward at the hands of him to whose elevation to power he contributed so much." Villard added that Koerner was "an excellent linguist and a first-class lawyer—qualifications which would certainly go a great way towards redeeming American diplomacy from the disgrace into which it has fallen in Europe; owing to the ignorance and boorishness of some of its present representatives." Receiving no further encouragement, Koerner headed to Springfield himself in quest of the honors he believed his due. Lincoln welcomed him "with his accustomed cordiality," Koerner reported, "as jovial and even as droll as usual" despite "all the anxiety and perplexity of the situation."[17]

In a show of respect, Lincoln received his visitor not at his crowded statehouse headquarters but at a quiet office "in one of the side-streets, where he met a few of his nearer friends for conversation."[18] Later, the President-elect knocked unannounced on Koerner's hotel room door while the startled visitor was dressing and there informally solicited his opinion regarding Simon Cameron's fitness for the U.S. Treasury Department. "I unbolted the door," Koerner recalled, "and in came Mr. Lincoln." The President-elect, Koerner afterward convinced himself, "would do his best for me." The post he truly coveted was minister plenipotentiary to the Kingdom of Prussia, in what would have been a glorious return to his native land.[19]

Unfortunately, "widespread" rumors of Koerner's expectations found their way into the press in Germany, stimulating premature "congratulatory letters from friends" there. "The entire Press, American & German mentioned the appointment as almost a positive fact," Koerner confessed to Lincoln, as if the leaks were the President-elect's fault. Koerner even received applications from prospective private secretaries, along with letters from his Illinois legal clients asking for recommendations for new counsel.[20] Needless to say, the embarrassment did not help Koerner's cause. Lincoln ultimately awarded the prize post instead to his longtime, native-born Illinois ally Norman Judd. "You will do me the Justice to say," Koerner later reminded Lincoln, "that I did not utter a word of complaint to you."[21]

Gustave Koerner, Republican by political conversion, became one of Lincoln's most devoted German supporters. This rare portrait is one of the few surviving photographs of the camera-shy Illinois politician.

Although stung by the rejection, Koerner gamely insisted he "did not at all think hard of Mr. Lincoln, who had personally promised me nothing."[22] To his wife, he added unconvincingly: "You know that I do not care anything about this matter. It is only that it was so generally taken for granted that I would get the mission, which is disagreeable."[23] Lincoln's old friend Ward Hill Lamon might have come closest to explaining Lincoln's unsentimental attitude on matters like repaying political debts by observing, "He did nothing out of mere gratitude, and forgot the devotion of his warmest partisans as soon as the occasion for their services had passed."[24]

In the end, no foreign-born appointee entered the Lincoln cabinet, either, although several Germans had strongly advocated for Schurz— the best "representative of the German sentiment of the party," in the words of one Pennsylvanian. That particular correspondent reasoned that "Schurz's appointment would be a guarantee, not that Germans should get many offices, but that our three cardinal principles, the exclusion of slavery, the tariff, and the homestead bill, should be *equally* favored by our influence, and no one of them postponed any longer."[25] The argument failed to sway Lincoln.

Onetime German presidential favorite William Seward did become secretary of state. Yet some observers whispered that Edward Bates, Lincoln's other convention rival but anathema to so many Germans at Chicago, earned the post of attorney general as a final gesture toward former Know-Nothings who had supported the Republicans in 1860. Then, after a widely publicized delay, caused more by rumors of his corruption than by his own history of nativism, Simon Cameron won appointment not to the Treasury but as secretary of war. Even as President-elect, Lincoln was not about to ostracize allies tainted by former dalliances with the Know-Nothing movement.

A few weeks later, as if to prove this point, Lincoln accepted a "valuable" and "beautiful" bronze medallion bearing a likeness of his "revered . . . teacher and leader," Henry Clay. The gift came from Daniel Ullmann, who had been the Know-Nothing nominee for governor of New York back in 1854 but more recently had campaigned for Lincoln. The President-elect no doubt preferred to focus not on the donor's nativist past but rather on his rationale for the gift: Ullmann told Lincoln he had reserved the memento for that "citizen of the school of Henry Clay, who should first be elected to the Presidency of the United States."[26]

. . .

One observer who believed the times demanded "a Jackson," not a Clay, was Henry Villard.[27] And his opinion now became important. Soon after the election, James Gordon Bennett hired Villard to take up temporary residence in Springfield and file regular dispatches for the *New York Herald* and Associated Press on Lincoln's preinaugural activities.[28] For the next three months, the longtime Lincoln skeptic remained embedded with the transition office. Villard produced by far the richest account of the beleaguered President-elect as he built his cabinet, rejected concessions to the slave states, welcomed visiting dignitaries, accepted gifts, greeted admirers, wrote letters, deflected office seekers, and, most important of all, steeled himself to face the existential crisis that began when South Carolina seceded from the Union on December 20.

If Villard worried that Lincoln might hold the correspondent's previous support for Douglas against him, he was quickly relieved of concern. Lincoln was too strategic in his thinking to keep a grudge. As he later told his new assistant private secretary, John Hay: "A man has not time to spend half his life in quarrels. If any man ceases to attack me, I never remember the past against him."[29] Quickly grasping that Villard could prove useful to him—after all, Democratic as well as Republican support would be needed to preserve the Union, and the *Herald* was read by members of both parties—Lincoln granted him wide access. "I was present almost daily . . . a silent listener . . . during his morning receptions," Villard attested, and "could get him at other hours when I was in need of information."[30]

Although he judged the President-elect to be "a man of good heart and good intention," Villard at first worried—in print—that Lincoln might not be up to the job for which he had been chosen. "I doubt Mr. Lincoln's capacity for the task of bringing light and peace out of the chaos that will surround him," Villard reported. "Instead of saving the Union, he may be called upon to bury it. . . . [T]he chances for utter wreck are equal to those for safe landing."[31] Yet the reporter soon warmed to his subject, especially as Lincoln deftly disposed one after another of the "Republican tuft-hunters" lured to Springfield by "the 'lust of spoils.'" By December, further impressed by Lincoln's refusal to conciliate the secessionists, Villard seemed sure that he would "do his duty fearlessly in any emergency that may arise."[32] The once-dubious immigrant journalist now prophesied of the incoming President: "He will not be frightened by the hurly-burly of the fire-eaters; and while he does not possess an aggressive disposition, he has a sufficiency of nerve to see the laws of the country respected."[33]

Hitherto irked by Lincoln's frequent reliance on humor, Villard did an about-face on that subject as well, coming to view it as a coping tool that benefited both the President-elect and the office seekers who usually came away from job interviews with less than they had antici- pated. "His never-failing stories helped many times to heal wounded feelings and mitigate disappointments," Villard marveled. "None of his hearers enjoyed the wit—and wit was an unfailing ingredient—of his stories half as much as he did himself. It was a joy indeed to see the effect upon him. A high-pitched laughter lighted up his otherwise melancholy countenance with thorough merriment. His body shook all over with gleeful emotion, and when he felt particularly good over his performance, he followed his habit of drawing his knees, with his arms around them up to his very face."[34] Back in 1858, such displays had struck Villard as almost vulgar. Now he gushed, "I think it would be hard to find one who tells better jokes, enjoys them better and laughs oftener than Abraham Lincoln."[35] By this time Villard might have regarded appreciation of Lincoln's already legendary joke telling as a kind of patriotic duty. Only when he assembled his memoirs forty years later did Villard complain anew, and with renewed "disgust," that Lincoln had a "fondness for low talk" and "never hesitated to tell a coarse or even outright nasty story if it served his purpose."[36]

German-born journalist Henry Villard, onetime Douglas supporter, covered Lincoln during the 1860–1861 transition and grew to respect the man he once thought vulgar and unfit.

Certainly not all subjects amused the President-elect. "Every newspaper he opened," Villard reported, overflowed "with clear indications of an impending national catastrophe."[37] With the disunion crisis worsening—Mississippi seceded from the Union on January 9, Florida on the tenth, and Alabama on the eleventh—Lincoln faced mounting pressure to assure the South he posed no threat to slavery in the areas where it already existed. Instead, he made clear to Illinois congressman William Kellogg that he would say nothing conciliatory at all. "I will suffer death," he thundered, "before I will consent or will advise my friends to consent to any concession or compromise which looks like buying the privilege of taking possession of this government to which we have a constitutional right."[38] Villard published the artfully orchestrated outburst on January 28, prompting Carl Schurz to exult the next day, "Glory to him! (Long live Lincoln!)"[39]

Lincoln's defiance evidently rekindled not only Schurz's admiration but also his ambition. In one final attempt to place himself before the President-elect in advance of his departure for Washington, Schurz returned to Springfield on February 10, Lincoln's last full day in his hometown. There, Lincoln welcomed him "with the utmost distinction" and set aside a few precious hours to explore "everything that was of common interest." Lincoln paid Schurz the ultimate honor, inviting him to examine and make suggestions to the draft of his eagerly anticipated inaugural address, whose contents remained a carefully guarded secret. "Now you know better than any other man in the country how I stand," Lincoln then told Schurz, adding, "and you may be sure that I shall never betray my principles and my friends." Whether Schurz suggested any changes is lost to history. But the German leader did claim that Lincoln also urged him to recommend names "for a few offices" and even invited him to join the traveling party embarking for Washington the next morning. Citing his obligation to keep several appointments to give speeches, Schurz declined, forfeiting the precious chance to spend hours, even days, in close and continuous contact with the man he was trying so hard to impress.[40]

Other immigrants pursued their interests more aggressively.[41] A week before Lincoln was scheduled to leave his hometown, a group of Hungarians, Bohemians, and Slavs wrote from Chicago to tell him they had "organized a company of Militia" and "as the first company formed in the United States, of such nationalities, we respectfully ask leave of your Excellency to entitle ourselves 'Lincoln Riflemen of Sclavonic [sic] Origin.'" Did the incoming president already sense that he might require the services of such well-armed volunteers—and that the best defense of the Union would necessarily involve foreign- as well as native-born Americans? Tellingly, he scrawled on the bottom of the "Sclavonic" letter: "I cheerfully grant the request."[42]

. . .

After an almost unbearably tense, three-month-long interregnum that Henry Adams grimly dubbed the "Great Secession Winter," Lincoln scheduled his departure from Springfield for February 11, 1861, the day before his fifty-second birthday.[43] At first light, despite a cold drizzle, a throng of neighbors gathered at the city's small rail depot, hoping their favorite son might address them before leaving for Washington. For what must have seemed an eternity, so one remarkable story goes, Lincoln was nowhere to be seen.

According to this vivid, though likely misdated, explanation for the alleged delay, Lincoln and his wife had yet to leave the downtown hotel where they had spent their final days in town after renting out their home.* In search of the President-elect came Herman Kreismann, the German-born Republican who had once comforted Lincoln on the Jonesboro debate stage—and who had expected to meet with him early that morning to discuss, not surprisingly, a patronage appointment for himself. Kreismann claimed he found Lincoln sitting forlornly in the parlor as his wife writhed "on the floor in a sort of hysterical fit caused by L's refusal to promise" a government job to Isaac Henderson, the copublisher of the *New York Evening Post*, who had allegedly promised Mary a costly bauble in return for her support. "Kreismann," Lincoln declared helplessly, "she will not let me go until I promise her an office for one of her friends." Mrs. Lincoln's uninhibited "fit continued," the mortified Kreismann remembered, "until the promise was obtained."[44]

Only then, supposedly, did the President-elect and his spouse set

---

*Other versions of this recollection corroborate the details of the episode but assign it to a somewhat earlier date and place the Lincolns at their own house.

out for the depot, where Lincoln indeed delivered a brief, poignant farewell speech. (Kreismann got his government post, too: secretary to the Berlin legation in support of Norman Judd.) Whether or not this appalling scene unfolded on the morning of Lincoln's departure, or previously, at his residence, the incident itself would be confirmed in time by both Kreismann and William Herndon, who disliked Mary Lincoln as much as she despised him. "I suppose that in this case Lincoln did not know what to do," Herndon rationalized. "The devil was after him & he stumbled."[45] (As for Isaac Henderson, the beneficiary of Mary's reported tantrum, he became naval agent in the New York Custom House but lost the job when accused of official misconduct.)[46]

Before his departure, and with no promises exacted in return, Lincoln accepted a gift of his own from a Bavarian-born Jewish friend: Abraham Simon Kohn, the Chicago city clerk. Kohn had created "an exquisitely executed picture of the American flag" that was "gracefully" adorned with verses from the book of Joshua in Hebrew writing: "Be strong and of a good courage; be not afraid, neither be thou dismayed: for the Lord thy God is with thee whithersoever thou goest. . . . I will not fail thee or forsake thee."[47] Lincoln, who knew his bible, surely asked for and received a translation of that inscription. When he appeared outside the rear car of his train to bid his extemporaneous good-bye to his old friends, he adroitly summoned the essence of the biblical inscription. His parting remarks included the cannily adapted paraphrase: "Without the assistance of that Divine Being . . . I cannot succeed. With that assistance I cannot fail. Trusting in Him, who can go with me, and remain with you and be every where for good, let us confidently hope that all will yet be well."[48] Once more, an Illinois immigrant had helped Lincoln along his journey to political success— and this time to rhetorical immortality. Although it took Lincoln six months to acknowledge Kohn's unique gift, John Hay would report in late 1862 that the flag had remained on display "in the Executive Mansion ever since the President's inauguration."[49] Perhaps even the well-informed Hay did not comprehend how much the immigrant's gift had inspired Lincoln's widely praised Farewell Address.

Once underway, unaware that an *Illinois State Journal* reporter had transcribed these evocative remarks at the Springfield depot, Henry Villard excused himself from the train's press car, called on Lincoln in his special compartment, and requested a text of the speech so that he could telegraph it to the wire services at their first stop. "Mr. Lincoln at once complied," Villard proudly recalled, not only writing out but also deftly massaging the impromptu version into a masterpiece.[50] As the train picked up speed and began to lurch, Lincoln handed the task over to John Nicolay and dictated the next few lines; then for some reason he took back the sheet of paper and completed the manuscript in his own hand. The final result: a document written down not only by an incoming president but in part by a German national who had been raised not far from Villard's own birthplace in the Rhineland.

The Springfield speech proved the first of many that Lincoln would deliver en route to Washington. The thirteen-day inaugural journey liberated the long-silent President-elect to begin addressing the secession crisis, even if he still felt he could offer only assurances without specifics. One newspaper likened him to "a pent up furnace that must blow off or burst up."[51] He "had done much hard work in his life," Lincoln told Ward Hill Lamon, who accompanied him on the trip, "but to make speeches day after day, with the object of speaking and saying nothing, was the hardest work he ever had done."[52] Would he conciliate the South to reverse secession, or confront the disunionists and coerce the slave owners? As Lincoln explained at one stop, he preferred to "wait until the last moment"—meaning his inauguration—". . . before I express myself decidedly [on] what course I shall pursue." He made that particular comment in Cincinnati to an immense crowd of foreign-born workingmen representing eighteen German industrial associations who marched to his hotel on the night of February 12.[53]

"Germans in battalions" had cheered Lincoln from the moment he arrived in the thickly German city.[54] Riding from the train station along Vine Street, he was serenaded with the national anthem by two dozen "little girls dressed in white," one of whom "was taken in the arms of a brawny German and carried to the carriage." There the child handed Lincoln a single flower and received a kiss in return, an "incident so touching and beautiful" that it reportedly "filled every eye with tears."[55] Providing comic relief farther along the boulevard, "a large German sitting on a huge beer barrel, with a glass of lager in his hand," belched a welcoming toast: "Got be mit you. Enforce the laws and save our country. Here's to your health."[56]

BURNET HOUSE ⚡ HÔTEL BURNET
CINCINNATI, OHIO.

The Burnet House, Cincinnati's best hotel, where Lincoln met the city's German workingmen and resoundingly embraced immigration.

After darkness fell, the two thousand German laborers massed at Lincoln's Cincinnati hotel with "flags flying, music playing and torches burning." Packing the street outside the Burnet House "as close as man could stand to man," they jeered the mayor when he begged them to excuse the exhausted President-elect from receiving them. According to an eyewitness, a "big Dutchman with a flaming tar stick and a stentorian voice, kept crying out 'you shust brings him out, cumes out you honest old Abe.'"[57]

Finally, his hosts cleared a path and Lincoln edged his way toward the balcony to greet the impatient well-wishers below, his great height making him visible to all as he appeared outside. On cue, a twenty-five-year-old immigrant iron molder named Frederick H. Oberkline stepped forward and recited a formal greeting likely prepared for his use by local German editor August Willich. The remarks hailed Lincoln as a "champion of free labor and free homesteads" and pledged that "German free workingmen, with others, will rise as one man at your call, ready to risk their lives in the effort to maintain the victory already won by freedom over slavery."[58]

Although he was unwilling to encourage a premature martial response to secession—although by this time a total of seven Deep South states had quit the Union—Lincoln's reply seemed, to one journalist on the scene, "pleasant and playful" and, more important, "satisfactory to the large body of patriotic working men and genuine Republicans to whom if was addressed."[59] Expressing himself carefully, Lincoln declared, "I agree with you . . . that the working men are the basis of all governments." He had no prepared speech for the Germans, much less a rallying cry to counter a looming rebellion, he told them, but he would happily celebrate the patriotic ardor of the foreign-born. "I am happy to concur with you in these sentiments," he added, "not only of the native born citizens, but also of the Germans and *foreigners from other countries*" (emphasis added). All men, Lincoln assured his admirers, shared a responsibility "to improve not only his own condition, but to assist in ameliorating mankind." Like the Germans, he favored "cutting up the wild lands into parcels, so that every poor man may have a home"—in other words, fulfilling the Republican promise of a homestead law.

Then, assuming a grave tone, Lincoln, unshackled now from the restraints of the campaign and free to share his most deeply held beliefs, turned to the ever-divisive issues of immigrants and immigration. "In regard to the Germans and foreigners," he volunteered, "I esteem them no better than other people, nor any worse. [Cries of good.] It is not my nature, when I see a people borne down by the weight of their shackles—the oppression of tyranny—to make their life more bitter by heaping upon them greater burdens; but rather would I do all in my power to raise the yoke, than to add anything that would tend to crush them." Before bidding the group "an affectionate farewell," Lincoln provided his most ringing and specific endorsement of European immigration yet.

"Inasmuch as our country is extensive and new, and the countries of Europe are densely populated," he concluded to cheers, "if there are any abroad who desire to make this the land of their adoption, it is not in my heart to throw aught in their way, to prevent them from coming to the United States."[60]

The next day, sensing an opportunity to drive a wedge between Lincoln and the foreign-born, a Democratic daily reported that the "Carl Squirtz red Republicans" had "got just what they deserved, a snub in the nose." Claiming the Germans had believed "they had him in a tight place, and that he would be compelled to define his position as to the 'irrepressible conflict,'" the *Cleveland Plain Dealer* judged that the President-elect proved "to[o] old a bird to be caught with chaff. He snubbed them on that point, and gave them to understand that they were no better for being German than other people, and no worse. This was as much to say: 'You have acted improperly in addressing me as Germans, and not as American citizens.' The outside crowd appreciated the rebuke even if 'We the German' free working men did not."[61] In truth, Lincoln undoubtedly rejoiced that he could depart Cincinnati the next day without either forfeiting his popularity among the Germans or exacerbating the secession crisis. Plus he had openly touted European immigration to America.

Yet he did not escape another disparaging reaction, this one from Rabbi Isaac Mayer Wise of Cincinnati's Congregation Bene Yeshurun, a native of Bohemia and a Democrat in politics. The influential rabbi, who edited the city's German-language Jewish paper *Die Deborah*, as well as the English-language *Israelite*, had earlier reacted to Lincoln's election by lamenting, "The People of the United States just committed one of the greatest blunders a nation can commit."[62] Now he decried the "humbug" of both the workingmen's rally and Lincoln himself. "We can not say what Mr. Lincoln has done for this country in politics, warfares, science or art," he sneered. "[B]eing a foreigner we can not be expected to know every man's biography; hence we can not tell you why these extraordinary demonstrations, processions, banquets, &c., should be made. Wait till he has done something, then show him the honor due to the man." The only certainty, Wise's brutal assessment concluded, was that Lincoln "will look queer in the white house, with his primitive manner."[63] Perhaps the rabbi's dyspeptic reaction owed something to the fact that so many people had assigned a decidedly nonkosher nickname to the hog-slaughtering center he called home: "Porkopolis."[64]

Influential Cincinnati rabbi Isaac Mayer Wise, whose anti-Lincoln sentiments reached beyond the pulpit to the German- and English-language Jewish newspapers he edited.

Lincoln's foreign-born Cincinnati admirers might have been surprised to learn that when he reached Buffalo a few days later—unleashing another warm greeting by a German delegation, to whom he replied "pleasantly in a little speech"—he attended church and dined with the 1856 Know-Nothing presidential candidate, Millard Fillmore.[65] His Cincinnati declaration notwithstanding, Lincoln still remained fixed on unifying the disparate elements who had voted for him—and whose support he would continue to require once he took the presidential oath. Reluctant as he was to placate the secessionists who dismissed the legitimacy of his victory, he was still willing to conciliate the Old Whig nativists who supported the Union.

Arriving in largely Irish New York City on February 19, Lincoln received another enthusiastic welcome along flag-festooned Broadway. The crowd was judged nearly as large as the immense throng that had greeted the visiting Prince of Wales a few months earlier. As the President-elect made his way downtown in an open carriage, ladies waved handkerchiefs and men cheered, though at one immigrant-owned emporium, Isador, Bernhard & Son, a banner in the front window declared: "Welcome, ABRAHAM LINCOLN, we beg for compromise." Eyewitness Walt Whitman insisted he observed an "ominous silence" from the "vast" crowd when Lincoln stepped from his carriage outside his favorite local hotel, the Astor House. Lincoln remained grateful simply to be greeted with respect "by a people who do not by a majority agree with me in political sentiments."[66]

A few days later, it was off to the site of the 1844 anti-Irish riots: Philadelphia, where his press contingent had diminished by one. After reporting almost daily on the progress of the inaugural journey, Henry Villard chose to remain behind in New York when the presidential special continued south on February 21. Thus he missed the biggest story of the entire journey: the President-elect's overnight passage through hostile Baltimore on the twenty-second to thwart an assassination threat, traveling in secret and allegedly disguised in what the *New York Times* inventively described as a Scotch cap and military cloak.[67] According to another wildly exaggerated account, Lincoln had worn the foreign-style attire often associated with Villard's publisher, James Gordon Bennett: a knee-baring kilt.

Lincoln had first learned about the purported murder plot from yet another immigrant: Scottish-born detective Allan Pinkerton, who approached him with the disquieting news on his final night in Philadelphia. As he informed the President-elect, Pinkerton's operatives in Baltimore had uncovered a ring of pro-slavery zealots plotting to stab Lincoln to death when he disembarked to change trains there. Pinkerton, who as a young man in Glasgow had affiliated with the workingmen's reform-minded Chartist movement, was originally a cooper by trade. In America, he had graduated to detective work and earned an enviable reputation for exposing counterfeiting gangs and apprehending train robbers. Now he was determined to "save the life of Mr. Lincoln and prevent the revolution which would inevitably follow his violent death."[68] Pinkerton warned him that among the conspirators was a particularly dangerous immigrant barber named Cipriano Ferrandini, a Corsican who had fought with Benito Juárez's army in Mexico. Ferrandini now belonged to the extremist Knights of the Golden Circle, a secret society that favored annexing Mexico to spread American slavery southward. The Knights hoped to overturn the 1860 election by insurrection and install defeated Southern Democrat John C. Breckinridge as president.[69]

Reluctantly accepting the urgent recommendation that he bypass Baltimore, Lincoln nonetheless insisted on first fulfilling commitments to raise the American flag in front of Independence Hall the next morning and to address the Pennsylvania state legislature in Harrisburg later in the day. He told Pinkerton that "he would fulfill those engagements under any and all circumstances, even if he met with death in doing so."[70] Only then would he place himself in Pinkerton's hands, though he still worried: "What would the nation think of a president stealing into the capital like a thief in the night?"[71]

One of the military men providing security for the inaugural journey, the aptly named Captain George W. Hazzard, had once lived in Baltimore himself. Now he concurred that Lincoln could not be protected there. As early as January, Hazzard had recommended that the President-elect either "avoid the city" entirely or consider "*Passing through Baltimore incognito*," recommending a "false mustache, an old slouched hat and a long cloak or overcoat for concealment."[72] In the end, except for the mustache, this was precisely the costume Lincoln chose: a coat, a shawl, and short-brimmed "Kossuth"-style headwear. "This was all there was of the 'Scotch cap and cloak' [story], so widely celebrated in the political literature of the day," insisted Ward Hill Lamon, who saw Lincoln in his actual traveling attire when the two men departed Harrisburg. Thus dressed, Lincoln admitted, "I was not the same man."[73] Also guarding him on the final, hushed leg of his trip was Pinkerton operative Kate Warne, a pioneering female law officer from Erin, New York, a town originally founded by Irish immigrants and named for the old sod.

In hindsight, Lincoln came to regret his decision to bypass Baltimore, particularly after the press excoriated him for the undertaking—a shaming that cartoonists intensified in a series of merciless caricatures. These included *The MacLincoln Harrisburg Highland Fling*, a lampoon in *Vanity Fair* showing him dancing a jig, hand on hip, and clad in beribboned plaid socks, a feathered tam, and a short kilt that exposed his scrawny legs.[74] Among the subtlest but sharpest, pictorial attacks was the skillfully rendered etching *Passage Through Baltimore*, in which Lincoln, riding in a freight car attired in an ankle-length military greatcoat, recoils at the mere sight of a hissing black cat.[75] It was the work of Baltimore dentist turned artist Adalbert Volck, a native of Augsburg, Germany, who had fully embraced the pro-slavery, anti-Union sentiments of his adopted city.

Fortunately for Lincoln, Volck's hostile etchings would remain under wraps until war's end.[76] The derogatory images that did circulate through the North proved humiliating enough. Pennsylvania journalist Alexander K. McClure testified that Lincoln bore unending

Passage Through Baltimore, Adalbert Volck's scathing cartoon mocking President-elect Lincoln's secret nighttime flight through that hostile city.

"mortification" over his decision to travel in secret—and regarded it as "one of the grave mistakes in his public career."[77]

. . .

The Baltimore embarrassment did nothing to discourage a new round of office seekers from heading to Washington in further search of the new president's beneficence. Establishing his latest transition headquarters in a suite at Willard's Hotel on February 24, Lincoln faced "the hungriest-looking crowd with which the President elect has ever been bored," one newspaper reported, including a "Dutch element" that "poured in thick and fast" before they "vamoosed in disappointment."[78] It had been "bad enough in Springfield," Lincoln complained to Henry Villard when the reporter reached the capital to cover the inauguration, "but it is child's play compared to this tussle here."[79]

Though he spent the entire war in Union-controlled Maryland, dentist turned artist Adalbert Volck "espoused the Confederate cause," said one contemporary, from "its incipiency." His etchings remained unpublished in the United States during the rebellion.

Villard had always believed that "Germans, as a rule, run less after office than the natives." To his surprise, he now discovered that those of his countrymen who had "made themselves conspicuous" during the 1860 campaign "both on the stump and otherwise" were proving just as rapacious as others.[80] Back in December, Villard had named on the pages of the *New York Herald* some of those he labeled "Teutonic expectants." He would always insist he identified these aspirants not to embarrass, much less disqualify them. Rather, knowing the incoming president could not read German, Villard hoped to ease "the difficulty of making Mr. Lincoln acquainted with the drift of the German wishes as reflected in their press." Likely Villard hoped to be influential, too. Lincoln "expects to be just to his German friends," the journalist confidently predicted, "and will doubtless act upon the hints herein thrown out."[81] In this prophecy, Villard proved correct.

Soon enough, Lincoln offered the post of consul general of

Elsinore, Denmark, to his long-faithful Chicago ally George Schneider of the *Illinois Staats-Zeitung*. Editor August Thieme became a pension agent, Hermann Tzchirner secured a post at the New York Custom House, and Reinhold Solger got a job in the Treasury Department.[82] After condemning the "spectacle" of hungry office seekers, gadfly Adam Gurowski, a German-educated count from Poland, became a State Department translator. After witnessing Lincoln's March 4 inauguration, Gurowski seemed "sure that a great drama will be played out, equal to any one known in history."[83] Always willing to report an observation or opinion, Gurowski would spend the war floating above the fray like a blade of grass on a stream.

Gurowski had written a few articles for the *New York Tribune*, but foreign-born applicants needed no journalistic credentials to seek and receive patronage jobs, particularly German Republicans. As consul at Rotterdam, Lincoln named Bavarian-born Dr. George E. Wiss of Baltimore, a former Maryland elector who had campaigned for the Republican ticket in 1860 (though Lincoln received almost no votes in that state). Other consular jobs went to August Alers (at Brunswick), a Californian by way of Oldenburg; Francis Klauser (Amsterdam), an Ohioan born in Württemberg; Prussian-born John P. Hatterscheidt of Kansas (Moscow); and August L. Wolff (Basel), an Iowan born in Lippe-Detmold. At landscape designer Frederick Law Olmsted's suggestion, Prussian-born Charles N. Riotte, a rarity among rarities as an abolitionist Texan, became minister to Costa Rica.[84] An exception to the Teutonic sweep came when Irish-born Brooklyn Democrat Patrick J. Divine became consul at Cork—to the dismay of local Republicans.[85]

In one of Lincoln's quietest patronage appointments for immigrants, the incoming chief executive named his "valued" old friend and advisor, the English-born Jewish lawyer Abraham Jonas, as deputy postmaster of his hometown of Quincy, Illinois. Jonas would hold the job until his death in 1864, after which Lincoln magnanimously awarded it to his widow, Louisa—even though four of their six sons fought for the Confederacy.[86]

. . .

Once sworn into office, besieged though he was by "Teutonic" and other "expectants" who now queued up daily outside his new White House office, Lincoln found himself otherwise surrounded there by members of the ethnic group with whom he remained the least popular politically: the veteran Irish servants who had long worked on the executive mansion's staff. Lincoln could easily replace consuls and postmasters, but apparently not long-serving White House retainers.

Among them were doorkeepers Edward "Ned" Burke and the ancient and colorful Edward McManus, the latter called *Old* Edward to distinguish him from his younger colleague. McManus, who had the insectile habit of rubbing his hands together "and looking penitent"— when he wasn't occupying himself in the mansion's vestibule cracking and chewing nuts—had worked in the White House since the Jackson administration, and by the Lincoln era rarely seemed impressed by the dignitaries who entered the building on his watch. One foreign visitor seemed shocked that the "old Irishman" not only let him pass through the entrance door with "no questions" but impertinently urged that he carry his coat with him, "all kinds of people being about."[87]

Newly hired presidential clerk William O. Stoddard remembered "the antediluvian" McManus as the "short, thin, smiling, humorous-looking elderly Irishman in the doorway . . . the all but historic doorkeeper, who has been so great a favorite through so many administrations." It was McManus who handed Stoddard the big brass front-door key in use since the days of John Adams. "It's like meself," the doorkeeper wheezed at him, "it can open the door as well as ever it could."[88] Under Lincoln, according to John Nicolay's daughter, the veteran doorkeeper became "a host in himself . . . trusted equally with state secrets, or with the diplomatic management" of the President's irrepressible young sons, ten-year-old Willie and seven-year-old Tad—who plagued the servants with pranks like sabotaging the mansion's bellpull system, setting off "all bells, and human answerers of bells, in futile motion."[89]

More importantly, as Stoddard attested, it was Old Edward who became "the first man met in the White House by Mr. Lincoln who succeeded in making him laugh." As the joke-loving President appreciatively commented, "There is no end of quiet fun in him."[90] One night as Lincoln prepared to depart the White House, the heavens opened for a drenching rain. The President dispatched McManus upstairs to fetch him an umbrella, "telling him whereabouts he might find it. In a few minutes he came back, announcing a fruitless search, explaining: 'Sure, yer Excellency, it's not there. I think the owner must have come for it!' The President laughed heartily."[91]

One of Lincoln's favorite Old Edward stories dated back a decade to Zachary Taylor's 1850 death in office and the subsequent arrival of his White House successor, Millard Fillmore. "Fillmore needed to buy a carriage," Lincoln quoted the doorman, so McManus took him to inspect a previously used model on sale nearby. "Fillmore looked it carefully over and then dubiously asked Edward: 'How do you think it will do for the President of the United States to ride in a second-hand carriage?' Replied Old Edward: 'Sure, your Excellency, you're only a second-hand President you know.'"[92] Lincoln still adored Irish humor.

Stoddard conceded that Old Edward harbored "his own ideas of presidential dignity," standards Lincoln did not always meet. For example, McManus "did not approve of the fact that Mr. Lincoln had roped his own trunks and boxes in Springfield and marked them, 'A. Lincoln, Washington, D.C.,' the night before starting his trip to the capital. 'The President, no less!'" McManus tutted.[93] The doorkeeper again expressed dismay when he spied Lincoln one morning, "too early for any respectable president to be up," wearing "his old linen wrapper, and with his shuffle slippers and blue socks" so "he didn't have the look of a regular president at all." As McManus watched in horror, Lincoln ventured outside onto Pennsylvania Avenue, shouting to a passerby: "Good-morning, good-morning. I am looking for a news-boy; when you get to that corner, I wish you would send one up this way." McManus disapproved. "Sure he was only waving his arm and shouting

at a newsboy to bring him the morning paper," the doorkeeper exclaimed, repeating his disparaging mantra: "The President of the
United States, no less."[94]

Lincoln, all but addicted to newspaper reading, was likely forced
into direct action that day when another Irish servant balked at undertaking the task. Journalist Noah Brooks complained that the President
had "succeeded in getting about him a corps of attaches of Hibernian
descent, whose manners and style are about as despicable as can be."
To illustrate the point, Brooks reported: "One morning, the President
happened to meet his Irish coachman at the door, and asked him to go
out and get the morning paper. The Jehu departed, but, like the unfil-
ial party of whom we read in Scripture, he said, 'I go,' but went not,
and the anxious President went out himself and invested five cents in
a *Morning Chronicle*."[95] In this case, the coachman "did not consider it
his business to run errands." This was no doubt the same incident Mc-
Manus had observed. Lincoln said nothing at the time, but the next
morning he ordered the carriage (and its driver) for 6:00 A.M. and "sent
a number of his household in the equipage up the Avenue" to procure
a newspaper, "with the mortified coachman in the box."[96]

As for Old Edward, the man John Hay described as "chatty" perhaps became too much so. McManus would lose his job in early 1865
after running afoul of the mercurial Mary Lincoln, who angrily
branded him as one of the "*serpents* that have crossed our pathways."
When McManus appealed his dismissal, she icily described herself as
"more shocked than ever, that anyone can be so *low* as to place confidence in a discarded menial's assertions." McManus's replacement, fellow Irishman Cornelius O'Leary, fell from grace more rapidly, exposed
by newspaperman Noah Brooks as a "swindler" who sold presidential
pardons.[97] And coachman "Ned" Burke, who had "outlived the storms
of two reigns," lasted only a year, until accused by Mary of appropriating a hat sent to her husband as a gift.[98] Burke at least departed with a
handwritten presidential job recommendation: "Edward Burke, the
bearer of this, was at service in this Mansion for several months now

last past; and during all the time he appeared to me to be a competent, faithful and very genteel man. I take no charge of the servants about the house," Lincoln hastened to add, recognizing that his wife jealously guarded her prerogatives in supervising (and firing) the household staff, "but I do not understand that Burke leaves because of any fault or misconduct."[99]

Burke was not the only Irish staff member to gain Lincoln's favor. "President Lincoln was a grand man," remembered Laurance Mangan, who substituted for his coachman brother during a week's sick leave, long enough to cherish his brief service more than sixty years later. "Quiet and gentle in every respect," Mangan recalled of the President, "he was always thoughtful of those who served him, and though I was a youngster in those days and not very long over from Ireland, Mr. Lincoln treated me with the same consideration he always bestowed on his regular men." One night, likely in the summer of 1863, Mangan drove the President up Massachusetts Avenue to examine the "big new telescope" recently installed at the U.S. Naval Observatory. An ardent astronomy enthusiast, Lincoln delighted in the powerful instrument that brought the heavens so close to the viewer. Resident astronomer Asaph Hall helped him focus it to locate a distant star. And then, as the stand-in coachman fondly remembered, Mangan was "permitted to look through the telescope," too.[100]

On at least one occasion, if one can believe the rather sadistic tale, the President supposedly had the last laugh on another Irish servant. Riding through the city with footman Charles Forbes, "who had but recently come from Ireland," according to doorman Thomas Pendel, Lincoln mischievously inquired: "'What kind of fruit do you have in Ireland, Charles?' To which Charles replied, 'Mr. President, we have a good many kinds of fruit: gooseberries, pears, apples, and the like.' The President then asked, 'Have you tasted any of our American fruits?' Charles said he had not, and the President told [Ned] Burke, the coachman, to drive under a persimmon tree by the roadside. Standing up in the open carriage, he pulled off some of the green fruit, giving some to Burke and some to Charles, with the advice that the latter try some of it." Lincoln apparently made no mention of the fact that the fruit was unripe and probably inedible. "Charles, taking some of the green fruit in his hand, commenced to eat, when to his astonishment he found that he could not open his mouth. Trying his best to spit it out, he yelled, 'Mr. President, I am poisoned! I am poisoned!' Mr. Lincoln fairly fell back in his carriage and rolled with laughter."[101]

As for servants of color, they were at first invisible, and additional Black hires unwelcome, on a White House staff so long dominated by resistant Irishmen. "No colored persons are employed about the Executive Mansion," Noah Brooks reported in 1862.[102] He was mistaken: several Black women already worked as domestics or cooks belowstairs, and under the Lincolns further barriers fell, though not without resistance. "The old help"—the Irish servants—strenuously objected, for example, when the new President sought to hire the African American valet who had accompanied him from Springfield, William Johnson. "In this case," reported author John E. Washington, "there was almost an open rebellion," owing to "a social distinction," for "Johnson's color was very dark."[103]

Lincoln persevered, first securing Johnson a menial but regular job stoking the White House furnace, then asking Secretary of the Navy Gideon Welles to find him work as a departmental messenger. As Lincoln explained matters, "the difference of color between him and the other servants is the cause of our seperation [sic]." When nothing could be found for Johnson at Navy, even though American warships had long been integrated, Lincoln turned to the War Department, where Johnson finally secured employment as a messenger with the added responsibilities of shaving the commander in chief and attending to his wardrobe each morning—all at twelve dollars per week. Only later did Johnson regain his standing as presidential valet, a promotion, as noted, for which he ultimately paid with his life after catching smallpox from the President. Lincoln occasionally referred to Johnson, a married man, as "a colored boy" but, when it came time to preserving

"William's" livelihood, insisted that his "integrity and faithfulness" be acknowledged.[104]

Not even a White House backstairs staff dominated by the Irish-born could be totally devoid of Germans—not after Lincoln had swept to office with so much German American support. Louis Burgdorf filled that unstated quota, serving as the guard posted outside Lincoln's second-floor office and occasionally assigned to messenger duty as well. Noah Brooks described him as "German, crusty, pragmatical, pertinacious; proud of his position and authority, and little tolerant of interference; both trustworthy, and, on the whole, capable." And John Hay jokingly described the man "who guards the door of the Abolitionist despot" as "a Teutonic worthy whose memory runs back to" the days of the Pierce administration.[105]

One more immigrant who became essential to the household was German-born Gustav E. "Gus" Gumpert, though he spent most of his time working at his family's tobacco business in Philadelphia. Following middle child Willie Lincoln's tragic death at age eleven in February 1862, his lonely brother, Tad, found comfort in Gumpert's company—at a time when the boy's father turned increasingly to his work and his mother remained in the "fiery furnace of affliction" that overtook her after Willie's passing. The President expressed his gratitude by presenting Gumpert with an amethyst ring and cuff links and ultimately naming him an assessor of internal revenue, a patronage plum Mary Lincoln described as "an especial favor upon me"—even if she mistakenly referred to the beneficiary as "Gumfert."[106]

. . .

Of all the qualified and loyal "Teutonic expectants," Henry Villard always ranked Carl Schurz's claims "the strongest, in consideration of his having delivered over a hundred campaign speeches and spent a small fortune for the cause."[107]

Schurz, who would have agreed, arrived in Washington in time to attend the March 4 inaugural. "The air was still thick with rumors of 'rebel plots' to assassinate Mr. Lincoln, or to capture him and carry him off before he could take hold of the reins of government," Schurz remembered. ". . . But the inauguration passed off without disturbance. . . . I saw Lincoln step forward to the desk upon which the Bible lay—his rugged face, appearing above all those surrounding him, calm and sad, but so unlike any other in that distinguished assemblage that one might well have doubted how they could work together. . . . I heard every word pronounced by Abraham Lincoln's kindly voice, of that inaugural address which was to be a message of peace and good will."[108] Soon, Schurz began "working like a beaver" to secure a diplomatic post for himself.[109] He met with Lincoln "repeatedly" in the weeks after the swearing in, proud that the new President never failed to receive him "with great cordiality."[110]

Schurz now usefully remembered something Lincoln had allegedly told him when they had met in Springfield the previous summer: "Men like you, who have real merit and do the work, are always too proud to ask for anything; those who do nothing are always the most clamorous for office. . . . But if I am elected, they will find a tough customer to deal with, and you may depend upon it that I shall know how to distinguish deserving men from the drones." At least that was how Schurz recounted the conversation to his wife in a recap that surely owed much to wishful thinking. In tone and content, the statement sounds much more like Carl Schurz than Abraham Lincoln.[111]

With a cabinet position out of reach, Schurz made it clear he would settle for a prestigious diplomatic posting to Mexico or somewhere in Europe, preferably Italy, which had been making progress toward liberal unification.[112] Although Lincoln was inclined to oblige him, he led Schurz a merry dance for weeks, shuttling him between the White House and the State Department to make and remake his case. Ironically, Secretary of State William Seward, whom Schurz had so loyally backed at the Chicago convention, now seemed disinclined to see his old supporter rewarded. Less than a year earlier, Seward had lauded "the important and responsible part" Schurz was "acting in the Republican cause."[113] But as secretary of state, Seward worried that the royal courts would be offended if the new administration sent a one-time revolutionary as a diplomat in residence. (In retrospect, Schurz generously thought Seward was "clearly right.")[114] Some observers, however, believed Seward simply opposed appointing any foreign-born aspirants to meaningful posts in the diplomatic corps.

No doubt learning that Seward was standing in the way of Schurz's ambitions, Horace Greeley belatedly took up the case, arguing that no man was "more admirably qualified to represent the greatest republic on earth at the court of the Liberal and popular ruler of uprisen and regenerated Italy." Besides, Greeley added, as if to remind the White House of its political debts, "We believe the speeches of no other man gained so many votes for Lincoln and Hamlin as did those of Carl Schurz."[115] Pressured from all sides, Seward let his still-raw emotions flare when a visitor eager to see Schurz satisfied pointed out that German Americans would be disappointed if he was not appointed. "Disappointed!" Seward exploded. "You speak to me of disappointment. To me, who was justly entitled to the Republican nomination for the presidency, and who had to stand aside and see it given to a little Illinois lawyer!"[116]

Meanwhile, a genuinely explosive crisis brewed in South Carolina. In the weeks following Lincoln's inauguration, anxious attention had turned to Fort Sumter, the thirty-two-year-old federal installation that still guarded Charleston Harbor, manned by a garrison of U.S. troops under orders to stand their ground. As federal and Confederate forces bickered over which "country" legitimately owned the installation, the fort's guardians began running out of food. Confederate authorities had made it clear that any attempt by Lincoln to resupply it would invite a hostile response from the mainland. Not everyone was sure the South Carolinians would cross that line. One Charleston resident sneered, "We don't want to risk our handsome, genteel, educated young fellows against a gang of Irishmen, Germans, British deserters, and New York roughs" defending the fort.[117] As tensions mounted, the *New York Herald* managed to josh, "Next to the difficulty about Fort Sumter, the question as to what is to be done with Carl Schurz seems to bother the administration more than anything else."[118]

Having lobbied for the U.S. mission at Sardinia or Turin without success, Schurz now adjusted his sights to Madrid. But the administration had promised Spain to the influential Kentucky abolitionist Cassius Marcellus Clay. Fortunately for Schurz, incoming postmaster general Montgomery Blair, no friend of the secretary of state's, alerted Clay: "It seems that Seward has contrived to fill every first-class mission in Europe, which Carl Schurz could accept, without providing for that particular gentleman." Unless Clay would "take Russia instead of Spain," Blair warned him, Schurz would "be left out in the cold altogether." And as Blair saw matters, "It is imperative that Schurz should have a place in Europe."[119]

After days of further uncertainty, Clay indeed accepted the post of U.S. minister to Russia. Over Seward's continuing objections, Lincoln then ordered Schurz's appointment as minister to Spain, a country ruled by just the sort of despotic monarch Schurz had fled Germany to escape. Delighted, Schurz believed Lincoln's decision would show foreign governments—even those ruled by despots—that the United States stood for liberty. "Seward's influence has been defeated, and I am master of the battle field," Schurz rejoiced to his wife. ". . . This outcome is better than the Turin mission would have been. It is a victory. Next to Mexico, Spain is the most important diplomatic post—and it is mine."[120]

As Schurz was preparing to leave for Madrid, however, a U.S. ship at last approached Charleston stocked with supplies for beleaguered Fort Sumter. In the predawn hours of April 12, Confederate forces commenced a bombardment, unleashing more than three thousand shells across the harbor. Sumter surrendered thirty-four hours later. Within four days, Lincoln called for seventy-five thousand volunteers to fight the rebellion.[121]

Almost immediately, and despite his long quest for a diplomatic plum, Carl Schurz decided that he should be one of them.

CHAPTER SEVEN

I Fights Mit Sigel

Not everyone—not even everyone in Carl Schurz's home state—rejoiced when Lincoln named the onetime revolutionary as American minister to Spain. "Impudence has triumphed," carped the pro-Democrat *Milwaukee Daily News*. "With an audacity that could not be repulsed . . . and a shamelessness that knew no blush this foreign adventurer and mercenary soldier takes the President of the United States by the throat . . . and with taunting words and threats demands a place to which only distinguished citizens and accomplished statesman have a right to aspire."[1]

Had Schurz truly been motivated by adventurism, he no doubt would have proceeded directly to Madrid to present himself triumphantly at court. Instead, after returning to Wisconsin for a brief visit home, he learned of Fort Sumter's capitulation, Lincoln's call for volunteers, and the capital's sudden peril in the absence of troops to defend it. The news had an "electric effect" on Schurz, who packed the pistols he had once carried in Europe and headed back east. "I thought it my duty," he explained, "to hurry to Washington at once, and offer what service I could render" to save the country.[2] Hastening to the White House, he told a dubious Lincoln that he now wished to abandon his hard-won diplomatic post and instead raise a cavalry regiment to fight the Rebels.[3]

Schurz was not the only German American to respond with enthusiasm to the call for volunteers to defend the country. At a New York City rally at which the traduced Sumter flag proved the central attraction—flying from the bronze equestrian statue of George Washington at Union Square—speaker after speaker, among them leaders of the immigrant community, pledged loyalty to the Union "in tones of thunder." "We may be born Germans," one orator roared to the throng of one hundred thousand, "and many dear old ties hold us still to the Fatherland, but, having adopted this county as our home, we are now American citizens . . . second to none in patriotism—to none in love to our glorious flag."[4]

In Washington, a city bursting with the same sense of urgency, Schurz found the President largely unaltered by the crisis. "Those who visited the White House—and the White House appeared to be open to whosoever wished to enter," he marveled—still found there "a man of unconventional manners, who, without the slightest effort to put on dignity, treated all men alike, much like old neighbors . . . always seemed to have time for a homely talk and never to be in a hurry to press business."[5] Yet Schurz also learned that "Washington fairly buzzed with criticism. . . . [T]he question was frequently asked in that atmosphere of discontentment, whether Abraham Lincoln was really the man to cope with a situation bristling with problems so perplexing."[6]

Lincoln, "surprised, but glad to see" him, listened "with attention and evident sympathy" to Schurz, who wrote, "I opened my heart . . . about my troubles of conscience." At first, however, the President remained unmoved. He strongly advised Schurz not to "give up the Spanish mission," insisting it presented "a greater field of usefulness" than military service. Besides, Lincoln pointed out overoptimistically, "the war might be over very soon."[7] Schurz pleaded for at least a brief leave of absence so he could recruit a unit of "able-bodied immigrants from Germany who had served in German cavalry regiments, and who had only to be armed and put upon horses" to make them "immediately fit for active service."[8] Surely the resident chargé d'affaires in Madrid could substitute for him awhile longer?

As John Hay chronicled the conversation, Schurz "spoke with wild enthusiasm of his desire to mingle in the war. He had great confidence in his capability of arousing the enthusiasm of the young."[9] According to Hay, Schurz returned to the White House on May 10, voiced his belief that slavery was "the cause of all our woes," then reappeared the very next day to join the President on the White House balcony, where together they enjoyed a Marine Band concert. This brought out another of Schurz's talents. "After the President had kissed some thousand children and retired," Hay reported, "Carl went into the library and . . . played [Beethoven on the piano] with great skill & feeling, sitting in the dusk at twilight until the President came by and took him down to tea. Schurz is a wonderful man. An orator, a soldier, a philosopher, an exiled patriot, a skilled musician, he has every quality of romance and dramatic picturesqueness."[10]

Ultimately, Lincoln acquiesced, against the advice of both the newly installed secretary of war, Simon Cameron, and the veteran general-in-chief, Winfield Scott (who, like Lincoln, believed "the war would be over before a cavalry regiment could be made fit for active service in the field").[11] Lincoln offered Schurz a three-month reprieve from the diplomatic corps, and on May 1 Cameron formally, if still reluctantly, authorized the German leader to "organize a volunteer regiment of cavalry."[12] The aspiring commander rushed to New York to launch his recruiting efforts, only to discover that in response to Lincoln's initial call for volunteers, many Germans there had already joined the infantry. So Schurz tried appropriating cavalry units from nearby states, including a German battalion already outfitted in Hoboken. At one point, he even proposed absorbing the Eleventh New

York, an infantry unit under the command of Lincoln's protégé and inaugural journey bodyguard, Elmer E. Ellsworth, and destined for glory of its own. Schurz added to this presumptuous (and unsuccessful) request by insisting that it be arranged "*forth with.*"[13] Within days, though making little headway in forming his dream regiment, Schurz began fancying himself a brigadier general and asked Lincoln to expedite a promotion to that rank by cutting through "the red-tape . . . which rests like an incubus on our whole military business."[14]

Lincoln, a man who paid his political debts, had already rewarded Schurz but remained willing to accommodate him. "Why should it not be done at once?" he prodded Cameron, still eager to see Schurz satisfied, if only to put an end to his badgering. "I am for it."[15] Yet the promotion did little to spur Schurz's power to recruit additional cavalrymen. Not until June did he turn over "his" regiment to another commander and at last head off to Spain. He was not the only German American who felt unfulfilled. While the newspapers reported widely on Schurz's reluctance to take up his choice assignment abroad, the still-neglected Gustave Koerner increasingly felt "like the client who never knew how hard a case his was, until he heard his lawyer unfold the tale of his wrongs." Unable to forget that he had been embarrassed in his recent quest for a diplomatic post while the now-reluctant Schurz had been splendidly rewarded, he finally gave voice to his pent-up envy and frustration. "When I left Washington," he confessed to Lincoln in a rambling, maudlin letter, "I was in hopes, that it might occur to you to offer me the Austrian or Swiss Mission. As I know the language of those countries, in addition to the French, the diplomatic language of the world, as I know the history of the people, their manners, their laws, and by my vast acquaintance with men now high in office, could have done something just at this crisis to retain for our Country their sympathy, I considered myself as being in any mission in Germany more useful, than perhaps many others who aspired to the respective places."[16]

Instead, Koerner had watched in dismay as men he considered less

qualified earned overseas appointments. "I am of your age," he continued in his agonized letter to Lincoln. "Have worked very hard in my
profession. My health has been greatly shattered. . . . Young active Germans, of merits, undoubtedly, but not half so well known to the Germans of the United States, and who had great prospects before them at
home in the sphere, in which they excel, were favored in the [diplo-
matic] missions. I stood disgraced in the eyes of others . . . had done
nothing to forfeit your friendship . . . being considered every where as
neglected & spurned by your administration. . . . I have never before
troubled you about myself[.] I hope you will be indulgent."[17]

His bitterness aired, but still ignored, Koerner ultimately, and
ironically, chose the path Schurz now preferred to diplomatic service:
he joined the army and went to war.

. . .

Schurz's ill-fated quest to assemble an all-German cavalry unit coincided with—and perhaps even helped inspire—a historic decision Lincoln made regarding nationwide recruitment. Quickly sensing that a
war to save the Union must not be an exclusively Republican or entirely
native-born undertaking, the President launched a concerted effort to
recruit marquee commanders from various political and ethnic backgrounds (though he did resist Frederick Douglass's early calls for the
enlistment of free Blacks).[18]

A German-born orator at New York's Union Square in April had
noted the presence of "old German Democrats and Republicans" in the
huge crowd, admitting that "whenever there are two Germans together, there are differences of opinion among them." But when it
came to "preservation of this great Republic, which is as dear to the
Germans as to any other men," the speaker added, "past differences
are forgotten."[19] Acting in the same hope, Lincoln reached out to both
the foreign-born and well-known Democrats to lead regiments, in the
latter category commissioning men like John A. Logan of Illinois,
who at least had military experience, and Benjamin F. Butler of

Massachusetts, a former Breckinridge supporter who did not.[20] The first three men Lincoln named as generals of volunteers—Butler, Nathaniel P. Banks, and John Adams Dix—were all Democrats. Koerner and other Republicans noted "the remarkable fact" that at the beginning of the war "the most noted generals were of Democratic antecedents."[21]

Intuitively sensing a wellspring of Union sympathy among the foreign-born, and eager to tap into the enormous manpower within their communities, Lincoln simultaneously sought to swell the military's leadership ranks with the nation's immigrants. The U.S. population at the time was 13 percent foreign-born—and more than nine out of ten of those newcomers dwelled in the North.[22]

In one of his first recruitment moves, even as he was dealing with the prickly Carl Schurz, Lincoln ordered his secretary of war to appoint "Col. Julian Allen, a Polish gentleman, naturalized," who "proposes raising a Regiment of our citizens of his nationality, to serve in our Army," adding, "I am in favor of accepting."[23] Once again, Cameron hesitated, prompting Allen to nudge the President eleven days later. "Your kind and friendly attention to our call, have [sic] endeared you to all the Polish-American citizens. Now, I, in the name of all my country-men beg you will not let that which you gave life to, die. . . . Do not turn us aside but accept our Patriotic offer."[24] Allen got his commission and began to raise a Polish regiment.

Although the most recently issued army regulations explicitly stated, "No volunteer will be mustered into the service who is unable to speak the English language," that rule would quickly be disputed.[25] The *Illinois Staats-Zeitung* ridiculed the idea that a soldier had to "pass an English examination before he can receive permission to let himself be shot for the Union."[26] Lincoln himself raised no objections to enthusiastic fighting men who lacked English. It was said that some of the earliest Illinois regiments issued orders only in German, and that New York's Fifty-Fifth Infantry Regiment—the *Gardes Lafayette*—

communicated exclusively in French. The impractical language regulations would henceforth be ignored, much to the relief of recruiters.

As Schurz's own recruiting efforts were languishing in the East,
his old acquaintance, Baden-born Franz Sigel, a saturnine thirty-six-
year-old Missouri resident whom Thurlow Weed admiringly labeled
"the strongest German in the Union," enjoyed far better luck in the
West.[27] The situation in Sigel's adopted state had grown desperate.
Missouri's governor, Claiborne Fox Jackson, had cast his lot with the
Confederacy and raised troops to fight against the Union even though
the state had not formally seceded.[28] The governor's treachery ignited
a bloody statewide civil war within the larger conflict about to roil the
nation.[29] The most contested of Missouri's resources was the city of St.
Louis, home to one of the country's largest concentrations of German-
born residents, almost all of them loyal to the Union—and most of
them to the Republican Party. Aware of these demographics, Lincoln
ordered Major General John C. Frémont, a favorite among German
Americans, to take command of the federal army's new Department
of the West, with St. Louis as his headquarters.

Yet it was Sigel, more than Frémont, who became a magnet for
German military recruitment in Missouri. Sigel was not only popular;
unlike Frémont, who had served in uniform chiefly as an explorer, he
also possessed genuine battle experience. Born in the Grand Duchy of
Baden, Sigel had trained at the Karlsruhe Military Academy and served
as a lieutenant in the German armed forces before siding with the revolution of 1848. Compelled to flee after the uprising collapsed, Sigel
immigrated to the United States in 1852 (following a brief sojourn in
England). He became a teacher at St. Louis's German American Institute and by the year of Lincoln's election was director of the city's entire
public school system. Usefully, he had also campaigned for the Republicans in 1860. With his prominent cheekbones and spruce mustache
and goatee, he looked every inch a romantic commander.

After the bombardment of Fort Sumter, Congressman Francis

Preston Blair Jr. organized the Third Missouri Infantry, and Sigel was elected its colonel. Then on May 10, he supported General Nathaniel Lyon in ousting a small Rebel garrison from Camp Jackson, on the outskirts of St. Louis. The Confederate defenders surrendered quickly, but the aggressive Union action ignited a civilian riot among Rebel sympathizers, punctuated by shouts of "Damn the long-eared Dutch." Showered with stones, federal troops fired on the crowd, causing a number of deaths, among them two females. Some newspapers branded the incident a massacre, with a few blaming excitable German officers like Sigel for the overwrought response. By contrast, the German press insisted that the seizure had kept Missouri from falling into Confederate hands.[30] The fact that the editor of the widely read St. Louis *Anzeiger des Westens*, Henry Boernstein, believed General Lyon harbored a "nativist hatred of foreigners"[31] made it easier for the paper to assign principal credit for this triumph to Sigel.

Ironically, this controversial episode would prove one of the highlights of Sigel's record in the field. On July 5, he commanded a small Union force in an inconclusive skirmish at Carthage in southwestern Missouri—the first real engagement of the war—but impressed observers chiefly by managing a well-executed withdrawal that inspired anti-German wags to begin referring to him as "Hell on Retreat."[32] In August, his command was again compelled to pull back after the much larger Battle of Wilson's Creek. This time, the retreat proved less orderly. Sigel himself admitted to witnessing "panic" in his ranks, and a report by a subordinate added, "Many of Sigel's men . . . turned to plunder," allowing the enemy to recapture artillery that Union forces had earlier seized—charges Sigel vehemently denied.[33] Critics derisively labeled him the "Flying Dutchman."

These setbacks neither diminished German enthusiasm for Sigel nor reduced the Lincoln administration's dependence on the flawed commander to maintain German American enthusiasm for the Union. Though General John Schofield filed an official complaint faulting Sigel as "unfit . . . deficient" and unable "to gain the confidence of

General Franz Sigel cuts a dashing figure at the July 5, 1861, Battle of Carthage—at least in the eyes of a fellow German, lithographer Feodor Fuchs of Philadelphia. Among the German-born, Sigel's popularity far exceeded his wartime accomplishments.

American officers and men," the *Anzeiger des Westens* countered, "Long Live Frémont! Long live Sigel!" and urged fellow Germans to "flock to the brave Sigel to join with his band of heroes to destroy the foe."[34] To at least one of his immigrant admirers, Sigel remained "far superior to many of our Major Generals" and worth "100 Fremonts."[35]

Consequently, instead of fading from the Union command structure, as he deserved, Sigel won appointment to the rank of brigadier general on August 7, and Lincoln made the promotion retroactive to mid-May to give Sigel more seniority. Sigel's real value, of course, came in serving as a touchstone for German enlistment and remaining a symbol of pride that fueled German Unionism. Indeed, he achieved almost the status of cult hero to German immigrants. "Fight Mit Sigel" became a patriotic rallying cry, and the general inspired poetry, musical tributes like "General Sigel's Grand March," and at least two songs entitled "I'm Going to Fight Mit Sigel," including this

stereotype-laden but affectionate example by New York composer-poet
John F. Poole:

> I've come shust now to tells you how
> I goes mit regimentals,
> To SCHLAUCH dem voes of Liberty,
> Like dem old Continentals,
> Vot fights mit England, long ago,
> To save de Yankee Eagle;
> Un now I gets mine sojer clothes,
> I'm going to fight mit Sigel.
> Chorus: Yaw! daus is drue, I shpeaks mit you,
> I'm going to fight mit Sigel.[36]

Picture publishers enhanced Sigel's growing legend with portraits
showing him in dramatic action, usually on horseback. Not surprisingly, the most flattering of these were aimed at German customers
and came from German-born lithographers: Louis Prang of Boston,
Feodor Fuchs of Philadelphia, and Ehrgott, Forbriger & Co. of Cincinnati. A measure of Sigel's importance—and the ongoing danger that his talismanic image and recruiting prowess posed to the
Confederacy—could be glimpsed in the slanderously anti-Union, anti-
German etching *Valiant Men "Dat Fite Mit Sigel,"* which accused the
general of atrocities against civilians. It showed a Teutonic-looking
Sigel (much stouter than in real life), hands defiantly on hips, cruelly
ignoring a kneeling woman's plea that he rescue children trapped in a
nearby home set afire by his soldiers. The print was the work of
Bavarian-born Marylander Adalbert Volck, the caricaturist who had
portrayed a trembling Lincoln passing through Baltimore in a freight
car. Despite his own ancestral roots, Volck's support for slavery and
secession clearly outweighed any pride he felt in his fellow German.
His incendiary etching failed to dent Sigel's reputation if only because,
like Volck's other works, it remained unpublished once Union forces

occupied his Baltimore hometown early in the war and suppressed anti-Union propaganda.[37] The *Anzeiger des Westens* perceptively acknowledged of Sigel—with pride as well as concern—that "since he is now the highest ranking military German he has to bear the cross of Germany as well."[38]

Among Germans other than Volck, Sigel remained a demigod; whatever his deficiencies in battle, Lincoln could ill afford to sacrifice him. As one Missouri Republican reminded the President, "The whole German element among us clings to and adores him."[39] That adoration gave Sigel leverage in dealing with the government, and he used it to his advantage when Lincoln reorganized the command in the western theater in response to the insubordination of commanding general Frémont. On August 30, 1861, acting on his own authority, Frémont declared all enslaved persons in his military department to be free, well ahead of administration policy and without consulting or even notifying his superiors. Lincoln not only countermanded the order after Frémont refused to retract it; he removed Frémont altogether and replaced him with General Henry W. Halleck, who thereupon reorganized the department and bypassed Sigel for promotion. The resulting brouhaha ensnared Halleck, Lincoln, Sigel, and even Gustave Koerner in a struggle for influence and power in the West that at one point endangered the President's standing among all the German American soldiers fighting under federal colors.

The fracas began when General Halleck overlooked Sigel for a new command opportunity. "Old Brains," as he was known, appointed Iowan Samuel R. Curtis instead, outraging Sigel's admirers. Halleck insisted that he bore "no personal prejudice" toward Sigel or other German officers—Halleck's own father, after all, had been born in Germany—claiming he had promoted Curtis only because he had served in the army longer. Viewing this instead as an assault on his honor, Sigel abruptly tendered his "absolute and immediate resignation" in January 1862, although, as he soon complained to Koerner, the President simply ignored his request.[40]

Republicans in Missouri were aghast, insisting, "We cannot really afford to lose his services. . . . A blow struck at Sigel will be considered a blow at the whole German people, not only in Mo. but throughout the Union." His absence would hurt "our cause" both "in the field and at the polls.[41] Before long, Sigel's discontent provoked "indignation meetings" among alienated Germans as far away as New York.[42] At one such rally at Cooper Union, orator after orator blamed "low jealousy and narrow-minded nativism" for Sigel's problems and demanded the general be given "an honorable sphere of action." Organizers duly forwarded the transcripts to the President.[43]

The crisis gave Lincoln what he considered a brilliant idea for an intervention. Why not console Sigel with a new command elsewhere, demonstrate renewed appreciation for the neglected Koerner, and placate the Missouri Germans all at once? His solution was to promote Koerner himself from colonel to brigadier general—but in characteristically secretive fashion, without telling Koerner of the scheme in advance. Instead, Lincoln dispatched Koerner to carry his written instructions to Halleck in a sealed envelope. First the President cleared the mission with the recently elevated commanding general George B. McClellan, hailing Koerner as "an educated german, once Lieut. Govr, one of the best men" in Illinois.[44]

In truth, Koerner was by now a fine candidate for promotion. He had already served in uniform for nearly a year, having raised the Forty-Third Illinois Regiment and become its colonel soon after Lincoln received his whining letter in 1861. Following Bull Run, Koerner had tried to organize a brigade composed of his fellow "Dutch," noting with excitement that "a great many Germans who had not yet served . . . were anxious to show their love for the Union by joining the army." Like Schurz, however, he learned to his disappointment that so many had already volunteered that few Germans remained left to recruit. "One of the great perplexities of the government," Lincoln had admitted in July, was "to avoid receiving troops faster than it can provide for them."[45]

In August, Lincoln harshly told Koerner that the awkward situation "embarrasses us." As the President elaborated: "We have promises out to more than four hundred Regiments, which, if they all come, are more than we want. If they *all* come, we could not take yours, if they do *not* all come we shall want yours; and yet we have no possible means of knowing whether they will all come or not." Koerner had met with Lincoln at the White House without resolving the problem, then spent a few more days in Washington advocating federal legislation designed to fast-track American citizenship for foreign-born soldiers who served in the Union military, after only a year's residence in the United States. An immigration reform that had divided the country when Winfield Scott first proposed it back in 1852 now sailed through Congress at Koerner's initiative.[46]

Subsequently, Koerner served for a time as an aide-de-camp to Frémont, who treated him "as cordially as his nature allowed," ever wary of Koerner's close "relations with Mr. Lincoln." And though Koerner in turn found Frémont "ambitious and vain," he came to understand that the onetime presidential candidate retained considerable popularity of his own among foreign-born soldiers. "For some reason or another," he told the President, "there is a charm around his name particularly with the Germans and Irish which is astounding." To remove him from command, Koerner advised his old friend, would be "suicidal."[47] That warning did not prevent Frémont's downfall. And as Koerner prophesied, his dismissal ignited so much "indignation" among Germans—both anti-civilians and troops—that, in Koerner's view, soldiers began flirting with "mutiny." The rebuke to Frémont left Koerner believing that he, too, had been "thrown out of the service."[48]

This was the crisis that prompted Lincoln to arm Koerner with his sealed, handwritten letter and instruct him to hand it sight unseen to Halleck, then presumably to examine it together with the general and thereafter "confer with him as to its contents." The presidential message Halleck dutifully opened in Koerner's presence included a fulsome paean to all Germans loyal to the Union: "The Germans are true

General John C. Frémont, "Pathfinder of the West" and 1856 Republican presidential candidate, remained remarkably popular among Missouri's antislavery Germans.

and patriotic," it began, "and so far as they have got cross in Missouri it is upon mistake and misunderstanding." Lincoln praised Koerner as "an educated and talented German gentleman, as true a man as lives," and advised Halleck: "With his assistance you can set everything right with the Germans." Only then did Lincoln lay out his elaborate plan: "[Y]ou should have Governor Koerner with you; and if agreeable to you and him, I will make him a brigadier-general so that he can afford to so give his time. He does not wish to command in the field, though he has more military knowledge than many who do . . . he will simply be an efficient, zealous, and unselfish assistant to you. I say this upon intimate personal acquaintance with Governor Koerner."[49]

The rest of the face-to-face meeting did not go exactly as Lincoln had hoped. For one thing, the chronically insecure Halleck was suspicious of potential rivals (he would shortly begin trying to steal credit from Ulysses S. Grant); he surely did not want the President's personal friend looking over his shoulder in St. Louis.[50] As for Koerner's promotion, a week after their meeting Halleck defiantly reported to Lincoln that he could not award Koerner a rank higher than colonel and would assign him a brigadier generalship only if the President insisted. Halleck added that discontent among German soldiers in Missouri had nothing to do with alleged "ill-treatment of Genl. Sigel, which is without the slightest foundation"; rather, it had arisen from "want of pay" and the interference of "designing politicians in and out of service"— among whom he implicitly included Koerner. "Being a German myself by descent," Halleck closed, "I know something of the German character, and I am confident that in a few weeks, if the Govt does not interfere, that I can reduce these disaffected elements to order & discipline."[51]

To add to Lincoln's woes, a stubborn Koerner now declared himself unwilling to abandon Sigel, even if it meant declining the promotion the President wanted to bestow on his old Illinois colleague. In a confidential nine-page letter penned in his usual neat hand on his customary blue stationery, Koerner told Lincoln that he had briefed Halleck on "the German element under his command" without agreeing to join it. Acting on his own, he had then taken a separate meeting with Sigel, and found the disgruntled general "a most modest, cool and reflecting man possessed . . . of great military sensibility."[52]

Koerner added that Halleck now agreed that had he known of the "enthusiasm" for Sigel among Germans—"particularly of the many thousand old Companions in arms, who followed him to this country and who allmost [sic] to a man are now in our ranks"—Halleck "would never have made the unfortunate move" of superseding him with Curtis. Koerner echoed Lincoln's suspicion that Germans were "smarting under some real and partly imaginary wrongs consequent upon the charges wrought by Fremonts [sic] removal." But Koerner continued to insist that Sigel remained "the embodiment of *action* in this war"—the representative of "the Millions of People who are desirous of seeing this damnable insurrection throttled at once and utterly crushed to dust." Koerner complicated matters further by claiming that Sigel's reputation had been besmirched by an Irishman—Brigadier General Thomas W. Sweeney—who had "interfered in the most ignorant manner with Sigels [*sic*] command."⁵³ This was hardly the result Lincoln had hoped for.

On February 7, Koerner followed up by demanding that Lincoln assign Sigel to the top command in either the West or the East, once again blasting the decision to name a non-German to outrank him as "a very gross outrage." Otherwise, Koerner warned, Sigel was "bound to resign, in justice to himself and the Germans."⁵⁴ Unwilling to risk further rifts with the community, Lincoln abandoned his Koerner scheme and arranged for Sigel's reassignment to a prestigious command in the East. As it turned out, the change of scenery would do the general little good.

For his part, hearing rumors in late 1862 that Carl Schurz was now pining to return to America and enlist in the military after all— following just a few months in Spain—Koerner once again set his own sights overseas.

. . .

Although no military figure ever rivaled Franz Sigel for the admiration of fellow German immigrants, others participated just as earnestly in the conflict—and helped shape it as a multiethnic crusade, as Lincoln hoped. Their eagerness to serve helped sustain "Dutch" enthusiasm for the Union despite occasional disputes. In the bargain, satisfying their ambitions helped Lincoln redeem political debts to German leaders who had campaigned for him in 1860. When Reinhold Solger, for example, sought an academic post at West Point, a supporter reminded Lincoln not only of the academic's recent pledge of "devotion" to the war effort but also his "services to the Republican cause," noting that Carl Schurz "can hardly be said to have done more to secure to the present administration the vote of the Western Germans" than had Solger.⁵⁵

The onetime revolutionary did not get the post at West Point but settled for a government job as assistant registrar in the Treasury Department.

However, Solger spoke for many foreign-born—and perhaps many native-born Americans as well—when he admitted of the nation's immigrants shortly after the fall of Fort Sumter: "A stranger is never a full citizen. . . . [H]is very accent defeats the most generous intentions. . . . [B]lood is stronger than naturalization papers." Now, with the opportunity to defend their adopted country, Solger accurately predicted that Germans would demonstrate "a sacrificial spirit, shared by all ranks," adding: "They all may bless the war for that knowledge."[56]

Standing in stark contrast to Sigel from a publicity standpoint was Prussian-born Alexander Schimmelfennig (sometimes mockingly called "Shiny Penny"), another former revolutionary whom both Schurz and Sigel had known in the old country. The onetime military instructor became colonel of a Philadelphia infantry regiment in September 1861 and soon thereafter was deemed eligible to rise in the ranks strictly because of his Teutonic moniker. A few months later, when Lincoln met with his new secretary of war, Edwin M. Stanton, to review a list of potential new brigadier generals, the President insisted that "there has to be something done that will be unquestionably in the interest of the Dutch, and to that end, I want Schimmelfennig appointed." The formidable Stanton tried pointing out, "Perhaps this Schemmel-what's-his-name is not as highly recommended as some other German officer." Lincoln shot back, "No matter about that, his name will make up for any difference there may be, and I'll take the risk of his coming out all right."[57] The risk proved higher than Lincoln expected.

A particularly inglorious record was notched by the President's old friend Friedrich Hecker, a native of Baden-Württemberg. A leading German revolutionary who resettled in Illinois, Hecker had served alongside Lincoln as a Frémont elector-at-large in 1856 and later benefited from Lincoln's charity when arsonists destroyed his Belleville home. By June 1861, he was a colonel in command of an Illinois regiment, but his staff, consigned to tedious guard duty, soon grew restive and resigned en masse. The mutiny succeeded in proscribing Hecker's military career, but not until he, like Sigel in Missouri, had served a useful purpose as a recruiter of German volunteers.[58]

Among the other prominent German Union commanders was the Prussian-Jewish Frederick (Friedrich) Salomon, who volunteered for the army in May 1861 and three months later "fought mit Sigel" at Wilson's Creek. (His brother Herman, a cabinetmaker, served as an enlisted man in a Missouri regiment of engineers.[59]) That defeat notwithstanding, Frederick became a full colonel by November and a brigadier general in July 1862. Neither brother is to be confused with Edward S. Salomon, a young Jewish volunteer from Chicago by way of the Duchy of Schleswig who served contentedly under Hecker but left the service after his commander fell from grace.*

In Ohio, filling two "quotas" at once—both as a German-born Jew and a Democrat who had campaigned against Lincoln in 1860— Colonel Marcus Spiegel commanded two different regiments before succumbing to battle wounds in Louisiana on May 4, 1864. Spiegel, who began the war committed to preserving the Union but opposed to emancipation, at first judged Lincoln "an honest man if let alone" by abolitionists and radicals.[60] But after seeing "the horrors of slavery" firsthand in the South, Spiegel became "glad indeed" to help to destroy "the accursed institution."[61] At his death, Spiegel was the highest-ranking Jewish officer in the federal military. Long after the war, the Bavarian-born Ohio lawyer Simon Wolf attested to the "spontaneous and cheerful alacrity with which our citizens of Hebrew faith entered their country's service in the hour of its need." Four out of every five Jewish enlistees were European-born.[62]

The roster of non-Jewish German commanders also boasts the name of Ohioan August Valentine Kautz, a West Point graduate who,

---

*Edward Salomon would later become governor of Washington Territory.

after serving in the infantry early in the war, became a Union cavalry captain, living Carl Schurz's unrealized dream. Lincoln later breveted Kautz a major general of volunteers. Prussian-born Peter Osterhaus became a major in the Second Missouri Volunteer Infantry, serving with distinction throughout the Civil War and beyond. Though his military record exceeded Sigel's, Osterhaus never achieved Sigel's unrivaled popularity.[63] Adolph von Steinwehr commanded the all-German Twenty-Ninth New York Volunteer Infantry at the Battle of Bull Run. And Prussian-born political radical August Willich, who composed the greeting that German workingmen had offered then President-elect Lincoln at Cincinnati in 1861, held commands in both Ohio and Indiana. When first commissioned, the onetime editor memorably warned the enemy, "We shall show them what German patriots can do!" His soldiers affectionately called him "Papa."[64] One wonders whether similar endearments were extended to German-born Wisconsin commanders with forbidding names like Adolphus Bush-beck and Leopold von Gilsa. In fact, von Gilsa had begun his American life as a singing piano player in a Bowery beer garden. Yet battle turned him into a raving tyrant known for spewing swear words at his men—in German.[65]

Then there was Brigadier General Louis Blenker, a native of the Rhineland city of Worms, who, like so many other Union officers, had notched considerable military service in Germany before embracing the revolution there in 1848. As a leader of the Baden uprising, he had once seized and briefly occupied his own birthplace city. Later forced into exile, Blenker made his way to the Empire State. A month after war broke out, he formed the New York infantry regiment known as the "German Rifles," which mustered into service in mid-May 1861 at a huge rally outside city hall. Lincoln's outreach to Democrats was working well at the time, for the troops were saluted that day by German-born Democratic Party chairman August Belmont, who praised the unit as "one of the finest corps [*sic*—it was a regiment] yet furnished in the noble quota from New York." Blenker responded by assuring the crowd that his men, "although adopted citizens," would proudly defend "this land of the free and home of the brave." He then called for three cheers for Lincoln and led his men south to defend Washington.[66]

Two German-born Union generals, each unpopular with his troops, strike similarly defiant poses early in the war: Louis Blenker (left) and Prince Felix Salm-Salm.

On July 6, the German Rifles serenaded Lincoln himself outside the White House.[67] General Scott generously called it "the best regiment we now have here."[68] Just two weeks later, the unit helped maintain as much order as possible during the Union's frenzied flight from the battlefield at Bull Run. Yet something about Blenker irked his fellow Germans. The following winter, Gustave Koerner warned Lincoln that Blenker "by no means" enjoyed "the confidence of the German population," and indeed the general's reputation later plummeted amid rumors of financial misconduct.[69] Though the U.S. Senate confirmed his promotion to major general, Blenker never recovered his early status. By 1863, Lincoln appeared to have forgotten his name. Blenker was subsequently kept out of the hard fighting in Pennsylvania and ultimately relegated to an inconsequential command in West Virginia.

Henry Boernstein of the *Anzeiger des Westens* served for the first three months of the war as the colonel of a Missouri volunteer regiment before taking up Lincoln's offer to serve as consul to Bremen. Boernstein had not only joined Sigel for the May 1861 march against Camp Jackson; he all but guaranteed its bloodless capitulation by helping empty the militia camp of Rebel weaponry before federal troops arrived. Boernstein also witnessed the civilian uprising that followed and claimed he wrote directly to Lincoln to report on the tragedy, although his letter does not survive in Lincoln's official papers. He later insisted that the violence against slaveholding civilians "made a deep impression on President Lincoln, by nature a gentle, good-natured man who only hardened in the course of events."[70]

A shroud of mystery surrounds another commander, born Baron Adolph Wilhelm August Friedrich von Steinwehr, who led the largely German Twenty-Ninth New York at Bull Run as part of Blenker's brigade. Despite that initial setback, von Steinwehr eventually rose to the rank of brigadier general, and elements of his command helped slow the attack of Richard Ewell's Confederate Corps at Gettysburg. (The main street of Gettysburg is still called Steinwehr Avenue.) After that, he was transferred to the western theater, where he was reorganized out of his job and never again held an important command.

The most elaborately named and most ethically challenged of all the German-born Union generals was Prince Felix Constantin Alexander Johann Nepomuk of Salm-Salm, who also served on Blenker's command staff. The nobleman had trained for the military in Berlin and seen action in the Austro-Sardinian War of 1859. Burdened with gambling debts and estranged from his wealthy family, he drifted to America and, when war broke out, volunteered his services to the Union. With experienced officers at a premium, Prince Salm-Salm (as he was known) quickly secured a commission as a colonel commanding the Eighth New York Infantry—which infuriated those German-born soldiers who despised the nobility. The remainder of Salm-Salm's military career can most charitably be described as checkered. In 1864, he was arrested for misrepresenting his rank, only to be reinstated and given another command, remaining in the army through war's end. Having fought in the Prussian, Austrian, and American armies, Salm-Salm would end his military career fighting for a French puppet, Emperor Maximilian, in Mexico and, later, back in Europe, in the Franco-Prussian War, during which he was killed in action.

This litany of widely publicized officers represents only part of the story of German participation in the Union war. Historians have estimated that some hundred and fifty Union military units, including militia, batteries, and cavalry, boasted rosters of all or nearly all German soldiers. By one count, twenty-four came from New York, eighteen each from Missouri and Illinois, fifteen from Ohio, and thirteen from Wisconsin. Among the other well-known units were the Koerner Regiment—an Illinois infantry force named for the former lieutenant governor—and the so-called Fremont Rifles (Forty-Sixth New York Infantry), commanded by Rudolph Rosa.[71]

A proliferation of rallies, public orations, and published broadsides effectively lured big-city immigrants to military service. A typical German-language recruitment poster published in New York stirringly proclaimed "*Bürger, Euer Land ist in Gefahr! Zu den Waffen!*"—"Citizens, your country is in danger! To arms!"—and offered a $160 bounty for volunteers.[72] Some of the earliest and most enthusiastic Western enrollees came out of St. Louis–based social clubs like the Turnverein and the Freie Gemeinde (Freethinkers), whose members found inspiration at rousing community gatherings where "bravado and beer flowed freely."[73] English writer Anthony Trollope expressed astonishment at the "vehement" antislavery sentiment he encountered among German volunteers training in Illinois. "They all regard slavery as an evil" that "should be abolished at once." But enthusiasm for the Union was personal, too. Before long, "Dutch" soldiers began referring to themselves as "*Lincolniten*"—Lincoln Men.[74]

Not all Germans agreed; in fact, not all Northern Germans responded positively to Lincoln's original 1861 call (and this book does not deal at all with Southern German Americans who enlisted to fight for the Rebels).[75] One German-born New Yorker mocked the "stupid people who sign up" for the Union, later enlisting only because the pay came to a healthy $1,200 a year.[76] In Wisconsin, when yet another Edward Salomon, this one the Prussian-born governor of Wisconsin, proposed a military draft in 1862 to meet his state's recruitment quotas, German Catholics in Ozaukee County launched a riot.[77] And Colonel Franz Wilhelm, who joined a Pennsylvania artillery unit soon after emigrating to America, branded the federal government "a disorganized state headed by a president who is not more than a figure head." Wilhelm also fretted that a quick Union victory would leave "40,000 unrestrained soldiers roaming the North," along with "80,000 stinking, lazy Negroes" who "wouldn't want to work any more" in the South.[78] Racism was not limited to the Confederacy, or to the nativist native-born.

For all the courage shown by most German volunteers, they were often subject to discrimination: taunted with expletives like "the Damned Dutch" and charged with drinking too much and fighting too little. Yet, as one soldier in the largely German Ninth Ohio Infantry lamented, its men had "no beer, no wine, and even no schnapps" to lubricate July Fourth celebrations that first year of fighting. The traditional festivities might have been more spirited, the thirsty soldier suggested, by observing "German customs."[79] Handicapping the Germans further, communication between officers and their superiors proved challenging: some of the recruits spoke only German, meaning that orders had to be translated before they could be understood, much less followed, often costing valuable time and causing confusion on the battlefield.

Although historian James M. McPherson has argued that, contrary to long-standing myth, Germans and other immigrants actually served the Union military in numbers *less* than their proportion in the Northern population—other scholars have since questioned that calculation—the "Dutch" nonetheless contributed powerfully to the sense that Lincoln's diverse nation was worth fighting for. Even given McPherson's caution that "only" 25 percent of Union men in arms qualified as immigrants—5 percent less than their presence in the population—their participation added significant raw numbers to the fighting force and, of enduring importance, helped expand the definition of American citizenship. In total, half a million of the two million white men who served in the Union armed forces were born overseas. And of these, 175,000 hailed from Germany.[80]

. . .

On the same day the Ohio German soldier bemoaned the absence of spirits—July 4, 1861—Lincoln told Congress that the war to suppress the rebellion was "a People's contest," a "struggle for maintaining in the world, that form, and substance of government, whose leading object is, to elevate the condition of men."[81] Naturalized Americans in the North seemed to understand that Lincoln meant to include them in this promise, as he always had; that he trusted they would fight to sustain democracy in America as courageously as they once had rebelled against monarchical oppression in Europe.

Germans were by no means the only ethnic group who so responded. Foreign-born Northerners from a range of European countries rushed into the Union armed forces. Alfred Napoleon Alexander "Nattie" Duffié, for example, born in Paris to a noble family, had served in Africa and the Crimea before immigrating to the United States in 1859 and bringing his military experience to the American Civil War two years later. Volunteering for Lincoln's army in 1861, he started with a captain's commission and rose steadily to major, colonel, and eventually the rank of general under Franz Sigel. Duffié's devotion stood in marked contrast to the indifference—at best—of the French government toward the Union. The long list of European-born recruits proceeds from there.

Among the Polish Americans who earned Union commands—in addition to Julian Allen, who had corresponded with Lincoln soon after the war began—were Albin Francisco Schoepf from Podgroz and Wladimir Krzyżanowski, a nobleman from Rożnowo. Krzyżanowski became the leader of the Polish Legion of the New York Fifty-Eighth but, as Carl Schurz liked to jest, failed to win Senate confirmation of a later promotion because "there was nobody there who could pronounce his name."[82] The first such units often outfitted themselves in red-and-white uniforms topped with four-pointed *rogatywka* caps, seemingly unafraid that such gaudy regalia would make them easy targets in battle.[83] Adam Gurowski, the Polish-born nobleman who had liberated serfs on his family estate before heading to America, offered to lead a "Negro regiment" before there were any to lead.[84]

Swiss Americans also raised companies in several states, the most famous among them Berdan's Sharpshooters, commanded by immigrant carpenter turned architect Casper Trepp. Eager to meet these particular foreign-born troops, Lincoln visited the Berdan unit when it encamped near Washington in October 1861, and he watched with delight as its crack marksmen engaged in a target-shooting competition.[85] "Such high visits," soldier Rudolf Aschmann wrote touchingly, "made us proud and awakened in [*sic*] us the desire soon to justify in battle the expectations which were cherished from us."[86]

As many as ten thousand Italian Americans, most from New York, also served in the federal armed forces, manning units like the "Spinola Brigade" (named for Colonel Francis Spinola, a local politician), and the Fifty-First New York under Brigadier General Edward Ferrero, born in Spain to Italian parents. A professional dance instructor in civilian life, Ferrero went on to command a unit of the newly formed U.S. Colored Troops. However, at the 1864 Battle of the Crater near Petersburg, Virginia, he would reportedly remain sheltered behind the lines, guzzling rum as his Black troops marched to their slaughter. He was breveted a major general anyway.

This multicultural Union recruiting poster from 1861 urged immigrants of many backgrounds to join the newly formed Garibaldi Guard.

Yet another well-known unit, the Thirty-Ninth New York Infantry, named itself the Garibaldi Guard in honor of the fifty-five-year-old Italian military hero Giuseppe Garibaldi. It became the army's first multiethnic regiment, appealing for recruits under the slogan: *Patrioti Italiani! Honvedek! Amis de la liberté! Deutsche Freiheits Kaempfer.* Reminding "Italians, Hungarians, and French, patriots of all nations" that the "aid of every man is required for the service of his ADOPTED COUNTRY!" This unique call to arms solicited 1,150 volunteer *bersaglieri* (Italian for "sharpshooters"), *honvedek* (Hungarian for "soldiers"), *chasseurs* (French for "cavalry"), and *Scharfschutzen* (German for "snipers").

Correspondent Henry Villard could not help noticing the "foreign elements" parading with other early recruits on the streets of New York, among them "the 'Garibaldi Guards,' in the legendary red blouses and bersaglieri hats . . . with some fanciful American features grafted upon them."[87] In the words of a "Garibaldi War Song" under which they marched:

> Ye come from many a far off clime,
> And speak in many a tongue
> But Freedom's song will reach the heart
> In whatever language sung.[88]

The flamboyant organizer of the Thirty-Ninth, Colonel Frederick D'Utassy, claimed to be a Hungarian nobleman schooled at the Austrian military academy and exiled from his native country after fighting heroically in the revolution. Only later was it learned that the colonel was in truth a Jewish-born horse trader named David Strasser, whose only military experience had been notched in selling steeds to Hungarian troops in the old country. Two years after forming the Garibaldi Guard, "D'Utassy" would be convicted of fraud—not surprisingly, involving horse trading—and imprisoned at Sing Sing.[89] Even this embarrassment did not count as the most awkward chapter in the Union's embrace of Giuseppe Garibaldi.

A week after the federal humiliation at Bull Run, Secretary of State Seward—likely acting with Lincoln's blessing—tendered Garibaldi himself a military commission in the Union army. Garibaldi had lived for a time in America during the previous decade and at one point even filed his naturalization papers—prematurely, as it turned out. Now he was home in Sardinia, a global celebrity but nursing battle wounds and reluctant to return to the United States for a mere major generalship. In an unauthorized attempt to sway him, a "cunning" American diplomat in Antwerp informed Garibaldi that Lincoln was prepared to offer him supreme command, explaining, "There are thousands of Italians and Hungarians who will rush to your ranks, and . . . tens of thousands of American citizens who will glory to be under the command of the 'Washington of Italy.'" When the U.S. minister to Brussels hastened to Garibaldi's side to set the record straight, the old general merely added another stipulation: he would accept American command only "with the additional contingent power . . . of declaring the abolition of slavery."[90] Needless to say, Garibaldi remained in Sardinia.

No such preconditions were required by Luigi Palma di Cesnola, a native of Parma and Crimean War veteran who founded a military school in New York to train Italian Americans for the Union army. Cesnola would go on to earn the Medal of Honor for gallant service at the Battle of Aldie, Virginia, in June 1863. (Sixteen years later, he became the first director of the recently formed Metropolitan Museum of Art.)

Meanwhile, Chicago's Scandinavian community responded without reservation within a week to Lincoln's original call for volunteers, "determined to a man," the *Chicago Tribune* reported admiringly, "to stand or fall in defense of American liberties, laws, and institutions." Among the "Norsemen" were veterans "well versed in military tactics from years of constant service in the armies of their country."[91] One such soldier, Swedish-born Eric Young, proudly noted that by 1862 his largely German company of the Minnesota Fourth Regiment boasted "11 Swedes and 11 Norwegian."[92] Among such Scandinavian volunteers, Lincoln was held in wide esteem, for when Nels H. Peterson enlisted in a predominantly Swedish company, he encountered so many like-named Petersons that he rechristened himself "Nels Lincoln." And so his name would be incised on the Civil War veterans' monument later erected in his adopted hometown of McPherson, Kansas.

Some fifty thousand English-born Americans also served in Union ranks, and another fifty thousand from British America, including Canada—and these included British citizens who had never even visited the United States but enlisted because they viewed Union service as an economic opportunity or a romantic lark.[93] The naturalized volunteers included the Scottish American Highlanders of the Seventy-Ninth New York Militia, who posed at Mathew Brady's Washington gallery attired in tartan kilts, silver-buckled shoes, horsehair sporrans, and Glengarry caps, but prudently changed into regulation uniforms to fight at Bull Run. As Scotsman James Todd of Ohio explained his patriotic impulse, "This is the Country of my adoption, and I am ready to sacrifice my life or all I possess in protecting the honor of my Country."[94]

Such volunteers joined the U.S. military despite suspicion abroad that they had been unlawfully impressed into American service or were mercenaries whose enlistments violated Britain's 1860 foreign enlistment ban. Indeed, Canadian legislator and former militia ensign Arthur Rankin traveled to Washington in 1861 with an eye to joining the Union army, secured a meeting with Lincoln, volunteered his services to fight against the Rebels, and received a commission to raise a regiment of British North American lancers. But when Rankin returned to Toronto later that year, local officials arrested him for recruiting for a foreign government. Authorities ultimately dropped the charges, but Rankin never served again in either the British or American military.[95]

The Union proved more aggressive when it came to recruiting in Ireland, unleashing protests from Confederate emissaries in London. Reports persisted throughout the war that unauthorized federal recruiters often met ships bearing Irish passengers at New York docks and plied young arrivals into the military with gifts of whiskey and tobacco, often splitting or stealing the financial bounties. Even if such stories exaggerated the situation at the waterfront, the Lincoln administration made no secret of the fact that it welcomed foreign volunteers if legitimately enrolled. Writing to American consul to Paris John Bigelow, Secretary of State Seward acknowledged that "to some extent this civil war must be a trial between the two parties to exhaust each other." Under such circumstances, the "immigration of a large mass from Europe would of itself decide it." Soon enough, with Lincoln's approval,

Seward began flooding American embassies with "Circular Number 19," inviting the poor of Europe to immigrate to the United States.[96]

Added to this total were seventy-five thousand soldiers listed as "other" foreign-born.[97] These included Hungarians with names ranging from Albert Anzelm to Sigismund Zsulavsky (both of whom enlisted in 1861, from Missouri and New Hampshire, respectively).[98] Lincoln and Mary demonstrated their respect for these enlistees in late June 1861 by attending the funeral of a Hungarian private who had served briefly in the multiethnic Garibaldi Guard.[99]

Not long thereafter, Lincoln's old acquaintance Julian Kuné, now a major in the Twenty-Fourth Illinois Infantry, turned up at the White House dressed in a Jaeger regimental uniform to hand the President a request to keep the Hungarian-Slav "Lincoln Riflemen" in the field after their original ninety-day enlistments had expired. Lincoln seemed grateful for this expression of patriotism but explained that the government had already reached its recruiting goal of seventy-five thousand men in arms, and that if he added more troops, "we would not be able to feed them." Kuné summoned his nerve and replied: "Permit me to tell you that it will take many times seventy-five thousand before this rebellion is put down." As to feeding them, "the prairies of our own State of Illinois can raise more than enough to feed a million soldiers." Lincoln "quietly handed our application" to John Hay and directed him to send it to the War Department with instructions "to accept this regiment." Kuné remembered being "startled" by Lincoln's "haggard appearance." As he put it: "The buoyant spirit which had kept him up during the late political campaign had left him. I had never seen such a change within so short a time in the appearance of a man."[100] (Kuné is not to be confused with George Kuhne, a Prussian-born Jewish former barber who was among five Union soldiers from the 118th Pennsylvania Volunteers executed for desertion at the order of General George G. Meade—after Lincoln himself denied an appeal "for mercy," calling their crimes "very flagrant"—on August 29, 1863.[101])

To inspire additional Magyar recruits, William Seward embarked on another international talent hunt, seeking to lure to America the Hungarian freedom fighter György Klapka, a veteran of his country's war for independence. Outdoing even Garibaldi's demands, Klapka agreed to entertain the offer only if he received supreme command, a $100,000 bonus, and an annual salary equal to the President's: $25,000. Then Klapka wrote to the recently named commander of the Army of the Potomac, George McClellan, to say he hoped soon to meet and evaluate him. McClellan acidly commented, "He failed to state what provision he would make for me, that probably to depend on the impression I made upon him." McClellan showed Klapka's presumptuous letter to Lincoln, who assured his general that "he would see that I should not be troubled in that way again."[102] That was the last that Lincoln's army heard of György Klapka.

Among the foreign-born soldiers who did fight for the United States were even, by some accounts, a smattering of Asians and Pacific Islanders, including a handful of Union volunteers from Indonesia and the Philippines. Recently unearthed records suggest that three of the thirty-five thousand Chinese immigrants then living in California— all of them lacking civil rights or a path to legal American citizenship— nonetheless served in the Union armed forces, two in the army and one in the navy. Even this represented a remarkable commitment from a people who, a decade after the war, would still be considered by Congress as "pagan in religion, inferior in mental and moral qualities . . . an undesirable element in a republic."[103] By one account, Lincoln even approved a venture aimed at recruiting Californios—Hispanic citizens of California—to form their own federal cavalry regiment under Don Andrés Pico, though he had fought against the United States in the Mexican–American War.[104] Yet, as noted, Lincoln continued to resist tapping another huge potential resource: the African American community. Not until the spring of 1863, following issuance of the Emancipation Proclamation and passage of enabling legislation by Congress, would the "U.S. Colored Troops" begin recruiting Black men to fight for their own freedom.

Troops from New York's multi-ethnic Garibaldi Guard parade past President Lincoln (standing beneath American flag) and General Winfield Scott (seated) on July 4, 1861 in Washington.

The vast majority of foreign-born soldiers saw action without accolades, some surviving with debilitating physical and emotional wounds that hobbled them for the rest of their lives. The incident lists of the war overflow with both mundane and bizarre casualty reports involving foreign names like E. Olsen, "killed in a draft riot" at New Lisbon, Wisconsin, in 1863; John Hoffman, "killed by lightning" at Cashtown, Maryland; and Augustus Meyer, who "left camp while insane and not heard from afterwards."[105]

CHAPTER EIGHT

God Bless the Irish Flag

If German Americans contributed the largest foreign-born contingent to the federal army, Irish Americans proved a close second. Some 150,000 Irishmen took up arms for the Union during the four-year-long Civil War.[1]

Such a patriotic response from this overwhelmingly pro-Democratic community could not have been predicted before the attack on Fort Sumter. Then, at New York's massive Union Square rally on April 20, lawyer Richard O'Gorman rose to address the crowd of one hundred thousand. "I am an Irishman, and I am proud of it," declared the one-time Young Ireland nationalist who had become an American, but "when I assumed the rights of a citizen, I assumed, too, the duties of a citizen." Abraham Lincoln, he admitted, "is not the President of my choice. No matter. He is the President chosen under the Constitution. . . . That flag is my flag." The attack in Charleston was "more to be regretted than if the combined fleets of England had threatened to devastate our coast."[2]

Not yet completely reassured, Lincoln summoned another prominent Irish New Yorker, criminal attorney James T. Brady, to the White
House and beseeched him to raise and lead the first Irish brigade;
patriotic oratory was fine, but an actual unit of Irish soldiers would
make a truly important statement about unity. Brady "protested earnestly" that he possessed neither experience in military matters nor
confidence in his ability to manage soldiers. "You know plenty of Irishmen who do know about such matters," Lincoln countered, "and as to
the appointment of officers, did you ever know an Irishman who would
decline an office or refuse a pair of epaulets, or do anything but fight
gallantly after he had them?" Like O'Gorman a longtime Democrat,
Brady became an instant convert and began recruiting. One contemporary gave credit for the initiative to the President, explaining, "Mr.
Lincoln's immediate object was fully realized by the exercise of that
keen practical insight and knowledge of human nature which shone so
conspicuously in him." As a result, "the smoldering discontent among
the Irish which had threatened to break into flame was replaced by an
air of enthusiasm."[3] The *Irish-American* newspaper now called on its
readers "to be true to the land of your adoption in this crisis of her
fate."[4]

As Lincoln knew, martial enthusiasm would go only so far. Most
Irish in the North remained faithful to the Democratic Party though
true to their adopted country—as long as federal war goals remained
fixed on defending the flag and restoring the Union, not on eradicating
slavery; and as long as deference was extended to immigrants. Fearing
that freed African Americans might compete for the low-paying jobs
that, for them, made the difference between subsistence and starvation, many Irish found no inconsistency in melding patriotism with
racism. To Lincoln's relief, their abundant nationalism manifested
almost immediately, starting in New York.

Already in existence for ten years, the overwhelmingly Irish Sixty-
Ninth Regiment of the New York State Militia marched down Broadway en route to the defense of Washington on April 23, 1861—barely

two weeks after the attack on Sumter—accompanied by the "stormy cheers" and "passionate prayers" of some half a million onlookers.[5] James T. Brady's recruitment efforts had paid off handsomely: Lincoln had called for volunteers on April 15, and it had taken only days to muster the Sixty-Ninth. "So great was the anxiety to join the ranks" that three times more men volunteered than could be accommodated in the regiment.[6]

Leading the Sixty-Ninth downtown that day, its emerald-green regimental flag rippling in the springtime breeze, was the slender, delicately bearded thirty-three-year-old Colonel Michael Corcoran. The onetime tavern clerk from County Sligo had led the unit since 1859. Then in 1860 he had aroused both municipal fury and ethnic pride by refusing to assemble his men to welcome the Prince of Wales to New York, arguing that the heir to the British throne represented "the oppressor of Ireland."[7] *Harper's Weekly* promptly denounced the move as "a step which can not but exasperate public feeling against the Irish race," warning "our Irish fellow-citizens not to presume too far upon the forbearance of our people"—a reminder that, to many, the Irish remained second-class Americans perpetually required to prove their loyalty.[8] Corcoran's anti-British gesture also earned him a court-martial that was still pending, only to be quietly shelved once the rebellion began. He was too well suited to his new role to be discarded for prewar insubordination.

A member of the three-year-old American organization the Fenian Brotherhood, which supported Irish independence, Corcoran was also a politically active ward heeler who served as an elected New York City school inspector, a Democratic district leader, and a member of a powerful political committee that chose party nominees for judgeships. Above all, New York archbishop John Hughes believed that "Corcoran should be appointed" to lead the first Irish regiment in defense of the Union, and Lincoln quickly replied that "my own judgment concurs."[9] In an uncirculated memorandum he composed sometime in 1861, the President identified Corcoran and two other noted

Period photograph of the thin, ascetic Colonel Michael Corcoran of New York (by way of County Sligo, Ireland), who became a living Union martyr among Irish Americans in the North.

Irishmen, Thomas Francis Meagher and James Shields, as ideal Union commanders. Lincoln managed to recruit all three.

After heading south to Washington via ship and rail, Corcoran and the Sixty-Ninth made camp above the capital on picturesque Arlington Heights. Assigned to build its own 650-by-450-foot redoubt slated to be named Fort Seward, the men insisted on christening it instead for their commander, and the installation became known as Fort Corcoran. Then the colonel asked the regimental chaplain, Catholic priest Thomas Mooney, to baptize its newly installed cannon with holy water. Father Mooney captured the spirit of the moment by declaring, "Parents look forward to the first words of their children. I look forward to the first roar from the mouth of this babe."[10] When Archbishop Hughes learned about the unorthodox ceremony, he replaced Mooney with another chaplain. Hughes might have considered the sanctifying of weaponry blasphemous, but he did begin flying the American flag over St. Patrick's Cathedral and urged his parishioners to "be patriotic, to do for the country what the country needs." And he vowed that "the blessing of God will recompense those who discharge their duty."[11] Yet no roar was heard from the Sixty-Ninth's cannon for months. Its men dug entrenchments, cut down trees, and finished constructing their wood-and-earthwork citadel as the Lincoln administration continued to recruit foreign-born troops.

In late June, Lincoln paid tribute to another predominately Irish regiment, New York's Thirty-Seventh Infantry—the "Irish Rifles"—by reviewing their encampment near the U.S. Capitol. There he was "most enthusiastically cheered" by both enlisted men and officers with names like Doherty, Murphy, O'Beirne, and Maguire.[12] New York was not the only heavily Irish city to recruit soldiers to fight for the Union. The boys of the Ninth Massachusetts, most of whom had probably not left Boston since their arrival from Ireland, now found themselves passing through Washington and viewing inspiring sights like Mount Vernon and the Capitol building for the first time.

Irish-born soldiers from the West enjoyed similar experiences. Strolling through downtown Washington on Independence Day 1861, enlistee Daniel Crotty, a shoemaker assigned to the Third Michigan Infantry, found himself before a grandstand outside the White House "covered with a canopy of Stars and Stripes" and surrounded by "a great multitude" of onlookers. As Crotty soon discovered, the nation's leaders had gathered there to review the troops. To his delight, Crotty caught a glimpse of "the honest and homely face of our good President Lincoln" surrounded by members of his cabinet and General Scott. "Hurrah for the Fourth of July!" he rejoiced.[13] As historians have pointed out, such nationalizing experiences might not have converted Irish soldiers to the ranks of the Republicans, but they helped further assimilate them—made them feel for the first time that they were a vital part of both cause and country.[14] Perhaps most important of all, the organization of Hibernian units under distinguished Irish officers promised to immunize these immigrants from the violent prejudices of the past.

Another prospective Irish commander of great promise, James Shields—Lincoln's onetime Illinois dueling foe and a former senator—had been for several years a resident of California. When Fort Sumter fell, Shields was even farther from home: in Mazatlán, Mexico, on a business venture and extended honeymoon with his Irish-born bride.[15] Shields's experience in the Mexican–American War plus his nativity and status nonetheless made him an ideal political general. When the fugitive Irish hero Thomas Meagher, among others, concurred, Lincoln recommended Shields for a command.[16] The Democrat, whom Lincoln had once publicly mocked, is said to have immediately "tendered his services to his old friend, now President of the United States"—probably an exaggeration on several counts: Shields neither responded quickly nor regarded Lincoln as a particular friend (though Gustave Koerner thought of the general as such).[17] For a time, in fact, Shields remained frustratingly out of reach.

For one thing, official word of his commission, issued in August, did not reach Mexico for months. Contrary to claims later advanced by his early biographers, Shields did not then rush back to the United States to take up arms. Claiming he was still hindered by a wound he had suffered in Mexico—which apparently did not limit his prolonged attentions to his much younger new wife—he delayed his return for weeks. This gave critics who doubted his loyalty ample time to mount a campaign to block his appointment. When Shields finally started for home in late November 1861, making it known he was finally ready to return to the army, newspaperman F. B. Murdock wrote to Lincoln from San Jose, California, to warn that Shields had "declared his opposition to you & the Republicans." Murdock was convinced that "if civil war should break out on the Pacific coast, Gen. Shields would be found on the Rebel side."[18] In what was obviously a coordinated effort, San Francisco businessman Ira P. Rankin wrote that same day to alert

Secretary of War Cameron that Shields remained "in full sympathy with those conspiring to break up the government" and, should war break out, "would fight for the south . . . to the spending of the last drop of his blood." Cameron made sure Lincoln got to see this disturbing message.[19] Yet the President remained committed to recruiting both Democrats and the foreign-born for Union commands—even one of his own former enemies.

Shields at last reached the national capital around New Year's Day 1862, and on January 8 met with Lincoln and Secretary of State Seward at the White House to clear the air. There Shields apparently convinced them of his "earnest, intelligent, and self-sacrificing cooperation with the government." What must have been a tense reunion ended with the President expressing "hearty and unreserved confidence" in Shields, whose appointment went through as planned.[20] His enlistment garnered nearly as much enthusiastic coverage in the Irish and Democratic press as Sigel had inspired in the German.[21] In New York, a special committee began recruiting men to serve under Shields as "a distinctive representation of Irish valor and patriotism."[22]

Shields's war, however, did not go as he and his admirers hoped. Initially assigned to serve under General Nathaniel Banks in the Department of the Shenandoah, he soon ran into what Gustave Koerner excused as "his usual bad luck." On March 23, Shields suffered a serious wound at the First Battle of Kernstown and had to be carried from the field.[23] In his absence, Union forces there achieved a modest victory over Stonewall Jackson that prompted Shields's friends to claim he was cheated out of credit for the success—once again a "political martyr." Shields remained disabled and out of action for five weeks. Then, in a June rematch at Port Republic, Jackson easily outmaneuvered him. Major John J. Coppinger nevertheless claimed that were it not for "the blunder of a subordinate," Shields might have been remembered as "one of the Shermans, Sheridans, and Meades" of the war.[24] Instead, he thereafter earned few command opportunities. In the summer, Lincoln offered some solace by promoting his old political rival to the rank of major general, but in an extraordinary rebuff to a onetime colleague, the Senate refused to confirm him.

Back in uniform and fighting ingloriously for the Union: Lincoln's onetime Irish nemesis and former U.S. senator James Shields.

Shields's military career never rebounded. Yet a period biographer claimed that after dismissing McClellan as commander of the Army of the Potomac later in 1862, Lincoln offered the top post to Shields. Supposedly, Shields turned the job down "owing to his strained relations"—not with Lincoln, the former Whig he had once threatened to kill on the field of honor, but with the new secretary of war, Edwin M. Stanton, a fellow Democrat, albeit a former one.[25] The tale is almost certainly fiction. More likely, with no military options remaining, Shields desired only to return to California, and Lincoln magnanimously arranged to provide him a soft landing there. Officially, the President transferred him to the military's Department of the Pacific in San Francisco. Shields thus enjoyed a government-funded transcontinental trip home and, once there, no doubt by prearrangement, resigned from the service. Before him lay yet another brief term in the U.S. Senate and his enshrinement in Statuary Hall.

The third Irish military leader mentioned in Lincoln's 1861 "Irish" memo was Corcoran booster Meagher, a celebrated onetime resistance fighter in Ireland who counted a devoted following on both sides of the Atlantic. Handsome, "rather stout," with "a clear high-colored complexion" and a "heavy, dark brown moustache, closely trimmed," Meagher was already an international celebrity.[26] Once banished to a Tasmanian penal colony by the British, he had made a daring escape, sailed to America, helped found an Irish newspaper in Boston, and arrived in New York to be greeted as an "apostle of freedom."[27] Like Shields, he had expressed initial sympathy for Southern independence but, after the Fort Sumter attack, advised his Irish American admirers that Union loyalty was "not only our duty to America, but also to Ireland."[28] Meagher then raised a Zouave company—his advertising slogan was "Young Irishmen to Arms!"—and headed south as part of Corcoran's Sixty-Ninth, his soldiers' colorful Middle Eastern–style regalia a startling contrast to the drab uniforms worn by the regiment's other Irish-born volunteers.[29]

That July, Meagher's Zouaves fought under Corcoran at Bull Run. All told, the Sixty-Ninth lost thirty-eight killed, fifty-nine wounded, and ninety-five missing, but endured none of the humiliation heaped on the Union army by the press over its frenzied retreat from the field. Englishman William Howard Russell of the *London Times*, who covered the battle and was hardly inclined to celebrate the Irish, did report privately, "Young Meagher of the Sword . . . ran away & appeared in Centreville [Virginia] at the end of the day declaring that 'We're whipped like dogs!'"[30] Yet Russell said nothing condemnatory about Meagher in print, though his scathing reports of the battle got him banned from the press corps. In truth, the Sixty-Ninth fell back only after making repeated assaults on a Confederate artillery position, and at one point Meagher's horse was shot out from under him. Well-to-do

New Yorker George Templeton Strong, no friend of the Irish, either, lamented that the Union had been "utterly and disgracefully routed" at Bull Run but acknowledged that "Corcoran's Irishmen are said to have fought specially well, and to have suffered much."[31] Indeed, even in withdrawing from the battlefield, the Sixty-Ninth helped safeguard the Army of the Potomac's rear flank in the midst of its wild flight.[32] Despite the smoke-filled chaos, Meagher managed to reorganize his soldiers and lead them back toward Washington to fight another day.

COL. MICHAEL CORCORAN AT THE BATTLE OF BULL RUN. VA. JULY 21ST 1861.
The desperate and bloody charge of the Gallant Sixty Ninth, on the Rebel Batteries.

Lithographers Currier & Ives issued this colorful but misleading print of the Battle of Bull Run in 1861, emphasizing Colonel Corcoran's bravery without acknowledging the Union's humiliating defeat.

Michael Corcoran was not so fortunate. Toward the end of the battle, "standing like a rock in the whirlpool" while bearing the regimental colors, he fell into Confederate hands. Sent south as a prisoner of war, he became, in effect, a living Irish American martyr. From captivity, he issued a stirring message that sounded at once pro-Union and pro-immigration: "One half of my heart is Erin's, and the other half is America's. God bless America, and ever preserve her as the asylum of all the oppressed of the earth."[33] In Corcoran's absence, overall command of the Sixty-Ninth fell to Meagher, who encamped his men back on Arlington Heights while Lincoln bestowed a sentimental promotion to the rank of brigadier general on "Col. Michael Corcoran, now a prisoner at Richmond."[34]

A few days later, on July 23, Lincoln and Secretary Seward paid further tribute to the regiment by riding up to Fort Corcoran, where the exhausted troops summoned "the greatest enthusiasm" in welcoming their commander in chief. As Lincoln knew, these and other battle-scarred volunteers were now eligible to leave the service, as their original three-month enlistment period was about to end. According to one newspaper account, "The President asked if they intended to re-enlist? The reply was that 'they would if the President desired it.' He announced emphatically that he did, . . . complimenting them upon their brave and heroic conduct. . . . This was received with cheers and the determination expressed to go in for the war and stand by the government and the old flag forever."[35] Meagher confirmed that his troops greatly enjoyed Lincoln's "affable manner and cheerful badinage," which "made him an especial favorite with these rough-and-ready appreciators of genuine kindness and good humor."[36] He was certain that once his veterans reached home, they would re-enroll in the military.

Demobilized a few weeks later, the Sixty-Ninth even earned the privilege of encamping briefly on the White House grounds before returning to New York. Yet neither Meagher nor his men could have imagined the joyous reception that awaited them back home. On July 27, thousands of well-wishers massed at Bowling Green on the southern tip of Manhattan to provide the kind of jubilant welcome usually reserved for those who won battles. In New York, however, ethnic pride still counted for more than martial accomplishment, and sustaining Irish loyalty remained the highest of priorities. As one writer observed, "The entrance of the 69th" after "its first brief and bloody campaign" produced "a popular ovation . . . in the hearts of the people. The return . . . of its shattered and hard-worn remains was regarded as a fete."[37] Accompanied by the elite, largely Protestant Seventh Regiment, the men of the Sixty-Ninth paraded up Broadway to Union Square, then marched back downtown to the Essex Market Armory to deposit their weapons before disbanding.

For months, Corcoran remained imprisoned in the Confederate capital. Throughout his confinement, however, he inspired celebratory portraiture, including a Currier & Ives lithograph whose caption honored "The desperate and bloody charge of the Gallant Sixty Ninth on the Rebel Batteries."[38] Advocating for Corcoran's release, *Frank Leslie's Illustrated Newspaper* published a clever Thomas Nast cartoon that managed to be both offensive and sympathetic at the same time. Basing his work on the legend of Saint Patrick driving the snakes from Ireland, Nast titled his woodcut *The American St. Patrick Driving Out the Reptiles.*

This Thomas Nast cartoon meant to salute modern Irish American warriors battling Confederate "reptiles" but, in depicting his hero wearing a miter, he reminded viewers of Catholic troops' feared allegiance to the pope.

The print depicted a simian-looking Irish warrior wearing a crucifix and papal miter and wielding a bishop's crozier laden with spikes and cannonballs to strike at Rebel alligators, snakes, and frogs. Brandishing his weapon, the Irishman shouts: "And yer won't give up Corcoran, won't yer? But I'll make yer, ye spalpeens! Now take this!"[39] On a higher artistic plane, the return of the Sixty-Ninth to Manhattan inspired German-born painter Louis Lang, who witnessed the scene, to produce a mammoth canvas showing Meagher on horseback, his troops following behind him as he waved his cap to the cheers of admirers. The viewers' attention is directed to a newsboy in the foreground hawking portraits of the imprisoned Corcoran. Lang's painting went on exhibit in 1863, earning praise from art critics and serving as an inducement to further Irish recruitment—and, it must have been hoped, compliance with that summer's military draft.[40]

Top: Colonel Thomas Francis Meagher posed for a New York photographer exactly as artist Louis Lang would depict him in his painting of the return of the Sixty-Ninth (bottom). Lang undoubtedly supervised the camera sitting. The canvas proved a popular and critical sensation when it went on exhibit in 1863.

As for the charismatic Meagher, a supremely gifted orator, he quickly reemerged for a huge rally at Jones's Wood on Manhattan's then-rural Upper East Side; the event was organized to raise funds for Bull Run widows. There he echoed Lincoln's recent plea for reenlistment: *"I ask no Irishman to do that which I myself am not prepared to do. My heart, my arm, my life is pledged to the national cause, and to the last it will be my highest pride, as I conceive it to be my holiest duty and obligation, to share its fortunes."*[41] A few days later, Archbishop Hughes conveyed his undiminished confidence in Meagher to Secretary Seward, with whom he had long maintained cordial relations. No doubt Seward in turn advocated Meagher's virtues to Lincoln, who soon offered him a fresh commission as a major general—as long as Meagher agreed to raise another all-Irish regiment. The President believed such units provided as much symbolic impact as the German companies Sigel had raised in the West—perhaps more, since most Irish enlistees were Democrats whose loyalty reflected the nonpartisan nature of the Union war effort.[42] Yet, in November, a member of the Irish Brigade's organizing committee, John T. Doyle, all but pleaded with Lincoln for "a word of kindness & encouragement" to the "Irish adopted citizens . . . furnishing a large proportion of the recruits." There is no record that he ever provided a reply.[43]

That same month, however, with the issues of ethnic unity and foreign neutrality much on Lincoln's mind, his administration named Archbishop Hughes as an unofficial envoy to overwhelmingly Catholic France. Seward instructed Hughes to "promote healthful opinions concerning the great cause in which our country is now engaged in arms"—in other words, to dissuade France from recognizing Confederate independence or interfering with Union efforts to put down the Southern rebellion. At first reluctant to undertake this "special mission"—the archbishop began considering it only when assured that Lincoln himself had "made it a special request"—Hughes ultimately accepted, believing his service "would redound to the benefit" of American Catholics and the Church. Though hobbled by arthritis and rheumatism, he spent six months abroad, visiting England, France, Italy, and Ireland. In each country, the prelate made a strong case for nonintervention, at one point taking his case directly to the French emperor (who complained about American tariffs and the Union blockade). France remained neutral, and at Easter in Rome, the pope himself told the archbishop he had done good work. It would not be lost on Catholics—nor their detractors—that the first-ever Irish American archbishop had performed valuable service to his adopted country, although he had done so by assuring Europeans that Lincoln meant only to restore the Union, not emancipate the slaves.[44]

Back in New York, even in Hughes's absence, Meagher's recruitment efforts among the Irish expanded. By mid-1862, he proudly reported to Lincoln that "thousands upon thousands cheer me as I entreat and exhort them to rally round and stand to the last by the Glorious Flag of the Union." Yet Meagher worried that "with all my popularity," recruiting had become "an up-hill work"—due to James Shields's humiliation at the hands of the U.S. Senate. "The Irish-born citizens not only in this city, but throughout all the loyal states," Meagher protested, "are fiercely indignant at the action of the Senate in regard to their gallant countrymen, and keenly feel it as an injustice to him, and an insult to them."[45] Like Koerner's defense of Sigel, Meagher's loyalty to Shields reminded Lincoln that his ethnic officers would never abandon their own, even those who failed to deliver victories. For his part, Shields expressed gratitude that Meagher "called the attention of the President to me." Both men disputed rumors that they had become rivals for both Lincoln's attention and the Irish public's affection. "We love each other," Shields insisted.[46]

Meagher's fidelity to his fellow Irishman did not forestall Shields's fall from grace. In fact, Shields faded from view as Meagher ascended, and the latter proved a fabulously successful recruiter despite his occasional misgivings. In response to rousing appeals in Boston and New York, three thousand Irishmen enrolled for three years' service in his newest brigade, prompting the *Irish-American* to declare that the name of Meagher had become "a word of talismanic power."[47] (It was perhaps no coincidence that Meagher in turn described the editor to Lincoln as "one of the earliest, most persistent and powerful champions of the National cause."[48]) Meagher proudly described his latest unit as "ready, sturdy, hearty, fiery, headlong, fearless fellows, whose bayonets are to clear a way for the returning authority of the American Republic."[49] During a July 1862 visit to General McClellan at Harrison's Landing, Virginia, Lincoln made sure to pay a call on the Irish Brigade. One soldier there swore he saw the President grasp the edge of the unit's green battle banner "and kiss it, exclaiming, 'God Bless the Irish Flag!'"[50]

Later that year—three full weeks after the Battle of Antietam—it would still be possible for an immigrant soldier to come into personal, unexpected contact with his commander in chief. One quiet October evening, Irish-born Private William McCarter of the Pennsylvania 116th Infantry, assigned to the defense of Washington but granted a few hours of leisure, headed downtown with a fellow soldier and strolled toward the White House. "There, standing near one of the entrances and leaning against a small tree with a little cane in his hand," McCarter claimed, "stood a man whom I at once recognized as Abraham Lincoln." Dressed in his characteristic black suit and stovepipe hat, Lincoln appeared "deep in thought," absent-mindedly slicing at the grass with his cane. As McCarter and his friends edged toward him for a better look, Lincoln suddenly noticed them. "Seeing two soldiers, only privates, he raised his hat to us and said in a polite and friendly manner, 'Good evening boys. What regiment?'

"My comrade replied, 'The 116th Pennsylvania, sir.'"

Lincoln answered, "God bless you." The privates thanked him, saluted smartly, and proceeded on their way, "much pleased, gratified and encouraged at such an unexpected interview with such a great and good man." But could this really have been the President? they began to wonder as soon as he was out of their sight. Passing another White House gate, they asked a sentinel if the man they had met was indeed

Lincoln. "Yes," they were told, "he comes out here nearly every evening that he is at home . . . for study and a quiet walk."[51]

Seven months later, just before the May 1863 Battle of Chancellorsville, Lincoln visited the Army of the Potomac and at one point, during a review of more than a hundred thousand assembled troops— perhaps recalling his encounters with common soldiers like McCarter—slowly and deliberately rode up to the largely Irish Pennsylvania 116th. Then, "reaching out his arms towards the ranks, he exclaimed within earshot of a Belfast-born private: 'My God, men, if I could save this country by giving up my own life and saving yours, how gladly I would do it.' As he spoke, the tears stole down his furrowed cheeks, and his great heart seemed bursting."[52]

From the beginning of the war, the Lincoln administration also saw to it that Catholic priests were available to offer the troops religious succor. By 1863, the Irish Brigade boasted a distinguished new chaplain, Father William Corby, a Notre Dame professor. Publicly, Corby proved an inspiring pastor. Privately, he worried about Colonel Meagher's growing fondness for alcohol. The chaplain noted that "at times, especially when no fighting was going on, his convivial spirit would lead him too far," though Corby hastened to add that, "brave as a lion," Meagher retained "the bearing of a prince" and was "by no means . . . a drunkard."[53]

Nonetheless, reports of insobriety among Irish soldiers persisted throughout the war. One Pennsylvania soldier admitted that "whiskey ran like water" wherever the Irish Brigade marched or encamped.[54] After the Battle of Fredericksburg, a Confederate soldier from South Carolina named J. J. McDaniel claimed that the Irish Brigade was "half drunk with liquor," a condition that "led them into the 'slaughter pen.'" Though acknowledging their "valor," McDaniel prayed that the heavy casualties they endured would discourage "all of the beastly, drunken, thievish foreigners who pollute our Southern soil in the company of their employers, the Yankees."[55]

As if in answer to a prayer from Father Corby, the Confederacy freed Michael Corcoran in the summer of 1862 after a year of captivity—as part of a prisoner swap—and the colonel at last made his way back to Washington. On August 18, the President hosted a White House dinner in honor of the now-emaciated Corcoran and three other recently exchanged Union officers.[56] Thereafter Corcoran's fame far exceeded his useful service. Although he went on to recruit and command a new unit that became known as Corcoran's Legion, he fought in only a few more minor engagements and achieved notice only when he shot and killed a fellow officer who tried to bar him from crossing into Union lines without invoking the required password. Corcoran somehow avoided punishment for that crime, but shortly before Christmas 1863, he fell from a runaway horse near Fairfax, Virginia, and suffered a fatal head injury.

Despite his absence, the Irish Brigade achieved immortality on the battlefield. At one of those engagements, observing its troops in action, Confederate general Robert E. Lee purportedly gave them their enduring nickname: "The Fighting Irish." But after the Union's morale-deflating loss at Lee's hands at Chancellorsville—at which the Irish Brigade took more than its share of casualties—a dispirited Meagher abruptly resigned his commission. Barely a week later, apparently refreshed, he wired Lincoln from New York to assure him, "If called upon and authorized by the Govt I shall proceed at once to raise three thousand (3000) Irish Soldiers in this city to act as Cavalry & Infantry wherever they may be ordered." Lincoln immediately replied: "Shall be very glad for you to raise 3000 Irish troops, if done by the consent of, and in concert with, [New York] Governor [Horatio] Seymour."[57] Both Meagher and Lincoln still believed strongly in ethnic recruitment. As Meagher put it, "an Irishman never fights so well as when he has an Irishman for his comrade."[58]

Whatever the name under which they did battle—the Sixty-Ninth, the Irish Brigade, Corcoran's Legion, or Meagher's Own—the legendary exploits of the Fighting Irish would continue, albeit at a staggeringly high cost in human life. As Meagher would modestly put it in a speech at Boston between the battles of Chancellorsville and Gettysburg, "It is not exaggeration for me to say, that the Irish have distinguished themselves pre-eminently."[59] In the appreciative words of the newspaper the *Irish People*, the Irish Brigade "[gave] us back our military reputation in its pristine luster . . . made manifest to the world the might of Irish prowess."[60] No one could argue otherwise. Lincoln, who had once looked on the Irish as menials, drinkers, vote stealers, or objects of ridicule, now deeply appreciated their willingness to fight. Sadly, Meagher's own final months in uniform in Union-occupied North Carolina would prove anticlimactic, soured by reports that he was frequently inebriated on duty. Ulysses S. Grant, no stranger to rumors of excessive drinking, quietly nudged Meagher out of the service before the war's end.

. . .

At the same time as the Irish were making their initial impact on the Union war effort, Germans and other foreign-born Americans sought their own paths to military glory in their adopted country. Impatiently marking time halfway around the world, Carl Schurz had decided almost immediately upon his arrival in Spain that he could resist the American conflict no longer. Though he did not take up his post at Madrid until early summer 1861—a consequence of leisurely sojourns to England and France en route—he had no sooner settled down there before he began pining for home and yearning anew for military service, especially once he read the disquieting news about the Union defeat at Bull Run.

He had quickly secured an audience with Queen Isabella (dressing in evening clothes because his specially ordered dress suit, court sword, and cocked hat had failed to arrive in time). But what Schurz soon described as "a life of ease and luxury and comparative idleness" in Europe became more and more "intolerable . . . while the Republic was fighting for its life, and most of the men of my age were in the field at the post of danger" back in America. The war might soon evolve into a fight to destroy slavery, and, simply put, Schurz once again grew "anxious to enter the army."[61] By early 1862, he was back in the United States, delivering an antislavery speech at Cooper Union just as Lincoln began urging border-state congressmen to accept a plan of compensated emancipation that would have gradually extinguished the institution in Southern areas still loyal to the Union. (Schurz would claim he had cleared his Cooper Union message with Lincoln and in turn received advance word that the President himself intended to speak out soon on the subject.[62]) Though Schurz still counted himself, like many Germans, an abolitionist at heart, he expressed a profound understanding of Lincoln's slow but sure path toward Black freedom. In August 1862, Lincoln had reminded Americans that his "paramount object" was to reunite the country and not either "to save or to destroy slavery." Schurz claimed he believed that, for Lincoln, "the destruction of slavery would turn out to be the necessary means for the salvation of the Union." So Schurz said—though not until 1908.[63]

From New York, Schurz headed to Washington determined to liberate himself from the diplomatic post he had occupied so briefly. To his surprise, he found that Secretary of State Seward, who had originally opposed his diplomatic appointment, now wanted him to remain in Spain, where his stature still served as an ongoing reminder to European governments that they must not recognize Confederate independence. Adamant about joining the war effort, Schurz took his case to the White House. There, Lincoln, eager to renew his own popularity among Germans still chafing over the recent controversies involving Sigel, Frémont, and Koerner, again overruled Seward. After reminding Schurz one last time that he was "giving up a large salary and a distinguished and comfortable place," and asking him if he had consulted his "handsome, dear wife," the President promised: "I shall send your name to the Senate with the next batch of brigadiers, and I trust we can find you a suitable command."[64] As Schurz concluded of the outmaneuvered secretary of state, "Seward must have felt that he was at the mercy of a superior man."[65] Whether he meant Lincoln or himself, Schurz left unsaid.

While the Senate considered his military nomination (confirmation was a mere formality), Schurz found himself flooded with applications from fellow Europeans eager to serve on his staff of officers. "Being myself of foreign birth," he explained, "I was approached by many of those who came from Germany, or Austria, or France, with the expectation that I would naturally be disposed to make especial exertions in their behalf. In some cases, having satisfied myself as to their antecedents and qualifications, I willingly did so." As his "antecedents" requirement suggests, Schurz proved something of a snob when it came to evaluating these applications. A Bavarian officer who had fought with Garibaldi and a captain who had served in the artillery for the Grand Duchy of Baden both earned his favor. A self-described count exposed as the offspring of a mere washerwoman and valet did not.[66]

One supposedly authentic "foreign nobleman" who wished to take the field with Schurz insisted he must first meet Lincoln, believing an audience with the commander in chief would earn him a prestigious rank. Against his better judgment, Schurz escorted him to the White House, where, in his "moderately" good English, the aspiring officer "explained to Mr. Lincoln how high the nobility of his family was, and that they had been counts so-and-so many centuries. 'Well,' said Mr. Lincoln, interrupting him, 'that need not trouble you. That will not be in your way, if you behave yourself as a soldier.'" As Schurz recalled, the "poor count looked puzzled, and when the audience was over, he asked me what in the world the President could have meant by so strange a remark." Although Schurz left no record of what became of the latest Count So-and-So, he received his own formal commission from the Senate shortly after the encounter at the White House. By May 1862, he joined the Army of the Potomac to serve as a brigadier general under Frémont, who, since his dismissal in Missouri, had been investigated, vindicated, and reassigned to Virginia's Shenandoah Valley. It was not to be an entirely happy return to military service for the ex-diplomat. Carl Schurz's American army career would be marked by accusations of poor leadership and by a series of disputes with his old friend Abraham Lincoln.[67]

Meanwhile, Gustave Koerner, earlier denied his dream job in Berlin and still frustrated by the recent contretemps with Halleck over Franz Sigel, received a belated honor, tainted by the knowledge that he was second choice for the position: Lincoln named him to replace Schurz in Madrid. Koerner had always looked upon Spain as "a land of romance and song," but now he insisted, "I should have preferred some other mission." Koerner never cited Schurz's previous occupancy as a reason for his misgivings; rather, he groused that it was prohibitively expensive to live in Madrid and he could not afford "to spend the little capital" he had "accumulated" to maintain a household there. Knowing that the current American ministers to Germany and Austria were far wealthier, Koerner dared ask if Lincoln would entertain "an exchange of missions." The President told his old ally that he would have no objections to a swap if another diplomat agreed; but not surprisingly, Norman Judd declined to leave Berlin for Madrid, explaining he knew no Spanish, and John L. Motley elected to remain in Vienna, pointing out proudly that he had begun to learn German. Faced with a Hobson's choice, Koerner agreed to accept the post in Spain.[68]

First Koerner paid a farewell call at the White House, where he found Lincoln surprisingly "at ease" even though General McClellan's army had made little progress on the Virginia Peninsula in an ill-fated campaign to capture Richmond. Koerner then sailed to Europe, but remained in Madrid only until word reached him in 1863 of the lengthy casualty lists from the battles of Lookout Mountain and Missionary Ridge, which included the names of one relative killed and several friends wounded. The sad news prompted Koerner to ask Lincoln for a leave of absence. Worried that his departure would again disrupt delicate American relations with Spain, Lincoln instructed Seward to consent only if he failed to convince Koerner that it was in the public interest that he remain at his post. Unpersuadable, Koerner set forth for home, terminating once and for all the diplomatic career he (like Carl Schurz) had long sought as a reward for his work in rallying German votes for Abraham Lincoln.

. . .

As the war widened, Lincoln came to rely increasingly on a new cadre of European immigrants who soon revolutionized the nature of the conflict: designing modern tools of war, providing sophisticated military espionage, codifying the laws of combat amid fighting that reached a barbaric scale yet unknown in world history, and fixing Lincoln's avuncular image in American hearts. Among the photographers who took the best wartime pictures of the President, for example, were three of Mathew Brady's foreign-born employees: Scotsman Alexander Gardner (who soon opened a gallery of his own); German Anthony Berger; and Frenchman Thomas LeMere.

One immigrant innovator of note was Allan Pinkerton, the Scottish-born former detective who had planned Lincoln's secret preinaugural passage through Baltimore. Early in the war, Pinkerton reemerged as a kind of spy in chief for General McClellan and the Army of the Potomac. Establishing and managing what he memorably called "a secret service," Pinkerton deployed "shrewd and daring operatives" to "make observations within the rebel lines."[69]

These scouts did not always provide good intelligence. Rather, Pinkerton's inflated estimates of Confederate manpower on the Virginia Peninsula in the spring of 1862, and at Antietam that September, only nourished McClellan's paralyzing sense of caution, especially when he found himself face-to-face with the aggressive—and, contrary to Pinkerton's calculations, outnumbered—Robert E. Lee. Yet, when Lincoln visited McClellan near Antietam on October 3, 1862, two weeks after Lee had retreated from Maryland back to Virginia, it was clear that the detective who dubbed himself the "Spy of the Rebellion" remained in the President's good graces. Pinkerton posed for two

General Carl Schurz poses during the war—in uniform and
sporting a thick, newly grown beard.

remarkable photographs that day, standing outdoors at Lincoln's side,
hand thrust inside his coat as if he had a pistol at the ready. Here was
not only the first time a commander in chief had been photographed on
a battlefield of war but the first time a president had posed alongside an
espionage agent.[70] Perhaps it was no accident that the photographer
who took the historic pictures that day was Pinkerton's fellow Scotsman
and Mathew Brady's principal camera operator, Alexander Gardner.

Another immigrant celebrity who had posed before Brady's camera was Francis (Franz) Lieber. Few philosophers of war exerted more
influence on the Lincoln administration than the Prussian- and
Jewish-born college professor who in 1863 authored A *Code for the
Government of Armies in the Field*—later commonly known as the Lieber Code. Lieber understood excessive wartime vengeance from
painful personal experience; as a young man, he had been imprisoned
at Cöpenick, Germany, for his anti-monarchical activities. After fleeing his homeland, he worked as a tutor in England. When he arrived
in the United States, he settled in Boston and launched his American

career as a gymnasium instructor while working on editing and translating encyclopedias. For years, Lieber taught history at South Carolina College, and owned slaves until he departed the region in 1856 to join the staff of New York's Columbia College (and its new law school). There, he taught not only history but political science—and was credited with defining and naming that new field of study.

Immigrant political scientist Francis Lieber, who codified the laws of war, as he looked during the rebellion.

Lieber had always been opposed to secession, and as a result his family became a house divided during the rebellion; one of his sons even joined the Confederate army and died in battle. "Behold in me," he anguished, "a symbol of civil war."[71] As Lieber explained his Union loyalty to an audience of South Carolinians: "This is my country from the choice of manhood, and not the chance of birth."[72] He cemented his Union ties by helping establish the Loyal Publication Society of New York, a civilian propaganda organization that produced and distributed pamphlet editions of pro-Union editorials and orations.[73] It was then that the War Department recruited the gifted academic to draft General Orders No. 100—the world's first comprehensive legal framework for waging so-called civilized war.

Although his code of military conduct was informed by the need for restraint, Lieber never wavered in his conviction that the Confederacy must be defeated by any legitimate means necessary. "Strike, strike and strike again," he argued; use the Union "sledgehammer" to inflict a "death blow" on the Rebels. Yet it was Lieber who created the rules under which captured Rebels would be treated—as prisoners of war, not criminals—regulations Lincoln would later insist be applied equally to Black Union soldiers captured by the Confederacy and threatened with execution or enslavement.[74]

Lieber developed solid relationships with Lincoln administration officials, especially General Halleck and Secretary of War Stanton, and soon had "the ear" of many other "influential men," including abolitionist senator Charles Sumner of Massachusetts. Even before Lincoln issued the Emancipation Proclamation, Lieber came to share Sumner's belief "that negroes coming into our lines must be, and are by that fact, free men." Surviving records, however, suggest that Lieber's influence had its limits: he apparently met Lincoln face-to-face but once, early in the war, before he commenced working on the code that would make him famous and indispensable. That singular encounter occurred on June 26, 1861, when Lieber visited the White House to present Lincoln with an honorary degree from Columbia Law School.[75] By 1864, Lieber would grow disenchanted with the President, confiding his belief that Lincoln should "patriotically and gracefully" abandon his bid for a second term. Whatever Lieber's political inconsistencies, one cannot underestimate the importance of his code of war, which its author grandiosely but accurately called "a contribution by the United States to the stock of common civilization."[76]

In terms of impact, the only immigrant civilian to rival the importance of the German-born architect of military civility was the Swedish-born architect of an entirely new class of military technology: engineer John (born Johan) Ericsson, who designed the revolutionary ironclad warship USS *Monitor*. The son of a factory manager from Värmland, east of Oslo, Ericsson had already perfected a new "caloric" engine capable of maintaining steady air temperatures below the waterline.

In August 1861, the inventor wrote to Lincoln that he was ready to deploy the process to power a new low-lying, "steel-clad" warship immune to "land batteries" and capable of destroying "the Rebel fleet at Norfolk." Added Ericsson, "I seek no private advantage or emolument of any kind."[77] The idea prompted Lincoln to attend a September 13 meeting of the Navy Ironclad Board at which experts considered Ericsson's design. Just when it seemed the hidebound board might reject the proposal, Lincoln weighed in with a characteristically humorous— but telling—observation: "All I can say is what the girl said when she put her foot into the stocking. It strikes me there's something in it."[78] The board approved the design and production went forward, quickly

This singular lithograph celebrated not only the triumph of the ironclad USS *Monitor* (center) at Hampton Roads but also the decisive contribution of inventor John Ericsson and his "caloric" engine (top).

240 BROUGHT FORTH ON THIS CONTINENT

enough for Ericsson's "cheese box on a raft" to appear dramatically in the waters off Norfolk just one day after the armored Confederate warship *Virginia* (previously known as the *Merrimack*) sank two of the federal navy's wooden warships.

For three smoke-filled hours on March 9, 1862, the sleek *Monitor* exchanged shells in a protracted duel with the *Virginia* that ended without either vessel prevailing. Still, the *Monitor*'s arrival enabled McClellan's Peninsula Campaign to proceed and caused a sensation in the press.[79] Two months later, Lincoln himself made a brief, unannounced visit to the ironclad, appearing "well acquainted with the mechanical details" of its construction.[80] The President, who had once secured a patent of his own for a device to lift rivercraft over shoals, found the high-tech vessel far more appealing than did Nathaniel Hawthorne, who glimpsed it around the same time and likened it to "a gigantic rat-trap." To the New England author, who was not much impressed with Lincoln, either, the innovative *Monitor* seemed "ugly, questionable, suspicious, evidently mischievous,—nay, I will allow myself to call it devilish." How, Hawthorne wondered, "can an admiral condescend to go to sea in an iron pot?"[81] Yet Ericsson's "rat-trap" had blocked the *Virginia* from doing further damage at a time Secretary of War Stanton worried that the Confederate ironclad might "come up the Potomac and . . . destroy the Capitol."[82] Lincoln finally got to meet the Swedish inventor the day he embarked on a riverboat excursion to Mount Vernon, a cruise that might never have been planned had not Ericsson's miraculous invention secured Virginia's inland waters.[83]

Not until the final months of the war did Lincoln also come face-to-face with the most renowned scientist of the day, the Swiss-born zoologist and biologist Louis Agassiz, whom a Massachusetts congressman ushered to the White House for a private meeting in January 1865. Two years earlier, Lincoln had signed a bill, promoted by Agassiz, establishing the National Academy of Sciences. Clearly nervous in Agassiz's presence, the President spent their first few minutes together asking "the great man" how to pronounce his name, then "prattled on about curious proper names in various languages, and odd correspondences between names of common things in different tongues." Afterward, Lincoln rambled further about an unfinished lecture he had prepared in the 1850s on "Discoveries and Inventions." Agassiz gently urged him to complete the talk one day. Asked later why he had raised such eccentric issues with Agassiz, Lincoln explained, "Why, what we got from him isn't printed in the books; the other things are."[84] Presumably the scientist did not bring up his belief in the theory of "polygenesis," which, he argued, substantiated the racial inferiority of the Black man.*

. . .

Lincoln's closest, and perhaps unlikeliest, wartime immigrant acquaintance was Dr. Issachar Zacharie, a vain, enigmatic, and possibly fraudulent British-born Jewish chiropodist. The *New York Herald* described him as "distinguished by a splendid Roman nose, fashionable whiskers, an eloquent tongue, a dazzling diamond breastpin, great skill in his profession, an ingratiating address, a perfect knowledge of his business and a plentiful supply of social moral courage."[85] Not everyone was similarly charmed.

Although there is no record that he ever formally trained in the specialty we now call podiatry, and while he may have plagiarized an 1860 book on diseases of the foot that appeared under his name, Zacharie was unquestionably an expert practitioner boasting a roster of renowned, satisfied clients. In autumn 1862, he successfully treated Lincoln's chronically painful corns along with other ailments and designed comfortable boots to cushion the President's enormous feet. On September 20, even as he was polishing the final draft of his preliminary Emancipation Proclamation, the grateful patient took time to

---

*Nor is it likely that Agassiz told Lincoln about the dehumanizing, now hotly contested daguerreotypes he had commissioned for his own use in South Carolina in 1850. The images, meant to illustrate Agassiz's theories of racial inequality, showed naked and half-naked enslaved Blacks undoubtedly ordered to pose for the scientist without their consent. See Brian Wallis, "Black Bodies, White Science: The Slave Daguerreotypes of Louis Agassiz," *Journal of Blacks in Higher Education* 12 (Summer 1990): 102–105.

write a testimonial to the healer's wide-ranging skills. "Dr. Zacharie has, with great dexterity taken some troublesome corns from my toes," Lincoln wrote. "He is now treating me, and I believe with success, for what plain people call back-ache." The President ended with the inevitable joke: "We shall see how it will end."[86]

Just two days later, on the same historic date he announced emancipation and issued another proclamation suspending the writ of habeas corpus, Lincoln penned a second endorsement letter for Zacharie to show to prospective customers, attesting that the chiropodist had "operated on my feet with great success, and considerable addition to my comfort."[87] Then, on September 23, Lincoln and Seward cosigned yet another note commending Zacharie's "surprising skill" in "operating upon corns, bunions and other troubles of the feet" and expressing the hope that "the Soldiers of our brave Army" might have "the benefit" of the doctor's care.[88] The *New York Herald* acknowledged Zacharie's growing prominence by observing: "The President has been greatly blamed for not resisting the [emancipation] demands of the radicals; but how could the President put his foot down firmly when he was troubled with corns?"[89] (That story appeared in print the same day Lincoln posed with Pinkerton at Antietam.) Yet, for all the publicity and despite Lincoln's recommendation, Zacharie failed to convince the War Department to retain his services to treat the thousands of soldiers whose chronically sore feet reflected—and sometimes impeded—their life on the march. That did not stop the doctor from describing himself afterward as the "Late Chiropodist-General, United States Army."[90]

What some Washington insiders wondered was how Lincoln could not only befriend such a self-aggrandizing figure but also award him additional, quasi-official assignments on behalf of the government. Ignoring such criticism, which he probably believed reflected the reigning animus toward Jews, the President sent Zacharie to Union-occupied New Orleans, where the doctor served as Lincoln's eyes and ears on the ground as the army worked to rebuild Union loyalty there after its April 1862 capture.

Zacharie's efforts in New Orleans focused on the city's Jewish residents, some of whom he may have enlisted to serve as informants against Rebel sympathizers. Zacharie emerged as a harsh critic of the anti-Semitic general Benjamin F. Butler, who had earlier overseen the city's harsh occupation and in the process cleaned up some of the city's most squalid immigrant districts. Yet, in arresting Jewish blockade-runners there, Butler had revealed his bigotry by vilifying the accused men as "Jews who betrayed their Savior & also have betrayed us."[91] Zacharie earned the contempt of Butler's loyal but equally prejudiced aides. "In season or out of season," the outgoing supervisor of customs alerted Salmon Chase, the "vulgar little scoundrel" typified the "whole crowd" of Jews in New Orleans. Zacharie, the officer elaborated, "fails not to announce himself as the *Confidential Agent*, or *Correspondent*, of the President," paraphrasing Milton's *Paradise Lost* to add contemptuously that "his presence distills continual perfume sweeter than the winds that blow from Araby the blest."[92]

In 1863 Zacharie visited Richmond, again with Lincoln's blessing, allegedly to test the waters for peace. The doctor claimed he met "the Chief of the Confederate Govern[men]t" there—meaning Jefferson Davis—and grandiosely reminded Lincoln of the "great responsibility resting on me" to end the war. While electioneering in Lincoln's behalf the following year, Zacharie reminded him, "I flatter myself I have done one of the sharpest things that has been done in the champaigne [*sic*]."[93] When he was not singing his own praises, the doctor was showering Lincoln with edible gifts: a box of "fine Pine apples" from New York, a "Barral of Homminy" [*sic*] from Philadelphia, and bananas from the South.[94]

Zacharie would spend a good part of autumn 1864 traveling to Pennsylvania and Ohio to drum up Jewish support for Lincoln's re-election bid. "I thank you again for the deep interest you have constantly taken in the Union cause," Lincoln wrote to him in gratitude.[95] The following January, Lincoln asked the secretary of war to provide the doctor a pass to visit his family in the newly conquered city of

Savannah, Georgia. (The President began his memorandum of instructions with the careless line: "About Jews.")[96] The historical jury is still out on Zacharie. He likely exaggerated his wartime exploits as smoothly as he padded his medical résumé. Yet his letters to Lincoln, unctuous as they were, do reflect a familiarity and trust between them, even though Lincoln's faith in the "doctor" appalled many of the President's other confidants.

Lincoln's foreign-born Jewish doctor: the enigmatic, controversial chiropodist and presidential emissary Isaachar Zacharie.

Zacharie's activities did not constitute Lincoln's first or sole involvement with wartime matters of concern to Jews. As early as 1861, religious groups had alerted him that long-standing regulations authorized the military to appoint only chaplains "of a Christian denomination."[97] A challenge soon arose from the Cameron Dragoons, a unit of Pennsylvania cavalry that defied the restriction by electing an unordained Jewish liquor salesman named Michael Allen to serve as an unofficial company chaplain. When it learned of this arrangement, the War Department put an end to it after a month. The story, which made its way onto the pages of the *New York Tribune,* might have been exaggerated. The unit's commander, Colonel Max Friedman, later insisted the regiment "had never expressed a desire to have a Jewish chaplain," pointing out that "there are not more than twenty Jews in his whole corps." Friedman, who was himself a Bavarian-born Jew, instead maintained that Allen had resigned his quasi-chaplaincy because "feeling against him was so strong in the regiment." Or perhaps because he was suffering from bad health.[98]

Whatever the particulars, the episode spurred Dr. Arnold Fischel, a native of Holland who taught at a New York synagogue, to accept (or seek) the position Allen had vacated and then to visit Washington to lobby the President for a formal congressional remedy. After a long wait, Fischel finally gained access to the President's office, where Lincoln received him with "marked courtesy" and "fully admitted the justice of my remarks."[99] The President, who claimed he knew nothing of the restrictions against Jewish chaplains, promised Fischel: "I shall try to have a new law broad enough to cover what is desired by you in behalf of the Israelites."[100] Within three months, Congress duly amended the chaplaincy regulations to permit the appointment of ordained spiritual advisors of all faiths. A half year later, on September 18, 1862, around the same time he was first treated by Dr. Zacharie, Lincoln named German-born cantor Jacob Frankel as the first official Jewish chaplain in American military history.[101] A more existential crisis "about Jews" would erupt just two months later.

· · ·

In December 1862, vexed by a proliferation of cotton traders and speculators operating within his military lines—some, but hardly all, of them Jewish—General Ulysses S. Grant issued his astonishingly ill-advised, deeply prejudicial General Orders No. 11. The edict mandated the forced removal of Jewish residents from Grant's entire command, which embraced the vast region between the Tennessee and

Mississippi Rivers, and from the northern borders of Mississippi to the southern counties of Illinois. "The Jews, as a class, violating every regulation of trade established by the Treasury Department," Grant's chilling manifesto began, ". . . are hereby expelled from the Department. Within twenty-four hours from the receipt of this order by Post commanders, they will see that all of this class of people be furnished passes and required to leave, and any one returning after such notification will be arrested and held in confinement."[102]

Accordingly, on Sunday, December 28, Cesar Kaskel, a Prussian-born Jewish merchant from Paducah, Kentucky, answered a summons from the local provost marshal's office and there received official notice ordering him "to leave the city" within a day. Thus a loyal Jewish Unionist found himself suddenly enveloped in what amounted to a pogrom that mandated the expulsion of dozens of Paducah's naturalized Jews and their families.[103] As friends and neighbors began resignedly packing their portable belongings to head north, Kaskel organized a group of fellow Jews to protest the forced exodus to the highest authorities even as they, too, abandoned their homes and headed to safety in Cincinnati. As "good & Loyal Citizens of the U. S. & residents of this town for many years engaged in legitimate business as Merchants," Kaskel and his friends at once wired President Lincoln, they felt "greatly insulted & outraged by this inhuman order" and prayed in the name of "law & humanity" for the President's "effectual & immediate interposition."[104]

Although the urgent telegram arrived at the White House by December 30, Lincoln might not have seen it; he was understandably focused at that moment on the monumental decision he faced within forty-eight hours: whether to sign the final Emancipation Proclamation, due to be issued on January 1. Thus, Kaskel's initial plea went unanswered, while Grant's order escaped press scrutiny for days.[105] When the *New York Times* did catch up with the story, the paper lambasted Grant for "stigmatizing a class, without signalizing the criminals," arguing: "Men cannot be condemned and punished as a class, without gross violence to our free institutions."[106]

In the meantime, Isaac Mayer Wise, the rabbi who had written so caustically of Lincoln's prepresidential visit to Cincinnati, undertook his own mission of grievance to the White House. As it turned out, Kaskel arrived in Washington before Wise did and, with the assistance of his local congressman, a lame-duck Republican, immediately secured a White House meeting of his own. There, Kaskel made Lincoln painfully aware of Grant's recent actions. Now Lincoln faced another crucial decision: whether to uphold an order issued by one of his few successful field commanders and aimed at only a tiny part of the voting population, or risk embarrassing the general by countermanding what was clearly an obnoxious act.

According to a legendary account of the historic White House meeting, Lincoln opened the dialogue by drawling, "And so the children of Israel were driven from the happy land of Canaan?" Kaskel retorted, "Yes, and that is why we have come unto Father Abraham's bosom, asking protection."

To which Lincoln answered: "And this protection they shall have at once."[107]

True to his word, in a swift response issued the following day—just as the story began exploding in the press—Lincoln mandated that General Orders No. 11 be voided. To soften the blow—and avoid the appearance that he had directly chastised his general—the President shrewdly instructed General Henry Halleck to break the news to Grant, thus sparing his general the humiliation of a public rebuke by the commander in chief. As Halleck explained the decision to Grant: "The President has no object[ion] to your expelling traders & Jew pedlars, which I suppose, was the object of your order; but, as it in terms proscribed an entire religious class, some of whom are fighting in our ranks, the President deemed it necessary to revoke it."[108]

In fact, Lincoln surely knew that the American army had a long and disgraceful tradition of anti-Semitism, perpetuated by the ongoing hostility of current generals like Butler and Sherman. For his part, Grant had months earlier ordered speculators entering his lines to be searched for contraband, emphasizing that "Jews should receive special attention."[109] If Grant's overreach received the greatest notoriety, and elicited the strongest condemnation, it grew out of ongoing discrimination against Jews, who had suddenly become conspicuous, though certainly not alone, among those who sought to trade in cotton wherever the Union army encamped in the South. For more than a year, Northern picture weeklies had unjustly targeted Jews as the sole purveyors of "shoddy," a word originally meant to describe substandard goods but suddenly made synonymous with Jewish gougers. Repugnant cartoons showed hook-nosed, bearded Jews—in one of the most infamous examples assuring officials they made no profit from their inferior merchandise, "s'elp me got!"[110]

For once, Rabbi Wise had approached the situation cautiously—telling Secretary of War Stanton that he "[did] not wish to pour oil on the fire."[111] Now, as he and his own delegation approached Washington, he learned that Grant's onerous order had been overturned. Having come so far, the rabbi marshaled his own congressman to arrange a White House meeting, if only to thank the President for his prompt and compassionate response. According to Wise, who quickly published an account of the session in his Cincinnati newspaper, Lincoln assured the group that he "knows of no distinction between Jew and Gentile . . . feels no prejudice against any nationality," and would not allow any citizen to "be wronged on account of his place of birth or religious confession." Few if any American presidents had so clearly declared themselves opposed to anti-Semitism, and Wise left Washington with new respect for the leader he had previously denigrated. In truth, Lincoln had been quite narrow in his reasoning for overturning Grant. "To condemn a class," Lincoln told the rabbi, "is, to say the least, to wrong the good with the bad. I do not like to hear a class or nationality condemned on account of a few sinners."[112]

Although at least one prominent Jewish officer resigned in the wake of the "taunts and malice" provoked by Grant's order, the Union army—at least a significant portion of it, Jews included—continued to speak and fight with a foreign accent.[113] Jews might have stimulated little public sympathy, but at least other foreign-born Unionists had made inroads against bigotry.

Gratefully acknowledging the massive immigrant participation in Lincoln's war, the *New York Times* expressed the hope by 1862 that "all 'nativism'—all proscription of foreigners" would in gratitude be "forever broken up" in the United States. The Union itself remained "broken up," but perhaps the war had at least defeated Know-Nothingism. The paper editorialized that only "when names like SIGEL and CORCORAN are dropped from the American memory" could we again "begin to speak of restricting the rights of our foreign-born citizens." Meanwhile, the newspaper asserted—omitting Blacks and women from the equation—"Universal suffrage has justified herself."[114]

Still, as the recent officially sanctioned discrimination against Jews demonstrated, immigrant security remained a tenuous privilege in America, not a fully established right. Inequities between native- and foreign-born citizens persisted even as the country now hastened at last toward atoning for its original sin of slavery—a policy that had begun in the seventeenth century with the forced immigration of Africans.

As it turned out, Lincoln's decisive rejection of the expulsion of immigrant Jews established no precedent against wartime exile and deportation. When General Thomas Ewing Jr. issued his own harsh orders in late August 1863 mandating the removal of families of Rebel guerrilla fighters in Missouri—and concurrently freeing the slaves of disloyal residents—Lincoln made no move to countermand him. Aware that the Ewing order might sweep up innocent civilians along with genuine Rebel sympathizers, Lincoln nonetheless told General Francis Preston Blair Jr., a Missourian who visited the White House to discuss the potentially controversial order, that "his position could very well be illustrated by an anecdote." It turned out to be an Irish-drunk story.

Blair told Ewing that Lincoln spun this yarn: "An Irishman once asked for a glass of soda water and remarked at the same time that he would be glad if the Doctor could put a little brandy in it '*unbeknownst to him*.' The inference is that old Abe would be glad if you would dispose of the Guerillas and would not be sorry to see the negroes set free, if it can be done without his being known in the affair as having instigated it."[115]

Lincoln might have been eager to kiss and bless the Irish flag in a display of reverence, but he still made some of his most salient and serious points by reaching for his bottomless supply of ethnic humor. This particular story he had told before—and would deploy several times again in the future to dispose of an equally fraught policy matter just before the war ended.[116]

When his cabinet members bristled at his penchant for funny stories in the midst of so much death, destruction, and displacement, Lincoln tried explaining: "With the fearful strain that is upon me night and day, if I did not laugh I should die."[117]

At least the President remained serious about ethnic diversity where and when it counted most: in recruiting officers and soldiers to defend the Union. His attitude proved a refreshing contrast to the prejudice that had long afflicted the armed services. During the Mexican-American War fifteen years earlier, General George Mc-Clellan, for one, had confessed his disgust over "wretched Dutch and Irish immigrants" in the ranks. Now, like it nor not, he and other Union commanders came to rely on foreign-born troops; thanks to their sheer numbers, not to mention their fighting spirit, they could spell the difference between victory and defeat on the battlefield.[118]

CHAPTER NINE

More of the Quarrel

The winter of 1862–1863 had brought scant improvement to Lincoln's standing among Germans, though the German-language press did cheer the New Year's Day announcement of the Emancipation Proclamation. "Hurrah for Old Abe!" ran one appreciative headline in Cleveland's *Wächter am Erie*. Six days later, a "large delegation of Germans" from five different states called on Lincoln to express support for a daring next step in promoting black freedom: Congressman Eli Thayer's bold plan to arm and lead twenty thousand black soldiers, and send them to Florida to put down the rebellion there and then "colonize" the state with freedmen. The impractical scheme went nowhere, but after "cordially welcoming his visitors," Lincoln acknowledged "the indebtedness of the country to the stable loyalty of the German element of our population." Yet many leading "Dutch" editors, most of them Republicans, still found it difficult to forget, much less forgive, the administration's perceived hostility toward German general Franz Sigel and German favorite John C. Frémont.[1]

Never as broadly popular as either man, Carl Schurz had been ensconced with the Union army in Virginia's Shenandoah Valley since his return from Spain. Despite his lack of military experience, he now commanded a predominantly German American division serving in the Union corps led by Frémont, and alongside perennial favorite Sigel. Schurz got along well enough with both generals but soon began bypassing the chain of command by sending his observations from the front directly to the President.

In the first of these, a seven-page-long "confidential report," Schurz made excuses for Frémont's reluctance to pursue Stonewall Jackson, telling Lincoln that Frémont's men were "in a starving condition and literally unable to fight."[2] Lincoln politely expressed gratitude for this "valuable," though unsolicited, information, but also made it clear he did not agree with it. He even tried to stir a bit of ethnic rivalry by rebutting Schurz's contention that Jackson's Confederates had recently demonstrated their invincibility by whipping the Irish-born general James Shields. No, Lincoln insisted, taking the Irish general's side: Jackson "did not beat Shields" at all; Stonewall had merely repulsed Shields's advance force, only to be driven back himself by Union reinforcements.[3] Schurz wrote again to expound further. Lincoln ignored him.

At the end of August 1862, Schurz finally saw action for the first time—and experienced his initial defeat—at the Second Battle of Bull Run. Prominent among the other German officers who participated in this Union catastrophe was Sigel, who by then had replaced Frémont in command of the corps, along with Alexander Schimmelfennig and Henry Bohlen, the latter killed in action by a sharpshooter. As one Civil War scholar later put it, perhaps too harshly, Bohlen ended his career, and his life, "under the command of the dubious [Louis] Blenker and then of the scholarly but inept Carl Schurz in the corps of the even more hapless Franz Sigel."[4] Ethnic recruiting did not always produce victories, enhance reputations, or elicit presidential recognition. By then, Lincoln had taken to referring to Blenker as "Blecker."[5]

Most of the blame fell on Union commander John Pope, who in

Photographer Alexander Gardner posed Lincoln during a visit to Union headquarters near Antietam, Maryland, on October 3, 1862. The President is flanked by Union spy Allan Pinkerton (left) and General John McClernand, an Illinois Democrat.

turn tried placing at least some of the responsibility for Bull Run on Sigel. His corps was "composed of some of the best fighting material we have," Pope pointed out, but would "never do much service under that officer," whom he rated as "perfectly unreliable."[6] Once again, Sigel found himself reassigned. Responding predictably to this latest slight, a crowd of German Americans thronged a "Sigel Mass Meeting" in Philadelphia on September 30, making clear they still ranked their idol "one of our best generals." It was the Lincoln administration, Sigel's admirers charged, that "rendered it it impossible for him to apply his great talents . . . for the welfare of the Union."[7]

As his devotees forwarded this overripe assessment to the White House, Sigel reached out directly to the President to express resentment at now being placed under the command of General Samuel P. Heintzelman—American-born despite his Teutonic name—who, Sigel bitterly pointed out, "is my junior."[8] Once again, the touchy Sigel asked to "be immediately relieved." And once again, he allowed himself to be talked out of quitting, mainly because, despite his indifferent military credentials, he remained (doubtless to Lincoln's growing frustration) politically invaluable. Only days later, as if to punctuate Sigel's unique status, a New York Republican leader urged Lincoln to grant Sigel a leave of absence to campaign for the party's gubernatorial candidate, James S. Wadsworth, a general who refused to return home to stump in his own behalf. "Gen. Sigle [*sic*]," enthused the New Yorker, "would take the Germans by storm." Lincoln decided the request could not, as he put it, "safely be granted."[9] The President seemed willing to sacrifice even Wadsworth's candidacy in New York to avoid further burnishing Sigel's standing among fellow Germans everywhere.

While Sigel faced mounting scrutiny over his performance at the Union's most recent defeat, Schurz immodestly assigned himself "honor" for "covering" the retreat from Second Bull Run, though he conceded he had done "nothing particularly brilliant" on the battlefield. And, like other Germans, Schurz remained obstinately blind to Sigel's faults, failing to recognize even how that general's recent postbattle mistakes served as a metaphor for the "Flying Dutchman's" entire sorry wartime record. After withdrawing from the field, Sigel's corps had stumbled in the dark along a road crowded with other troops, causing a traffic snarl of "men and guns and caissons and wagons and ambulances." Amid this "nightmare" disorder, some of the soldiers groping their way forward ended up in the wrong units. Even a simple night march far from the menace of enemy guns had proved too much for General Sigel.[10]

Once Lincoln restored George McClellan to command of the Army of the Potomac in the wake of Bull Run, Schurz's corps redeployed to the defense of Washington. The old revolutionary's sudden proximity to the capital for a time denied him further combat experience but gave him opportunities to hobnob once again with civilian dignitaries. Welcoming him back at a White House reception, Lincoln himself conspicuously congratulated Schurz on his recent battlefield experience: "I heard you have fought first rate. Good luck to you!"[11] Schurz's new assignment kept him away from the Battle of Antietam, Maryland, on September 17, but he rejoiced when the President followed this modest but costly success by issuing his preliminary Emancipation Proclamation.[12]

The joy did not long endure. In a crucial test of public support less than two months later, voters shellacked Lincoln's party in the midterm elections. Republicans lost twenty-two seats in the House of Representatives, forfeiting their outright majority.[13] Democrats picked up governorships in both New Jersey and New York (where, absent help from Sigel, General Wadsworth fell to administration critic Horatio Seymour), and won legislative majorities in two states where Lincoln had spent most of his life: Indiana and Illinois. In Lincoln's own home county, his onetime law partner and cousin by marriage, Democrat John Todd Stuart, won the previously Republican-held House seat the President himself had once occupied.[14]

These setbacks disappointed but likely did not shock Lincoln, who had anticipated that war fatigue and hostility to emancipation would hurt Republican chances at the polls.[15] Yet the election results sent Schurz into a panic, and though he remained in camp, he determined to share his chagrin as dramatically as possible. On November 8, his attractive and accomplished wife, Margarethe, turned up at the White House armed with a new letter from her husband, which she proceeded to recite aloud to a doubtless flabbergasted President. After reminding Lincoln "I am your friend," Schurz's text remonstrated: "The defeat of the Administration is the Administration's own fault. . . . The people felt the necessity of a change."[16]

The Schurz message elaborated on Lincoln's main failure: he had placed political "enemy's" [sic] in top command posts—meaning Democrats like Butler and McClellan. "Let us be commanded by generals whose heart is in the war," Schurz now demanded, "and only by such. . . . If West-Point cannot do the business, let West-Point go down. Who cares?"[17] In tone, the advice must have sounded to Lincoln like that of an older man lecturing a much younger one, rather than the other way around: Schurz, only thirty-three at the time, was in fact Lincoln's junior by a full twenty years.

Lincoln had expanded his own notions of why Republicans had fared poorly on Election Day, and now he decided to get some of them off his chest. His written reply to Schurz came in what the general called Lincoln's "peculiar clean-cut, logical style" but replete with "an undertone of impatience, of irritation, unusual with him—this time, no doubt, induced by the extraordinary harassment to which he was subjected from all sides." Schurz seemed clueless to the fact that the most recent "extraordinary harassment" had come from his own pen.[18]

"Certainly, the ill-success of the war had much to do with" the recent vote, Lincoln patiently acknowledged in his response. But he reminded Schurz that, back in 1861, Democrats had been "left in a majority by our friends going to the war"—thus reducing Republican voting strength at home. (Absentee voting had not yet been widely introduced.) Then it was Lincoln's turn to deliver a lecture. The war simply could not be waged by members of only one political party, particularly one that had won less than 40 percent of the popular vote in the most recent presidential election. As Lincoln tartly put it, "It was mere nonsense to suppose a minority could put down a majority in rebellion. Mr. Schurz (now Gen. Schurz) was about here [in Washington] then & I do not recollect that he then considered all who were not republicans, were enemies of the government, and that none of them must be appointed to military positions." Besides, the President pointed out, he had also elevated a good many Republicans to high command and failed to see "that their superiority of success has been so marked as to throw great suspicion on the good faith of those who are not Republicans."[19]

Once again, Schurz sought the last word, and his follow-up letter proved more insolent than the first. "I am far from presuming to blame you for having placed old democrats into high military positions. . . . But it was unfortunate that you sustained them," he imperiously noted.

"No, sir, let us indulge in no delusions as to the true causes of our defeat in the elections. . . . The people had sown confidence and reaped disaster and disappointment. They wanted a change." In a misguided attempt to praise his battle-weary troops, he haughtily added: "I do not know, whether you have ever seen a battlefield. I assure you, Mr. President, it is a terrible sight."[20]

Lincoln had ignored Schurz's previous attempts to prolong such debates, but this audacity he could not overlook. "I have just received, and read, your letter of the 20th," Lincoln began his acid response. "The purport of it is that we lost the late elections, and the administration is failing, because the war is unsuccessful; and that I must not flatter myself that I am not justly to blame for it. I certainly know that if the war fails, the administration fails, and that I *will* be blamed for it, whether I deserve it or not. And I ought to be blamed, if I could do better. You think I could do better; therefore you blame me already. I think I could not do better; therefore I blame you for blaming me."[21]

Turning to Schurz's demand that only men with "heart" be entrusted with command, Lincoln piled on: "[B]e assured, my dear sir, there are men who have 'heart in it' that think you are performing your part as poorly as you think I am performing mine."[22] Stung as he was by the criticism, Schurz's heart sank further when, just a few days later, a messenger arrived in camp bearing a note summoning him to the White House. Schurz headed to the mansion expecting further reprimand. But the President still harbored affection and respect for him, and certainly knew that the overwrought general continued to hold the admiration of tens of thousands of German American voters whom Lincoln could ill afford to offend further after his latest dustup with Franz Sigel.

Entering the President's office, Schurz found the weary Lincoln "seated in an arm chair before the open-grate fire, his feet in his gigantic morocco slippers." Unexpectedly, he greeted Schurz "cordially as of old and bade me pull up a chair and sit by his side. Then he brought his large hand with a slap down on my knee and said with a smile: 'Now tell me, young man, whether you really think that I am as poor a fellow as you have made me out in your letter!'" As Schurz recalled, "I looked into his face and felt something like a big lump in my throat." After struggling to find words to express his "sorrow," Lincoln gently cut him off by exclaiming jocularly: "Didn't I give it to you hard in my letter? Didn't I? But it didn't hurt, did it? I did not mean to, and therefore I wanted you to come so quickly."[23] Lincoln thus reestablished the natural order of their father-son relationship. "He laughed again," recalled Schurz, "and seemed to enjoy the matter heartily," adding: "I guess we understand one another now, and it's all right." Before they parted, the irrepressible Schurz dared ask Lincoln if "he still wished that I should write to him. 'Why, certainly,' he answered; 'write me whenever the spirit moves you.' We parted as better friends than ever."[24]

Schurz emerged from the feared showdown feeling relief as well as remorse for troubling a man he still admired. Worse, he returned to the field in time to join General Ambrose E. Burnside's humiliating "Mud March," the rain-soaked retreat in foot-deep "liquid slime" that followed the Union's latest devastating defeat at the Battle of Fredericksburg in December. Self-servingly, Schurz later claimed he had opposed Burnside's plan to engage Lee there.[25]

In the Fredericksburg campaign, Irish, not German, troops had emerged from the carnage with honors—demonstrating extraordinary courage in the face of overwhelming Confederate resistance. As one captain reported of his brigade's "shattered condition" after a futile attack on the fiercely defended Confederate stronghold on Marye's Heights: "Irish blood and Irish bones cover that terrible field today. . . . We are slaughtered like sheep, and no result but defeat." Added an Irish-born New York private: "Our men were mowed down like grass before the scythe of a reaper . . . and sorrow hangs like a shroud over us all."[26]

Despite the humiliating setback, not everyone in the Union focused that month on the war in the East, or on the immigrants engaged in fighting it. Two weeks later—the day after Christmas—thirty-eight

Dakota Sioux who had waged a bloody uprising against white settlers were hanged by federal authorities in Mankato, Minnesota. It was the largest mass execution in American history. Lincoln had personally authorized the punishment against those found guilty of murder or rape, though he also commuted the death sentences of 264 others and resisted calls from local Republicans to allow the hangings to proceed before Election Day for maximum political effect. In justifying his decision, Lincoln insisted the condemned had "manifested a spirit of insubordination . . . with extreme ferocity, killing, indiscriminately, men, women, and children."[27] He subsequently reported to Congress, without any hint of unease, that white Minnesotans now hoped "for the removal of the tribes beyond the limits of the State as a guarantee against future hostilities."[28] Did Lincoln see the irony of pursuing policies that closed doors on Native Americans while opening them to new Americans? If so, he never said as much.

A few months later, a delegation of Cheyenne, Apache, and other Indian chiefs—all colorfully "dressed in their war regalia" and carrying "tomahawks, lances, bows and arrows"—entered the White House, not in anger but for a peaceful summit with the President. As the visitors sat cross-legged on the floor of the East Room, Lincoln described Washington's public buildings as "big wigwams" and then recommended that they forsake hunting and turn to "the cultivation of the earth." Finally, he assured them he desired peace with "our red brethren." Witnessing this remarkable scene by chance was one Louis Hensel, a German-born spear-carrier for a visiting German opera company whose Washington performances Lincoln had recently attended. During a backstage visit, the President had casually extended an open invitation (allegedly "in very broken German") to the entire cast and crew, and now Hensel, mistaken for a translator, had stumbled into the executive mansion during a historic meeting. He would never forget the moment one chief rose and swung a tomahawk perilously close to Lincoln's face—but threatened only to "split the heads of your enemies."[29]

Native Americans were not the only "outsiders" excluded that year from Lincoln's expanding vision of pluralism. Congress also passed an Act to Prohibit the "Coolie Trade," barring Chinese laborers from immigrating to the United States notwithstanding the acute need for workers to extend the transcontinental railroad to the Pacific coast. (The borderline racial slur "Coolie" originated as a Chinese slang term for "rented muscle.")[30] Lincoln had been urging legislation to stem the "Asiatic coolie trade" since 1861, and his foreign-born secretary, John Nicolay, had urged similar restrictions even earlier.[31] Yet, just nine years before, the governor of California had referred to the Chinese as the "most desirable of our adopted citizens" and proposed free land grants "to induce further immigration."[32] Now federal lawmakers justified this precursor to the future Chinese Exclusion Act as a righteous effort to curtail another potentially dehumanizing slave trade before it could expand unregulated. But bigotry lurked not far from the surface. One senator made a point of volunteering his view that people of a supposedly "inferior race . . . should not be transported" to America, a highly selective argument that had never precluded earlier slavery apologists from embracing the forced importation of Africans.[33]

· · ·

In the military shake-up that followed Fredericksburg, Lincoln named General Joseph Hooker to succeed Burnside in command of the Army of the Potomac, whereupon Carl Schurz decided he was entitled to a promotion of his own to the rank of major general. As to qualifications, Schurz reminded Lincoln not of his military acumen but of his "influence with a large class of citizens, which would undoubtedly be impaired by a letting down." Conveniently forgetting that he had demanded to be released from his diplomatic assignment in order to enlist, he rewrote history to claim: "I gave up a first-class position in the civil service . . . merely for the purpose of serving the Republic on a more dangerous field at home."[34] Magnanimously, Lincoln opted to reward Schurz—and, in the bargain, elevate Hungarian American cavalry officer Julius Stahel (born Gyula Számvald). Even after a dispiriting battlefield loss, ethnic appointments remained the order of the day. Foreign-born officers might not produce military success, but they provided political cover.

As Lincoln now instructed Secretary of War Stanton: "Schurz and Stahl [*sic*] should both be Maj. Genls. Schurz to take Sigel's old corps, and Stahl to command Cavalry." That these significant rewards represented Lincoln's latest attempt to soothe ruffled feathers among the foreign-born became clear when he added: "They, together with Sigel, are our sincere friends; and while so much may seem rather large, any thing less is too small. I think it better be done."[35] Although Congress would not ratify Schurz's promotion until July, Hooker assigned him to take over the Eleventh Corps from Sigel right away—in effect exchanging one German commander for another.

When Sigel learned he had once more been superseded, this time in favor of a *landsmann*, he responded as if wounded by friendly fire. He obeyed the order but protested the "misunderstandings" that had allowed Schurz to succeed him before formally attaining his new rank. Sigel also gossiped that a "humiliated" Stahel had come out the worse from the reorganization, generating "much dissatisfaction among the officers, which might be damaging to our interests in case of a battle." Stahel must be given more manpower for his new cavalry contingent, Sigel insisted, as well as seniority higher than Schurz's. This was too much, even for the forbearing Lincoln. "I have tried, in regard to Gen. Schurz & Gen. Stahl," the exasperated President wrote Sigel, "to oblige all around; but it seems to get worse & worse. If Gen. Sigel would say distinctly, and unconditionally, what he desires done, about the command of the forces he has, I should try to do it; but when he has plans, conditioned upon my raising new forces, which is inconvenient for me to do, it is drawing upon me too severely."[36]

Here this latest dispute might have ended, but on February 5, Lincoln inexplicably rekindled it with an apology to Sigel—apparently at Schurz's behest, and likely again for purely political reasons. As Lincoln almost meekly told Sigel: "Gen. Schurz thinks I was a little cross in my late note to you. If I was, I ask pardon. If I do get up a little temper I have no sufficient time to keep it up." As a concession, Lincoln agreed to "give an increased Cavalry command to Gen. Stahl" after all. Yet even this did not satisfy Sigel. On February 12—Lincoln's fifty-fourth birthday—Sigel once again asked to be reassigned elsewhere. Exasperated with the entire German problem—though he tellingly took time that day to recommend the promotion of two officers in the Irish Brigade—Lincoln made clear that he "has given General Sigel as good a command as he can, and desires him to do the best he can with it." Sigel refused. On March 11, the general demanded that "either I be relieved of my command or that my resignation be accepted, as my present position and relations . . . are so unsatisfactory and dispiriting to me, that it would be in the highest degree unpleasant for me to continue in command of my Corps."[37] At last, Lincoln called his bluff and transferred him to an outpost far from the main action—and the journalists who covered it.

Schurz never admitted that his own elevation might have been used to ease Sigel out of the command hierarchy. Rather, Schurz maintained (long after his opinion might have benefited Lincoln) that Sigel hurt his career by coming across to colleagues as "pretentious . . . reserved, even morose." As a result, Schurz maintained, Sigel "was always regarded as a foreign intruder who had no proper place in the Army of the Potomac and whose reputation, won in the West, was to be discredited. Whenever he did anything that gave the slightest chance for criticism, he could count upon being blamed without mercy."[38] Nonetheless, Schurz rose as Sigel fell.

Schurz was never one for self-awareness. In spring 1863—exhibiting the kind of high-handedness for which he criticized Sigel—he asked Lincoln to shift his own corps from his latest commander, General O. O. Howard, to either General William S. Rosecrans or General Ambrose Burnside in the western theater. Schurz argued that his German soldiers "have always been outsiders in this Army," adding, "I have no doubt this Army will see us leave without regret." But Schurz had failed to rally his fellow German officers around the transfer scheme, and one of them, Adolph von Steinwehr, demurred, telling General Howard, "I hope the time is not far of[f] when these political moves may cease." Unexpectedly, Lincoln took Steinwehr's side. "I do not myself see a good reason why it should be done," he wrote to Schurz of the proposed reassignment. "The Division will do itself, and its officers, more honor; and the country more service, where it is. . . . I always wish to oblige you, but I can not in this case."[39]

After a brief April 1863 visit to the front, Lincoln did make a conspicuous show of placating Schurz: the President invited him to steam back to Washington with him and the next day prolonged their conversation over dinner at the White House—to little avail. Although Schurz had boasted just a few weeks earlier that he had "become something of an American and not altogether dependent upon the endorsement of any class of foreign born people," Lincoln found him as reliant as ever on his German connections, roots, and grievances. After the general returned to camp, Lincoln confided that his old ally seemed convinced he would always be treated as a second-class American. "Did you notice how glum Schurz is?" Lincoln asked journalist Noah Brooks. "He is dissatisfied. Poor Schurz! He seems never to forget that he is an adopted citizen of the country."[40]

Unfortunately, Lincoln's decision to keep Schurz and his corps of adopted citizens in place left them to face their greatest military challenge—and their most brutal condemnation—at the Battle of Chancellorsville that May. Only days before that encounter, Lincoln paid a morale-building return visit to Union headquarters in Virginia and reviewed Hooker's splendid-looking army, his trademark black stovepipe hat fully visible to the lines of assembled troops. This was the day he also honored the all-Irish Pennsylvania 116th, but Lincoln also took pains to pay special attention to the Eleventh Corps, telling a proud Schurz that his German unit seemed "the best drilled and most soldierly of the troops that passed before him."[41] Yet, as the spruce McClellan had demonstrated a few months earlier at Antietam, well-drilled soldiers did not always win decisive victories.

Instead, at Chancellorsville, Union forces suffered another cata-
clysmic defeat. And for his part, Schurz proved helpless to quell the
hysteria that war correspondents claimed overtook his ranks in the
heat of battle. General Hooker deserved most of the blame for this
latest rout, but recriminations fell heavily on German commanders
and their troops, draining public confidence in their fighting ability.
The *New York Times* heaped particular abuse on the "panic-stricken
Dutchmen" under Schurz's command. "Without waiting for a single
volley from the rebels," the paper charged, "this corps disgracefully
abandoned the position behind their breastworks." In the report's un-
flinching words, "Thousands of these cowards threw down their guns"
and stampeded. (A German paper in Pittsburgh attributed the criticism to the *Times* correspondent's "nativist perfidy.")[42]

BATTLE OF CHANCELLORSVILLE, Vᴬ MAY, 3ᴿᴰ 1863.

This terrific Battle was fought between the "Army of the Potomac" under Gen! Hooker; and the Rebel Army, under command of Generals Lee, Stonewall Jackson, Longstreet and Hill ... The Rebels advanced in overwhelming numbers, but the Brave Union Soldiers fought with desperate gallantry, holding the Rebels in check, and inflicting dreadful slaughter among them.

Currier & Ives's view of the Battle of Chancellorsville offered no hint of reported
German cowardice under fire. Rather, it showed Union troops chasing Confederates
and featured a caption insisting that federal forces had "fought with desperate gallantry,
holding the Rebels in check." In fact, the encounter proved a Union fiasco
and a crushing blow to the reputation of German troops.

In an equally scathing account, the *New York Herald* also singled out "the disastrous and disgraceful giving way of General Schurz's division" and claimed his men had "fled from the field in a panic, nearly effecting the total demoralization of the entire army." This gave the paper an opportunity to remind readers of the superiority of "Anglo-Saxon blood" in battle, singling out for special praise those soldiers who hailed from Scotland (not coincidentally the birthplace of its publisher James Gordon Bennett). For good measure, the *Herald* excoriated the administration for "inconsiderately removing the general to whom the German troops were attached and whom they would follow to their death"—Sigel, of course—and replacing him with "more of a talker than a fighter," meaning Schurz.[43] Taking the abuse another step further, the *New York Tribune* declared: "We hope that swift justice will overtake the regiments that broke" and "if it be deemed too rigid to shoot them all, they may at least be decimated and then dissolved." Horace Greeley could not quite bring himself to attack someone he had once praised; the worst his paper said of Schurz was that he had failed to "arrest the panic."[44] Then Hooker himself condemned the "stampede of the 11th corps" in an appearance before Congress's Joint Committee on the Conduct of the War—which unaccountably declined to hear rebuttal testimony from Schurz.[45] Among detractors, the slogan of the day became "I Fights Mit Sigel und runs mit Schurz."[46]

Schurz did not take the criticism quietly. Describing himself as "deeply pained" by reports he had "led the disgraceful flight in person," he demanded that General Howard state for the record "what troops threw themselves flying upon the rest" and "what I was doing while you saw me on the field of battle." Knowing better than to further agitate a friend of the President's, Howard replied that he regarded the rumors as "false and malicious," adding with diplomatic vagueness: "I do not believe you could have done more than you did."[47]

This clarification did little to quell the opprobrium against the Germans. Schimmelfennig, too, endured criticism for the Chancellorsville debacle. "Just what I expected," he sniffed to a subordinate after one newspaper singled out his flawed battlefield performance.[48] The continuing attacks prompted the German-language Philadelphia *Freie Presse* to anguish, "Have we not sent able generals and a hundred thousand German soldiers into the field?"[49] In later years, Schurz would try ascribing blame for the Chancellorsville catastrophe on Hooker's insobriety, alleging he was "accustomed to the consumption of a certain quantity of whiskey every day," an explosive charge the Joint Committee dismissed as "unfounded."[50] Instead, the "flying Dutch" continued to shoulder major blame for the disheartening loss. The German-language Highland, Illinois, *Bote* ("Messenger") lamented that "bigots, witch-burners, temperance men, and Know-Nothings that hate the German population from the bottom of their soul" relished their "much wished-for opportunity to attack the 'cowardly' Dutchmen." Unless the German community "unifies a little," warned the paper, ". . . we will be spied upon, criticized, and labeled 'traitors' right and left."[51]

In an unexpected way, it is possible that the scapegoating of one corps of foreign-born soldiers helped restore the overall élan of the Army of the Potomac. That may have been crucial in the weeks before it next confronted Lee's army at Gettysburg under yet another new commander, George G. Meade. If so, its revived confidence came at the expense of a dispirited but still politically potent German community. As Pittsburgh's *Freiheits Freund* ("Friend of Freedom") *und Pittsburger Courier* reported after its correspondent visited corps headquarters, "morale is quite depressed, especially among the officers, who without exception feel offended and outraged in the aftermath of the strenuous denunciation of the American press."[52] Not surprisingly, as German troops absorbed the stigma of cowardice and dereliction, their disenchantment with their commander in chief spiked. With another battlefield defeat in the history books and another election—this one for president—looming the following year, the scapegoating did Lincoln as little good as it did the Germans.

German restiveness found an outlet in yet another revival of Sigel lionization. One German-born soldier speculated in a letter home that "if Sigel had been in command the 11th Corps would not have been so badly defeated."[53] Charging into the vacuum, the failed general encouraged his press supporters to suggest afresh that he—again and alone—represented the answer to Union defeatism. Even Schurz supported his return. A few days after Chancellorsville, as the rest of the New York press railed against the Eleventh Corps, William Cullen Bryant, the graybeard poet who edited the pro-administration *New York Evening Post*, wrote Lincoln to urge "that General Sigel should be again placed in command" of "German soldiery." To Bryant, Sigel's return would be "equal to the addition of ten thousand men to the army."[54]

Lincoln had reached the point of no return. "I kept Gen. Sigel in command for several months, he requesting to be resign, or be relieved," he reminded Bryant. "At length, at his urgent & repeated solicitation, he was relieved. Now it is inconvenient to assign him a command without relieving or dismissing some other officer, who is not asking, and perhaps would object, to being disposed of."[55] It was the second time in a matter of weeks that Lincoln had used the word "inconvenient" to characterize his growing unwillingness to placate Sigel and his advocates.

Still, the latest Sigel boom would not fade. Even as Lincoln was exchanging views with Bryant, yet another mass meeting, this one attracting thousands of "loyal citizens of St. Louis," assembled to promote a Sigel comeback. Organizers hoped to mark the second anniversary of the capture of Camp Jackson—Sigel's 1861 pinnacle—by sending Lincoln a package of resolutions critical of the war effort since.[56] The petition, likely drafted by German-born state legislator and editor Emil Preetorius, an outspoken critic of slavery, called for the ouster of Sigel's most persistent detractor, General Halleck, and the firing of cabinet members still unenthusiastic about emancipation. Not surprisingly, the Germans also demanded the reinstatement of generals who supported a "policy of freedom," namely Frémont and Sigel. One can almost hear Lincoln sighing as he refolded the document and marked it: "More of the quarrel."[57]

Just a few weeks later, St. Louis attorney James Taussig—born Jakob Taussig in what is now Czechia—visited the White House to submit the St. Louis demands in person. He found the President in an irritable mood. After listening to Taussig, Lincoln erupted that "it may be a misfortune for the nation that he was elected President. But, having been elected by the people, he meant to be President, and to perform his duty according to *his* best understanding, if he had to die for it. No general will be removed," he made clear, "nor will any change in the Cabinet be made to suit the views or wishes of any particular party, faction, or set of men."[58]

As for his alleged hostility to German military leaders—or those non-Germans whom the Germans admired—critics were wrong, Lincoln insisted, to suppose that such men were "systematically kept out of command. . . . [O]n the contrary, he fully appreciated the merits of the gentlemen named . . . [and] was not only willing but anxious to place them again in command as soon as he could find spheres of action for them, without doing injustice to others, but at present he 'had more pegs than holes to put them in.'"[59]

Then the conversation turned to slavery, which remained legal in border states like Missouri even after the Emancipation Proclamation struck it down in Rebel territory, where the President enjoyed the power to liberate as a military measure. Taussig, like Preetorius a Republican with advanced views on race, urged immediate abolition in his home state. Lincoln insisted he still preferred a "gradual" approach in order to keep Missouri out of the Confederacy. He graphically illustrated his preference for incrementalism by comparing the situation to the "case of a man who had an excrescence on the back of his neck, the removal of which, in one operation, would result in the death of the patient, while tinkering it off by degrees would preserve life." Taussig was "sorely tempted" to reply with his own story of "the dog whose tail was amputated by degrees," eliciting a "fresh howl of agony at every blow of the cleaver struck," but held his tongue.[60]

Such tension had become almost routine during Lincoln's recent meetings with antislavery men. After one particularly fraught session, he had admitted privately that he admired their cause more than he did its advocates: "They are nearer to me than the other side, in thought and sentiment, though bitterly hostile personally . . . but after all their faces are set Zion-wards."[61] Lincoln terminated the Taussig meeting by declaring that "there was evidently a serious misunderstanding springing up between him and the Germans of St. Louis, which he would like to see removed"—and removed promptly (unlike the "excrescence" of slavery). He was growing weary of these disputes, Lincoln lectured Taussig as they parted. Indeed, as he put it, "the two sides ought to have their heads knocked together."[62]

Instead, German obsession with Sigel lingered. When Lee aimed his army toward Pennsylvania in late June, Sigel's stubborn admirers alerted Lincoln that the idle general might now prove that state's savior—if not through his military acumen, then via his still-magical allure to prospective recruits. A group of New York Germans, including Lincoln's old acquaintance Sigismund Kaufmann, urged that the White House unleash Sigel to "issue a call for volunteers at once to march" to Pennsylvania's defense. Lincoln curtly replied that if New York's Democratic governor wished Sigel's assistance in raising troops, "he can have it."[63] The assignment never materialized. Rather, the administration banished Sigel to an obscure command in the Department of West Virginia.

As for Alexander Schimmelfennig, he would once more ignite scorn after his corps broke under hammerblows from Confederate forces just north of Gettysburg a few weeks later. This time, the German general invited ridicule by taking shelter in a pigsty as his men beat a hasty retreat through town—and for remaining there until Lee's entire army retreated south three days later.[64] The star-crossed, four-syllable general had also managed to tumble from a horse and contract smallpox, malaria, and tuberculosis, limiting further field service. His health shattered but his tongue-twisting name immortalized among students of the Civil War, Schimmelfennig survived the conflict by only five months.

Carl Schurz's military career did not end in similar ignominy, despite the uproar over his Chancellorsville performance. He would go on to lead his corps ably at Gettysburg and in the autumn transferred to Tennessee to join Rosecrans's Army of the Cumberland—just as he had wished. Although he thereafter saw little meaningful action in the West and disliked the region intensely, he stuck it out for months. Only in 1864 did the ever-restive Schurz write again to the President suggesting he might be better utilized in another war: the battle for Lincoln's reelection.

. . .

If the reputation of German soldiers plummeted at Chancellorsville in May, the prestige of Irish troops reached its zenith at Gettysburg in July—on both sides of the epic battle that engulfed the small, predominantly German village in scorching summer heat.[65]

New York's Sixty-Ninth, the Fighting Irish, reached the small Pennsylvania crossroads under a new command. Following the Battle of Fredericksburg seven months earlier, Thomas Meagher had accused the War Department of "discrimination against the adopted citizens" of his brigade for failing to grant its men passes home during the idle winter. Thereafter, Meagher felt he could not "in self-respect—or in justice to his command submit any longer to the treatment which both were subjected by the official dictators . . . Stanton and Halleck." His resignation was quickly accepted, but Meagher lingered on through a raucous celebration of St. Patrick's Day in March 1863 and the deadly fighting at Chancellorsville that May, departing only after a round of elaborate ceremonies and speeches. Colonel Patrick Kelly, a battle-tested native of Ireland's County Galway, took over the unit before it marched into Pennsylvania.[66]

As the Gettysburg fighting commenced, Irish Brigade chaplain William Corby held a divine service for the Catholic troops. Standing "upon a large rock in front of the brigade," a spellbound eyewitness recalled, "Father Corby reminded the soldiers of the high and sacred nature of their trust . . . and the noble object for which they fought." At the conclusion of his remarks, "every man fell on his knees," and "stretching his right hand toward the brigade," the chaplain offered the men general absolution. Even corps commander Winfield Scott Hancock, a Protestant of English and Welsh stock, removed his hat at this solemn moment in the Catholic Mass. "The scene was more than impressive; it was awe-inspiring . . . ," marveled an onlooker. "I do not think there was a man in the brigade who did not offer up a heart-felt prayer. For some, it was their last."[67]

Father William J. Corby (right) offers Catholic soldiers "absolution under fire" before the second day of fighting at Gettysburg, July 2, 1863. Artist Paul Henry Wood reimagined the legendary religious service three decades later.

Their ranks already thinned by the horrendous losses at Fredericksburg and Chancellorsville, the Fighting Irish could muster only five hundred or so able-bodied men for the three-day contest at Gettysburg. But they made an oversize difference. The already legendary infantry unit proved key to the fierce struggle for the Wheatfield on the battle's second day, charging across dangerous terrain and into the woods shouting their war cry, *Faugh a Ballaugh!* ("Clear the way"). Their aggressive action secured the Union line and staved off a complete and early rout by Confederate forces.[68]

Then, on the climactic third day of fighting, Irish units from both New York and Pennsylvania helped defend the center of the Union position against the largest assault of the entire war: Pickett's Charge. One Irishman, Colonel Dennis O'Kane, a native of County Derry, steeled the defenders, nicknamed Paddy Owens's Regulars, against the onslaught of Rebels at what became known as the "high water mark of the Confederacy."[69] At the furious climax of the struggle, O'Kane's men held the high ground against Irish troops of the Virginia Brigade—their fierce, all-Gaelic, hand-to-hand combat epitomizing the brother-against-brother nature of the entire war as seen later through the lens of Lost Cause mythology. As one veteran put it forty years after the battle, "The [Union] Irishmen stood immovable, unconquerable, fearless and splendid in their valor, the green flag waving side by side with the colors of their adopted country, both held aloft by the stone wall until the victory was assured and the hosts of the enemy crushed."[70]

The Irish Brigade sacrificed a quarter of its already depleted roster on the first day of Gettysburg alone—men with names like Cavanagh, Degnan, Mulligan, and Reilly. On the battle's third and final day, the company's well-liked second-ranking officer, Captain James M. Rorty, died in action while manning federal artillery on Cemetery Ridge. In total, the brigade lost 198 of its 532 remaining men at Gettysburg, a casualty rate that approached a staggering 40 percent. Their fortitude earned high honors for Hibernian troops in a monumental battle that for once ended with a Union victory.[71]

. . .

The reputational apogee lasted only days. The war's next battleground also involved the Irish, but this time in deadly civilian riots that convulsed an unlikely field: the cobblestoned streets of New York City.

The violent disturbance erupted soon after the government commenced enforcing the recently passed federal Enrollment Act. Under the law's fiercely disputed terms, all men between the ages of twenty and forty-five fell subject to a military conscription lottery, with those randomly picked compelled to serve in the armed forces for three years—unless they could afford $300 for an exemption or substitute. The statute unleashed legitimate charges that Lincoln's crusade against secession had descended into a "rich man's war and poor man's fight" and stirred additional anxiety by taking effect just days after the press reported the carnage at Gettysburg. Just as trainloads of the battle's wounded survivors began streaming into the city, authorities scheduled the first draft call.

One pseudonymous "Adopted Citizen" bitterly complained—in a letter that made its way to Lincoln himself—"I have not got 300 dollars[.] I must go and fight and dapper Mr Smirk with his stainless linen [undergarments] and fashionable clothing can stay home and strut round because forsooth he has 300 dollars." Such inequity would breed anger "not confined to the German 'Arbeiter Vereine' [workingmen]," warned the angry writer, and "materially interfere with Republican prospects at the coming elections."[72] Nor was it lost on the eligible manpower pool that the government now required that conscripts risk life and limb not only to preserve the Union but also to secure Black freedom, a goal many New Yorkers did not deem worth fighting for, much less dying for. Another new law had authorized the recruitment of "colored" troops, igniting additional fear among many poor whites that Black military service would result in racial equality and decreased wages once the war ended.[73]

Still, the first round of the draft in New York began and ended peacefully. After a one-day pause for the Sabbath, it recommenced amid rising tensions on the steamy Monday morning of July 13. As a Union officer prepared to pull the names of that day's first draftees at the provost marshal's office on Third Avenue between Forty-Fifth and Forty-Sixth Streets—above which a number of immigrant German families lived—resentment came to a boil outside.[74] No one knows who hurled the first brick through the window, but within minutes a mob ransacked the office, scattered draft cards, and smashed the wooden wheel housing them. The largest civil disturbance in American history—save for the Civil War itself—was underway.[75] Similar riots broke out elsewhere in the North, but national attention focused on the city with the most newspapers to report on the uprising.

The New York riot had not erupted without abundant incitement. Dennis Mahony's book *The Prisoner of State* castigated the administration for "kidnapping American freeman" through so-called arbitrary arrests, reminding readers that Lincoln's executive actions were thought unconstitutional by Catholic chief justice Roger B. Taney.[76] For days preceding the outbreak, the Democratic press had blared inflammatory warnings that the conscription act was about to deprive struggling white families of their breadwinners. Declaring the draft "profoundly repugnant to the American mind" and "a dangerous experiment to insult the popular will," the *New York World* (now owned by Democratic National Committee chairman August Belmont) all but predicted—and perhaps helped stir—"manifestations of popular disaffection." The anti-administration *New York Daily News* was even more incendiary, warning, "A free people will not submit to the conscription."[77] The *News* ghoulishly predicted that "one out of about every two and a half of our citizens are destined to be brought off into Messrs. Lincoln & Company's charnel house."[78]

Anger was directed not only at the government but at innocent African Americans, viewed as special beneficiaries of administration policy. At a "States Rights and Peace Demonstration" in one of the city's poor Irish wards, speaker Lindley Spring, a fierce opponent of racial equality, further aroused residents against what he branded "a far more ignominious despotism than your fathers escaped from" in Ireland, likening the draft to "a highwayman's call on every American citizen for $300 or your life."[79]

Whatever the trigger, the July 13 attack on the Third Avenue draft office quickly mushroomed. The mob surged uptown, headed west along the southern fringes of the new Central Park, then stormed down Manhattan's West Side, cyclonically gathering strength in numbers along the way. Boys and women joined the mob, which turned southward and began breaking into factories to seize weapons. Others took up improvised arms: sticks, clubs, rocks, and paving stones pried from the streets. Rioters plundered shops, torched buildings, attacked known abolitionists, pillaged private homes, and assaulted policemen and firefighters who tried to intercede. The marauders aimed particular fury against people of color, driving them from their houses, attacking them randomly on the streets, and killing unknown numbers by pummeling them, lynching them, or driving them off the docks to drown in the river.

As one journalist reported: "Wherever a negro came in sight he was pursued, and if caught was beaten till the crowd was satisfied. . . . One of the crowd said, 'I don't know that the n——s themselves is responsible for this here trouble, but by God there is a war about 'm, damn 'm, and we'll pound 'm.'" A horrified observer watched as a white woman emerged from a house on West Thirty-Second Street to alert the mob "that there was a row of negro tenements in the rear." Thereupon, one rioter "carried a coil of rope to hang the negroes whom they expected to find. The torch was applied, and in a few minutes the houses were on fire."[80] Blacks unfortunate enough to fall victim to the mob faced torture. Some corpses were sexually mutilated, other bodies dragged through the streets or hanged from lampposts. One witness saw a Black man strung up from a tree, then watched in disbelief as a group of "men and women set him on fire as he dangled from the branches."[81] Uncounted hundreds perished.

One of the vilest attacks took place late on the first afternoon of the outbreak, when a predominantly Irish American mob plundered and then set fire to the well-appointed "Colored Orphan Asylum" on the northwest corner of Fifth Avenue and Forty-Third Street. At one point, rioters trapped more than two hundred helpless youngsters inside as flames licked the walls, only grudgingly allowing their escape, and not before forcing them past a gauntlet of hecklers screaming racial epithets. Finally, one friendly "Irish" voice called out: "If there is a man among you, with a heart within him come and help these poor children." In return, the mob "laid hold of him . . . ready to tear him to pieces." Only then did another "young Irishman, named Paddy M'Caffrey," step forward and, with the aid of a handful of firemen and coachmen, escort the orphans to safety at a nearby police precinct. "Had it not been for the courageous conduct" of these good Samaritans, the *Times* reported, "there is little doubt that many, and perhaps all of these helpless children, would have been murdered in cold blood."[82]

Increasingly fueled by drink, the rioters turned further wrath on private and sacred property alike, sacking emporiums like Brooks Brothers, which catered to the elite; desecrating Protestant churches; and crashing into "colored" schools. Diarist George Templeton Strong watched one band of "Irish blackguards" set upon Mayor George Opdyke's home on Fourteenth Street—twice. Strong felt relieved when a group of passing "gentlemen" rushed to the scene and used "their walking sticks and their fists" to disperse the "uprising." After watching a nearby precinct house go up in flames, Strong overheard "a crowd of Celtic spectators . . . exulting over the damage to 'them bloody police.'" Strong had no doubt the mob was "perfectly homogenous," asserting, "Every brute in the drove was pure Celtic."[83] By Tuesday, the second day of unrest, the city's German Americans organized to fend off attacks on their own community.[84]

In the turmoil, some of the most unspeakable violence transcended ethnic and racial enmity. On July 14, a mob plundered the home of Irish-born colonel Henry F. O'Brien, a veteran of Corcoran's Legion who had bravely supported the draft. Rushing to the scene on Second Avenue and Thirty-Fourth Street, O'Brien was struck by a flying rock and sought treatment at a neighborhood pharmacy, aptly named the Union Drug Store. Rioters promptly shattered the shop's window, stormed inside, and pulled the colonel into the street by his hair. There they trampled him and beat him "in the most merciless manner with stones, bars of iron, bludgeons, and sling shots, stabbed him in several parts of his body and then dragged him through the gutters by a cord around his neck." (See illustration, page 281.) Children set flaming paper under his head while adults kicked his face to a pulp. The rioters then strung O'Brien from a nearby lamppost, left him dangling for a few minutes, and cut him down. Somehow, he was still breathing, so he was stripped of the remnants of his scorched and tattered uniform, whereupon the beatings resumed. It took hours for the mangled colonel to die.[85]

The rioters directed additional outrage against the pro-Republican newspapers headquartered just south of city hall. Shouts of "Down with the *Tribune*!" resounded through Printing House Square as a mob broke into that pro-emancipation daily. "Down with the old white coat [as editor Greeley was known] that thinks a naygar as good as an Irishman!"[86] Only when a peace officer fired his gun outside did the invaders retreat into the street, do battle with policemen wielding clubs, and finally disperse into the darkness, leaving in their wake smashed furniture and scattered paperwork. The attackers never reached the editorial rooms upstairs, where Greeley's employees huddled, poised for confrontation, clutching weapons they had acquired from a nearby arsenal.

For seventy-two hours, the riots engulfed large swaths of the city. By July 16, a day before Union troops finally arrived to restore order, immigrant James Gordon Bennett's pro-Union but racist *New York Herald* suggested that "n——head" newspapers deserved as much blame as antiwar journals for inciting New Yorkers "to the pitch of passion."[87] That same day, the most prominent of the city's antiwar "Copperhead" dailies, Belmont's *New York World*, joined in blaming abolitionist papers like the *Evening Post* and the *Tribune* for the heinous attacks on African Americans. "Negroes are cruelly beaten in New-York," the *World* perversely argued, "because mock philanthropists have made them odious by parading them and their emancipation as the object to which peace first, and the Union afterward, with the lives of myriads of Northern men, are to be sacrificed."[88]

To most other observers, fault for the violence rested squarely with the Irish. The *Times* reported it as "a fact, patent to everyone who has seen anything of the mob, that it is composed almost exclusively of Irishmen and boys."[89] Such shaming was expected from the British consul in New York, who alerted the prime minister "that the rioters have been almost entirely Irish," their anger directed primarily "at the poor Negro people."[90] George Templeton Strong, who described the "*jacquerie*" as the worst since the anti-Catholic nativist riots of the 1840s, called for "heroic doses of steel and lead" to subdue the "Irish anti-conscription, N——r-murdering mob."[91]

Orestes Brownson, a onetime Protestant minister who had converted to Catholicism in the 1840s—but still held the Irish in low regard—estimated that "nearly nine-tenths of the active rioters were Irishmen and Catholics . . . from the lowest and most degraded social class." Brownson perceptively noted that the mob "did not Act as Catholics or as Irishmen, but as adherents of the DEMOCRATIC PARTY." Yet the fact remained: even if only a small minority of the city's Irish had engaged in the rioting, an overwhelming majority of the rioters was indeed Irish. In something of an understatement, Strong noted that the "generous and chivalric sons of Erin are under a cloud just now."[92]

The *Irish-American* did try refuting the "abolition papers," which, "without a single exception, continue their assaults on the Irish-born population of New York, attributing to them, with all the exaggeration that prejudice and malignity can impart to the slander, the worst excesses committed during the late riots in the city."[93] Yet the Irish-born Sergeant Peter Welsh of the Twenty-Eighth Massachusetts spoke for most contemporaries when he admitted in a letter home: "I am very sorry that the Irish men of New York took so large a part in them disgraceful riots." His fellow Irishmen, he worried, "are too easily led into such snares which give their enemies an opportunity to malign and abuse them."[94] Taking refuge through humor, as usual, the President was said to be amused when he learned that Union general Hugh Judson Kilpatrick was headed to New York to quell the uprising. Lincoln responded to the news with a rather feeble pun by noting of "kill Patrick's" assignment that "his name has nothing to do with it."[95]

Only when federal troops did take back New York's streets—under the command of General Dix, not Kilpatrick—did the aging, ailing Archbishop John Hughes finally appear on the balcony of his Madison Avenue residence to deliver a pacific speech that both friends and critics had been awaiting for days. As a large crowd listened respectfully, some men standing on barrels for a better view, the prince of the New York Catholic Church belatedly sought to put an end to the riot while at the same time absolving Irish American Catholics of total guilt for the violence. "I know of no people on earth who have not had their grievances," he began, to shouts of "That's so."

"When I cast my eyes back to the land of my nativity," he continued, "and when I think of its oppressions . . . I thank God that I came to a country where no such oppression exists. If you are Irishmen, as your enemies say the rioters are, *I* am an Irishman, but not a rioter. If you are Catholics, as they have reported, probably to hurt my feelings, then I am a Catholic too." Then he asked: "Do you want my advice? ('Yes.') Is there not some way in which you can stop these proceedings and support the laws, of which none have been enacted against you as Irishmen and Catholics?" Otherwise, he warned his flock, "military force will be let loose on you. The innocent will be shot down, and the guilty likely to escape. Would it not be better for you to retire quietly?"[96] Hughes helped calm the crowd, but his remarks also confirmed that his fellow Irishmen had started the upheaval.[97] It was probably the archbishop's finest public moment and also one of his last. He would be dead within six months.

Perhaps the most nuanced commentary on the violence came from an unexpected source, the pictorial newspaper *Harper's Weekly*, which at first insisted, "There was nothing peculiar to . . . the Irish race in this riot." Indeed, the paper took pains to laud the courageous Irishmen who had come forward to save the children of the orphans' asylum, and heaped praise on Archbishop Hughes and "the entire Roman Catholic priesthood to a man" for condemning the outbreak. Like Orestes Brownson, *Harper's* instead faulted the "despicable politicians and their newspaper organs"—meaning Democrats—for provoking the mob. "They denounced Mr. Lincoln as an imbecile tyrant," the weekly reminded readers. "They denounced the war as a needless, fratricidal, and abolition war. . . . Under these circumstances," *Harper's* concluded, "who can wonder at riots breaking out?"[98]

Just a week later, however, as the city began clearing debris, even *Harper's* succumbed to the festering resentment against Irish New Yorkers. On August 1, the paper published a two-page spread featuring engraved images of the grisliest scenes of horror, including "Sacking a Drug Store in Second Avenue" (where Colonel O'Brien was killed) and "Charge of the Police on the Rioters at the 'Tribune' Office." The thugs portrayed in these scenes bore stock features long familiar in derogatory caricatures of Irishmen: simian facial structure, noses swollen by drink, and battered plug hats. Such clichés contradicted the narrative advanced by the paper only days earlier, but likely provoked more attention. *Harper's* readers subscribed to the paper for illustrations, not editorial content, and each of its harsh anti-Irish pictures was surely worth at least a thousand of its earlier conciliatory words.[99]

Not long after the riot, the pro-Union Southerner James R. Gilmore, editor of the magazine *Continental Monthly*, spent three hours at the White House trying to persuade President Lincoln that New York governor Horatio Seymour had seditiously plotted the uprising to give antiwar Democrats control of the nation's largest metropolis. Now Gilmore urged that Lincoln name an investigator—a kind of special prosecutor—to conduct an official inquiry into the insurrection.[100] The President demurred. "You have heard of sitting on a volcano," he explained. "We are sitting upon two. One is blazing away already, and

SACKING A DRUG STORE IN SECOND AVENUE.

Among the grisly illustrations of the New York draft riots published in
Harper's Weekly was this woodcut of the drugstore rampage that claimed the life
of Irish pro-conscription Union colonel Henry F. O'Brien.

the other will blaze away the moment we scrape a little loose dirt from
the top of the crater. Better let the dirt alone, at least for the present.
One rebellion at a time is about as much as we can conveniently handle."[101] Especially if a second front might ensnare immigrant Americans in further ethnic unrest.

In mid-October, Lincoln finally received one piece of cheering
news from New York's Irish community: an unexpected letter from
some young men he had not seen for more than three years. The note
bore the signatures of the "poor boys" of the Five Points House of
Industry, the facility he had visited after speaking at Cooper Union in
1860. The youngsters—Patrick McCarty, John Donahue, William
Ryan, and John O'Neil, claiming to speak for more than a hundred of
their fellow students—fondly remembered that Lincoln had once told
them that "the way was open to every boy present, if honest, industri-
ous, and perserv[er]ing, to the attainment of a high and honorable
position." Now the boys wanted belatedly to "congratulate" the visitor

who had gone on to win "the highest honors in the gift of a free people." As the young correspondents put it, "[Y]our own life history illustrates the truth of the words you then addressed to us." The students assured Lincoln they were praying that God "to further honor you as His instrument in liberating a race, and in leading your countrymen through present troubles, to righteousness, peace, and prosperity."[102] The note no doubt lightened Lincoln's mood.

In political terms, however, both the draft and the riots hardened Irish opposition to Lincoln and the Republicans. As a measure of consolation, the bloody milestone might have temporarily relieved Lincoln of political pressure from the "Dutch." When Emil Preetorius of the St. Louis *Westliche Post* visited the White House at the end of September, he arrived determined, like Taussig and other German visitors before him, to lobby for immediate emancipation in Missouri. But unlike previous advocates, Preetorius left convinced that Lincoln was correct in emphasizing border-state loyalty. "We Germans," he claimed, "had not felt so kindly toward Mr. Lincoln since he had set aside Fremont's proclamation of emancipation."[103]

That sympathetic attitude would not last, but for now it helped Lincoln over the rocky shoals of ethnic politics in Missouri and elsewhere in the West. That fall, Ohio voters overwhelmingly rejected a Copperhead candidate for governor—ironically, the same man, Democrat Clement L. Vallandigham, who a year earlier had championed the right of Jewish soldiers, most of them immigrants themselves, to select their own chaplains.

· · ·

Resistance to the draft ebbed only when Congress passed a Conscription Act amendment that did away with substitution-for-pay. Irish opposition to Black recruitment, however, remained fevered. It took the Irish-born poet, humorist, and Union officer Charles Graham Halpine to make a macabre but incontrovertible point about "colored" troops. "Every black regiment in garrison would relieve a white regiment for service in the field," he pointed out, and "every ball stopped by a black man would save the life of a white soldier." Halpine, who wrote comic articles and verse under the pseudonym "Private Miles O'Reilly," drove home the argument in a blatantly racist poem with a double entendre title: "Sambo's Right to Be Kilt."[104]

Reportedly Lincoln enjoyed the verse so much that he convinced himself it might help reconcile the Irish to Black recruitment. According to fellow Halpine admirer John Hay, himself a gifted writer, the poem inevitably reminded the President of a joke—about the prostitute who dropped a valuable half eagle into a church collection plate to atone for her sins. Though she had earned the coin by doing bad, as the pious but impecunious deacon conceded, her donation would do good; hence he would keep it. "I have no doubt, Hay," the President reportedly remarked, "that O'Reilly, in whom you seem to take such an interest, might be a great deal better man than he is" (Halpine was a Democrat). Meanwhile, "that song of his is good and will do good."[105] According to newspaper correspondent Noah Brooks, the President "had a dread of people who could not appreciate the fun of such things." Funny stories, particularly those of the ethnic variety, "gave him refuge from himself and his weariness."[106] Though Halpine had lampooned Lincoln in the past, the President bore the writer no malice—particularly since he made him laugh.

Halpine had been an associate editor of the *New York Times* and part owner of a literary newspaper called the *New York Leader* before, in the words of an early chronicler, he "laid down the pen and took up the sword." In truth, while he did serve in the New York Sixty-Ninth, he never entirely abandoned his writing. In fact, he based his most acclaimed fictional character, the dense, hard-drinking "O'Reilly," on soldiers he encountered in his own Hibernian regiments.[107] The humorist comically described Miles as six feet seven inches in height, "a brawny, large boned, rather good-looking young Milesian [Celt], with curly reddish hair, gray eyes, one of which has a cataract upon it, a cocked nose . . . and the usual strong type of Irish forehead." In

Halpine's account, O'Reilly's "whole countenance beams with a candor and unreserve equal to a mealy potato which has burst its skin or jacket by too rapid boiling."[108] Despite such hyperbole, many readers remained unsure whether the comical figure was real or fictional.

Halpine quickly became one of Lincoln's favorite humorists. In turn, Halpine, now writing primarily for the *New York Herald*, began including Lincoln himself in some of "O'Reilly's" imagined adventures. In one such tale, Miles convinces the President to pardon him after he is imprisoned for attempting to bribe the secretaries of war and the navy. In another mock situation, O'Reilly gets recruited by the administration to adapt the President's funniest stories into songs.

Then, in November 1863, Halpine published a *Herald* satire situating O'Reilly at a White House reception, greeted there by its legendary Irish—or, in Halpine's hands, Italian—doorkeeper, who at the time was nearing the end of his long service at the mansion. According to the absurdist story, "there was a great scene of handshaking at the door between Private O'Reilly and Edward McManus, the chatty old grayhaired gentleman from Italy—where O'Reilly knew him—who has kept watch at the gate through five administrations, now assisted by Mr. Thomas Burns, also from Italy, who has out lived the storms of two reigns. It was 'God bless you, Miles,' and 'God bless you kindly, Edward,' for as many as ten minutes, the handshaking being fast and furious all the time."[109]

Then, the deadpan hoax continued, General Thomas Meagher (described as having known the O'Reilly clan back on "the Green Isle which was their common birthplace") presents O'Reilly to Lincoln, remarking "that he was happy to have the honor of introducing to one who was regarded as the Father of the Army this *enfant perdu*, or lost boy of the Irish race." Lincoln disdains making a formal speech, explaining, "In this position it was not wise to talk foolishly, and he would, therefore, but rarely talk at all"—a remark taken from a widely reported line he had actually ad-libbed the day before his Gettysburg

Address.[110] Instead, the President relates a racist "story about the Widow Zollicoffer's Darkey," replete with the n-word, to the uproarious laughter of the diplomats, military men, government officials, and other guests, while O'Reilly continues standing awkwardly at attention. Ultimately, Miles heads upstairs to chief of staff John Nicolay's office for a sip of whiskey-laced water, then joins the Lincoln family for Thanksgiving turkey. The burlesque seemed at some level so believable that many readers concluded that Halpine, if not O'Reilly, had actually visited the White House.[111]

A spectral Abraham Lincoln uncoils from his chair to greet the fictional Irish private Miles O'Reilly in a fanciful illustration from humorist Charles G. Halpine's 1864 book of comic essays.

For the next few weeks, however, Halpine worried that he had crossed a line with the satire. No word had come back from his friends in the administration regarding Lincoln's reaction, and Halpine feared he had perhaps been "too funny" this time. He need not have worried.

The simple truth was that Lincoln had come down with smallpox after returning from Gettysburg and remained bedridden, for once in no mood for jokes.

At last, John Hay wrote to assure the satirist, "The President was immensely amused with Miles's last," adding with his own humorous touch: "He is too sick to read and not well enough to object to anything. So I had him at my mercy and read him into a fever."[112] If such were the case, Hay must have been as relieved as Halpine, for the secretary had actually supplied the author with much of the comic material for O'Reilly's imagined "visit," including "the *personnel* of the White House"—like the hilarious idea of doorkeeper McManus's supposedly Italian heritage. At first, Hay had cautioned Halpine, "You had better far get up your own jokes than ask anything authentic from me" but in the end invented and leaked raw material that "O'Reilly" adapted verbatim.[113] Hay probably dared do so only because Lincoln remained distracted by his illness. Yet there was a more sober aspect to Lincoln's appreciation for Halpine: the hope that the humorist might boost overall Union morale and, in the bargain, soothe the still-angry Irish community. In the wake of the New York City draft riots, Lincoln named Halpine an assistant adjutant general on the staff of General Dix. If anything could convince the residents that the President was serious about enforcing conscription while reestablishing respectful relations with the Irish, perhaps it was the elevation of an Irish humorist. (Halpine, his eyesight failing, spent the rest of the war fulfilling the "congenial duty of arresting bounty swindlers"—rascals who accepted bonuses for enlisting but then vanished without serving.[114])

Halpine embraced his new military assignment with tongue-in-cheek gratitude by having Miles O'Reilly bless Lincoln for his recent phantom pardon in verses that turned out to be both amusing and prophetic:

> Long life to you, Misther Lincoln!
> May you die both late an' aisy;

An' whin you lie wid the top of aich toe
Turned up to the roots of a daisy,
May this be your epitaph, nately writ—
"Though thraitors abused him vilely,
He was honest an' kindly, he loved a joke,
An' he pardoned Miles O'Reilly."[115]

Amid the painful thoughts of German disenchantment and Irish sedition, perhaps healed a bit by this dose of rib-tickling blarney, Lincoln thereafter roused himself from his post-Gettysburg sickbed to work on his Annual Message to Congress, and, with it, his history-altering initiative on immigration.

CHAPTER TEN

This Noble Effort

Under Lincoln, the door to America would open wider at last—though at some cost to immigrants who were already here. The President's December 8, 1863, Annual Message to Congress indeed proposed landmark reform, but through initiatives at once welcoming and forbidding. On the one hand, Lincoln called for the first-ever federal legislation to encourage foreign immigration. On the other, he sought to codify the obligation of foreign-born American residents—including those who had only filed for, but not yet earned, citizenship—to serve their adopted country in the military. With rights, he argued, should come responsibilities.

He was consistent in this belief. Seven months earlier, Lincoln had tried cracking down on immigrants who sought exemptions from the draft through pleas of "alienage"—loyalty to their countries of origin that unsurprisingly grew more ardent once the conscription law took effect. To avoid military service, some immigrants had even renounced their newly obtained American citizenship or withdrawn pending applications for their papers. In response, Lincoln issued a proclamation declaring it unlawful for foreigners to shirk the draft if they had already declared "their intention to become citizens" or had previously voted in any American election.[1]

Now, in one of the opening passages of his Annual Message, Lincoln asked that Congress codify this executive order in federal law. There was "reason to believe," he insisted, "that many persons born in foreign countries, who have declared their intention to become citizens, or who have been fully naturalized," still "evaded the military duty required of them by denying the fact." Conversely, Lincoln suggested, some "foreigners frequently become citizens of the United States for the sole purpose of evading duties imposed by the laws of their native countries." Once naturalized, they might "repair" to their homeland and claim that their new American citizenship excused them from legal obligations in their country of origin. To close this loophole as well, Lincoln urged Congress to bar any naturalized American citizen and most resident foreigners from sidestepping "other civil obligation, on the ground of alienage."[2]

Only then did the President turn to the matter of "encouraging" immigration—what amounted to the first federal effort to stimulate foreign settlement in America since the repeal of the Sedition Act at the dawn of the century. Here was a president making good on his preinaugural vow to "throw aught" in the way of "any abroad who desire to make this the land of their adoption."* The timing for reform seemed ideal.

As Lincoln pointed out, the war-torn country now faced labor shortages across many industries, while "tens of thousands of persons, destitute of remunerative occupation," stood ready "to emigrate to the United States if essential, but very cheap, assistance can be afforded them." In the President's view, immigrants "ought to receive the

---

*From Lincoln's remarks in Cincinnati, February 12, 1861.

attention and support of the government."[3] And Lincoln meant such "support" to be tangible. The government itself would allocate federal funding to underwrite relocation, an all but revolutionary idea and surely the apex of Lincoln's own long evolution on the immigration issue.

Lincoln poses at photographer Alexander Gardner's Washington gallery with his chief aides, John Nicolay (left) and John Hay, just weeks before he began work on his 1863 Annual Message to Congress.

Some have speculated as to why Lincoln prefaced this generous proposal with the rather chilling ones that preceded it. They need look no further for an explanation, or at least a precedent, than his Annual Message of the previous year. His 1862 text had featured Lincoln's stirring declaration, "In *giving* freedom to the *slave*, we *assure* freedom to the *free*." Yet, a few paragraphs earlier, he had proposed appropriating federal funds "for colonizing free colored persons, with their own consent," reiterating: "I cannot make it better known than it already is, that I strongly favor colonization." And as he icily justified what sounded like a call for reverse immigration for Blacks: "With deportation, even to a limited extent, enhanced wages to white labor is mathematically certain. . . . Reduce the supply of black labor, by colonizing the black laborer out of the country, and, by precisely so much, you increase the demand for, and wages of, white labor."[4] Now, a year later, he had abandoned his longtime commitment to colonization with the mass recruitment of Black troops; yet he still felt the need to satisfy both enlightened and retrograde constituencies in tandem—just as he had once labored to balance conflicting interests by appealing to both foreign-born and Know-Nothing voters back in Illinois. By late 1863 he was eager to swell the white domestic workforce by stimulating European immigration, but simultaneously he wanted to assure those who feared an influx of undesirable—or at least undesired—aliens that, like the native-born, new citizens would be required to meet their obligations as Americans.

These society-altering proposals, it must be said, generated little public attention. The press focused instead on a far bigger bombshell in the 1863 Annual Message: Lincoln's generous (some charged overly lenient) proposals on both amnesty for Rebels and postwar reconstruction for the South. Newspapers that did publish summaries of the full message referred to the immigration initiative only in passing. One Western daily noted merely that the President had mentioned "the expediency of establishing a system for the encouraging of immigration," condensing Lincoln's justification by paraphrasing: "In the fields of industry there is a great deficiency of laborers."[5] Secretary of State Seward thought the message was generally "well received" but as yet made no comment on the immigration initiative himself.[6]

One publication that did enthusiastically endorse the President's proposal was John Williams's New York–based *Hardware Reporter*—a trade and labor monthly whose technical-sounding name belied its considerable reach. "Future historians," Williams predicted, would "assign a most important place in history" to immigration reform. "Surely no more profitable use of the people's money could be made in expending a moderate sum in facilitating emigration of a large number of laborers, especially of skilled workers, to this country." The editorial urged that "Congress . . . promptly do its duty."[7]

The response from Capitol Hill proved mixed. Although Lincoln had specifically urged the House and Senate to set a time limit beyond which no foreign-born "Citizen of the United States residing abroad" could cite his rights as an American to avoid obligations in his homeland, Congress never acted on this request.[8] On February 24, 1864, however, it did amend the 1863 Conscription Act to refuse draft exemption to any naturalized citizen or foreign resident who had held public office or cast votes in a local, state, or territorial election.

As for Lincoln's main initiative, an Act to Encourage Immigration, it too moved through Congress expeditiously. Within days, the Senate Agriculture Committee began consideration of a bill to extend the benefits of the 1862 Homestead Act to foreign immigrants (it subsequently passed). Concurrently, the House Agriculture Committee took up a proposal to create a federal bureau to underwrite transatlantic passages. Emphasizing its potential economic benefits, Congressman Ignatius L. Donnelly, Republican of Minnesota, argued: "Throw wide the doors to emigration . . . and in twenty years the results of labors of the immigrant and their children will add to the wealth of the country a sum sufficient to pay the entire debt created by this war."[9]

Not everyone agreed. Democratic congressman Daniel W. Voorhees of Indiana, grandly describing himself as "a friend to the stranger who seeks our shores to enjoy liberty or to increase his stores," denounced the notion of offering immigrants "pecuniary inducements to come and take the places of our lost and dead—to fill the empty chairs around bereaved firesides."[10] Antiwar Copperheads like Voorhees were not about to debate immigration without denouncing the administration over the battlefield casualties endured by native-born Americans. In castigating Lincoln's proposal, Voorhees and his followers thus introduced what anti-immigrant forces would later derisively call the "replacement theory."

Democratic objections did not deter Republican floor managers from referring Lincoln's proposals to a House Select Committee on Emigration, which happened to be chaired by the President's old friend, Illinois representative Elihu Washburne (who a year earlier had hailed Grant's expulsion of the Jews as "the wisest order yet made by a military command"). Quickly, the Washburne committee began marking up its own bill to create a Bureau of Immigration. As the committee's report argued, "Never before in our history has there existed so unprecedented a demand for labor as at the present time," from "the agricultural districts of the northwest" to "the coal and iron mines of Pennsylvania" and the "gold and silver mines of California." Such manpower needs, it agreed, could be filled only by "those of the Old World who seek new homes in this country of free institutions, where land is cheap, food is plenty, and labor remunerative."[11]

Then, on February 18, 1864, Senator John Sherman of Ohio, younger brother of the increasingly prominent Union general, introduced a Senate version of the bill but added a cautionary note. Sherman worried that individual government bounties to immigrants might attract "the idle, very poor, or vicious of foreign populations" while making no tangible difference to "the thrifty" who had already saved enough money to book passage to America.[12] The government-financing proposal had hit a roadblock.

A month later, when Secretary of State Seward brought up the pending bills at a March 18 cabinet meeting, both Treasury Secretary Salmon P. Chase and Interior Secretary John P. Usher voiced support. But Navy Secretary Gideon Welles "quietly" expressed reservations. The blond-wigged, white-bearded New Englander whom Lincoln called "Neptune" fretted that too much government "meddling" might scare off ongoing private investment in efforts to woo foreign workers here and thus "retard instead of promoting emigration." As Welles put it: "Millions are now contributed to aid friends to emigrate, but this would wholly stop if the Government came in to assist. . . . As a general thing, I am averse to government bounties."[13] Seward seemed persuaded. By then he harbored objections of his own.

Afterward, Seward, too, began encouraging congressional leaders to modify their approach to Lincoln's proposal. Citing his prerogatives on matters of foreign policy, he made clear in a lengthy and widely published letter to the Washburne committee that he did not want an independent immigration bureau operating outside his purview.[14] He also implied that offering European laborers federally funded inducements to migrate might offend the foreign governments the administration had worked so hard to keep neutral in the American war. There was irony in this cautionary view, since Seward himself had only recently urged diplomatic and consular representatives abroad to promote American opportunity—generating a "perfect 'rush'" of prospective emigrants to the Paris legation and unleashing renewed Confederate charges that the Union planned to replenish its ranks with foreign mercenaries.[15]

Now Seward added that underwriting immigration might be an imprudent use of federal funding, too. He estimated it would cost fifteen dollars to transport each foreign passenger, and with "100,000 needy immigrants" yearning to cross the ocean, the government would have to set aside a million and a half dollars each year just to finance their voyages. (To put that supposedly prohibitive number in perspective, the war was already costing the government a million dollars—daily.) Even though Seward acknowledged that the country "derives incalculable advantages from every considerable accession to its population," he made clear that he "could not recommend such an appropriation."[16] Far better, he advised, to let private industry lend travel funds directly to potential immigrants if they agreed to a fixed term of employment here. If Lincoln raised any objections to watering down his original proposal, his concerns remained unrecorded. A gradualist by nature, Lincoln likely saw the wisdom in the more cautious approach—even if it threatened to substitute a system akin to indentured servitude for his original vision of direct government aid to lure foreign workers.

Not surprisingly, Seward's longtime newspaper ally Henry Raymond also began advocating this alternative. Government payment "of the passage of the emigrant," his *New York Times* opined in mid-April, would be "injudicious." Raymond warned in the purplest of prose that "the moment our Government has a hand in it, the odium of all this will taint it in every country of Europe. We shall be called a Union of sharpers. Every man who is fleeced of his earnings on the voyage, every woman debauched, every unfortunate emigrant landing in a pestiferous swamp . . . every unlucky and disappointed foreigner reaching these shores, will have a tale of horrors and disgraceful rascality to relate against the Government of America."[17]

Worse, Raymond shamelessly adopted the ugliest tropes about the foreign-born, cautioning that "a system of hired emigration would export to us the very refuse of the sinks of Germany and Ireland. Every parish or principality that had some peculiarly lazy and wretched subjects, and who were a burden on the community, would be sure to send them to the nearest seaport, and there let them quietly take advantage of this generous offer of our Government." Raymond advised merely regulating ocean travel more rigorously and enlarging New York's overcrowded Castle Garden arrival center into "a national institution" that provided "a great inducement" to emigrants.[18] Castle Garden, the emigrant landing depot that sat at the southern tip of Manhattan on the site of a onetime fort and former theater, had begun serving as an entry point in 1855.

In response to Seward's concerns, and now those of the newspaper widely considered a quasi-official administration organ, both houses of Congress obligingly scaled back the landmark legislation. Instead of creating a new emigrant bureau, the tamped-down but still sweeping bill authorized the President only to name a $2,500-per-year commissioner of immigration reporting directly to the State Department. Rather than provide federal funds to subsidize travel, it encouraged

Union officers recruit newly arrived German and Irish immigrants
as they exit the landing depot at Castle Garden on
the southern tip of Manhattan.

private employers and agencies to lend foreigners the money to come
to America. And it obliged workers to repay the resulting debt on time
or else risk, among other penalties, forfeiting whatever free land they
might acquire here through the Homestead Act.[19]

New immigrant workers would be required to set aside up to
twelve months of their labor to pay off private cash advances for their
transport to the United States. But to spur migration, now no foreign
arrival would be subject to compulsory military service after all, until
he voluntarily renounced his allegiance to the country of his birth and
declared "his intention to become a citizen of the United States." The
U.S. Emigrant Office in New York, the city where most new arrivals
were expected to disembark, would be tasked with helping to link
foreign workers to American jobs and arranging transportation for
them within the United States.[20]

At least the compromise would mandate additional regulations to
safeguard passengers traveling aboard ship to American shores. And
acting against his own recommendations, Seward would soon establish a separate Immigration Bureau after all. In turn, the new bureau

would begin contracting with private firms like the dominant New York–based American Emigrant Company, to recruit skilled foreign laborers, advance the money to fund their voyages, and place them in good jobs. Though it burdened these workers with substantial debt, the law at last placed the federal government squarely in the immigration-oversight business, upending century-old traditions under which states and localities governed the flow of new arrivals.

By late June, Horace Greeley's *New York Tribune* belatedly joined in opposing any "scheme of furnishing a free passage at the expense of the Government," citing a potential "drain upon the treasury" that would attract a class of *"governmental immigrants"* from "the poor-houses and jails of Europe," destined to become "a charge upon public charity."[21] Added to the *Times'* earlier misgivings, the salvo ended all talk of re-kindling Lincoln's generous original proposal. A week later, the paper at least acknowledged that immigrants and immigration had "constantly strengthened" the Union war effort, denying Confederate claims that Union recruiters had been busy luring—or "crimping"—foreigners into the military. No, Greeley insisted, for every immigrant who hoped to "share our destiny . . . there are ten who would gladly follow."[22]

After the House and Senate each passed slightly different versions of the compromise immigration bill at the end of June, a conference committee reconciled remaining differences and both chambers passed a final law on July 2.[23] Just two days later—on Independence Day, the holiday on which Lincoln had once saluted foreign-born Americans in Chicago—he put his signature on the milestone legislation. Even adulterated, it remained the most proactive federal immigration reform in generations. A month later, the President ordered the secretary of the Treasury to send the required $25,000 to the State Department to fund the new program.[24]

Otherwise, the law left the financing aspect to for-profit entities like the aforementioned American Emigrant Office—which soon confirmed its preeminence by subletting some of its New York office space to the nascent federal bureau. Surely that odd transaction reminded many reformers that Lincoln's hoped-for overhaul was less than ideal.[25] But it was a start. And even before the law took effect, marketplace forces kicked in: mine owners, for example, began reaching out directly to American consulates abroad to invite workers here from Scandinavia. By June, more than five hundred skilled copper miners were headed to Michigan and Maine without any government benefaction.[26]

That summer, convinced that the Lincoln administration was still luring the Irish here to ensnare them in the Union army, Sir Robert Peel, Britain's secretary for Ireland, testified before Parliament that as many as thirty thousand Irishmen had been misled into immigrating to the United States and then all but dragooned into its armed forces. In the face of persistent reports that the military solicited enrollees right off the boat, the *Irish-American* newspaper warned that the army recruiting station that indeed stood near Castle Garden encouraged the British and French, along with "rebel emissaries and sympathizers," to think the military ranks "were being filled by the forced enlistments of arriving emigrants."[27] Still the new arrivals poured into the city, with a number of young men indeed joining the service.

Whether all these population-swelling developments would resonate to Lincoln's benefit politically remained to be seen. By the time the President affixed his name to the federal immigration act, he had only recently become his party's nominee for reelection. Yet he was widely expected to lose his bid for a second term, in part, ironically, because immigrant voters had been souring on him for months. "If we come triumphantly out of this war, with a presidential election in the midst of it," the German-born Francis Lieber nonetheless predicted late that summer, "I shall call it the greatest miracle in all the historic course of events."[28]

. . .

The race for president had begun to take shape even before Lincoln's 1863 trip to Gettysburg. Who, a curious White House visitor asked

Lincoln that year, would most likely win the White House the following November? Lincoln looked no further for a politic nonreply than
to the trove of Irish stories he had been committing to memory since
his days in Illinois.

"My opinion as to who will be the next President," he replied with
a smile, "is very much the opinion that Pat had about the handsome
funeral. You see Pat was standing opposite the State House in Springfield, with a short black pipe in his mouth and his hands in his empty
breeches pockets. 'Pat, whose funeral is passing?' inquired old Jake
Miller, who seemed impressed with a belief that an Irishman must
know everything. 'Plaize your honor,' replied Pat, removing his pipe
for a moment, 'it isn't meself can say for sartin, but to the best o'my
belief, the funeral belongs to the gintleman or lady that's in the coffin!'

"Now it's very much the same about the next presidency," Lincoln
concluded. "I can't say for certain who will be the people's choice; but
to the best of my belief, it will be the successful candidate!"[29]

A few months later, when Lincoln's supporters brought him the
disquieting news that Ohio Republicans might bolt to their native son,
Treasury Secretary Salmon Chase, for the Republican nod, Lincoln
turned not to morbid thoughts of cabinet disloyalty but again to his
vast storehouse of Irish humor. He told this story to artist-in-residence
Francis B. Carpenter:

"Some years ago, a couple of 'emigrants,' fresh from the 'Emerald
Isle,' seeking labor, were making their way toward the West. Coming
suddenly, one evening, upon a pond of water, they were greeted with a
grand chorus of bull-frogs,—a kind of music they had never before
heard. 'B-a-u-m!' 'B-a-u-m!' Overcome with terror, they clutched their
'shillelahs,' and crept cautiously forward, straining their eyes in every
direction, to catch a glimpse of the enemy; but he was not to be found!
At last a happy idea seized the foremost one,—he sprang to his companion and exclaimed, 'And sure, Jamie! it is my opinion it's nothing
but a *noise!*'"[30] So, Lincoln believed, was the talk of a Chase White
House boom.

In this case, however, the noise produced genuine political reverberations. Just days after the President released his pro-immigration December 1863 Annual Message, the St. Louis *Neue Zeit* ("New Times") renewed German demands that Lincoln dismiss General Henry Halleck along with conservative postmaster general Montgomery Blair and attorney general Edward Bates (himself a Missourian)—or else face a revolt in the party. "His creatures work like ants to secure his candidacy," the paper bitterly complained of the President, "and will finally deceive the people with wonderful tales of Lincoln's liberal sentiments and future intentions, unless the eyes of the people are previously opened concerning Mr. Lincoln's very equivocal political and public character."[31] Even Joseph Medill of the *Chicago Tribune* privately urged Lincoln to jettison Bates and Halleck and restore Sigel, reminding Lincoln that "Germans of all classes" remained "deeply offended" by the treatment the general had endured. Give Sigel a new command, Medill believed, and German hostility to Lincoln would "slacken and then mostly cease."[32]

For months, buoyed by Republican disaffection, Salmon Chase pursued the party's nomination—not quite publicly, as overt political ambition was seldom rewarded by nineteenth-century voters or convention delegates—but through the efforts of congressional radicals and their press allies. These now included Horace Greeley, who preferred Chase for the nomination, and if not the Treasury secretary, then Generals Benjamin Butler, William Rosecrans, John C. Frémont, Ulysses S. Grant, William T. Sherman, or just about any alternative to Lincoln. But the Chase effort collapsed by March 1864, and the mortified secretary offered (not for the first time) to quit the cabinet—only to be stunned when Lincoln actually accepted his resignation.[33]

The most serious threat to Lincoln's reelection instead arose from Frémont, again a White House aspirant despite his all but disqualifying failures in both the western and eastern theaters of the war, not to mention his unsuccessful 1856 race for the presidency. Because he had once attempted to emancipate slaves within his Missouri command—

an order squelched by Lincoln—he remained the darling of abolition-ist forces (particularly Germans) in that border state, where Lincoln's own Emancipation Proclamation still did not apply. By spring 1864, Frémont emerged as a potential third-party spoiler. Unlikely as he was to win the presidency himself, he threatened to siphon off enough German votes in the West to split the Republicans and elect a Demo-crat to the White House. The beneficiary of the rift would be the likely Democratic nominee, another discarded general: George McClellan, dismissed by Lincoln back in November 1862.

It was not only that Lincoln now seemed too conservative for the abolitionists. Germans in the West already also chafed under Lincoln's continued use of war powers to suppress free expression and the free press. To the further chagrin of progressives, the administration now authorized the military to intervene in labor strikes if walkouts were judged detrimental to the war effort. In March 1864, defiant workers struck the Parrott gun foundry in Cold Spring, New York, just across the Hudson River from West Point. Lincoln had visited both the mil-itary academy and the munitions plant just two years earlier. In re-sponse to the work stoppage, federal troops took possession of the town and imprisoned strikers, many of them foreign-born. When iron molders struck for higher wages in St. Louis, a city under martial law, General Rosecrans issued a military order banning strikes there altogether—prohibiting even labor organizing—"in any manufactur-ing establishment where any article is ordinarily made which may be required for use in the . . . military, naval, or transport service."[34]

In protest, Charles Bernays, the German Jewish editor whom Linc-oln had named consul to Zurich three years earlier, urged the Presi-dent to allow the labor strife to "work out itself according to the natural laws of public economy and not by the sword of a military commander." Only in heavily German St. Louis, he protested, had an army officer placed "himself between the employers & employees" and ruled "in favor of the first. . . . We are not through with the destruction of slavery and we already begin to attack free labor." As Bernays saw matters, generals should never be "allowed to overstep even under the pretense of their orders being necessary to save the Union."[35] At his political peril, Lincoln ignored the plea.

Economic pressures multiplied Lincoln's woes. As inflation also took its toll and wages lagged, worker discontent spilled over to New York, Philadelphia, Albany, Troy, Cincinnati, and Pittsburgh. In late March, the German Workingmen's Association assembled for a tumultuous mass meeting at a Chicago hall "literally crammed with German citizens" and strongly denounced the administration. Under the headline "The Germans in Earnest Against Old Abe," a local paper reported attendees "unmistakably in favor of Fremont for their next President."[36] Returning to St. Louis following the rally, Emil Preetorius told another cheering crowd that he no longer wanted "a half and half radical like Abraham Lincoln" in the White House. Seconding the sentiment, Missouri legislator Caspar Butz roared that he "did not think that there was a single man present at the meeting who would stand up [and] say that Abraham Lincoln should be re-elected." To Butz, Lincoln suddenly seemed "the weakest and worst man that ever filled the Presidential chair."[37]

The anti-Lincoln brushfire spread rapidly. In New York, members of a key German American political club announced "that under no circumstances whatever will they support President Lincoln for a second term." A brand-new, pro-Frémont newspaper hit the city's streets under the name *New Nation*, denouncing Lincoln in each edition. Meanwhile a long-established newspaper, the *New York Herald*, mischievously suggested that Democrats "fuse" with the radicals and "adopt Fremont as their candidate."[38] From the President's own home state, the long-supportive Illinois *Staats-Anzeiger*, once owned by his friend George Schneider, opted to "cut loose decidedly and forever from Lincoln and his policy, and to *protest against his re-election under all circumstances and at any cost*." Instead, the paper "booked the name of JOHN C. FREMONT as candidate for the Presidency." Back in St. Louis, the *Volksblat* ("People's Newspaper") concurred that, where

Lincoln was concerned, one presidential term "ought to be sufficient," a potential second term "dangerous."[39]

Nor did Germans forget their aggrieved hero Franz Sigel. Still plagued by controversy and shackled by limited opportunities, Sigel had been transferred to the Department of the Susquehanna, where he continued to lead troops. Then, on May 15, 1864, he performed poorly at the Battle of New Market against teenage cadets from the Virginia Military Institute, prompting his removal from active command. After that humiliation, as John Hay reported from the White House with his usual panache, the long-feared "Dutch Revolt" over Sigel's downfall amounted to "very small beer."[40] In this instance, Hay proved naive. As the once-proud boast "I fights mit Sigel" yielded to the lament "I fights mit Sigel no more," Lincoln's rift with the German progressives only widened.[41]

Just two weeks after New Market, on May 29—with party stalwarts scheduled soon to gather for the Republican National Convention, and by then certain to renominate Lincoln despite widespread German discontent—a breakaway gathering of disaffected party men calling themselves the Radical Democracy assembled at Cleveland for a formal nominating convention of their own. There, a mere 158 delegates, many German-born, sent a thunderbolt through the 1864 race by formally naming Frémont as their candidate for president.[42]

Just a few days later, Republicans gaveled to order as scheduled in once-hostile Baltimore—with the organization now rebranded as the National Union Party to attract pro-war Democrats. As expected, delegates nominated Lincoln by acclamation on June 8.[43] Democrat Andrew Johnson, the only senator from a seceded state to remain in his chair during the war, became Lincoln's new running mate. In addition to applauding the incumbent president's "practical wisdom" and "unselfish patriotism," the party platform—with Lincoln's quiet but vital blessing—called for a constitutional amendment ending slavery everywhere in the United States, a plank expected to assuage German abolitionists among many others.[44]

Currier & Ives, which also offered campaign posters featuring
Lincoln and McClellan, issued this 1864 print to showcase the short-lived
third-party presidential candidacy of John C. Frémont.

Largely overlooked amid the attention given that monumental initiative was "Platform Plank Number Eight." It resolved that "foreign immigration, which in the past has added so much to the wealth, development of resources and increase of power to the nation, the asylum of the oppressed of all nations, should be fostered and encouraged by a liberal and just policy"—an acknowledgment that the bill then just making its way through Congress might come up short of this goal.[45] Thus did a second Lincoln administration promise society-altering new commitments to expand both Black freedom and foreign immigration—but only if Lincoln could become the first president since Andrew Jackson to win a second term. And for that, he again needed German votes, just as he had in 1860.

Immigration and abolition planks notwithstanding, liberal Germans, once ardent and crucial Lincoln supporters, clung tenaciously to

Frémont. In mid-June, the *New York Herald* reported that German Americans, still "exceedingly bitter against" the President, "would not, under any contingency, vote for Abraham Lincoln for another term."⁴⁶ The St. Louis *Neue Zeit* made the mass defection more personal, decrying "the organization of blood-suckers created by Mr. Lincoln for the perpetuation of his own unnatural power" and beseeching its readers to "raise the ticket of the Radical Democracy."⁴⁷

Lincoln's earliest German supporters could express only dismay. From Europe, outgoing American minister to Spain Gustave Koerner tried pointing out that foreign leaders still regarded Lincoln as "the only man who could pilot the ship of state safely through the raging storm." Yet the diplomat acknowledged the dissension back home. "What I most regretted was that so many Germans were found in opposition to him," Koerner declared. "They were most radical on the slavery question, and Lincoln was too slow for them. They were honest enough, but highly impractical idealists." A mortified Koerner acknowledged that the Radical Democracy convention had been "principally gotten up by some Germans in Illinois, Missouri, and New York." Whether or not they could be persuaded to return to the Republican fold before November, Koerner did not venture to guess.⁴⁸

By August, a Boston paper counted twenty-six German-language newspapers for Frémont and but six for Lincoln, predicting that "Lincoln's vote among the Germans will be limited and scattering. They are almost all against him."⁴⁹ Later that month, Union Party chairman Henry J. Raymond glumly advised Lincoln that he could not possibly win a second term, a prognosis the President himself echoed in a confidential memorandum that conceded it had become "exceedingly probable that this Administration will not be re-elected."⁵⁰

. . .

From his regimental headquarters in Virginia, Carl Schurz viewed the situation no less pessimistically—and had been trying to so warn Lincoln for months. Anti-administrant criticism "had assumed a virulent temper," he worried, and would "prevent" Lincoln from winning the race.

Unlike the unshakable Koerner, however, Schurz had begun to believe that some of Lincoln's policies and personality quirks might indeed be "open to criticism." The President lacked "energy." He had "loose ways of conducting the public business." And some (perhaps even Schurz—he had said as much back in 1861) found fault with "his rustic manners, and with the robust character of his humor, and concluded that the Republic must have a President more mindful of the dignity of his office."[51] Schurz made no mention of whether he, too, hoped Lincoln might yet bow out and yield to a more "dignified" nominee like Chase. It was not such a far-fetched scenario. From New York, Greeley now advanced a scheme under which the Union Party would indeed reconvene, dump Lincoln, and replace him with a more electable standard-bearer.[52]

As early as February 1864, Schurz had sought a private meeting with Lincoln to share his concerns about the race and provide what he thought would be expert advice on how to overcome them. "I should be glad to have a conversation with you about political matters," Schurz wrote the President from New York, where he had taken a brief leave to recover from that scourge of soldier life, diarrhea. Schurz requested not only authorization to visit Washington but an extended leave from the army "to take an active part in the presidential canvass." Hearing nothing from the White House after a week, Schurz impatiently renewed his call for "an interview" with Lincoln "on pending political questions."[53] The German leader had convinced himself he should be welcomed to Washington immediately and enthusiastically.

Perhaps because Schurz had recently asked a military court of inquiry to reexamine the criticism General Hooker had leveled against him after a night battle at Wauhatchie, Tennessee, Lincoln opted to keep his German ally out of Washington. As the President tried explaining, he had "found, on feeling around, I could not invite you here without a difficulty which at least would be unpleasant, and perhaps would be detrimental to the public service." As for Schurz's proposal to absent himself from the army to join the campaign, Lincoln bluntly advised him, "[I]f you wish to remain in the military service, it is very dangerous for you to get temporarily out of it; because, with a Major General once out, it is next to impossible for even the President to get him in again." Much as he wanted Schurz's "service" on the hustings, Lincoln had concluded that "we can not properly have it, without separating you from the military."[54] Just a month earlier, Belfast-born editor John Mulally's new Catholic paper, the *Metropolitan Record and New York Vindicator*, had fanned Irish–German rivalry by complaining that Lincoln had made Schurz "a general before he was fit to be a citizen."[55] The President was in no position to risk further criticism of this symbol of German American patriotism.

Somehow, Lincoln's cautionary instructions failed to reach Schurz, who now spiraled into one of his periodic frenzies. "You have entirely misapprehended my intentions," he lectured Lincoln on March 19. ". . . If I can take an active part in the political contest consistently with my position in the Army, I shall be glad to do so, expecting nothing for myself but to resume my old position and command after the election." Above all, he wanted that face-to-face meeting placed on Lincoln's calendar. "I must confess," he huffily added, "it is somewhat difficult for me to understand, why I did not receive that permission in reply to my letters."

Complicating matters further, Schurz sent Lincoln a copy of his active complaint to the court of inquiry.* And he seized the opportunity to renew his request to be transferred to a new command—no doubt rankling the President further by suggesting he be reassigned to Franz Sigel in West Virginia "unless he has already too many German generals with him." ("All but played out," according to a German-born colleague, Sigel would shortly thereafter lose his command there.)[56]

This time, Schurz did not even wait for an answer. Just two days

---

*The court ultimately exonerated Schurz of alleged misconduct in battle.

later he wrote indignantly to remind Lincoln: "I approached you with the feelings of a friend, not to ask for something but to offer something and I find myself turned off very much like an enemy or a suspicious character. I must confess, I cannot understand this." He found "incomprehensible" Lincoln's assumption that Schurz should "easily conjecture" the "difficulty" of visiting Washington. So the President sent Schurz yet another note—this one terser than his previous explanations, and leaving little room for further appeal. "I perceive no objection to your making a political speech when you are where one is to be made; but quite surely speaking in the North, and fighting in the South, at the same time, are not possible," Lincoln told Schurz. "Nor could I be justified to detail any officer to the political campaign during it's [sic] continuance, and then return him to the Army." The obviously harried President did not even bother to sign his name to this latest reply.[57]

Schurz would simply not let the matter die. A presidential meeting had become a matter of pride, yet even with critical German support in jeopardy, it took the President another two months to authorize Schurz to visit Washington for a conversation. Predictably, when their meeting finally took place, it proved a tonic for the general, who quickly forgot his grievances. Just as an earlier White House meeting had calmed his fury over the 1862 midterms, the long-sought 1864 interview reminded Schurz of "the whole tender generosity of Lincoln's great soul."[58]

Schurz called at the White House on a steamy July afternoon. Lincoln greeted him "cordially," but then explained he could not receive him at once—he had too much business on his schedule. Instead, the President proposed that Schurz wait and drive out with him later to his summer residence, the Soldiers' Home, a few miles north of the city. During their carriage ride that evening, Lincoln seemed calm, casually inquiring about the attitudes of "this and that group of people"— German voters doubtless among them. When the pair reached the presidential cottage, Lincoln invited Schurz to sit with him on a sofa in the "scantily furnished" parlor. There, the President's mood abruptly darkened, and he began talking heatedly of "the attacks made upon him by party friends, and their efforts to force his withdrawal" from the campaign, speaking with what Schurz described as bursts of "emphasis" interrupted by long pauses.[59]

"They urge me with almost violent language to withdraw from the contest, although I have been unanimously nominated," he said defiantly, "in order to make room for a better man. I wish I could. Perhaps some other man might do this business better than I. That is possible. I do not deny it. But I am here, and that better man is not here. And if I should step aside to make room for him, it is not at all sure— perhaps not even probable—that he would get here. It is much more likely that the factions opposed to me would fall to fighting among themselves, and that those who want me to make room for a better man would get a man whom most of them would not want in at all." Most painfully of all, Lincoln confided, "men who have been my friends and who ought to know me better"—meaning Germans—were now accusing him of doing things "hurtful to the common cause only to keep myself in office! Have they thought of that common cause when trying to break me down? I hope they have."[60]

As Lincoln continued his uncharacteristic rant, it seemed to Schurz almost as if he were "speaking to himself." When the summer sun set and the gaslight began casting shadows across the room, Schurz thought he glimpsed the President's "sad eyes moist and his rugged features working strangely, as if under a very strong and painful emotion." Finally, Lincoln paused his soliloquy, as if expecting a reply. As had happened at their tense meeting a few years earlier at the White House, a "deeply touched" Schurz melted, blurting out his "confident assurance that the people, undisturbed by the bickerings of his critics, believed in him and would faithfully stand by him." At once, Lincoln relaxed and grew more cheerful. The two men chatted amiably until Lincoln ended the session with a few of his characteristic "humorous remarks." Bidding Schurz good-bye, Lincoln seized his visitor's hand and declared: "Well, things might look better, and they might look worse. Go in, and let us all do the best we can."[61]

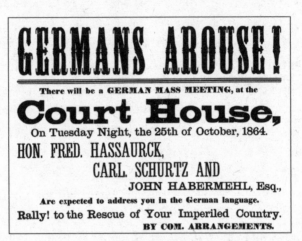

An October 1864 broadside promoting a "German mass meeting," no doubt to support Lincoln's reelection based on the roster of featured speakers: Carl Schurtz [sic], Friedrich Hassaurck [sic], and politician and memoirist John Habermehl, all Republicans. The location of the rally is unknown.

Schurz went in. No longer able to serve under General Hooker, whose judgment he had challenged before the court of inquiry, he finally secured his long-sought transfer west. And soon thereafter, he took the protracted leave he had requested and, with or without the President's blessing, campaigned vigorously for the Lincoln–Johnson ticket in New York, Pennsylvania, and Illinois, constantly looking over his shoulder for fear he would be called back to active duty before Election Day.[62] In Philadelphia, he railed against Democratic opposition to Black troops.[63] At the Academy of Music in Brooklyn, he gave a lecture called "The Treason of Slavery," hailing Lincoln as "a Union man of a true heart and a clear head" and, more importantly, a "Liberator."[64] He ended his swing in Wisconsin. Schurz had come home, and now he wanted his fellow German Americans to come home, too—to Abraham Lincoln.

. . .

Through much of the 1864 campaign, the rechristened National Union Party and its chairman, *New York Times* owner Henry Raymond, faced potentially fatal hostility from two powerful, foreign-born, New York–based newspaper rivals: Scotsman James Gordon Bennett of the *Herald* and the *World*'s new owner, German-born Democratic Party chairman August Belmont. (Had two publishers from the same metropolis ever before squared off as opposing party chairmen, as Raymond and Belmont now did? No one could remember a similar circumstance.) Under Copperhead editor Manton Marble, Belmont's *World* quickly became a lost cause. After the *World* published a spurious presidential proclamation in June, Lincoln briefly shut down the paper and ordered Marble imprisoned. Once the daily reopened, it resumed excoriating the President at full blast—and without further reprisal—and continued doing so for the rest of the campaign. The

One of the most inspired cartoons of the 1864 campaign, this print lampooned Lincoln as Shakespeare's disembodied court jester, Yorick, yet hinted that opponent McClellan was as indecisive a general as Hamlet was a prince.

World pitched much of its criticism to Irish-born voters by stoking fears about racial amalgamation—what the *World* now labeled, coining a new word, "miscegenation."[65]

Although many observers viewed the 1864 contest purely as a referendum on Lincoln's war policies, ethnic politics played a major role, too. This was evident in one of the period's cleverest cartoons, which portrayed McClellan as a flamboyantly costumed Hamlet in the play's grave-digging scene. Unearthing the skull of Lincoln (as the court jester Yorick), the prince utters the famous line, "I knew him, Horatio; a fellow of infinite jest. . . . Where be your gibes now?" The pox-on-both-their-houses image suggested that Lincoln had sullied his high office by spewing inappropriate jokes, yet also reminded voters that Hamlet-like McClellan had been a chronically indecisive general. Lurking in the scene's background is the gravedigger himself in the form of a tipsy Irishman, clay pipe protruding from his hatband, his smirk leaving the distinct impression that such unworthy individuals would play a decisive role in deciding which of the two candidates earned political burial.[66] In more openly partisan fashion, Currier & Ives's rendering of *The Chicago Platform and Candidate* showed McClellan's rotting campaign planks hoisted aloft by Jefferson Davis and Satan, and cheered on by a club-wielding, apelike Irishman raising a fist and declaring: "All right General! if yere in favor of resistin the draft, killing the n——rs, and pace wid the Southerners I'll knock any man on the head that'll vote aginye." The only patriotic dissent comes from a Union soldier who likens the Democrats' "blarney" to "brimstone."[67]

At least the White House soon neutralized cantankerous *Herald* editor Bennett. The man who had blamed the previous summer's draft riots on Blacks and abolitionists rather than the Irish never directly endorsed Lincoln's reelection. But his paper dialed back its usual hostility once intermediaries let it be known that in his second term, the President would name Bennett to the coveted post of American minister to France. Although Bennett likely assured the White House in advance that he would turn down the prestigious appointment, he desperately wanted it offered as a mark of long-withheld respect, and Lincoln proved all too willing to make the gesture if it earned him slack from the *Herald*.[68] Still, the President remained a long shot for reelection.

Then, abruptly, the political momentum shifted tectonically. Just as dispiriting war news had crippled administration chances in the midterms of 1862, a series of cheering military reports served to buoy Lincoln's standing in 1864. In June, the Union sloop of war *Kearsarge* sank the Confederate commerce raider *Alabama* in a picturesque duel outside Cherbourg harbor. The news took weeks to reach the United States from France, but soon after it did, in August, the Union navy scored another morale-building victory at Mobile Bay. That same day, the St. Louis *Staats-Zeitung* observed that "the Fremont movement is dying in Missouri."[69]

These naval triumphs were followed in short order by General Philip H. Sheridan's dramatic October ride from Winchester, Virginia, to Cedar Creek, twenty miles away, astride his foaming horse, Rienzi. "Little Phil's" inspiring gallop supposedly changed a battlefield defeat into a victory, inspiring a poem, a painting, and several popular prints. Coming just three weeks before Election Day, it did no harm to Lincoln's chances for a second term. Sheridan claimed Albany, New York, as his birthplace, but his parents had just arrived from County Cavan in Ireland.[70] Whether born in America or, as some have speculated, on board the ship that carried his father and mother here, Sheridan now took his place as an authentic Irish-American hero. As Lincoln appreciatively described him, "This Sheridan is a little Irishman, but he is a big fighter."[71]

Of all the timely 1864 Union triumphs, none proved more sensational—or politically consequential—than William Sherman's capture of Atlanta on September 1. Earlier that same day, a "gloomy" Francis Lieber had written General Halleck in the hope Lincoln might still be persuaded to drop out of the race. "Oh, that an angel could

Poet-artist Thomas Buchanan Read celebrated General Philip H. Sheridan's morale-boosting 1864 ride, both in verse and in this simple but iconic image.

descend," Lieber opined, "and show him what a beautiful stamp on his name in history such a withdrawal would be."[72] Within hours, Sherman's victory had made such a draconian move unnecessary.

The capture of Atlanta upended the opposition, too. Just one day earlier, after unwisely postponing their convention from July 4, Democrats had at last formally nominated George McClellan to oppose Lincoln. The delay ended up hurting the general's chances, since he formally entered the campaign only after the Union began winning military victories. Worse, the party saddled its candidate with a Copperhead running mate and a platform weighed down by a peace plank that McClellan quickly disavowed. Lincoln, asked whether he believed the political tide had turned because of the opposition platform or the capture of Atlanta, reportedly admitted, "I guess it was the victory."[73]

Democratic attempts to woo disaffected German voters fizzled, even after Philadelphian Max Langenschwartz boasted to McClellan that he had persuaded "the most influential german paper in the State" to "hoist our flag." Republicans in power had ways to punish such disloyalty. When the Illinois *Staats-Anzeiger* criticized the President, Isaac N. Arnold urged that the weekly "be dropped from those receiving advertisements of the War Department" and reinstated only *"on condition that it shall cease its assaults . . .* and support the nominees of the party." Meanwhile, Gustave Koerner, home from Spain, hit the campaign trail in its final days, sharing the stage at Chicago's Bryan Hall with Shakespearean actor James Hackett, a Lincoln admirer who recited a soliloquy from *Hamlet.* Appearing again a few days later to address "very enthusiastic" fellow Germans at a local Turn-Hall, Koerner spoke "as an American citizen, to strengthen the faith . . . convince the wavering" and "bring them over to our cause."[74]

It was obvious that the Lincoln campaign had taken on new life among the "Dutch." On September 3, G. Henry Voessler, a Lutheran minister from Maryland, pledged himself to the President, cautioning only that as "a poor man," he could not "spent [*sic*] a dollar in behalf of your re-election." Instead, he offered: "I will pray for you, and that don't cost a cent. Besides," he added, "I will work for the same purpose among the many hundred Germans here."[75] Over the next few weeks, previously hostile German newspapers began falling into line, too. The St. Louis *Staats-Zeitung* advised "the followers of Fremont to give up his cause as hopeless," and the wayward Chicago-based paper of the same name published a guest editorial so supportive of Lincoln that its author encouraged the President to buy and circulate a thousand copies.[76] On September 22, an exultant Gustave Koerner alerted Lincoln that "most leading Germans" in Ohio previously committed to Frémont were "rapidly beating a retreat" and "would vote for you." Even Colonel Friedrich Hecker, who still believed he had been "ill-treated" by the administration, came around and took "a decided stand" behind Lincoln "for the good of the country."[77]

Frémont, his support crumbling, remained in the presidential race for only a few days more, bowing out after his supporters struck a deal with the White House—the one that Germans had been advocating for months: the ouster of conservative postmaster general Blair. A few Germans remained "indignant that Fremont should now desert them," but had nowhere to go but to Lincoln.[78] For his part, Blair left the cabinet convinced "it is for the best all around" and proceeded to campaign vigorously for his former boss's reelection, as did Salmon Chase.[79]

Even Francis Lieber, who only recently had hoped the President might withdraw from the race, now authored a vigorous pro-Lincoln pamphlet targeted at his fellow German Americans. Lambasting the Democrats, Lieber asked: "Can you, Germans, vote on the same side with these men, whose only principle has been to shut in your faces the gates on this wide continent . . . Will you vote with those who, like their friends, the rebels, would load you with infamy, and who speak of you as the offscouring [*sic*] of the earth?"[80]

Still active on the campaign trail, Carl Schurz labored to sway even fellow Germans who could not yet vote. He told one boyhood friend who had just reached America but lacked appreciation for Lincoln: "You are underrating the President. I grant that he lacks higher education and his manners are not in accord with European conceptions of the dignity of a chief magistrate. He is a well-developed child of nature and is not skilled in polite phrases and poses. But he is a man of profound feeling, correct and firm principles and incorruptible honesty, and he possesses to a remarkable degree the characteristic, God-given trait of this people, sound common-sense. . . . He personifies the people." In a rare admission of imperfection, Schurz confided of his own, often contentious relationship with Lincoln: "I have criticized him often and severely, and later I found out that he was right. . . ."[81]

"I will make a prophecy that may now sound peculiar," Schurz capped his ringing endorsement. "In fifty years, perhaps much sooner, Lincoln's name will be inscribed close to Washington's on this American Republic's roll of honor. And there it will remain for all time. The children of those who now persecute him, will bless him."[82]

. . .

On Election Day, November 8, 1864, the multi-ethnic Company C of the Illinois Ninety-Sixth Volunteer Infantry—battle-weary veterans of Sherman's recent Atlanta campaign, nearly a third of their roster born in Germany, Ireland, Scotland, or England—voted 3–1 for Lincoln.[83] The outcome signaled that Germans had returned to the Republican fold. And so did most soldiers casting ballots in the field, 80 percent of whom supported Lincoln.

For the predominantly Democratic Irish—whether voting in camp or at home—the 1864 political contest had at first stirred mixed emotions. Troops on campaign, whatever their ethnicity or politics, struggled mightily to reconcile conflicting priorities, above all yearning that the war would end swiftly so that they could return to their families. That hope alone tempted allegiance to McClellan. Moreover, many Irish, civilian and military alike, remained opposed to emancipation and Black recruitment and feared the specter of racial parity in postwar America. They dreaded the mass migration of freed Blacks from the South to the North—a kind of internal immigration that stirred their nightmares of race mixing and wage competition. The Republicans had made universal abolition a cornerstone of their party platform, overriding the argument that Lincoln's Emancipation Proclamation had been a war measure meant only to restore the Union. Yet, against these prevailing sentiments, some Irish soldiers initially recoiled at the prospect of voting for a Democrat running on a platform that called for immediate armistice, endorsement of which implied that all their battlefield sacrifices had been for naught.

Still, as the campaign reached its final days, old party loyalties prevailed, just as they did among German Republicans. Influential Irish American newspapers like the *Boston Pilot*, the oldest Catholic journal in America, all but demanded support for McClellan. Longtime editor Patrick Donohoe was a fierce Unionist who had helped organize Irish regiments at the outset of the war. But now Donohoe told voters that Lincoln viewed Irish soldiers as good for nothing more "than being reduced to dust and being made food for gunpowder."[84]

Three days before the election, New York's *Irish-American* newspaper reiterated its own preference. McClellan alone, it argued, promised "the restoration of peace and Union." Warned the paper: "If the American people, in this election, through default or weakness, entrust the management of their affairs to Mr. Lincoln, they place their liberties at the mercy of a party who have proved themselves already faithless to every trust reposed in them."[85] A seemingly lone Hibernian dissent came from the still-admired Thomas Meagher, who decried that the Irish "to their own discredit and degradation . . . have suffered themselves to be bamboozled into being obstinate herds in the political field." Endorsing Lincoln, Meagher argued that Democratic success in 1864 "would cripple the national power."[86]

That argument failed to persuade voters in Manhattan's overwhelmingly Irish Sixth Ward, who cast 90 percent of their ballots for McClellan. Farther uptown, George Templeton Strong waited dutifully on line at his own, largely Protestant polling place for two long hours to vote for Lincoln, the tedium relieved only when none other than August Belmont, standing but a few spots in front of him, had his right to vote "challenged on the ground that he had betted on the election." When a poll inspector turned away the Democratic chairman, "Belmont went off in a rage," delighting Strong no end. As the partisan diarist justified the overt act of voter suppression, "[T]his foreign money-dealer has made himself uncommonly odious, and the bystanders, mostly of the Union [Republican] persuasion, chuckled over his discomfiture." The next morning, in a face-saving editorial, Belmont's *New York World* congratulated local McClellan supporters for maintaining order during the voting. Strong grumbled in turn that the "Democratic masses" who had earned that praise included "the liquor dealers, roughs, and brutal Irishry of the City."[87] Yet they had helped the Democrats rack up two-thirds of the city's votes.

All told, New York City Democrats rallied overwhelmingly for

Thomas Nast drew this imaginary scene of a New York polling place
showing elegant Republicans casting paper ballots for Lincoln alongside thuggish
Irishmen voting for Democrat George B. McClellan. As the woodcut reminds us, secret
balloting did not yet exist in 1864: voters openly and proudly deposited their color-coded
Republican or Democratic ballots into glass fishbowls for all to see.

McClellan on November 8—not in sufficient numbers to deny Lincoln
the state's electoral votes, but in an unmistakable reminder of unyield-
ing Irish opposition to the President and emancipation. Echoing
Strong, the *New York Tribune* acidly commented that the Democratic
majorities in Manhattan had materialized from "dens of debauchery"
and "Irish grogshops."[88] In a reminder that voters on all sides harbored
doubts about election integrity, the *Irish-American* wondered "what
frauds upon the electoral franchise were committed to win" New York
for Lincoln?[89]

The final national tally proved more than a vote of confidence
in the Republicans; it produced a mandate. Lincoln earned nearly
56 percent of the popular vote and a lopsided electoral majority of
212–21, winning every Northern state except New Jersey. The outcome
cheered Belgian-born Captain Charles Lucas of the Twenty-Fourth
Illinois, that "the majority of the people are determined to overthrow

the rebellion." There would "still be much blood spilled," Lucas predicted, "but I have complete confidence in the ultimate success of our army."[90]

Looked at another way, the results, it could be argued, in fact revealed a country still as starkly divided as it had been four years earlier when Lincoln won the presidency with only a plurality. Indeed, Lincoln's 1864 support in the North changed little from the vote four years earlier; it actually decreased in New York—but with Confederate states no longer participating, his national margin increased. What mattered most, Lincoln believed—unknowingly echoing Francis Lieber—was that the voting had occurred without incident. "It has demonstrated," the President told a crowd of well-wishers two nights after his victory, "that a people's government can sustain a national election, in the midst of a great civil war."[91]

In an advance Thanksgiving Day proclamation, Lincoln also acknowledged God's help in "the cause of Freedom and Humanity." As he put it, the Almighty had "largely augmented our free population by emancipation and by immigration," and these transformative factors would together prove crucial to a "happy deliverance from all our dangers and afflictions."[92]

. . .

One more time, Lincoln's latest reference to a "great civil war" (a phrase he had introduced at Gettysburg) would be followed just a few weeks later by an Annual Message to Congress. His latest "state of the nation" report, delivered to Capitol Hill on December 6, 1864, and "received with lively satisfaction," once again addressed the subject of foreign immigration.[93]

"The act passed at the last session for the encouragement of emigration," Lincoln reported, "has, so far as was possible, been put into operation." But he insisted it needed amending "to prevent the practice of frauds against the immigrants while on their way and on their arrival in the ports, so as to secure them here a free choice of avocations and places of settlement." Again he proposed "giving the immigrants effective national protection," this time by explicitly exempting new immigrants from the military draft.[94] Senator Sherman agreed that the President's proposed fixes would "repair evils" that persisted in New York and other disembarkation points.[95]

Lincoln made his growing empathy abundantly clear in his most emotional passages yet on the subject of immigration: "I regard our emigrants as one of the principal replenishing streams which are appointed by Providence to repair the ravages of internal war, and its wastes of national strength and health. All that is necessary is to secure the flow of that stream in its present fullness, and to that end the government must, in every way, make it manifest that it neither needs nor designs to impose involuntary military service upon those who come from other lands to cast their lot in our country."[96] He had once mused in a private meditation that God willed that the war must continue; now Lincoln implied that God ordained immigration as well, and perhaps even excused new arrivals from the army to make sure they "replenished" American farms and factories.[97]

Once again, the response to these latest proposals divided along party lines. One Democratic newspaper bitterly observed: "Mr. Lincoln believes in immigration. He advises Congress to hold out every inducement to foreigners to settle upon our shores and to excuse them, from involuntary military service. Whether he intends by this, that the conscription shall eat up all the native-born and leave the land free for aliens and negroes, we cannot say. This may be another little joke of his for aught we know."[98] Another antagonistic journal stoked revived fears of migrants by demanding that Lincoln "allow no more pirates, thieves, robbers and murderers to infest the land," arguing: "They are enemies of the human race."[99]

Despite such criticism, the House of Representatives, again with Elihu Washburne taking the lead, went on to craft an amended act that toughened the penalties for defrauding immigrants, authorized more rigorous inspections of shipboard passenger accommodations, and created new immigration offices in Baltimore, Boston, New Orleans, Philadelphia, and San Francisco.[100] Full House approval followed on March 3, 1865, just one day before the President was to take the oath of office for the second time. But despite John Sherman's support, the Senate version languished, and after Lincoln's death six weeks later, the legislation died, too. It would be revived only under his successor.[101]

. . .

Following his March 4 inauguration, Lincoln spent much of the next few weeks aboard the sidewheel steamer *River Queen* at General Grant's end-of-war riverfront headquarters at City Point, Virginia. The President visited troops in the field and discussed final strategy with Grant, Sherman, and Admiral David Dixon Porter. At a council of war aboard the presidential vessel on March 28, Sherman asked Lincoln how they should treat his Confederate counterpart when Union forces caught up with him.

One more time Lincoln was reminded of the joke he had deployed on earlier occasions when he wanted his instructions carried out without attribution. "As to Jeff. Davis," Sherman grasped, Lincoln "was hardly at liberty to speak his mind fully, but intimated that he ought to clear out, 'escape the country,' only it would not do for him to say so openly. As usual, he illustrated his meaning by a story." When Lincoln began to speak, Sherman recalled, the President's "care-worn and haggard" face "lightened up" and "his tall form, as it were, unfolded." As Lincoln spun the well-worn tale, "A man had once taken the total-abstinence pledge. When visiting a friend, he was invited to take a drink, but declined, on the score of his pledge; when his friend suggested lemonade, which was accepted. In preparing the lemonade, the friend pointed to the brandy-bottle, and said the lemonade would be more palatable if he were to pour in a little brandy; when his guest said, if he could do so 'unbeknown' to him, he would not object. From this illustration," Sherman concluded, "I inferred that Mr. Lincoln wanted

Mr. Davis to escape, 'unbeknown to him.'"[102] The only aspect of the story Sherman failed to record that day was whether it was recited in a brogue. In its past incarnations, Lincoln's irresolute teetotaler was Irish.

The President hosted one more conference at City Point—this one with Carl Schurz, who arrived unexpectedly, bearing a "confidential communication" from the secretary of war. The message delivered, the two men enjoyed a long, stress-free reunion. "I found Mr. Lincoln in excellent spirits," Schurz reported. "He was confident that the fall of Richmond, and with it the total collapse of the rebellion, would come in the near future." Turning to political affairs, Lincoln spoke "with great freedom . . . much in contrast with the depression of mind which he had shown at our last meeting during the presidential campaign." Weary but animated, Lincoln told Schurz he felt "that his triumphant re-election had given him a moral authority stronger than that which he had possessed before." He would use that power, Schurz believed, to apply a "magnanimous spirit" to reconstruction.[103]

When Schurz prepared to depart after spending an entire day with the President, Lincoln asked his visitor what kind of vessel he planned to take back to Washington. A "government tug," Schurz replied. "Oh, you can do better than that," Lincoln suggested. "Mrs. Lincoln is here, and will start back for Washington in an hour or two. She has a comfortable steamboat to carry her, on which there will be plenty of room for both of you, if you keep the peace."[104] (Mary had been quarreling with her husband and others so often in recent days that the President had insisted she return home.) Schurz accepted the challenge and took leave of Lincoln—as it turned out, for the last time.

. . .

On April 4, hand in hand with his twelve-year-old son, Tad, Lincoln entered the fallen Confederate capital of Richmond for an unannounced visit. It had been only two days since Jefferson Davis and the city's

defenders had indeed fled "unmolested."* Stepping off a skiff on an unseasonably hot day with only a dozen sailors to transport and guard
him, Lincoln drew a joyous greeting from the city's African Americans,
who cheered him as "the savior of the land."[105] From the riverbank,
Lincoln strolled almost casually toward the so-called Confederate
White House, from which Davis had run the Rebel government.

German-born Union general Godfrey Weitzel and his staff pose in Richmond
in early April 1865. Weitzel is the bearded officer in high boots standing on the porch
steps at left, right hand thrust into his coat pocket.

Breathlessly catching up with him there was a young German general not yet thirty years old. Born Gottfried Weitzel in Bavaria, he had
been brought to America at the age of two and raised in Cincinnati.
There, his father Americanized his given name to "Godfrey." Nicknamed "Dutch" by his West Point classmates—he had entered at age
fifteen—Weitzel had taught civil engineering at the academy before
joining the Army of the Potomac, serving principally under General
Benjamin Butler, and rising to the rank of major general of volunteers.

---

*Davis would be captured by Union troops in Georgia on May 10 and imprisoned for
two years at Fortress Monroe.

Assigned to command the U.S. Colored Troops of the Twenty-Fifth Corps, Weitzel had led them into Richmond and accepted the city's formal surrender on April 3, nearly four years after the war had begun. "Let history record," this immigrant general proudly reminded his Black soldiers, that "thirty thousand freemen, not only gained their own liberty but shattered the prejudice of the world and gave to the land of their birth, Peace, Union and Glory!"[106]

To his embarrassment, Weitzel had missed Lincoln's actual arrival at the conquered city. Hastening to the Davis mansion, now his own headquarters, he found the President already seated in his Confederate counterpart's office chair, having refused alcoholic refreshment, partaken of a glass of water, and enjoyed a tour of the abandoned home. Weitzel arranged for lunch, then joined Lincoln for an ambulance ride to see the sights. Sometime that long day, the two began discussing conditions in a city still literally smoldering from fires started by the Rebels before withdrawing.

Neither artists nor photographers bore witness to Lincoln's unannounced arrival at Richmond on April 4, 1865. Painter Dennis Malone Carter later imagined the greeting the President received when he rode through the former Confederate capital in an army ambulance. In truth, Lincoln elicited no such enthusiasm from the city's white residents, only from its newly emancipated Blacks.

As the general informed Lincoln, secessionist leaders who remained behind had already requested a meeting to discuss the future. Lincoln was amenable, but with the prerequisite that he and a designated Confederate emissary each be accompanied at such a conference by a single aide. "I shall have one friend with the same liberty to them," the President insisted. As his own "one friend," he designated a surprised Weitzel. The Virginians were represented by John A. Campbell, who had resigned from the U.S. Supreme Court and gone south as soon as Virginia left the Union. (Lincoln had only recently met with Campbell and two others for an aborted peace conference at Hampton Roads.)

With Weitzel looking on, Lincoln used the meeting to make his position clear to the judge. The administration would not deal with "any rebels until they had laid down their arms and surrendered; and that if this were first done, he would go as far as he possibly could to prevent the shedding of another drop of blood." He was "surfeited with this thing" and wanted the war to end.[107] But Lincoln reminded Campbell that peace could only come under three conditions: restoration of federal authority, acceptance of emancipation, and "the disbanding of all force hostile to the government."[108]

En route back to Washington aboard the steamer USS *Malvern*, Lincoln wrote out his final instructions to Weitzel. Should Virginia state legislators attempt to convene at Richmond, "give them permission and protection, until, if at all, they attempt some action hostile to the United States, in which case you will notify them and give them reasonable time to leave" and "arrest any who may remain." Lincoln never again wrote to a foreign-born American.[109]

. . .

Eight days later, on Good Friday, April 14, 1865, Lincoln and his wife took a carriage from the White House to Ford's Theatre, a repurposed brick church a few blocks away, to attend a benefit performance of a boisterous English comedy called *Our American Cousin*. Shortly after 10:00 P.M., the pro-secessionist, racist actor John Wilkes Booth crept into the presidential box above stage left, aimed a pistol at the back of Lincoln's head, and fired a single shot into his brain.[110]

A fellow conspirator, Prussian-born George Atzerodt, assigned by Booth to kill Vice President Johnson simultaneously, lost his nerve and failed to carry out his part of the bloody plot to decapitate the federal government before it could mandate Black voting rights.

The fatally injured Lincoln was tenderly borne across the street to a boardinghouse owned by a German-born immigrant tailor named William Petersen. There, in a tiny rear bedroom soon packed with government leaders, the President struggled against death for nearly nine hours. Among those who attended to him was Charles H. Liebermann, a Jewish ophthalmologist born in Russia, trained in Germany, and now the head of the Washington Medical Society. His fellow physicians at the bedside vigil likely summoned the noted "oculist"—and former slave owner—when Lincoln's right eye, behind which Booth's bullet had lodged, began to swell and blacken. Liebermann's sole contribution to the futile resuscitation efforts that night was to pour a shot of brandy down the inert Lincoln's throat—to no effect.[111] None of the doctors could do more than keep their patient warm and comfortable as his life ebbed away. Without ever regaining consciousness, the President breathed his last at 7:22 A.M. on April 15.

Over those same eventful days, several ships from Europe—including the *Golden Rule*, the *Edinburgh*, and the *Ocean Queen*—docked in New York City after long transatlantic voyages and disgorged their passengers onto the teeming streets of Manhattan. Dotting the lists of new arrivals were German and Irish names surely destined to join the ranks of new Americans in the months and years after Lincoln's death. Here were the very "Hanses" and "Patricks" Lincoln had all but invited here a few years earlier: men called Diedrich, Biemenstall, Rausch, and Heising—along with Muldoon, Sweeny, O'Brien, O'Neill, Kavanagh, and at least two fresh arrivals named Kelly.[112] Lincoln was gone, but his immigration plan lived on.

Eleven days after the assassination, Booth was cornered in a

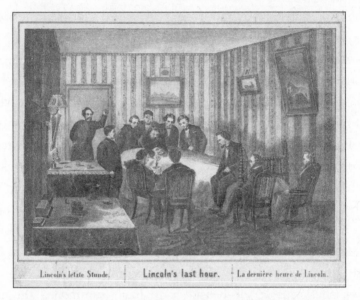

Lincoln's letzte Stunde. | Lincoln's last hour. | La dernière heure de Lincoln.

Lincoln's dying moments inspired many engraved and lithographed souvenir depictions, some—like this example by an unknown artist—whose German-language captions indicated they were designed for the martyr's foreign-born admirers.

Virginia barn by a unit of armed soldiers led by James Rowan O'Beirne, a colonel hailing from Kilrooskey, Ireland, and a veteran of the Union's Irish Rifles. There, a mentally unstable soldier, British-born religious zealot Thomas H. "Boston" Corbett, disobeyed orders to capture the assassin alive and shot Booth down. Corbett claimed God had commanded him to do so. George Atzerodt and four other conspirators fell into the hands of pursuers and went on trial in Washington.

. . .

In his final letter to Lincoln, Carl Schurz had focused on an issue that would animate his own later career in politics: civil service reform. Having learned that the President was being urged "to remove as large a number as possible of the civil officers of the government and to put new ones in their places," Schurz protested that "the system called rotation in office has done more than anything else to demoralize the body politic." As ardently as he had quested for political patronage himself, he now believed "high-toned reform" could become "one of the most important features of your administration."[113]

"This is one of those cases where all personal resentments ought to be forgotten," Schurz ended his latest and last policy recommendation. A few days later, as he had hoped, Lincoln indeed let political bygones be bygones and appointed his erstwhile challenger former Treasury Secretary Salmon Chase as the new chief justice of the Supreme Court. It seemed possible, even before Lincoln so expressed it, that "malice toward none" might indeed become the hallmark of his second term.

Attempting to express his grief to his wife after the shock of Lincoln's murder, Schurz found himself for once at a loss for words, unable to "shake off the gloom that has settled upon me since the arrival of the news." Finally, he summoned the energy to lament: "A thunderclap from the blue sky could not have struck us more unexpectedly and frightfully. Our good, good Lincoln!"[114]

Margarethe Schurz, who had once recited her husband's intemperate protest letter to a startled Lincoln at the White House, replied that her own "piercing sorrow" had been assuaged only by the thought that the President "could not have died more happily than now; without pain, in sight of his victories, to fall like a hero." Then she assured Carl that "what you have always said is true; that, after Washington, he is our greatest president and the greatest emancipator. How happy I am that you served him so loyally!"[115] Two months later, Schurz was still telling a friend, "Never was the sorrow of a nation more universal and more sincere."[116]

Gustave Koerner and his family were relaxing in their Belleville, Illinois, parlor on the night of April 14 when they heard the loud report of a gunshot outside. Hurriedly raising the window and peering out, Koerner could detect no sign of either a lurking perpetrator or any lingering smoke. Early the next morning, he set out as usual for his law office, shocked when he saw Main Street merchants lowering their flags to half-mast. Only then learning that Lincoln had been assassinated, he rushed back home, where his wife exclaimed, "That was the shot we heard last night!" For years after the event that the President's old friend called a "national calamity," Sophie Koerner would insist that the gunfire that startled the family in Belleville around the time Booth pulled the trigger in Washington was "a very remarkable coincidence"— or something more.[117]

Now came the tributes—from many sources and in several languages. In New York, Bennett's long-hostile *Herald* solemnly announced Lincoln's murder beneath the headline "Our Loss. The Great National Calamity."[118] Even to the unrelentingly critical New York *Irish-American*, the "Deplorable National Calamity" had left the country "stained with the blood of its Chief Magistrate, shed by an assassin's hand to glut the vengeance of faction."[119] And in Chicago, the Swedish-language paper *Hemlandet* ("Homeland") placed a front-page tribute within thick black borders, announcing: "Mournful tidings! Abraham Lincoln, father of the country is dead, fallen by an assassin's bullet, and

New York's city hall draped in black to receive Lincoln's remains on April 25, 1865. Note the banner above the entrance: "THE NATION MOURNS."

the entire country is in mourning. Death, thou has struck one of the cruelest blows. . . . [O]ur country has never had such a leader and will not soon again find another."[120]

Not all immigrants mourned, of course. It was said that a patriotic New York hotelier dismissed his entire workforce of Irish waiters over their "Celtic talk approving Lincoln's murder." Yet, on the day of Lincoln's Manhattan funeral procession, one diarist noted the unmistakable presence of Irish mourners ("in *inconceivable numbers . . . never ending*"), not to mention the expected turnout of Scots, Germans, and Jews.[121] Indeed, the participants included the survivors of Corcoran's Irish Legion along with German vocalists singing the "Pilgrim's Chorus" from Wagner's *Tannhäuser* in their native tongue—the choir situated just below Lincoln's open coffin. African Americans—belatedly granted permission to participate only when Secretary of War Stanton overruled stubborn local officials—marched under the protection of Police Chief John Kennedy, an Irish American who had been stabbed while trying to put down the 1863 draft riots. Yet, even on this day of near-universal lamentation, as the *Times* reported, "some of the Irish societies" refused to march at all "if a place in the procession was assigned to the colored men."[122]

In Philadelphia, the Polish-born printmaking brothers Max and Louis Rosenthal collaborated on a large hand-colored lithograph, *Last Moments of Abraham Lincoln*, depicting a trio of angels beckoning the dying president from his deathbed toward a heaven already occupied by George Washington. Less ambitious assassination and deathbed prints poured forth as well, some with captions in both German and English, designed for sale to the martyr's "Dutch" admirers on both sides of the Atlantic.[123]

And in Cincinnati, Rabbi Isaac Mayer Wise ascended the pulpit of the Lodge Street Temple to reflect on the man he had mocked so dyspeptically in 1861—and had then petitioned for relief from Grant's anti-Semitic purge in 1862. Now, Wise acknowledged, the fallen president had unleashed "the tears of countless myriads, and the dark

A German chorus performed a selection from Wagner's *Tannhäuser*
in the rotunda of New York's city hall. At the top of the stairway above, the
embalmed body of President Lincoln lay in state for public view.

clouds of mourning which envelop the great Republic." He did not
explain or apologize for his earlier disdain.

"Whenever our mission is fulfilled," Wise instead sermonized,
"God calls us hence. Abraham Lincoln fulfilled a great mission; he led
the country through this glorious struggle to glorious victory." Wise
now saw in him—too late to acknowledge while the President lived—
"purity of heart, honesty of purpose, confidence in the great cause, and
implicit faith in the justice of Providence." In retrospect, it seemed
obvious that these virtues had "endeared" Lincoln to "many millions
of hearts." He was now a martyr whom "myriads of freedmen consider their savior, and tens of thousands esteem as high as George

Washington, and feel as sincerely and affectionately attached to as Israel to her David."[124]

It seemed fitting somehow that so many tributes to the leader who had expanded immigration came from the foreign-born. In dramatic, if coincidental, ten-year intervals—from decrying the Philadelphia anti-Catholic riots of 1844, to confronting the Know-Nothings beginning in 1854, to signing immigration reform in 1864—Lincoln had slowly but surely helped expand the borders of American opportunity. And he had done so by opening the borders to America itself.

Destroying slavery had helped preserve the Union and set the country on a path to an expanded citizenry with expanded rights, but so had the work of rejecting nativism and spurring foreign immigration, which had swelled the armed forces during the existential fight to save American democracy and kept industry and agriculture humming despite the wartime loss of hundreds of thousands of men. In between these milestones, the country had endured but survived the rise of violent nativism, draft riots, and the conversion of German voters from Democrats into Republicans—the making of a new political majority that would keep Lincoln's party in the White House, with but one Democratic exception, until 1912.[125]

There was no erasing the fact that the same president who had encouraged immigration by Europeans also favored restrictions on Asian newcomers, the relocation and concentration of Native Americans, and, until late in his presidency, the voluntary emigration of African Americans. But as W. E. B. Du Bois would put it in 1922: "The scars and foibles and contradictions of the Great do not diminish but enhance the worth and meaning of their upward struggle." Lincoln "was a man—a big, inconsistent, brave man" who steadily evolved "upward."[126]

In New York, where Lincoln's body lay in state at city hall for more than twenty-four hours in late April 1865, some 150,000 mourners filed past the open coffin—including Irish immigrants who no doubt proudly recognized General Thomas Meagher standing at attention there as a guard of honor.

Among the grief-stricken visitors was a Dublin-born seventeen-year-old who for four years had been working as an apprentice cameo cutter while studying art at Cooper Union, where Lincoln had so memorably orated back in 1860. The son of a French shoemaker and an Irish mother, the teenager had lived in Manhattan since infancy and considered himself thoroughly American. So young Augustus Saint-Gaudens waited for hours in an "interminable" line for his chance to view the late President. By the time he approached the catafalque, the embalmed remains were showing unmistakable signs of deterioration. According to the *New York Times*, "The dust had gathered upon the features, the lower jaw somewhat drooped, the lips slightly parted, and the teeth visible. It was not a pleasant sight."[127] Yet once young Saint-Gaudens at last glimpsed the martyr's face, the aspiring artist rushed back to the end of the queue and awaited his turn for a second glance.[128]

He would put the experience to grand use. Twenty-two years later, by then the most acclaimed of all American sculptors, Saint-Gaudens installed his 1887 statue *Abraham Lincoln: The Man* at a Chicago park renamed for the sixteenth president—in a neighborhood originally dotted with Native American settlements and later home to Kashubian refugees fleeing from Prussian domination. Young Abraham Lincoln II—the President's only grandson, destined to die just three years later—unveiled the nineteen-foot-high bronze.

Nearly a century and a quarter afterward, Barack Obama stood not far from that same iconic statue to claim victory in the 2008 presidential election. There he quoted his idol, Abraham Lincoln, to reassure even those who had voted against him, as Lincoln once had declared to assuage a house dividing in 1861: "We are not enemies, but friends."[129]

America had again been transformed, and, just as Lincoln had hoped and planned, replenished. Obama was not only the first man of color elected to the White House. He was the first child of a foreign-born resident from Africa.

Scattered to the Winds

In June 1865—two months after Lincoln's death—Congress passed and the new president, Andrew Johnson, signed the immigration law refinements that Abraham Lincoln had proposed in his final Annual Message six months earlier. As it turned out, this would be the last federal legislation enacted to encourage foreigners to migrate to the United States until 1965, when Lyndon B. Johnson approved the Immigration and Nationality Act, reversing a century of government policy focused instead on restrictions, quotas, and exclusion.[1]

The 1865 pro-immigration enhancements did nothing to erase understandable Northern hostility toward the foreign-born who had supported the Confederacy or plotted the murder of the President. On July 7, after a quick trial before a military tribunal, German George Atzerodt and three of his co-conspirators in the Lincoln assassination died on the gallows in the walled-off courtyard of the Washington Arsenal. During the war, the facility had served as a munitions factory. Girls, many Irish-born, and some as young as thirteen, had been employed there to hand-sew cloth-covered cartridges, attracting little public notice until an accidental 1864 explosion claimed the lives of twenty-one workers.[2]

Taking charge of the July 1865 hanging of the assassination conspirators was General John Frederick Hartranft, a Medal of Honor recipient who gave the signal to release the trapdoor of the gallows. Hartranft had been born in Pennsylvania to recently arrived German parents named Herterranft. A lifelong Democrat, he had switched political allegiance after McClellan's 1864 nomination for president. "I would rather see the flag burned, and its ashes scattered to the winds," Hartranft had asserted, "than it should be disgraced by a dishonorable peace."[3]

One of the exclusive photographs made from a nearby window on that brutally hot day of reckoning shows Hartranft reading the death sentence aloud to the prisoners as they stand on the wooden gallows awaiting their punishment. This and an ensuing sequence of grisly execution pictures, culminating in a grotesque shot of the four corpses dangling from their nooses, were the work of Scottish-born Alexander Gardner. He had photographed Lincoln on the Antietam battlefield back in 1862, produced a suite of portraits a week before Lincoln left for Gettysburg in 1863, and taken the last studio poses of the haggard, doomed President two months before his assassination. Now he would assure the world through his sensational visual record of the hanging that his most famous sitter had been avenged.[4]

Lincoln was not the final casualty of the Civil War, which had been fought on so many fields by so many foreign-born combatants. Somehow appropriately, that distinction fell to an immigrant. Confederate captain Herman Wirz—born Hartman Heinrich Wirz in Zurich, and a resident of the United States since 1849—had been a homeopathic doctor and later a plantation manager in Louisiana before joining the Confederate army. For a year, beginning in April 1864, he had served as commandant of the barbaric military prison camp at Andersonville, Georgia, where some thirteen thousand Union captives died of starvation, disease, or brutal treatment. After the publication of shocking atrocity pictures depicting skeletal survivors who looked more dead than alive, followed by a trial nearly as widely publicized as that of Booth's co-conspirators, Wirz was hanged as a war criminal on November 10, 1865.

Reportedly his final words—conceivably uttered in German-accented English—were to remind his captors that he had merely followed orders.

. . .

Carl Schurz won a U.S. Senate seat in 1868—the first German-born American ever elected senator. He served for six years. Later, he became secretary of the interior in the Rutherford B. Hayes administration, championed civil service reform, opposed the enforcement of civil rights legislation for fear of race mixing, served as editor of the *Nation* and the *New York Evening Post*, and founded yet another newspaper in St. Louis. The postwar Schurz is perhaps best known for his utterance from the floor of the Senate: "My country, right or wrong."[5] He died in New York City in 1906 at age seventy-seven. A couple years later, his reminiscences appeared in three volumes.

Gustave Koerner, to his apparent "surprise," was invited to serve as a pallbearer at Lincoln's 1865 funeral at Springfield. In 1872, he ran unsuccessfully for governor of Illinois, then four years later backed Democrat Samuel J. Tilden in the New Yorker's failed bid for the presidency. That campaign ended in a controversial, arguably stolen election that took place the same day as grave robbers invaded Lincoln's tomb and tried stealing the body Koerner had once helped see to its rest. Soon thereafter, Koerner formally returned to the Democratic Party, which he had abandoned two decades earlier to join Lincoln's Republicans. He died in Belleville, Illinois, in 1896 in his eighty-seventh year. Koerner's two-volume memoirs were published posthumously. Its most compelling sections examined the "highly complex character" of the man he had so loyally supported and who had alternatively enthralled and disappointed him. Abraham Lincoln, Koerner ultimately concluded, "was the justest man I ever knew."[6]

Franz Sigel never totally lost his following among fellow Germans, but he never rekindled the ardor he had first inspired in the heady days of Union enlistment in 1861. After the war, Sigel became a newspaper editor in Baltimore and then New York. He ran and lost an 1869 race for New York secretary of state as a Republican, but he later served in appointive office as a collector of internal revenue under Democratic president Grover Cleveland. One of his last professional efforts came in launching a monthly German-language newspaper—the type of journal that had so faithfully defended him through much of the Civil War. He died in New York in 1902 at the age of seventy-seven.

Scottish-born espionage chief Allan Pinkerton returned to his detective agency after the war and earned unwanted national publicity for failing to capture Jesse James and his notorious gang of train robbers. Pinkerton's last case took him to Cuba at the behest of the Spanish government to help put down a revolution. He died in 1884. Francis Lieber became an arbitrator between the United States and Mexico on cases that were largely left unresolved at his death in 1872. And inventor John Ericsson turned his postwar attention to the development of submarine technology. He died on March 8, 1889—twenty-seven years to the day since the epic duel between his USS *Monitor* and the Confederate ironclad *Virginia*. Per his final wish, Ericsson was buried in his native Sweden.

Lincoln's White House successor, Andrew Johnson, rewarded the hard-drinking Irish hero Thomas Francis Meagher with the appointment as territorial governor of Montana. But in July 1867, under mysterious circumstances, a possibly inebriated Meagher toppled to his death—or, some believe, was pushed overboard by political enemies—from the deck of a steamboat near Fort Benton on the Missouri River. He was a month short of his forty-fourth birthday. The mystery of his demise has never been solved. When New Yorkers gathered at Cooper Union for a Meagher memorial service, the principal address came from Richard O'Gorman—the same Dublin-born orator who had rallied his fellow Irish Americans to the defense of the Lincoln administration and the American flag at Union Square six years earlier. O'Gorman died in 1895.[7] Meagher's admirers installed a statue of the general in front of the Montana state capitol in 1905. James T. Brady, the Democratic attorney Lincoln had once asked to raise the first Irish regiment, died of a stroke at age fifty-three in 1869.

After breaking a still-standing record by serving as a U.S. senator from a third state, Missouri (albeit for only three months), James Shields declined the chance to seek a full term and embarked on what he hoped would be a long and remunerative lecture tour. Early in his travels, however, he succumbed to an apparent heart attack and died in Iowa in 1879. He was seventy-three.

August Belmont remained chairman of the Democratic Party for another seven years without ever managing a successful presidential campaign, stepping down only after the landslide 1872 reelection of Republican Ulysses S. Grant. Belmont kept his hand in politics for the remainder of his life but concentrated mainly on business and high society. Thirty years after his 1890 death at age seventy-six, the novelist Edith Wharton purportedly used him as the model for the mysterious, status-seeking character Julius Beaufort in her book *The Age of Innocence*.

The art student who viewed Lincoln's remains in New York, Augustus Saint-Gaudens, went on to a spectacularly successful career as a sculptor. He produced statues of Sherman and Admiral David Farragut, and a replica of his *Abraham Lincoln: The Man*, which was later installed in Parliament Square, London. But Saint-Gaudens was not the first immigrant sculptor to craft a statue of the martyred Civil War President. That honor went to an Irish-born stonecutter named Lot Flannery, who designed a standing Lincoln that was unveiled outside the Washington, D.C., city hall in 1868.[8]

After the war, Dr. Issachar Zacharie invoiced the federal government for his supposed work as "chiropodist-general" of the United States Army—an honorific he used without authorization on the title page of one of his books. Officials summarily rejected the claim, and without his presidential benefactor to attest to his putative wartime service, Lincoln's onetime physician and friend returned to England, where he quietly resumed his medical practice. Zacharie lived until 1900, dying in Kent in his seventy-fifth year.

George Schneider, the German-born, Chicago-based newspaper-man who had crafted the bold anti-nativist resolutions passed with Lincoln's help at the 1856 Decatur editors' convention, had sold his remaining interest in the *Staats-Zeitung* newspaper back in 1862. He spent the last years of the Lincoln administration as collector of internal revenue for Chicago, a patronage job arranged by the White House. He later became president of the Illinois National Bank, so devoted to his profitable business that he turned down a Grant administration appointment as minister to Switzerland. He did attend the Republican National Convention that nominated Rutherford B. Hayes for the presidency in 1880 and five years later founded the still-vibrant Chicago Festival. After decades of success, Schneider saw his fortune suddenly wiped out in the 1896 collapse of his bank. He spent his final years living with a daughter in Kansas City, where he died in 1905 at age eighty-one.

Of Lincoln's two most prominent foreign-born photographers, Alexander Gardner died first, at age sixty-one in 1882, but not before he published his epic *Photographic Sketch Book of the War* (1865–1866) and secured government contracts to take pictures of Native Americans and the Far West. His onetime employer, Mathew Brady, outlived him, but, unable to obtain more than $25,000 from the government in exchange for his enormous trove of wartime pictures—a mere fourth of the money he had thrown into the enterprise—he eventually declared bankruptcy. Nearly blind, Brady was struck down by a Manhattan streetcar in 1896 and died a few days later in the charity ward of a New York hospital, somewhere around seventy-four years of age. At his passing, the man once considered the most famous photographer in the country lacked funds even for burial. The city's fabled Seventh Regiment paid for Brady's funeral.

Lincoln's Bavarian-born secretary and chief of staff, John Nicolay, was on board a ship bound for Washington from Charleston when the shocking news reached him of the President's murder. Nicolay had been on a long-overdue vacation to Cuba before heading home via South Carolina, where he had paused to attend a flag-raising ceremony at Fort Sumter on April 14—four years after its surrender and, unbeknownst to him, just hours before the assassination. Lincoln had earlier told his secretary that he planned to send him to Paris as U.S. consul, and Nicolay duly secured the appointment from Andrew Johnson and served there from 1865 to 1869. President Grant later recalled him, conceivably when he discovered that Nicolay had never obtained his American citizenship papers and was therefore ineligible to hold a diplomatic post.

Nicolay and his onetime White House deputy, John Hay, then obtained exclusive access to the files of incoming correspondence, memoranda, drafts, and the late President's handwritten manuscripts and copies—later known as the Lincoln Papers—that they had maintained for the President in Civil War Washington. The two used the material first as the primary source for a series of authoritative articles on Lincoln for *Century Magazine* (1886–1890) and then for a massive ten-volume, best-selling biography, *Abraham Lincoln: A History*, which appeared between 1890 and 1894. The onetime "Teutonic" guardian of Lincoln's White House door finished his government career serving in a similar but far less prestigious post as marshal of the U.S. Supreme Court. He died in 1901 at the age of sixty-nine.

Although he declared Lincoln "worthy of martyrdom," a guilt-ridden Nicolay always regretted that he had not been at the President's side on the fateful day he was attacked by John Wilkes Booth in Washington.[9] Fourteen years before his own death, he told the *Chicago Herald* that Lincoln had received countless warnings about his personal safety but always ignored them, insisting: "I see hundreds of strangers every day, and if anybody has the disposition to kill me, he will find the opportunity. To be absolutely safe I should lock myself up in a box."[10]

Sergeant "Boston" Corbett, the London-born soldier who defied orders and fired the shot that killed assassin John Wilkes Booth, became an instant Northern hero, lionized by the newspapers and immortalized by photographers and printmakers. What admirers did not yet know was that Corbett was a longtime religious fanatic who had castrated himself with scissors to avoid sexual temptation. Corbett was briefly jailed after killing Lincoln's killer. His behavior grew increasingly bizarre over the years, but in a nod to his fame he secured a conspicuous job in 1887 as a doorkeeper at the Kansas statehouse. After he threatened lawmakers there with a gun, however, authorities confined Corbett to a Topeka insane asylum. He somehow escaped, then apparently made his way into the Minnesota woods, at which point the authorities—and history—lost track of him.[11]

ACKNOWLEDGMENTS

Conducting research has changed so much since I began working on my first book more than forty years ago. Back in the 1980s, doing research always meant visiting libraries and repositories in person. Advance reservations had to be made, credentials presented, coats checked, file folders and card catalogs scoured, often-illegible documents transcribed, and large, brittle newspaper pages delicately turned (or hand-cranked on sour-smelling microfilm). One's success at unearthing long-buried new information required both perseverance and luck.

Some of the romance, and much of the grind, has since gone out of the research process, as many more sources have opened up remotely. The Abraham Lincoln Papers are all online and largely transcribed. The Papers of Abraham Lincoln (up to 1858) and an updated, ever-evolving Lincoln day-by-day chronology are similarly searchable. Newspaper articles from far and wide can be found and reprinted with but a click or two on the computer. Rare publications can easily be viewed digitally on Google Books. Even the massive *Official Records of the Union and Confederate Armies*, not to mention what we now call the *Congressional Record*, are now fully digitized and searchable. And so, my gratitude goes above all to the wizards who put so much material on the web in the first place, and the experts who make it possible to examine innumerable and constantly expanding sources without leaving the home or office computer. Thank you for a technological blessing that at first ranked as a convenience but became truly crucial during the pandemic lockdown, when most of the work on this book was undertaken and most libraries shut down.

Not that I did not enjoy and profit greatly from opportunities to visit research institutions pre- and post-COVID. I'm always thrilled to have the incomparable pleasure of seeing original material. For those opportunities, I'm grateful, as always, to colleagues like Michelle Krowl, Civil War and Reconstruction specialist at the Manuscript Division at the Library of Congress; and Louise Mirrer, Valerie Paley, and their team at the New-York Historical Society. Lacking the opportunity to make a personal visit for this project to Springfield, Illinois, I am greatly indebted to Christian McWhirter, Lincoln specialist at the Abraham Lincoln Presidential Library and Museum, who has been both a guide to sources and a sounding board for ideas. So has Sam Wheeler, the knowledgeable historian of the Illinois courts. Special salutes to Springfield's elder statesman, Lincoln scholar Wayne C. Temple, like me (and Lincoln's mother) a February 5 birthday boy. Nearing age one hundred at this writing, he gave his usual expert reading to some of my early chapters and generously shared new information on John Nicolay that enriched this book. Every Lincoln writer of my generation wants to grow up to be like "Doc" Temple.

I benefited equally from another helpful reading from my friend, the gifted and generous historian and Lincoln biographer Jon Meacham, who never met an adverb that he liked, much to my benefit. Thanks for another crucial reading from Professor Emeritus Craig L. Symonds of the U.S. Naval Academy, who may have turned recently to World War II studies but has retained more than enough Civil War knowledge to detect errors I might otherwise have committed here about its battles and leaders. My appreciation, too, goes to writer-producer Turlough McConnell for his sensitive reading of sections related to Irish and

Irish American history and, through Turlough, input from Professor Robert Schmuhl of Notre Dame.

Advice on other particulars, along with good conversations about Lincoln, the Civil War, American history, and publishing, came from: John Marszalek at Mississippi State University; Lincoln Forum vice chairman Jonathan W. White of Christopher Newport University; Rhode Island chief justice emeritus Frank J. Williams; Matthew Pinsker of Dickinson College; Douglas L. Wilson of Knox College; Daniel Stowell of the Papers of Abraham Lincoln; Jeff Ronsenheim, chief curator of the Metropolitan Museum's Department of Photography; writer-producer David Black; technology expert and Lincoln historian David Kent; Erin Carlson Mast of the Lincoln Presidential Foundation; as well as friends like Robert Caro, Judy Collins, Louis Nelson, Ron Chernow, Jean Powers Soman, Thomas Horrocks, Sidney Blumenthal, Rabbi Menachem Genack, and Rabbi Meir Soloveichik of Yeshiva University, with whom I've had the honor of teaching both undergraduates and law students.

For their help in finding and obtaining copies of illustrations, documents, and nineteenth-century newspapers, I have many curators, archivists, and administrators to thank: Kayla Gustafson at the Lincoln Financial Foundation Collection in Fort Wayne, and her beloved former colleague Sara Gabbard; Mary Mann and Samantha Berman at Cooper Union in New York; Emily Rolfs at the Quincy, Illinois, Public Library; Teri Barnett, Megan Klintworth, and Christopher Schnell at the Abraham Lincoln Presidential Library and Museum; Valerie Paley and Eleanor Gillers at the New-York Historical Society; Rabbi Gary Zola, Dana Herman, and Joe Weber at the Jacob Rader Marcus Center of the American Jewish Archives at Hebrew Union College in Cincinnati; Kathy L. Nichols at the Farmington Historic Plantation in Louisville; William P. Shannon IV at the St. Clair County Historical Society in Belleville, Illinois; Julie Zeftel at my old stamping grounds at the Metropolitan Museum of Art; Christine Kinealy at Ireland's

Great Hunger Institute at Quinnipiac University in Hamden, Connecticut; Caitlin Hogue at the Filson Historical Society in Louisville; Hannah Elder at the Massachusetts Historical Society; Zachary Palitzch at the State Historical Society of St. Louis; biographer Candice Shy Hooper; and Molly Riddick at the Gilder Lehrman Institute of American History.

Thanks, too, to all the organizational leaders who expressed an interest in scheduling me to speak on this book—even before it was published: Paul Ellis-Graham and Rob Kaplan of the Lincoln Group of New York; David Kent, Jon Willen, and others from the Lincoln Group of the District of Columbia; Dale Gregory and Alex Kassl of the New-York Historical Society; Peter Carmichael at the Civil War Institute, Gettysburg College; and my entire Lincoln Forum family, especially Jon White, Diane Brennan, and my good friends on the executive committee.

At my professional home, the Roosevelt House Public Policy Institute at Hunter College, I was fortunate to have the patient help of my chief assistant, AmyRose Yee, and of former staffer Jacki Summerfield, along with the opportunity to discuss history and book writing with many gifted members of the Hunter faculty. Above all, I am beholden to Jennifer J. Raab, who finished twenty-two extraordinary years as president of the college as this book headed to press. I will forever be grateful to her for unexpectedly recruiting me to work at Hunter in 2015. Her enthusiasm and support for my writing—never at the expense of her fierce devotion to, and expectations for, Roosevelt House—provided a constant source of inspiration, not to mention a wonderful place to cap my own career. Thank you, Jennifer.

Finally, much appreciation for the advice and guidance from my agent, John Schline, along with his predecessor at Writers House, my longtime representative, Geri Thoma, who shopped this book when it was a wisp of an idea. Thanks to my invaluable aide Kraig Smith and my research assistant Avi Mowshowitz for their usual fine work on yet another project. And a shout-out to Philip Market, the Roosevelt

House IT maven who constantly keeps my computers in working order and more than once helped me find imperfectly stored Word documents I feared I had lost, mangled, or infected.

For the second time I've had the great pleasure of working with the publishing team at Dutton, led by John Parsley and Christine Ball. My gratitude above all goes to my patient, creative, and collegial editor, Brent Howard, so savvy about the book world, so solid in his instincts, and so much fun to spend time with. Thanks, too, to assistant editor Grace Layer, who saved me from several disasters; senior production editor Andrea St. Aubin and senior designer Elke Sigal; director of marketing Stephanie Cooper and marketing assistant Diamond Bridges; the excellent copy editor Maureen Klier; and the PR team led by Sarah Thegeby.

I can always count on inspiration and understanding from my amazing and accomplished children and their spouses. In return, much love to Remy and Adam Kirsch and Meg Holzer and Rhiana Swartz. Thanks to them, my wife and I have been blessed with two spectacular grandsons who give us endless joy: Charles Kirsch and Leo Holzer-Swartz.

Above all, thank you to Edith, my adored wife of fifty-two years and fifty-six books. I love you more each day and remain ever grateful for, among many other gifts, traveling with me on research trips; examining old papers, documents, and microfilm side by side with me; and above all, for proofreading every word of this book more than once and then dealing patiently with me when I argued with you over your suggestions. I want to add a special word of gratitude to my late father-in-law, Leon Spiegel, who resisted and survived the Nazis and immigrated with his baby daughter to the United States after World War II. Had it not been for his yearning to reinvent himself in America, not unlike the earlier generations of refugees portrayed in this book, Edith and I would never have met as teenagers at high school in Queens.

As I hope readers notice, this book is dedicated to my grandparents, all four of them born to poverty and peril in Europe and all four reborn in New York at the end of the nineteenth century. I got to know only one of them: my father's strong and loving mother, Eva, who never let on that she could neither read nor write and who traversed the daunting subways of 1950s Brooklyn to visit us by counting station stops on her fingers. The others all died before, or shortly after, I was born. But during my childhood, the hypnotic stories I heard about their fraught voyages across the Atlantic, their struggles, sacrifices, and hard work here, their devotion to their children and commitment to both their inherited faith and their adopted country, enriched my life. They have formed and inspired me in ways I appreciate more than ever after working on this project and learning so much about the Europeans who migrated and thrived here half a century before them.

My late friend John O'Keefe loved to repeat (always deploying a thick brogue) the words his Irish-born mother always barked when asked how she was getting along: "Better than before we came here!"

Now, more than ever, I think I understand what she meant.

BIBLIOGRAPHY

Selected Newspapers

Anzeiger des Westens (St. Louis)

Boston Herald

Boston Pilot

Chicago Times

Chicago Tribune

Cincinnati Daily Commercial

Cincinnati Daily Gazette

Cleveland Plain Dealer

Daily Eastern Argus (Portland, ME)

Davenport (IA) *Gazette*

Douglass' Monthly (Rochester, NY)

Frank Leslie's Illustrated Newspaper (NY)

Freie Presse (Philadelphia, Indianapolis, and Alton, IL)

Harper's Weekly (NY)

Hartford Daily Courant

Illinois Staats-Zeitung (Chicago)

Illinois State Register (Springfield)

The Independent (New York)

Irish-American (New York)

The Israelite (Cincinnati)

Milwaukee Daily News

Milwaukee Daily Sentinel

Missouri Democrat (St. Louis)

Missouri Republican (St. Louis)

Neue Zeit (St. Louis)

New York Courier and Enquirer

New York Evening Post

New York Herald

New York Journal of Commerce

New York Observer

New York Times

New York Tribune

New York World

New-Yorker Demokrat

Philadelphia Inquirer

Phunny Fellow (New York)

Poughkeepsie (NY) *American*

Sangamo Journal (later the *Illinois State Journal* [Springfield])

Staats-Zeitung (St. Louis)

St. Louis *Volksblatt*

Washington Evening Star

Selected Internet Sites

American Jewish Archives: https://sites.americanjewisharchives.org

American Presidency Project: https://www.presidency.ucsb.edu

Essential Civil War Curriculum: https://essentialcivilwarcurriculum.com

Germans in the Civil War: http://www.geocities.com/Athens/Aylantis/2816/germans/units.html [archived]

The Immigrants' Civil War: https://longislandwins.com/immigrants-civil-war

Irish in the American Civil War: https://irishamericancivilwar.com

Jews in the Civil War: http://www.jewish-history.com

Scots in the Civil War: http://acwscots.co.uk

The Shapell Roster of Jewish Service in the American Civil War: www.shapell.org/civil-war-soldier-database

Government Publications

DeBow, J. D. B. *Statistical View of the United States: Compendium of the Seventh Census.* Washington, DC: Beverly Tucker, 1854.

Kennedy, Joseph C. G. *Population of the United States in 1860: Compiled from the Original Returns of the Eighth Census.* Washington, DC: Government Printing Office, 1864.

The Seventh Census: Report of the Superintendent of the Census for December 1, 1852. Washington, DC: Robert Armstrong, 1853.

U.S. House of Representatives, Committee on Foreign Affairs. *Report on Foreign Criminals and Paupers (Report No. 358). 34th Congress, 1st Session.* Washington, DC: Government Printing Office, 1856.

U.S. Secretary of the Interior. *Statistics of the United States, (Including Mortality, Property, &c.) in 1860; Compiled from the Original Returns and Being the Final Exhibit of the Eighth Census.* Washington, DC: Government Printing Office, 1866.

The War of the Rebellion: A Compilation of the Official Records of the War of the Union and Confederate Armies. 70 vols. Washington, DC: Government Printing Office, 1880–1901.

Manuscript Collections

Abraham Lincoln Papers (Robert Todd Lincoln Papers), Library of Congress

Papers of Abraham Lincoln, Abraham Lincoln Presidential Library and Museum, Springfield, Illinois

James Gordon Bennett Papers, Library of Congress

Horace Greeley Papers, Library of Congress

Horace Greeley Papers, New York Public Library

James Harper Papers, New-York Historical Society

Gustave Koerner Papers, University of Illinois Urbana-Champaign

George B. McClellan Papers, Library of Congress

John G. Nicolay Papers, Library of Congress

Records of the Order of United Americans, New-York Historical Society

Henry O'Reilly Papers, New-York Historical Society

Carl Schurz Papers, Library of Congress

William Tecumseh Sherman Family Papers, University of Notre Dame

Franz Sigel Papers, New-York Historical Society

Lyman Trumbull Papers, Library of Congress

Henry Villard Papers, Houghton Library, Harvard University

Selected records and documents, Gilder Lehrman Collection, New-York Historical Society

Primary Sources

Anonymous. *Fremont's Romanism Established. Acknowledged by Archbishop Hughes. How Fremont's Nomination Was Brought About. Hughes, Seward, Fremont, and the Foreigners—a Most Foul Coalition*. American Party pamphlet, n.p., 1856.

———. *A Full Account of the Late Awful Riots in Philadelphia*. Philadelphia: John B. Perry, 1844.

———. *The Full Particulars of the Late Riots, with a View of the Burning of the Catholic Churches, St. Michaels and St. Augustines.* Philadelphia: n.p., 1844.

Ayres, Stephen Cooper. *Sketch of the Life and Services of Vice Admiral Stephen C. Rowan, U.S. Navy.* Ohio Commandery of the Loyal Legion of the United States, 1910.

Barnes, David. *The Draft Riots in New York, July 1863.* New York: Baker & Godwin, 1863.

Bartlett, D. W. *The Life and Public Services of Hon. Abraham Lincoln [. . .].* Cincinnati: Moore, Wilstach, Keys & Co., 1860.

Bates, David Homer. *Lincoln in the Telegraph Office: Recollections of the United States Military Telegraph Corps During the Civil War.* New York: Century Co., 1907.

———. *Lincoln Stories Told by Him in the Military Office in the War Department During the Civil War.* New York: William Edwin Rudge, 1926.

Bates, Edward. *The Diary of Edward Bates, 1859–1866.* Edited by Howard K. Beale. Washington, DC: Government Printing Office, 1933.

Beach, William H. *The First (Lincoln) Cavalry from April 19, 1861, to July 7, 1865.* New York: Lincoln Cavalry Association, 1902.

Belmont, August. *A Few Letters and Speeches of the Late Civil War.* New York: privately printed, 1870.

———. *Letters, Speeches and Addresses of August Belmont.* [New York]: privately printed, 1890.

Bennett, James Gordon. *Memoirs of James Gordon Bennett and His Times by a Journalist* [Isaac L. Pray]. New York: Stringer & Townsend, 1855.

Börnstein, Heinrich [Henry Boernstein]. *Memoirs of a Nobody: The Missouri Years of an Austrian Radical, 1849–1866.* Edited and translated by Steven Rowan. St. Louis: Missouri Historical Society Press, 1997. Originally published 1881 as *Memoiren.*

Bright, John. *Speeches of John Bright, M.P. on the American Question.* With an introduction by Frank Moore. Boston: Little, Brown, 1865.

Brooks, Noah. *Abraham Lincoln and the Downfall of American Slavery.* New York: G. P. Putnam's Sons, 1894. First published 1888.

———. *Lincoln Observed: Civil War Dispatches of Noah Brooks.* Edited by Michael Burlingame. Baltimore: Johns Hopkins University Press, 1998.

———. *Mr. Lincoln's Washington: Selections from the Writings of Noah Brooks, Civil War Correspondent.* Edited by P. J. Staudenraus. South Brunswick, NJ: Thomas Yoseloff, 1967.

———. *Washington in Lincoln's Time.* New York: Century Co., 1895.

Brown, Marshall. *Bulls and Blunders.* Chicago: S. C. Griggs & Co., 1893.

Browne, Francis Fisher. *The Every-day Life of Abraham Lincoln*. New York: N. D. Thompson, 1886.

Browne, Junius Henri. *The Great Metropolis; A Mirror of New York. A Complete History of Metropolitan Life and Society, with Sketches of Prominent Places, Persons and Things in the City, as they Actually Exist*. Hartford, CT: American Publishing Co., 1869.

"Brutus." See Morse, Samuel F. B.

[Bunkley, Josephine M.] *The Escaped Nun: or, Disclosures of Convent Life; and the Confessions of a Sister of Charity, Giving a More Minute Detail; of their Inner Life and a Bolder Revelation of the Mysteries and Secrets of Nunneries than Have Ever Before Been Submitted to the American Public*. New York: De Witt & Davenport, 1855.

[Burr, Walter H.] *The Murder of Abraham Lincoln Planned and Executed by Jesuit Priests*. Indianapolis: Ironclad Age, 1893.

Busey, Samuel C. *Immigration: Its Evils and Consequences*. New York: De Witt & Davenport, 1856.

Cadwallader, Sylvanus. *Three Years with Grant*. Edited by Benjamin P. Thomas. New York: Alfred A. Knopf, 1955.

Canisius, Theodor. *Abraham Lincoln: Historisches Charakterbild*. Vienna: Christoph Reisser, 1867.

Carpenter, Francis B. *Six Months at the White House with Abraham Lincoln. The Story of a Picture*. New York: Hurd & Houghton, 1866.

Carr, Clark E. *My Day and Generation*. Chicago: A. C. McClurg, 1907.

Carroll, Anna Ella. *The Great American Battle; or the Contest Between Christianity and Political Romanism*. New York and Auburn: Miller, Orton & Mulligan, 1856.

Chambrun, Marquis Adolphe de. *Impressions of Lincoln and the Civil War: A Foreigner's Account*. Translated by Adalbert de Chambrun. New York: Random House, 1952.

Chase, Salmon P. *Inside Lincoln's Cabinet: The Civil War Diaries of Salmon P. Chase*. Edited by David Donald. New York: Longman's, Green & Co., 1954.

———. *Papers of Salmon P. Chase*. Edited by John Niven. 5 vols. Kent, OH: Kent State University Press, 1993–1998.

Chiniquy, Charles. *Fifty Years in the Church of Rome*. Chicago: Adam Craig, 1888.

Chittenden, L[ucius]. E. *Recollections of President Lincoln and His Administration*. New York: Harper & Bros., 1891.

Clay, Cassius Marcellus. *The Life of Cassius Marcellus Clay. Memoirs, Writings, and Speeches, Showing His Conduct in the Overthrowing of American Slavery, the Salvation of the Union, and the Restoration of the Autonomy of the States*. 2 vols. Cincinnati: J. Fletcher Brennan & Co., 1886.

Condon, William H. *Life of Major-General James Shields: Hero of Three Wars and Senator from Three States*. Chicago: Blakely Printing Co., 1900.

Conolly, Thomas. *An Irishman in Dixie: Thomas Conolly's Diary of the Fall of the Confederacy*. Edited by Nelson D. Lankford. Columbia: University of South Carolina Press, 1988.

Conyngham, D. P. *The Irish Brigade and Its Campaigns: With Some Account of the Corcoran Legion, and Sketches of the Principal Officers*. New York: William McSorley & Co., 1867.

Corby, W[illiam]. *Memoirs of Chaplain Life*. Chicago: La Monte, O'Donnell & Co., 1893.

Corcoran, Michael. *The Captivity of General Corcoran: The Only Authentic and Reliable Narrative of the Trials and Sufferings Endured During His Twelve Months' Imprisonment in Richmond and Other Southern Cities*. Philadelphia: Barclay & Co., 1865.

Crotty, D. G. *Four Years in the Army of the Potomac*. Grand Rapids, MI: Dygert Bros. & Co., 1874.

Daeuble, John, and Gottfried Rentschler. *Two Germans in the Civil War: The Diary of John Daeuble and the Letters of Gottfried Rentschler, 6th Kentucky Volunteer Infantry*. Edited by Joseph R. Reinhart. Knoxville: University of Tennessee Press, 2004.

Dahlgren, John A. *Memoir of John A. Dahlgren, Rear-Admiral of U.S. Navy*. Edited by Madeleine Vinton Dahlgren. Boston: James R. Osgood, 1883.

De Hauranne, Ernest Duvergier. *A Frenchman in Lincoln's America*. Translated and edited by Ralph H. Bowen. 2 vols. Chicago: R. R. Donnelly & Sons, 1974.

Dicey, Edward. *Spectator of America*. Edited by Herbert Mitgang. Chicago: Quadrangle Books, 1971.

Dickens, Charles. *American Notes for General Circulation*. New York: Harper & Bros., 1842.

Dix, John Adams. *Memoirs of John Adams Dix Compiled by His Son Morgan Dix*. 2 vols. New York: Harper & Bros., 1883.

Domschcke, Bernard. *Twenty Months in Captivity: Memoirs of a Union Officer in Confederate Prisons*. Edited and translated by Frederic Trautmann. Cranbury, NJ: Associated University Press, 1987.

Douglas, Stephen A. *The Letters of Stephen A. Douglas*. Edited by Robert W. Johannsen. Urbana: University of Illinois Press, 1961.

Downing, Major Jack [Seba Smith]. *Letters of Major Jack Downing of the Downingville Militia*. New York: Bromley & Co., 1864.

Fehrenbacher, Don E., and Virginia Fehrenbacher, eds. *Recollected Words of Abraham Lincoln*. Stanford, CA: Stanford University Press, 1996.

Fox, William F. *Regimental Losses in the American Civil War, 1861–1865. A Treatise on the Extent and Nature of the Mortuary Losses in the Union Regiments. With Full and Exhaustive Statistics Compiled from the Official Records on File in the State Military Bureaus and at Washington*. Albany, NY: Albany Publishing, 1889.

Franklin, Benjamin. *Information to Those Who Would Remove to America, and Remarks Concerning the Savages of North America*. London: John Stockdale, 1784.

———. *Observations Concerning the Increase of Mankind, Peopling of Countries, &c.* Boston: S. Kneeland, 1755.

———. *The Papers of Benjamin Franklin*. Vol. 4, *July 1, 1750, Through June 30, 1753*. Edited by Leonard W. Larabee. New Haven, CT: Yale University Press, 1961.

Frémont, John Charles. *Memoirs of My Life, Including in the Narrative Five Journeys of Western Exploration, During the Years 1842, 1843–4, 1845–6–7, 1848–9, 1853–4. [. . .] A Retrospect of Fifty Years, Covering the Most Eventful Periods of Modern American History*. Chicago: Belford, Clarke & Co., 1887.

Fry, James B. *New York and the Conscription of 1863: A Chapter in the History of the Civil War*. New York: G. P. Putnam's Sons, 1868.

Gilmore, James R. *Personal Recollections of Abraham Lincoln and the Civil War*. Boston: L. C. Page & Co., 1898.

Grant, Ulysses S. *The Papers of Ulysses S. Grant*. Edited by John Y. Simon and John F. Marszalek. 32 vols. Carbondale: Southern Illinois University Press, 1967–2012.

———. *Personal Memoirs of U. S. Grant*. 2 vols. New York: Charles L. Webster, 1885.

Greeley, Horace. *Recollections of a Busy Life: Including Reminiscences of American Politics and Politicians, from the Opening of the Missouri Contest to the Downfall of Slavery [. . .]*. New York: J. B. Ford & Co., 1868.

Gurowski, Adam. *Diary, from March 4, 1861, to November 12, 1862*. Boston: Lee & Shepard, 1862.

———. *Diary, from November 18, 1862, to October 18, 1863*. 2 vols. New York: Carleton, 1864.

———. *Diaries: 1863-'64-'65*. Washington, DC: W. H. and O. H. Morrison, 1866.

Guyer, I. D. *History of Chicago; Its Commercial and Manufacturing Interests and Industry [. . .]*. Chicago: Church, Goodman & Cushing, 1862.

Hall, Basil. *Travels in North America in the Years 1827 and 1828*. Edinburgh: Robert Cadell, 1830.

Halliday, Samuel B. *The Lost and Found; or Life Among the Poor.* New York: Phinney, Blakeman & Mason, 1860.

Halpine, Charles G. *The Life and Adventures, Songs, Services, and Speeches of Private Miles O'Reilly.* New York: Carleton, 1864.

[————.] *The Poetical Works of Charles G. Halpine (Miles O'Reilly). Consisting of Odes, Poems, Sonnets, Epics, and Lyrical Effusions Which Have Not Heretofore Been Collected Together, with a Biographical Sketch and Explanatory Notes.* Edited by Robert B. Roosevelt. New York: Harper & Bros., 1869.

Hancock, William. *An Emigrant's Five Years in the Free States of America.* London: T. Cautley Newby, 1860.

Hay, John M. *At Lincoln's Side: John Hay's Civil War Correspondence and Selected Writing.* Edited by Michael Burlingame. Carbondale: Southern Illinois University Press, 2000.

————. *Inside Lincoln's White House: The Complete Civil War Diary of John Hay.* Edited by Michael Burlingame and John R. Turner Ettlinger. Carbondale: Southern Illinois University Press, 1999.

————. *John Hay's Anonymous Writings for the Press, 1860–1864.* Edited by Michael Burlingame. Carbondale: Southern Illinois University Press, 1998.

————. *Lincoln's Journalist: John Hay's Anonymous Writings for the Press, 1860–1864.* Edited by Michael Burlingame. Carbondale: Southern Illinois University Press, 1998.

Hensel, Louis. *My Life in America Before, During, and After the Civil War: Includes Meeting President Abraham Lincoln.* Translated by Sigrid Wilshinsky. New York: Jo-An Books, 2009.

Herndon, William H. *Herndon on Lincoln: Letters.* Edited by Douglas L. Wilson and Rodney O. Davis. Urbana: University of Illinois Press, 2016.

————, and Jesse W. Weik. *Lincoln's Herndon: The True Story of a Great Life.* 3 vols. Chicago: Belford & Clark, 1889.

Hertz, Emanuel. *Abraham Lincoln: The Tribute of the Synagogue* [sermons ca. 1865]. New York: Bloch, 1927.

Johnson, Charles W., ed. *Proceedings of the First Three Republican National Conventions of 1856, 1860 and 1864, Including Proceedings of the Antecedent National Convention Held at Pittsburg in February, 1856, as Reported by Horace Greeley.* Minneapolis: Harrison & Smith, 1893.

Johnson, Robert Underwood, and Clarence Clough Buell, eds. *Battles and Leaders of the Civil War. Being for the Most Part Contributions by Union and Confederate Officers. Based upon "The Century War Series."* 4 vols. New York: Century Co., 1887–1888.

Johnston, James F. W. *Notes on North America*. Boston: Charles C. Little & James Brown, 1851.

Kamphoefner, Walter D., and Wolfgang Helbich, eds. *Germans in the Civil War: The Letters They Wrote Home*. Translated by Susan Carter Vogel. Chapel Hill: University of North Carolina Press, 2006. Originally published as *Deutsche im Amerikanischen Bürgerkrieg: Briefe von Front und Farm, 1861–1865*. Ferdinand Schöningh: Paderborn 2002.

Kaufmann, Wilhelm. *The Germans in the American Civil War*. Edited by Don Henrich Tolzmann and translated by Steven Rowan. Carlisle, PA: John Kallmann, 1999.

Kircher, Henry A. *A German in the Yankee Fatherland: The Civil War Letters of Henry A. Kircher*. Edited by Earl J. Hess. Kent, OH: Kent State University Press, 1983.

The Know Nothing Almanac 1855. New York: T. W. Strong, 1855.

Koerner, Gustave. *Memoirs of Gustave Koerner, 1809–1896: Life-Sketches Written at the Suggestion of His Children*. Edited by Thomas J. McCormack. 2 vols. Cedar Rapids, IA: Torch Press, 1909.

Kune [Kuné], Julian. *Reminiscences of an Octogenarian Hungarian Exile*. Chicago: published by the author, 1911.

Lamon, Ward Hill. *The Life of Abraham Lincoln as President: A Personal Account by Lincoln's Bodyguard*. Edited by Bob O'Connor. West Conshohocken, PA: Montclair, 2010.

———. *The Life of Abraham Lincoln, from His Birth to His Inauguration as President*. Boston: James R. Osgood, 1872.

———. *Recollections of Abraham Lincoln, 1847–1865*. Edited by Dorothy Lamon. Chicago: A. C. McClurg, 1895.

Laurens, J. Wayne. *The Crisis: or, The Enemies of America Unmasked*. Philadelphia: G. D. Miller, 1855.

Lee, John Hancock. *The Origin and Progress of the American Party in Politics: Embracing a Complete History of the Philadelphia Riots in May and July, 1844, With a Full Description of the Great American Procession of July Fourth, and a Refutation of the Arguments Founded on the Charges of Religious Proscription and Secret Combinations*. Philadelphia: Elliott & Gihon, 1855.

Leonard, Ellen. *Three Days' Reign of Terror, or the July Riots in 1863, in New York*. New York: Harper's, 1867.

Lieber, Francis. *The Life and Letters of Francis Lieber*. Edited by Thomas Sergeant Perry. Boston, James. R. Osgood, 1882.

———. *On Civil Liberty and Self-Government*. 3rd ed. Edited by Theodore D. Woolsey. Philadelphia: J. B. Lippincott, 1883.

Lincoln, Abraham. *The Collected Works of Abraham Lincoln*. 8 vols. Edited by Roy P. Basler. New Brunswick, NJ: Rutgers University Press, 1953–1955.

———. *The Collected Works of Abraham Lincoln: Supplement 1832–1865*. Edited by Roy P. Basler. Westport, CT: Greenwood Press, 1974.

———. *The Collected Works of Abraham Lincoln: Second Supplement 1848–1865*. Edited by Roy P. Basler and Christian O. Basler. New Brunswick: Rutgers University Press, 1990.

———. *Political Debates Between Hon. Abraham Lincoln and Hon. Stephen A. Douglas in the Celebrated Campaign of 1858, in Illinois; Including the Preceding Speeches of Each, at Chicago, Springfield, etc. [. . .] as Carefully Prepared by the Reporters of Each Party, and Published at the Times of their Delivery*. Columbus, OH: Follett & Foster, 1860.

Lincoln, Mary Todd. [*Letters*]. See Turner, Justin G., and Linda Levitt Turner.

Losing, Benson J. *Pictorial History of the Civil War in America*. 2 vols. Vol. 1. Philadelphia: George W. Childs, 1866.

Lyons, W. F. *Brigadier General Thomas Francis Meagher: His Political and Military Career; with Selections from His Speeches and Writings*. New York: D. & J. Sadlier & Co., 1870.

Mackay, Alexander. *The Western World; or, Travels in the United States in 1846–47 [. . .]*. 3 vols. London: Richard Bentley, 1850.

Maguire, John Francis. *The Irish in America*. London: Longmans, Green, 1868.

Mahony, D[ennis]. A. *The Prisoner of State*. New York: Carleton, 1863.

McCarter, William. *My Life in the Irish Brigade: The Civil War Memoirs of Private William McCarter, 116th Pennsylvania Infantry*. Edited by Kevin E. O'Brien. Cambridge, MA: Da Capo Press, 2003. Originally published 1896.

McNamara, M. H. *The Irish Ninth in Bivouac and Battle; or Virginia and Maryland Campaigns*. Boston: Lee & Shepard, 1867.

Meagher, Thomas F. *Memoirs of Gen. Thomas Francis Meagher, Comprising the Leading Events of His Career Chronologically Arranged, with Selections from His Speeches, Lectures, and Miscellaneous Writings, Including Personal Reminiscences [. . .]*. Edited by Michael Cavanagh. Worcester, MA: Messenger Press, 1892.

[Morse, Samuel F. B.]. *Foreign Conspiracy Against the Liberties of the United States*. New York: Leavitt, Lord & Co., 1835.

Mueller, Jacob. *Memories of a Forty-Eighter: Sketches from the German-American Period of Storm and Stress in the 1850s*. Edited and translated by Steven Rowan. Cleveland: Western Reserve Historical Society. Originally published 1896.

Mulholland, St. Clair A. *The Story of the 166th Regiment Pennsylvania Volunteers in the War of the Rebellion: The Record of a Gallant Command*. Philadelphia: F. McManus Jr. & Co., 1903.

Nicolay, John G., and John Hay. *Abraham Lincoln: A History*. 10 vols. New York: Century Co., 1890.

"One of 'Em," ed. *The Wide-Awake Gift: Know-Nothing Token for 1855*. New York: J. C. Derby, 1855.

Orr, Hector. *The Native American: A Gift for the People*. Philadelphia: Hector Orr, 1845.

Page, Charles A. *The Naturalization Question: From the Stand-Point of a United States Consul in Europe*. Washington, DC: Philip & Solomons, 1869.

Pendel, Thomas F. *Thirty-Six Years in the White House: Lincoln to Roosevelt*. Washington, DC: Neale Publishing, 1902.

Phisterer, Frederick. *New York in the War of the Rebellion, 1861 to 1865*. 2nd ed. New York: Weed, Parsons & Co., 1890.

Piatt, Donn. *Memories of the Men Who Saved the Union*. Chicago: Belford, Clarke & Co., 1887.

Pierce, Edward L. *Letter of Edward L. Pierce, Esq., of Chicago, Containing Important Statistics in Regard to the Foreign Vote at the Presidential Election*. Boston: Commercial Printing House, 1857.

Pinkerton, Allan. *The Spy of the Rebellion; Being a True History of the Spy System of the United States Army During the Late Rebellion Revealing Many Secrets of the War Hitherto Not Made Public. Compiled from Official Reports Prepared for President Lincoln, General McClellan, and the Provost-Marshal-General*. Philadelphia: H. W. Kelley, 1883.

Poore, Ben Perley. *Perley's Reminiscences of Sixty Years in the National Metropolis, Illustrating the Wit, Humor, Genius, Eccentricities, Jealousies, Ambitions and Intrigues of the Brilliant Statesmen, Ladies, Officers, Diplomats, Lobbyists and other noted Celebrities of the World that gather at the Centre of the Nation [. . .]*. 2 vols. Philadelphia: Hubbard Brothers, 1886.

Porter, Kirk H., and Donald Bruce Johnson, eds. *National Party Platforms, 1840–1960*. Urbana: University of Illinois Press, 1961.

Proceedings of the First National Convention of the Fenian Brotherhood Held in Chicago, Illinois, November 1863. Philadelphia: James Gibbons, 1863.

Proceedings of the Second National Congress of the Fenian Brotherhood Held in Cincinnati, Ohio, January, 1865. Philadelphia: James Gibbons, 1863.

Raymond, Henry J. *History of the Administration of President Lincoln: Including His Speeches, Letters, Addresses, Proclamations, and Messages, and with a Preliminary Sketch of His Life*. New York: Derby & Miller, 1864.

———. *The Life and Public Services of Abraham Lincoln, Sixteenth President of the United States; Together with His State Papers [. . .]*. New York: Derby & Miller, 1865.

Robinson, William E. *Speech of William E. Robinson, in Exposition of New Hampshire Democracy in its Relations to Catholic Emancipation, Including a Scrutiny of the Part Taken with Reference Thereto, by Gen. Franklin Pierce. An Exposure of the False Pretences and False Assertions of Geo. M. Dallas and Others, Respecting the Action of the Whigs of New Hampshire.* New York: New York Tribune, 1852.

Ryan, John. *Campaigning with the Irish Brigade: Pvt. John Ryan, 28th Massachusetts.* Edited by Sandy Barnard. Terre Haute, IN: AST Press, 2001.

Saint-Gaudens, Augustus. *The Reminiscences of Augustus Saint-Gaudens.* Edited by Homer Saint-Gaudens. 2 vols. New York: Century Co., 1913.

Savage, John D. *Fenian Heroes and Martyrs.* Boston: Patrick Donahoe, 1868.

Schade, Louis. *The Immigration into the United States of America, from a Statistical and National-Economical Point of View.* Washington, DC: Daily Union, 1856.

Schurz, Carl. *Abraham Lincoln: A Biographical Essay, with an Essay on the Portraits of Lincoln by Truman H. Bartlett.* Boston: Houghton Mifflin, 1907.

———. *Carl Schurz, Revolutionary and Statesman: His Life in Personal and Official Documents with Illustrations.* Edited by Rüdiger B. Wersich. Gräfelfing, Germany: Verlag Moos & Partner, 1986.

———. *Intimate Letters of Carl Schurz, 1841–1869.* Edited by Joseph Schafer. Madison: State Historical Society of Wisconsin, 1929.

———. *The Reminiscences of Carl Schurz.* 3 vols. New York: McClure Co., 1907–1908.

———. *Speeches, Correspondence, and Political Papers of Carl Schurz.* 6 vols. Edited by Frederic Bancroft. New York: G. P. Putnam's Sons, 1913.

Seward, Frederick W. *Reminiscences of a War-Time Statesman and Diplomat, 1830–1915.* New York: G. P. Putnam's Sons, 1916.

———. *Seward at Washington, as Senator and Secretary of State: A Memoir of His Life, with Selections from His Letters, 1861–1872.* New York: Derby & Miller, 1891.

Seward, William H. *Autobiography of William H. Seward, from 1801–1834. With a Memoir of His Life, and Selections from His Letters from 1831–1846.* Edited by Frederick W. Seward. New York: D. Appleton, 1877.

Sheridan, Philip H. *Personal Memoirs of P. H. Sheridan, General United States Army.* New York: Charles L. Webster & Co., 1888.

Sherman, William T. *Memoirs of General William T. Sherman by Himself.* 2 vols. New York: D. Appleton & Co., 1875.

Sparks, Edwin Erle. *The Lincoln–Douglas Debates of 1858.* Collections of the Illinois State Historical Library, Lincoln Series, Volume 1. Springfield: Illinois State Historical Library, 1908.

[Spiegel, Marcus]. *Your True Marcus: The Civil War Letters of a Jewish Colonel.* Edited by Frank L. Byrne and Jean Powers Soman. Kent, OH: Kent State University Press, 1985.

Stevens, C. A. *Berdan's United States Sharp Shooters in the Army of the Potomac, 1861–1865.* Edited by Stuart Vogt. Dayton, OH: Morningside, 1984. Originally published 1892.

Stoddard, William O. *Inside the White House in War Times.* New York: Charles L. Webster, 1890.

———. *Inside the White House in War Times: Memoirs and Reports of Lincoln's Secretary.* Edited by Michael Burlingame. Lincoln: University of Nebraska Press, 2000.

———. *Lincoln's Third Secretary: The Memoirs of William O. Stoddard.* Edited by William O. Stoddard Jr. New York: Exposition Press, 1955.

———. *Lincoln's White House Secretary: The Adventurous Life of William O. Stoddard* [memoirs]. Edited by Harold Holzer. Carbondale: Southern Illinois University Press, 2007.

[———]. *The Volcano Under the City by a Volunteer Special.* New York: Fords, Howard & Hulbert, 1887.

Strong, George Templeton. *The Diary of George Templeton Strong.* Edited by Allan Nevins and Milton Halsey Thomas. 4 vols. New York: Macmillan, 1952.

Sullivan, James P. *An Irishman in the Iron Brigade: The Civil War Memoirs of James P. Sullivan, Sergt., Company K, 6th Wisconsin Volunteers.* Edited by William J. K. Beaudot and Lance J. Herdegen. New York: Fordham University Press, 1993.

Thornton, John. *Diary of a Tour Through the Northern States of the Union, and Canada.* London: F. Barker, 1850.

Tisdale, W. S., ed. *Know Nothing Almanac and True Americans' Manual for 1856.* New York: De Witt & Davenport, 1855.

Tocqueville, Alexis. *Democracy in America.* New York: George Adlard, 1839.

Tocqueville, Alexis de. *Democracy in America.* Edited by Phillips Bradley. 2 vols. New York: Alfred A. Knopf, 1945. Originally printed 1835.

Townsend, George Alfred. *The Real Life of Abraham Lincoln: A Talk with Mr. Herndon, His Late Law Partner.* New York: Bible House, 1867.

Turner, Justin G., and Linda Levitt Turner, eds. *Mary Todd Lincoln: Her Life and Letters.* New York: Alfred A. Knopf, 1972.

Villard, Henry. *Lincoln on the Eve of '61: A Journalist's Story by Henry Villard.* Edited by Harold G. Villard and Oswald Garrison Villard. New York: Alfred A. Knopf, 1954.

———. *Memoirs of Henry Villard: Journalist and Financier, 1835–1900*. 2 vols. Boston: Houghton Mifflin, 1904.

———. *Sixteenth President-in-Waiting: Abraham Lincoln and the Springfield Dispatches of Henry Villard, 1860–1861*. Edited by Michael Burlingame. Carbondale: Southern Illinois University Press, 2018.

Von Borcke, Heros. *Memoirs of the Confederate War for Independence*. Edinburgh and London: W. Blackwood & Sons, 1867.

Wagner, William. *History of the 24th Illinois Volunteer Infantry Regiment (Old Hecker Regiment)*. Chicago: n.p., 1911. Originally published in German, 1864.

Ward, William Hayes. *Abraham Lincoln: Tributes from His Associates—Reminiscences of Soldiers, Statesmen and Citizens*. New York: T. Y. Crowell & Co., 1895.

Weed, Thurlow. *Memoir of Thurlow Weed*. Edited by Thurlow Weed Barnes. Boston: Houghton, Mifflin & Co., 1884.

Welles, Gideon. *Diary of Gideon Welles*. Edited by John T. Morse Jr. 3 vols. Boston: Houghton Mifflin, 1911.

Welsh, Peter. *Irish Green and Union Blue: The Civil War Letters of Peter Welsh*. Edited by Lawrence F. Kohl and Margaret Crosse Richard. New York: Fordham University Press, 1986.

Whitney, Henry Clay. *Life on the Circuit with Lincoln*. Boston: Estes & Lauriat, 1892.

———. *Lincoln the Citizen*. New York: Baker & Taylor, 1908.

Whitney, Thomas R. *A Defence of the American Policy, as Opposed to the Encroachments of Foreign Influence, and Especially to the Interference of the Papacy in the Political Interests and Affairs of the United States*. New York: De Witt & Davenport, 1856.

Williams, John. *Immigration: A Letter to Peter Cooper, Esq*. New York: Offices of the Hardware Reporter, 1864.

Wilson, Douglas L., and Rodney O. Davis, eds. *Herndon's Informants: Letters, Interviews, and Statements About Abraham Lincoln*. Urbana: University of Illinois Press, 1998.

Wolf, Simon. *The American Jew as Patriot, Soldier and Citizen*. Philadelphia: Levytype Co., 1895.

Wyse, Francis. *America: Its Realities and Resource; Comprising Important Details Connected with the Present Social, Political, Agricultural, Commercial, and Financial State of the Country [. . .]*. 3 vols. London: T. C. Newby, 1846.

Secondary Sources

Abinder, Tyler. *Nativism and Slavery: The Northern Know Nothings and the Politics of the 1850s*. New York: Oxford University Press, 1992.

Achorn, Edward. *The Lincoln Miracle: Inside the Republican Convention That Changed History.* New York: Atlantic Monthly Press, 2023.

Ackerman, Bruce. *We the People: Transformations.* Cambridge, MA: Harvard University Press, 2000.

Ahearn, Robert G. *Thomas Francis Meagher: An Irish Revolutionary in America.* Boulder: University of Colorado Press, 1949.

Allendorf, Donald. *"Your Friend, as Ever, A. Lincoln": How the Unlikely Friendship of Gustav Koerner and Abraham Lincoln Changed America.* Gretna, LA: Pelican Publishing, 2014.

Anbinder, Tyler. *Nativism and Slavery: The Northern Know Nothings and the Politics of the 1850s.* New York: Oxford University Press, 1992.

Anderson, Galusha. *The Story of a Border City During the Civil War.* Boston: Little, Brown & Co., 1908.

Anderson, George McCullough. *The Work of Adalbert Johann Volck, 1828–1912, Who Chose for His Name the Anagram V. Blada, 1861–1865.* Baltimore: George McCullough Anderson, 1970.

Anderson, Kristen Layne. *Abolitionizing Missouri: German Immigrants and Racial Ideology in Nineteenth-Century America.* Baton Rouge: Louisiana State University Press, 2016.

Angle, Paul M. *"Here I Have Lived": A History of Lincoln's Springfield.* Chicago: Abraham Lincoln Book Shop, 1971. Originally published 1935.

Appelbaum, Laura Cohen, and Claire Uzel, eds. *Jewish Life in Mr. Lincoln's City.* Washington, DC: Jewish Historical Society of Washington, 2015.

Baker, Jean H. *Affairs of Party: The Political Culture of Northern Democrats in the Mid-Nineteenth Century.* Ithaca, NY: Cornell University Press, 1983.

———. *Ambivalent Americans.* Baltimore: Johns Hopkins University Press, 1977.

Baron, Frank. *Abraham Lincoln and the German Immigrants: Turners and Forty-Eighters.* Topeka: Society for German-American Studies, University of Kansas, 2012.

Bennett, David H. *The Party of Fear: From Nativist Movements to the New Right in American History.* Chapel Hill: University of North Carolina Press, 1988.

Bensel, Richard Franklin. *The American Ballot Box in the Mid-Nineteenth Century.* New York: Cambridge University Press, 2004.

Bernstein, Iver. *The New York City Draft Riots: Their Significance for American Society and Politics in the Age of the Civil War.* New York: Oxford University Press, 1990.

Bilby, Joseph G. *The Irish Brigade in the Civil War: The 69th New York and Other Irish Regiments of the Army of the Potomac.* Cambridge, MA: Da Capo Press, 1997. Originally published in 1995 as *Remember Fontenoy!*

Billington, Ray Allen. *Protestant Crusade, 1800–1860: A Study of the Origins of American Nativism.* New York: Macmillan, 1938.

Black, David. *The King of Fifth Avenue: The Fortunes of August Belmont.* New York: Dial Press, 1981.

Blumenthal, Sidney. *The Political Life of Abraham Lincoln.* Vol. 2, *Wrestling with His Angel, 1849–1856.* New York: Simon & Schuster, 2017.

Brancaforte, Charlotte L., ed. *The German Forty-Eighters in the United States.* New York: Peter Lang, 1989.

Bremer, Robert H. *The Public Good: Philanthropy and Welfare in the Civil War Era.* New York: Alfred A. Knopf, 1980.

Brown, Thomas N. *Irish-American Nationalism.* New York: J. B. Lippincott, 1966.

Bruncken, Ernest. *The Political Activity of Wisconsin Germans, 1854–1860.* Madison: State Historical Society of Wisconsin, 1901.

Buccola, Nicholas. *Abraham Lincoln and Liberal Democracy.* Lawrence: University Press of Kansas, 2016.

Bunker, Gary L. *From Rail-Splitter to Icon: Lincoln's Image in Illustrated Periodicals, 1860–1865.* Kent, OH: Kent State University Press, 2001.

Burlingame, Michael. *Abraham Lincoln: A Life.* 2 vols. Baltimore: Johns Hopkins University Press, 2008.

———. *An American Marriage: The Untold Story of Abraham Lincoln and Mary Todd.* New York: Pegasus, 2021.

Burton, Orville Vernon. *The Age of Lincoln.* New York: Hill & Wang, 2007.

Burton, William L. *Melting Pot Soldiers: The Union's Ethnic Regiments.* Ames: Iowa State University Press, 1988. Originally published 1951.

Campanella, Richard. *Lincoln in New Orleans: The 1828–1831 Flatboat Voyages and Their Place in History.* Lafayette: University of Louisiana at Lafayette Press, 2010.

Carden, Allen, and Thomas J. Ebert. *John George Nicolay: The Man in Lincoln's Shadow.* Knoxville: University of Tennessee Press, 2019.

Carman, Henry J., and Reinhard J. Luthin. *Lincoln and the Patronage.* New York: Columbia University Press, 1943.

Carson, Oliver. *The Man Who Made News: James Gordon Bennett.* New York: Duell, Sloan & Pearce, 1942.

Carwardine, Richard, and Jay Sexton, eds. *The Global Lincoln.* New York: Oxford University Press, 2011.

Clarke, Duncan. *A New World: The History of Immigration into the United States.* San Diego: Thunder Bay Press, 2000.

Clayton, John. *The Illinois Fact Book and Historical Almanac, 1673–1968.* Carbondale: Southern Illinois University Press, 1970.

Clinton, Catherine. *Mrs. Lincoln: A Life.* New York: Harper, 2009.

Conroy, James B. *Lincoln's White House: The People's House in Wartime.* New York: Rowman & Littlefield, 2017.

Conzen, Kathleen Neils. *Immigrant Milwaukee, 1836–1860.* Cambridge, MA: Harvard University Press, 1976.

Cook, Adrian. *The Armies of the Streets: The New York Draft Riots of 1863.* Lexington: University Press of Kentucky, 1974.

Coolidge, Mary Roberts. *Chinese Immigration.* New York: Henry Holt, 1909.

Crissey, Elwell. *Lincoln's Lost Speech: The Pivot of His Career.* New York: Hawthorn Books, 1967.

Current, Richard N. *Speaking of Abraham Lincoln: The Man and His Meaning for Our Times.* Urbana: University of Illinois Press, 1989.

———. *Unity, Ethnicity, and Abraham Lincoln* (R. Gerald McMurtry Lecture). Fort Wayne, IN: Louis A. Warren Lincoln Library & Museum, 1978.

Daniels, Roger. *Coming to America: A History of Immigration and Ethnicity in American Life.* 2nd ed. New York: Harper Perennial, 2002. Originally published 1991.

———. *Guarding the Golden Door: American Immigration Policy and Immigrants Since 1882.* New York: Hill & Wang, 2004.

Dixon, David T. *Radical Warrior: August Willich's Journey from German Revolutionary to Union General.* Knoxville: University of Tennessee Press, 2020.

Davis, William C. *Lincoln's Men: How President Lincoln Became a Father to an Army and a Nation.* New York: Free Press, 1999.

Donald, David Herbert. *Lincoln.* New York: Simon & Schuster, 1995.

Doyle, Don H. *The Cause of All Nations: The International History of the American Civil War.* New York: Basic Books, 2015.

Efford, Alison Clark. *German Immigrants, Race, and Citizenship in the Civil War Era.* New York: Cambridge University Press, 2013.

Egan, Timothy. *The Immortal Irishman: The Irish Revolutionary Who Became an American Hero.* Boston: Houghton Mifflin, 2016.

Endes, David Jeffrey, and William B. Kurz, eds. *Soldiers of the Cross, the Authoritative Text: The Heroism of Catholic Chaplains and Sisters in the American Civil War.* South Bend, IN: Notre Dame University Press, 2019.

Engle, Stephen. *Yankee Dutchman: The Life of Franz Sigel.* Fayetteville: University of Arkansas Press, 1993.

Eric, Steven P. *Rainbow's End: Irish-Americans and the Dilemmas of Urban Machine Politics, 1840–1985.* Berkeley: University of California Press, 1988.

Erickson, Charlotte. *American Industry and the European Immigrant, 1860–1885.* Cambridge, MA: Harvard University Press, 1957.

Fanning, Charles, ed. *New Perspectives on the Irish Diaspora.* Carbondale: Southern Illinois University Press, 2000.

Faust, Albert Bernhardt. *The German Element in the United States.* 2 vols. Boston: Houghton Mifflin, 1909.

Fehrenbacher, Don E. *Prelude to Greatness: Lincoln in the 1850's.* Stanford, CA: Stanford University Press, 1962.

Feldberg, Michael. *The Philadelphia Riots of 1844: A Study of Ethnic Conflict.* Westport, CT: Greenwood Press, 1975.

Fellman, Michael. *Citizen Sherman: A Life.* New York: Random House, 1995.

———. *Inside War: The Guerrilla Conflict in Missouri During the American Civil War.* New York: Oxford University Press, 1989.

Fischer, LeRoy H. *Lincoln's Gadfly, Adam Gurowski.* Norman: University of Oklahoma Press, 1964.

Foner, Eric. *The Fiery Trial: Abraham Lincoln and American Slavery.* New York: W. W. Norton, 2010.

———. *Free Soil, Free Labor, Free Men: The Ideology of the Republican Party Before the Civil War.* New York: Oxford University Press, 1998. Originally published 1970.

———. *Politics and Ideology in the Age of the Civil War.* New York: Oxford University Press, 1981.

Franklin, George Frank. *The Legislative History of Naturalization in the United States from the Revolutionary War to 1861.* New York: Arno Press, 1969. Originally published 1906.

Freitag, Sabine. *Friedrich Hecker: Two Lives for Liberty.* Translated by Steven Rowan. St. Louis: St. Louis Mercantile Library, 2006. Originally published 1955.

Friedel, Frank. *Francis Lieber: 19th Century Liberal.* Baton Rouge: Louisiana State University Press, 1947.

Gavronsky, Serge. *The French Liberal Opposition to the American Civil War.* New York: Humanities Press, 1968.

Gazley, John G. *American Opinion of German Unification, 1848–1871.* New York: AMS Press, 1970. Originally published 1926.

Geitz, Henry. *The German-American Press.* Madison, WI: Max Kade Institute for German-American Studies, 1992.

Gerber, David A. *American Immigration: A Very Short Introduction.* New York: Oxford University Press, 2011.

Gibson, Florence E. *The Attitudes of the New York Irish Toward State and National Affairs, 1848–1922.* New York: Columbia University Press, 1951.

Gienapp, William E. *The Origins of the Republican Party, 1852–1856.* New York: Oxford University Press, 1987.

Gleeson, David. *The Green and the Gray: Irish in the Confederate States of America.* Chapel Hill: University of North Carolina Press, 2013.

Guelzo, Allen C. *Lincoln and Douglas: The Debates That Defined America.* New York: Simon & Schuster, 2008.

Gutman, Herbert G. *Power and Culture: Essays on the American Working Class.* New York: Pantheon, 1987.

Hagwood, John H. *The Tragedy of German-America: The Germans in the United States of America During the Nineteenth Century—and After.* New York: G. P. Putnam's Sons, 1940.

Hamilton, Charles Granville. *Lincoln and the Know-Nothing Movement.* Washington, DC: Public Affairs Press, 1954.

Hanchett, William. *Irish: Charles G. Halpine in Civil War America.* Syracuse, NY: Syracuse University Press, 1970.

Hansen, Marcus Lee. *The Atlantic Migration, 1607–1860: History of the Continuing Settlement of the United States.* Cambridge, MA: Harvard University Press, 1951.

———. *The Immigrant in American History.* Cambridge, MA: Harvard University Press, 1940.

Hayduk, Ronald. *Democracy for All: Restoring Immigrant Voting Rights in the United States.* London: Routledge, 2006.

Heidler, David S., and Jeanne T. Heidler. *Henry Clay: The Essential American.* New York: Random House, 2010.

Helbich, Wolfgang, and Walter D. Kamphoefner, eds. *German-American Immigration and Ethnicity in Comparative Perspective.* Madison: University of Wisconsin Press, 2004.

Hernon, Joseph M., Jr. *Celts, Catholics and Copperheads: Ireland Views the American Civil War.* Columbus: Ohio State University Press, 1968.

Herriott, F. I. *The Germans of Chicago and Stephen A. Douglas in 1854.* Reprinted from the *Transactions of the Illinois State Historical Society* (1912). Springfield: *Illinois State Journal*, 1913.

———. *The Premises and Significance of Abraham Lincoln's Letter to Theodore Canisius.* Reprinted from *Deutsch-Amerikanische Geschichtsblätter Jahrbuch der Deutsch-Amerikanischen Historischen Gesellschaft von Illinois*—Jahrgang 1915 (vol. 15).

Hertz, Emanuel. "The Conference of German–Republicans in the Deutsches Haus, Chicago, May 14–15, 1860." Reprinted from *Transactions of the Illinois State Historical Society*, 1928.

———. *Lincoln Talks.* New York: Viking Press, 1939.

Higham, John. *Strangers in the Land: Patterns of American Nativism, 1860–1925.* New Brunswick, NJ: Rutgers University Press, 1955.

Hofstadter, Richard. *The American Political Tradition and the Men Who Made It.* New York: Alfred A. Knopf, 1948.

———. *The Paranoid Style in American Politics.* New York: Vintage Books, 2008. Originally published 1952.

Hokanson, Nels. *Swedish Immigrants in Lincoln's Time.* New York: Harper & Bros., 1942.

Holloway, Anna Gibson, and Jonathan W. White. *"Our Little Monitor": The Greatest Invention of the Civil War.* Kent, OH: Kent State University Press, 2018.

Holt, Michael F. *The Rise and Fall of the American Whig Party: Jacksonian Politics and the Onset of Civil War.* New York: Oxford University Press, 1999.

Holzer, Harold. *Lincoln and the Power of the Press: The War for Public Opinion.* New York: Simon & Schuster, 2014.

———, Mark E. Neely Jr., and Gabor S. Boritt. *The Lincoln Image: Abraham Lincoln and the Popular Print.* New York: Charles Scribner's Sons, 1984.

———, and Edward Steers Jr. *The Lincoln Assassination Conspirators: Their Confinement and Execution, as Recorded in the Letterbook of John Frederick Hartranft.* Baton Rouge: Louisiana State University Press, 2009.

Honeck, Mischa. *We Are the Revolutionists: German-Speaking Immigrants and American Abolitionists After 1848.* Athens: University of Georgia Press, 2011.

Horrocks, Thomas A. *Lincoln's Campaign Biographies.* Carbondale, Southern Illinois University Press, 2014.

Hoyt, Joanna Michal. *A Wary Welcome: The History of US Attitudes Toward Immigration.* Lefkofia, Cyprus: Skinny Bottle Publishing, 2017.

Isenberg, Nancy. *White Trash: The 400-Year Untold History of Class in America.* New York: Random House, 2016.

Johannsen, Robert W. *Stephen A. Douglas.* New York: Oxford University Press, 1973.

Joyce, William L. *Editors and Ethnicity: A History of the Irish-American Press.* New York: Arno Press, 1976.

Katz, Irving. *August Belmont: A Political Biography.* New York: Columbia University Press, 1968.

Keating, Ryan W. *Shades of Green: Irish Regiments, American Soldiers, and Local Communities in the Civil War Era.* New York: Fordham University Press, 2017.

Keller, Christian B. *Chancellorsville and the Germans: Nativism, Ethnicity, and Civil War Memory.* New York: Fordham University Press, 2007.

Kellner, George H. *The German Element on the Urban Frontier: St. Louis, 1830–1860.* Columbia: University of Missouri Press, 1973.

Kettner, James H. *The Development of American Citizenship, 1608–1877.* Chapel Hill: University of North Carolina Press, 1977.

Keyssar, Alexander. *The Right to Vote: The Contested History of Democracy in the United States.* New York: Basic Books, 2009.

Kline, Michael J. *The Baltimore Plot: The First Conspiracy to Assassinate Abraham Lincoln.* Yardley, PA: Westholme Publishing, 2008.

Knobel, Dale. *"America for the Americans": The Nativist Movement in the United States.* New York: Twayne Publishers, 1996.

Korn, Bertram. *American Jewry and the Civil War.* Philadelphia: Jewish Publication Society of America, 1951.

Kurtz, William B. *Excommunicated from the Union: How the Civil War Created a Separate Catholic America.* New York: Fordham University Press, 2016.

Lapham, James Sigurd. *The German-Americans of New York City.* New York: St. John's University Press, 1977.

Laxton, Edward. *The Famine Ships: The Irish Exodus to America.* New York: Henry Holt, 1997.

Lea, J. Henry, and J. R. Hutchinson. *The Ancestry of Abraham Lincoln.* Boston: Houghton Mifflin, 1909.

Lehrman, Lewis E. *Lincoln at Peoria: The Turning Point.* Mechanicsburg, PA: Stackpole Books, 2008.

Lemire, Elise. *"Miscegenation": Making Race in America.* Philadelphia: University of Pennsylvania Press, 1992.

Leonard, Elizabeth D. *Benjamin Franklin Butler: A Noisy, Fearless Life*. Chapel Hill: University of North Carolina Press, 2022.

Leonard, Ira M., and Robert D. Parmet. *American Nativism, 1830–1860*. New York: Van Nostrand Reinhold, 1971.

Levine, Bruce. *The Spirit of 1848: German Immigrants, Labor Conflict, and the Coming of the Civil War*. Urbana: University of Illinois Press, 1992.

———. *Thaddeus Stevens: Civil War Revolutionary, Fighter for Racial Justice*. New York: Simon & Schuster, 2021.

Lincoln, Waldo. *History of the Lincoln Family: An Account of the Descendants of Samuel Lincoln of Hingham, England, Massachusetts, 1637–1920*. Worcester, MA: Commonwealth Press, 1923.

Lonn, Ella. *Foreigners in the Confederacy*. Chapel Hill: University of North Carolina Press, 1940.

———. *Foreigners in the Union Army and Navy*. Baton Rouge: Louisiana State University Press, 1951.

Luebke, Frederick C., ed. *Ethnic Voters and the Election of Lincoln*. Lincoln: University of Nebraska Press, 1971.

Mahin, Dean. *The Blessed Place of Freedom: Europeans in Civil War America*. Washington, DC: Brassey's 2002.

Mahon, John. *New York's Fighting Sixty-Ninth: A Regimental History of Service in the Civil War's Irish Brigade and the Great War's Rainbow Division*. Jefferson, NC: McFarland, 2004.

Maldwyn, Allen Jones. *American Immigration*. Chicago: University of Chicago Press, 1960.

Marcus, Jacob Rader. *United States Jewry, 1776–1985*. 5 vols. Detroit: Wayne State University Press, 1993.

Markens, Isaac. *Abraham Lincoln and the Jews*. New York: Isaac Markens, 1909.

Marszalek, John F. *Commander of All Lincoln's Armies: A Life of General Henry W. Halleck*. Cambridge, MA: Harvard University Press, 2004.

Masur, Kate. *Until Justice Be Done: America's First Civil Rights Movement, from the Revolution to Reconstruction*. New York: W. W. Norton, 2021.

McConville, Mary St. Patrick. *Political Nativism in the State of Maryland, 1830–1860*. Washington, DC: Catholic University of America, 1928.

McKenzie, R. D. *Oriental Exclusion: The Effect of American Immigration Laws, Regulations and Judicial Decisions on the Chinese and Japanese on the American Pacific Coast*. Chicago: University of Chicago Press, 1928.

McPherson, James M. *Battle Cry of Freedom: The Civil War Era*. New York: Oxford University Press, 1988.

Mehrlander, Andrea. *The Germans of Charleston, Richmond and New Orleans During the Civil War Period, 1861–1870: A Study and Research Compendium*. Berlin: Walter de Gruyter, 2011.

Mendelsohn, Adam D. *Jewish Soldiers in the Civil War: The Union Army*. New York: New York University Press, 2022.

Meredith, Roy. *Mr. Lincoln's Camera Man*. New York: Charles Scribner's Sons, 1946.

Miers, Earl Schenck, ed. *Lincoln Day by Day: A Chronology, 1809–1865*. 3 vols. Washington, DC: Lincoln Sesquicentennial Commission, 1960.

Miller, Kerby A. *Emigrants and Exiles: Ireland and the Irish Exodus to North America*. New York: Oxford University Press, 1985.

Miller, Sally M., ed. *The Ethnic Press in the United States: A Historical Analysis and Handbook*. Westport, CT: Greenwood Press, 1987.

Mitchell, Arthur J., ed. *Fighting Irish in the American Civil War and the Invasion of Mexico: Essays*. Jefferson, NC: McFarland, 2017.

Monaghan, Jay, ed. *Lincoln Bibliography, 1839–1939*. 2 vols. Springfield: Illinois State Historical Library, 1943.

Mulkern, John R. *The Know-Nothing Party in Massachusetts: The Rise and Fall of a People's Movement*. Boston: Northeastern University Press, 1990.

Mullan, Michael L. *The Philadelphia Irish: Nation, Culture, and the Rise of a Gaelic Public Sphere*. New Brunswick, NJ: Rutgers University Press, 2021.

Neely, Mark E., Jr. *The Fate of Liberty: Abraham Lincoln and Civil Liberties*. New York: Oxford University Press, 1981.

———. *Lincoln and the Democrats: The Politics of Opposition in the Civil War*. New York: Cambridge University Press, 2017.

Nicolay, Helen. *Lincoln's Secretary: A Biography of John G. Nicolay*. New York: Longmans, Green, 1949.

O'Connor, Richard. *The German-Americans: An Informal History*. Boston: Little, Brown, 1968.

O'Dowd, Niall. *Lincoln and the Irish: The Untold Story of How the Irish Helped Abraham Lincoln Save the Union*. New York: Skyhorse Publishing, 2018.

Overdyke, Darrell. *The Know-Nothing Party in the South*. Gloucester, MA: Peter Smith, 1968.

Panzer, Mary. *Mathew Brady and the Image of History*. Washington, DC: Smithsonian Institution Press, 1997.

Parker, Kunal M. *Making Foreigners: Immigration and Citizenship Law in America 1600–2000.* New York: Cambridge University Press, 2005.

Patterson, Benton Rain. *Lincoln's Political Generals: The Battlefield Performance of Seven Controversial Appointees.* Jefferson, NC: McFarland, 2014.

Paull, Bonnie E., and Richard Hart. *Lincoln's Springfield Neighborhood.* Charleston, SC: History Press, 2015.

Piványi, Eugene. *Hungarians in the Civil War.* Cleveland: Booklife, 2012. Originally published 1913.

Quatman, G. William. *A Young General and the Fall of Richmond: The Life and Career of Godfrey Weitzel.* Athens: Ohio University Press, 2015.

Reilly, Bernard F., Jr. *American Political Prints, 1760–1876: A Catalog of the Collections in the Library of Congress.* Boston: G. K. Hall, 1991.

Rosen, Robert N. *The Jewish Confederates.* Columbia: University of South Carolina Press, 2000.

Rowan, Steven. *Cleveland and Its Germans.* Translated by Steven Rowan. Cleveland: Western Reserve Historical Society, 1998.

Sarna, Jonathan D. *When General Grant Expelled the Jews.* New York: Shocken Books, 2012.

———, and Adam Mendelsohn, eds. *Jews and the Civil War: A Reader.* New York: New York University Press, 2010.

———, and Benjamin Shapell. *Lincoln and the Jews: A History.* New York: St. Martin's Press, 2015.

Schafer, Joseph. *Carl Schurz, Militant Liberal.* Madison: State Historical Society of Wisconsin, 1930.

Schecter Barnet. *The Devil's Own Work: The Civil War Draft Riots and the Fight to Reconstruct America.* New York: Walker, 2005.

Schneller, Robert J. *Quest for Glory: A Biography of Rear Admiral John A. Dahlgren.* Annapolis, MD: Naval Institute Press, 1995.

Scisco, Louis Dow. *Political Nativism in New York State.* New York: Columbia University Press, 1901.

Shalev, Eran. *American Zion: The Old Testament as a Political Text from the Revolution to the Civil War.* New Haven, CT: Yale University Press, 2013.

Sheahan, James W. *The Life of Stephen A. Douglas.* New York: Harper & Bros., 1860.

Shiels, Damian. *The Irish in the American Civil War.* Dublin: History Press Ireland, 2013.

Silbey, Joel H. *A Respectable Minority: The Democratic Party in the Civil War Era, 1860–1868*. New York: W. W. Norton, 1977.

Silverman, Jason H. *Lincoln and the Immigrant*. Carbondale: Southern Illinois University Press, 2015.

———. *When America Welcomed Immigrants: The Short and Tortured History of Abraham Lincoln's Act to Encourage Immigration*. Charleston, SC: Palmetto Publishing, 2020.

Smith, Adam I. P. *No Party Now: Politics in the Civil War North*. New York: Oxford University Press, 2006.

Smith, Dennis M. *Abraham Lincoln and the New Immigrant Irish in 1860s America*. Fort Lauderdale, FL: Nova Southeastern University Press, 2003.

Smith, William Ernest. *The Francis Preston Blair Family in Politics*. 2 vols. New York: Da Capo Press, 1969. Originally published 1933.

Soini, Wayne. *Abraham Lincoln, American Prince: Ancestry, Ambition and the Anti-Slavery Cause*. Jefferson, NC: McFarland, 2022.

Spickard, Paul. *Almost All Aliens: Immigration, Race, and Colonialism in American History and Identity*. New York: Routledge, 2007.

Stahr, Walter. *Salmon P. Chase: Lincoln's Vital Rival*. New York: Simon & Schuster, 2021.

Stauffer, John, Zoe Trodd, and Celeste-Marie Bernier. *Picturing Frederick Douglass: An Illustrated Biography of the Nineteenth Century's Most Photographed American*. New York: Liveright, 2015.

Steers, Edward, Jr. *The Lincoln Tree: 300 Years of Lincoln Ancestry, 1500–1837*. Privately printed, 2021.

Steiner, Mark E. *Lincoln and Citizenship*. Carbondale: Southern Illinois University Press, 2021.

Stephenson, George M. *A History of American Immigration, 1820–1924*. Boston: Ginn & Co., 1926.

Symonds, Craig L. *Lincoln and His Admirals*. New York: Oxford University Press, 2008.

———. *Stonewall of the West: Patrick Cleburne and the Civil War*. Lawrence: University Press of Kansas, 1997.

Szabados, Stephen. *Irish Immigration to America*. Privately printed, 2021.

Temple, Wayne C. *The Dinkels and the Lincolns*. Springfield, IL: Abraham Lincoln Association, 2020.

————. *Lincoln's Springfield/Pittsfield Connection: "A Tale of Two Cities."* Mahomet, IL: Mayhaven, 2017.

————, and Sunderine Temple. *Abraham Lincoln and Illinois' Fifth Capitol*, revised edition. Mahomet, IL: Mayhaven Publishing, 2006.

Thomas, Benjamin P. *Lincoln's New Salem.* Chicago: Lincoln's New Salem Enterprises, 1973. Originally published 1934.

Thomas, John L., ed. *Abraham Lincoln and the American Political Tradition.* Amherst: University of Massachusetts Press, 1986.

Thulesius, Olav. *The Man Who Made the Monitor: A Biography of John Ericsson.* Jefferson, NC: McFarland, 2007.

Trefousse, Hans L. *Carl Schurz: A Biography.* Knoxville: University of Tennessee Press, 1982.

————, ed. *Germany and America.* New York: Brooklyn College Press, 1980.

Tucker, Phillip Thomas. *The Irish at Gettysburg.* Charleston, SC: History Press, 2018.

————. *Irish Confederates: The Civil War's Forgotten Soldiers.* Abilene, TX: McWhiney Foundation Press, 2006.

Ural, Susannah J. *Civil War Citizens: Race, Ethnicity, and Identity in America's Bloodiest Conflict.* New York: New York University Press, 2010.

Ural Bruce, Susannah. *The Harp and the Eagle: Irish-American Volunteers and the Union Army, 1861–1865.* New York: New York University Press, 2006.

Van Tuyll, Debra Reddin, Mark O'Brien, and Marcel Broersma, eds. *Politics, Culture, and the Irish American Press, 1784–1963.* Syracuse, NY: Syracuse University Press, 2021.

Vasvary, Edmund. *Lincoln's Hungarian Heroes: The Participation of Hungarians in the Civil War, 1861–1865.* Washington, DC: Hungarian Reformed Federation of America, 1939.

Warner, Ezra J. *Generals in Blue: Lives of the Union Commanders.* Baton Rouge: Louisiana State University Press, 1992. Originally published 1964.

————. *Generals in Gray: Lives of the Confederate Commanders.* Baton Rouge: Louisiana State University Press, 1987. Originally published 1959.

Washington, William D. *They Knew Lincoln.* New York: E. P. Dutton, 1942.

Welling, A. Dallas. *The Praise of Lincoln: An Anthology.* Indianapolis: Bobbs-Merrill, 1925.

Wersich, Rüdiger, ed. *Carl Schurz: Revolutionary and Statesman—His Life in Personal and Official Documents with Illustrations.* Munich: Hans Moos, 1979.

White, Jonathan W. *A House Built by Slaves: African American Visitors to the Lincoln White House*. Landham, MD: Rowman & Littlefield, 2022.

White, Ruth Morris. *Yankee from Sweden: The Dream and the Reality in the Days of John Ericsson*. Whitefish, MT: Literary Licensing, 2015. Originally published 1960.

Widmer, Ted. *Lincoln on the Verge: Thirteen Days to Washington*. New York: Simon & Schuster, 2010.

Wilentz, Sean. *The Rise of American Democracy: Jefferson to Lincoln*. New York: W. W. Norton, 2005.

Wineapple, Brenda. *Ecstatic Nation: Confidence, Crises, and Compromise, 1848–1877*. New York: Harper, 2013.

Winkle, Kenneth J. *The Young Lion: The Rise of Abraham Lincoln*. Dallas: Taylor Trade, 2001.

Witt, John Fabian. *Lincoln's Code: The Laws of War in American History*. New York: Free Press, 2012.

Wittke, Carl Frederick. *The German-Language Press in America*. Lexington: University of Kentucky Press, 1957.

———. *Refugees of Revolution: The German Forty-Eighters in America*. Philadelphia: University of Pennsylvania Press, 1970.

Work, David. *Lincoln's Political Generals*. Urbana: University of Illinois Press, 2009.

Zola, Gary P. *They Called Him Rabbi Abraham: Lincoln and American Jewry*. Carbondale: Southern Illinois University Press, 2014.

Zolberg, Aristede R. *A Nation by Design: Immigration Policy in Fashioning America*. Cambridge, MA: Harvard University Press, 2006.

Zucker, A. E., ed. *The Forty-Eighters: Political Refugees of the German Revolution of 1848*. New York: Columbia University Press, 1950.

Book Chapters

Brinkmann, Tobias. "Jews, Germans, or Americans? German-Jewish Immigrants in the Nineteenth-Century United States." In *The Heimat Abroad: The Boundaries of Germanness*, 111–140, edited by Krista O'Donnell, Renate Bridenthal, and Nancy Rogin. Ann Arbor: University of Michigan Press, 2005.

Current, Richard N. "From Civil War to World Power: Perceptions and Realities, 1865–1914." In *On the Road to Total War: The American Civil War and the German Wars of Unification, 1861–1871*, 621–639, edited by Stig Forster and Jorg Nagler. Washington, DC: German Historical Institute, 1996.

Davis, David Brion. "Some Themes of Counter-Subversion: An Analysis of Anti-Masonic, Anti-Catholic, and Anti-Mormon Literature." In *The Fear of Conspiracy:*

Images of Un-American Subversion from the Revolution to the Present, 9–22, edited by Davis. Ithaca: Cornell University Press, 1971.

Holt, Michael. "The Antimasonic and Know-Nothing Parties." In *History of United States Political Parties*, 1:575–620, edited by Arthur M. Schlesinger Jr. New York: Chelsea House, 1973.

Jentz, John B. "The 48ers and the Politics of the German Labor Movement in Chicago During the Civil War Era." In *The German-American Radical Press: The Shaping of a Left Political Culture, 1850–1940*, 49–62, edited by Elliott Shore, Ken Fones-Wolf, and James P. Danky. Urbana: University of Illinois Press, 1992.

Keil, Harmut. "German Immigrants and African-Americans in Mid-Nineteenth Century America." In *Enemy Images in American History*, 137–157, edited by Ragnhild Fiebig-von Hase and Ursula Lehmkuhl. Providence, RI: Berghan Books, 1997.

Knobel, Dale T. "Beyond 'America for Americans': Inside the Movement Culture of American Nativism." In *Immigrant America: European Ethnicity in the United States*, edited by Timothy Walch. Milton Park, England: Routledge, 1994.

Maizlish, Stephen E. "The Meaning of Nativism and the Crisis of the Union: The Know-Nothing Movement in the Antebellum North." In *Essays on American Antebellum Politics, 1840–1860*, 166–198, edited by Maizlish and John J. Kushma. College Station: Texas A&M University Press, 1982.

Von Katzler, William. "The Germans in Newark." In *A History of the City of Newark, New Jersey*, 1057–1087, edited by F. J. Urquhart. New York: Lewis Historical Publishing, 1913.

Zacharias, Donald W. "The Know-Nothing Party and the Oratory of Nativism." In *Oratory in the Old South*, 218–233, edited by Waldo W. Braden and John J. Auer. Baton Rouge: Louisiana State University Press, 1970.

Journal and Magazine Articles

Abbott, Edith. "Federal Immigration Policy, 1864–1924." *University Journal of Business* 2 (March 1924): 133–156.

Abramitzky, Ran, and Leah Boustan. "Immigration in American Economic History." *Journal of Economic Literature* 55 (December 2017): 1311–1345.

Adams, Charles Francis [Jr.]. "Lincoln's Offer to Garibaldi." *Proceedings of the Massachusetts Historical Society*, 3rd ser., 1 (1908): 319–325; also *The Magazine of History* 78 (January–June 1908): 159–165.

Amundson, R. J. "Sanford and Garibaldi." *Civil War History* 14 (March 1968): 40–45.

Ash, Stephen V. "Civil War Exodus: The Jews and Grant's General Orders No. 11." *The Historian* 44 (August 1982): 505–523.

Baum, Dale. "The 'Irish Vote' and Party Politics in Massachusetts, 1860–1871." *Civil War History* 26 (1980): 117–141.

———. "Know-Nothingism and the Republican Majority in Massachusetts: The Political Realignment of the 1850s." *Journal of American History* 64 (March 1978): 959–986.

Bean, William G. "Economic Nativism During the 1840's." *New York History* 29 (April 1948): 170–186.

Benjaminson, Eric. "A Regiment of Immigrants: The 82nd Illinois Volunteer Infantry and the Letters of Captain Rudolph Mueller." *Journal of the Illinois State Historical Society* 94 (Summer 2001): 137–180.

Berger, Max. "The Irish Emigrant and American Nativism as Seen by British Visitors, 1836–1860." *Pennsylvania Magazine of History and Biography* 70 (April 1946): 146–160.

Betts, John R. "The Negro and the New England Conscience in the Days of John Boyle O'Reilly." *Journal of Negro History* 51 (1966): 246–261.

Borchard, Gregory A. "Revolutions Incomplete: Horace Greeley and the Forty-Eighters at Home and Abroad." *American Journalism* 27 (Winter 2010): 7–36.

Brooks, Noah. "Personal Recollections of Abraham Lincoln." *Harper's New Monthly Magazine* 31 (July 1865): 222–230.

———. "Personal Recollections of Abraham Lincoln." *Scribner's Monthly* 15 (February 1878): 561–569; (March 1878): 673–681.

Bruncken, Ernest. "The Political Activity of Wisconsin Germans, 1854–1860." *Proceedings of the State Historical Society of Wisconsin [. . .] December 12, 1901* (Madison: Democrat Printing, 1902).

Buchkoski, Courtney. "Luke-Warm Abolitionists." *Journal of the Civil War Era* 9 (June 2019): 249–274.

Bunker, Gary L., and John Appel. "'Shoddy,' Anti-Semitism and the Civil War." *American Jewish History* 82 (1994): 43–71.

Carlson, A. Cheree. "The Rhetoric of the Know-Nothing Party: Nativism as a Response to the Rhetorical Situation." *Southern Communications Journal* 54 (1989): 364–383.

Carman, Henry J., and Reinhard H. Luthin, "Some Aspects of the Know Nothing Movement Reconsidered." *South Atlantic Quarterly* 29 (1940): 213–234.

Carson, Jamie L., Jeffrey A. Jenkins, David W. Rhode, and Mark A. Souva. "The Impact of National Tides and District-Level Effects on Electoral Outcomes: The U.S. Congressional Elections of 1862–63." *American Journal of Political Science* 45 (October 2001): 887–898.

Carter, Edward C., II. "A 'Wild Irishman' Under Every Federalist's Bed': Naturalization in Philadelphia, 1789–1806." *Proceedings of the American Philosophical Society* 133 (June 1989): 331–346.

Castle, Henry A. "General James Shields: Soldier, Orator, Statesman." *Collections of the Minnesota Historical Society* 15 (May 1915): 711–730.

Clark, Allen C. "Lincoln in the National Capital." *Records of the Columbia Historical Society* 27 (1925): 1–174.

Cogan, Brian. "The Irish-American Press as an Agent of Change: The Transformation of the New York Irish, 1850–1880." *New York Irish History* (Annual Journal of the New York Irish History Roundtable) 14 (2000): 29–46.

Cohn, Raymond L. "Mortality on Immigrant Voyages to New York, 1836–1853." *Journal of Economic History* 44 (June 1984): 289–300.

———. "Nativism and the End of the Mass Migration of the 1840s and 1850s." *Journal of Economic History* 60 (June 2000): 361–383.

———. "Occupational Evidence on the Causes of Immigration to the United States, 1836–1853." *Explorations in Economic History* 32 (June 1995): 383–408.

———. "The Transition from Sail to Steam in Immigration to the United States." *Journal of Economic History* 65 (June 2005): 469–495.

Conzen, Kathleen Neils. "Immigrant Religion and the Republic: German Catholics in Nineteenth-Century America." *German Historical Institute Bulletin* 35 (Fall 2004): 43–56.

Cullop, Charles P. "An Unequal Duel: Union Recruiting in Ireland, 1863–1864." *Civil War History* 13 (1967): 101–113.

Curran, Thomas J. "Assimilation and Nativism." *International Migration Digest* 3 (Spring 1966): 15–25.

Dal Lago, Enrico. "Writing the US Civil War into Nineteenth-Century World History." *Journal of the Civil War Era* 11 (June 2021): 255–271.

Daniels, George J. "Immigrant Vote in the 1860 Election: The Case of Iowa." *Mid-America* 44 (July 1962): 146–162.

Deusner, Charles E. "The Know-Nothing Riots in Louisville." *Register of the Kentucky Historical Society* 61 (April 1963): 122–147.

Dicey, Edward. "Washington During the War." *Macmillan's Magazine* 6 (May 1862): 16–29.

Donner, Barbara. "Carl Schurz as Office Seeker." *Wisconsin Magazine of History* 20 (December 1936): 127–142.

Douma, Michael, Anders Bo Rasmussen, and Robert Faith. "The Impressment of Foreign-Born Soldiers in the Union Army." *Journal of American Ethnic History* 38 (Spring 2019): 76–106.

Dorpalen, Andreas. "The German Element and the Issues of the Civil War." *Mississippi Valley Historical Review* 29 (June 1942): 55–76.

Efford, Alison Clark. "Abraham Lincoln, German-Born Republicans, and American Citizenship." *Marquette Law Review* 93 (2010): 1375–1381.

———. "Race Should Be as Unimportant as Ancestry: German Radicals and African American Citizenship in the Missouri Constitution of 1865." *Missouri Historical Review* 104 (April 2010): 138–158.

Emory, Charles Wilson. "The Iowa Germans and the Election of 1860." *Annals of Iowa*, 3rd ser., 33 (October 1940): 421–453.

Ernst, Robert. "Economic Nativism in New York City During the 1840's." *New York History* 29 (April 1948): 170–186.

Fry, Joseph A. "Eyewitness by Proxy: Nelson M. Beckwith's Evaluation of Garibaldi, September 1862." *Civil War History* 28 (March 1982): 65–70.

Gay, H. Nelson. "Lincoln's Offer of a Command to Garibaldi: Light on a Disputed Point of History." *Century Illustrated Monthly Magazine* 75 (November 1907): 63–74.

Geffen, Elizabeth M. "Violence in Philadelphia in the 1840's and 1850's." *Pennsylvania Magazine of History* 36 (October 1969): 381–420.

George, Joseph, Jr. "Philadelphia's *Catholic Herald* Evaluates President Lincoln." *Lincoln Herald* 82 (Fall 1980): 447–453.

Gerber, Richard A. "Carl Schurz's Journey from Radical to Liberal Republicanism: A Problem in Ideological Consistency." *Mid-America* 82 (2000): 71–99.

Gienapp, William E. "Nativism and the Creation of the Republican Majority in the North Before the Civil War." *Journal of American History* 72 (December 1985): 529–559.

Graham, David. "A Fight for Principle: The 24th Volunteer Infantry Regiment." *Journal of the Illinois State Historical Society* 104 (Spring–Summer 2011): 38–55.

Gumpert, Gustave. "Tad Lincoln and Gus Gumpert." *Journal of the Illinois State Historical Society* 48 (Spring 1955): 40–44.

Hansen, Marcus Lee. "The Revolution of 1848 and the German Emigration." *Journal of Economic and Business History* 2 (August 1930): 620–630.

Hansen, Stephen L., and Paul D. Nygard. "Abraham Lincoln and the Know-Nothing Question, 1854–1859." *Lincoln Herald* 94 (Summer 1992): 61–72.

————. "Stephen A. Douglas, the Know-Nothings, and the Democratic Party in Illinois, 1854–1858." *Illinois Historical Journal* 87 (Summer 1994): 109–130.

Harrington, Fred Harvey. "A Peace Mission of 1863." *American Historical Review* 46 (October 1940): 76–86.

Harris, Sheldon W. "John Louis O'Sullivan and the Election of 1844 in New York." *New York History* 41 (July 1960): 278–298.

Hawthorne, Nathaniel [A Peaceable Man]. "Chiefly About War-Matters." *Atlantic Monthly* 10 (July 1862): 43–61.

Hellerstein, Kathryn. "A Letter from Lincoln's Jewish Telegrapher." *Jewish Quarterly Review* 94 (Autumn 2004): 625–636.

Higham, John. "Another Look at Nativism." *Catholic Historical Review* 44 (July 1958): 147–158.

Holland, Samuel H. "Charles H. Liebermann, M.D.: An Early Russian-Born Physician of Washington, D.C." *Medical Annals of the District of Columbia* 38 (1969): 499–504.

Holt, Michael. "The Politics of Impatience: The Origins of Know-Nothingism." *Journal of American History* 9 (September 1973): 309–331.

Iverson, Ian. "Conservative to the Last Degree: The Emerging Illinois Republican Party and the Election of 1856." *Civil War History* 68 (December 2022): 349–372.

Johns, Jane Martin. "A Momentous Incident in the History of Illinois." *Journal of the Illinois State Historical Society* 10 (January 1918): 548–560.

Johnson, Hildegard Binder. "The Election of 1860 and the Germans in Minnesota." *Minnesota History* 28 (March 1947): 20–36.

Johnston, Tyler V. "Punishing the Lies on the Rio Grande: Catholic and Immigrant Volunteers in Zachary Taylor's Army and the Fight Against Nativism." *Journal of the Early Republic* 30 (Spring 2010): 63–84.

Jung, Moon-Ho. "Outlawing 'Coolies': Race, Nation, and Empire in the Age of Emancipation." *American Quarterly* 57 (September 2005): 677–701.

Kamphoefner, Walter D. "German-Americans and Civil War Politics: A Reconsideration of the Ethnocultural Thesis." *Civil War History* 37 (September 1991): 232–246.

————. "German Language Persistence in Texas and Missouri." *Yearbook of German-American Studies* 55 (2020): 1–20.

————. "St. Louis Germans and the Republican Party, 1848–1860." *Mid-America: An Historical Review* 57 (1975): 69–88

Kanazawa, Mark. "Immigration, Exclusion and Taxation: Anti-Chinese Legislation in Gold Rush California." *Journal of Economic History* 65 (September 2005): 779–805.

Keeling, Drew. "The Transportation Revolution and Transatlantic Migration, 1850–1914." *Research in Economic History* 19 (1999): 39–74.

Keller, Christian B. "Pennsylvania and Virginia Germans During the Civil War: A Brief History and Comparative Analysis." *Virginia Magazine of History and Biography* 109 (2001): 37–86.

Kenny, Kevin. "Abraham Lincoln and the American Irish." *American Journal of Irish Studies* 10 (2013): 39–64.

———. "Mobility and Sovereignty: The Nineteenth-Century Origins of Immigration Restriction." *Journal of American History* 109 (September 2022): 284–297.

Kettner, James H. "The Development of American Citizenship in the Revolutionary Era: The Idea of National Allegiance." *American Journal of Legal History* 18 (1974): 208–242.

Klement, Frank. "Catholics as Copperheads During the Civil War." *Catholic Historical Review* 80 (January 1994): 36–57.

Knobel, Dale T. "'Native Soil': Nativists, Colonizationists, and the Rhetoric of Nationality." *Civil War History* 27 (December 1981): 314–337.

Kostecki, Joseph L. "Polish Medics of the Civil War." *Polish American Studies* 23 (July–December 1966): 110–111.

Kyle, Otto R. "Lincoln Steps Out: The Anti-Nebraska Editor's Convention." *Abraham Lincoln Quarterly* 5 (March 1948): 25–37.

Lacher, J. H. A. "Francis A. Hoffmann of Illinois and Hans Buschbauer of Wisconsin." *Wisconsin Magazine of History* 13 (June 1930): 327–355.

Laverdure, Paul. "Creating an Anti-Catholic Crusader, Charles Chiniquy." *Journal of Religious History* 15 (June 1988): 94–108.

———. "'The Jesuits Did It!' Charles Chiniquy's Theory of Lincoln's Assassination." *Historical Papers: Canadian Society of Church History* (2001): 125–139.

Levering, Noah. "Recollections of Abraham Lincoln." *Iowa Historical Record* 12 (July 1896): 495–497.

Levine, Bruce. "Conservatism, Nativism, and Slavery: Thomas R. Whitney and the Origins of the Know-Nothing Party." *Journal of American History* 88 (September 2001): 455–488.

———. "'The Vital Element of the Republican Party': Antislavery, Nativism, and Abraham Lincoln." *Journal of the Civil War Era* 1 (December 2011): 481–505.

Levine, Peter. "Draft Evasion in the North During the Civil War, 1863–1865." *Journal of American History* 67 (March 1981): 816–834.

Levstik, Frank. "Civil War Diary of Colonel Albert Rogall." *Polish American Studies* 27 (Spring–Autumn 1970): 33–79.

"Lincoln's Blood German? Allegations Made by a German Historian Living in Baltimore." *New York Times,* May 29, 1919.

Lohne, Raymond. "'Five Times as Enthusiastic': Abraham Lincoln and the Bloody Seventh of Chicago." *Yearbook of German-American Studies* 50 (2015): 105–128.

———. "Team of Friends: A New Lincoln Theory and Legacy." *Journal of the Illinois State Historical Society* 101 (Fall–Winter 2008): 285–314.

Luthin, Reinhard H. "Indiana and Lincoln's Rise to the Presidency." *Indiana Magazine of History* 38 (December 1942): 385–405.

———. "Lincoln Appeals to German-American Voters." *German-American Review* 25 (June–July 1959): 4–20.

Malin, James C. "The Motives of Stephen A. Douglas in the Organization of Nebraska Territory: A Letter Dated December 17, 1853." *Kansas Historical Review* 19 (November 1951): 321–353.

Marraro, Howard R. "Lincoln's Offer of a Command to Garibaldi: Further Light on a Disputed Point of History." *Journal of the Illinois State Historical Library* 36 (March 1943): 237–270.

Meckel, Richard A. "Immigration, Mortality, and Population Growth in Boston, 1840–1880." *Journal of Interdisciplinary History* 15 (Winter 1985): 393–417.

Monaghan, Jay M. "Did Abraham Lincoln Receive the Illinois German Vote?" *Journal of the Illinois State Historical Society* 35 (Summer 1942): 133–139.

Montgomery, David. "The Shuttle and the Cross: Weavers and Artisans in the Kensington Riots of 1844." *Journal of Social History* 5 (Summer 1972): 411–446.

Murdock, Eugene C. "New York's Civil War Bounty Brokers." *Journal of American History* 52 (September 1966): 259–278.

Nagler, Jörg. "The Lincoln Image in Germany." *American Studies Journal* 60 (2020). www.asjournal.org/60-2016/Lincoln-image-germany/.

Neely, Mark E., Jr. "'Unbeknownst' to Lincoln: A Note on Radical Pacification in Missouri During the Civil War." *Civil War History* 44 (September 1988): 212–216.

Nicolay, John G. "Abraham Lincoln." *Transactions of the McLean County Historical Society* 3 (1900): 95–101.

O'Keefe, Thomas M. "The Catholic Issue in the *Chicago Tribune.*" *Mid-America* 57 (1975): 227–245.

———. "Chicago's Flirtation with Political Nativism, 1854–1856." *Records of the American Catholic Historical Society of Philadelphia* 82 (September 1971): 131–158.

Olden, Peter H. "Anton C. Hessing: The Rise of a Chicago Boss." *Journal of the Illinois State Historical Society* 35 (September 1942): 260–287.

Paludan, Philip Shaw. "Lincoln and Colonization: Policy or Propaganda?" *Journal of the Abraham Lincoln Association* 25 (Winter 2005): 23–37.

Parker, Kunal M. "State, Citizenship, and Territory: The Legal Construction of Immigrants in Antebellum Massachusetts." *Law and History Review* 19 (Fall 2001): 583–643.

Paulin, Charles Oscar. "President Lincoln and the Navy." *American Historical Review* (January 1909): 284–303.

Pinhiero, John C. "'Religion Without Restriction': Anti-Catholicism, All Mexico, and the Treaty of Gaudalupe Hildago." *Journal of the Early Republic* 23 (Spring 2003): 69–96.

Pinsker, Matthew. "Not Always Such a Whig: Abraham Lincoln's Partisan Realignment in the 1850s." *Journal of the Abraham Lincoln Association* 29 (Summer 2008): 27–46.

Poage, George Rawlings. "The Coming of the Portuguese." *Journal of the Illinois State Historical Society* 18 (April 1925): 101–135.

Pupin, Michael. "The Revelation of Lincoln to a Serbian Immigrant." *Lincoln Centennial Association Papers*, (1926) Centennial Association Papers: 63–80.

Raskin, Jamin B. "Legal Aliens, Local Citizens: The Historical, Constitutional, and Theoretical Meanings of Alien Suffrage." *University of Pennsylvania Law Review* 141 (1993): 1401–1470.

Rietveld, Ronald D. "The Lincoln White House Community." *Journal of the Abraham Lincoln Association* 20 (Summer 1999): 17–48.

Roseboom, Eugene. "Salmon P. Chase and the Know Nothings." *Mississippi Valley Historical Review* 25 (December 1938): 335–350.

Rozanski, Edward C. "Civil War Poles of Illinois." *Polish American Studies* 23 (July–December 1966): 112–114.

Salomon, Herman. "The Civil War Diary of Herman Salomon." *Wisconsin Magazine of History* 10 (December 1926): 205–210.

Sanders, Neill F. "'Fairness, and Fairness Only': Lincoln's Appointment of James O. Putnam as Consul at Le Havre." *Lincoln Herald* 87 (Fall 1985): 76–82.

———. "'Unfit for Consul?': The English Consulates and Lincoln's Patronage Policy." *Lincoln Herald* 82 (Fall 1980): 464–474.

Schafer, Joseph. "Who Elected Lincoln?" *American Historical Review* 47 (October 1941): 51–63.

Schneider, George. "Lincoln and the Anti-Know-Nothing Resolutions." *Transactions of the McLean County Historical Society* 3 (1900): 87–94.

Segal, Charles M. "Isachar Zacharie: Lincoln's Chiropodist." *Publications of the American Jewish Historical Society* 43 (December 1953): 71–126.

———. "George Schneider." *Transactions of the Illinois State Historical Society* (1906), 329–331.

Selby, Paul. "The Editorial Convention of 1856." *Journal of the Illinois State Historical Society* 5 (October 1912): 343–349.

Senning, John P. "The Know Nothing Movement in Illinois, 1854–1856." *Journal of the Illinois State Historical Society* 7 (April 1914): 7–33.

Seraile, William. "The Struggle to Raise Regiments in New York State, 1861–1864." *New York Historical Society Quarterly* 58 (1974): 215–233.

Silverman, Jason H. "The Long Twisting Road: Abraham Lincoln's Evolving World with the Foreign Born." *Lincoln Lore* 1918 (Summer 2018): 14–18.

———. "Lost to History: Abraham Lincoln's Act to Encourage Immigration." *Lincoln Lore* 1923 (Fall 2019): 23–27.

———. "'One of the Principal Replenishing Streams': Lincoln and His Evolving Relationship with Immigrants and Ethnic Groups." *Lincoln Herald* 114 (Fall 2012): 159–177.

———. "The Short and Tortured History of Abraham Lincoln's Act to Encourage Immigration." *Lincoln Herald* 119 (Fall 2017): 148–166.

Smith, Donnal V. "The Influence of the Foreign-Born of the Northwest in the Election of 1860." *Mississippi Valley Historical Review* 19 (September 1932): 192–204.

Smith, George Winston. "Carpetbag Imperialism in Florida, 1862–1868." *Florida Historical Quarterly* 27 (October 1948): 99–130.

Soloveichik, Meir. "What the Bible Taught Lincoln About America." *Wall Street Journal*, February 15, 2020.

———. "When Lincoln Died on Passover," *Washington Examiner*, April 20, 2015.

Streitmatter, Rodger. "The Nativist Press: Demonizing the American Immigrant." *Journalism and Mass Communications Quarterly* 76 (Winter 1999): 673–683.

Strickland, Jeffrey. "How the Germans Became White Southerners: German Immigrants and African Americans in Charleston, South Carolina, 1860–1880." *Journal of American Ethnic History* 28 (Fall 2008): 52–69.

Stuckey, Clay W. "Lincoln and Garibaldi." *Lincoln Herald* 90 (Winter 1988): 140–143.

Swan, Patricia B., and James B. Swan. "James W. Sheahan: Stephen A. Douglas Supporter and Partisan Chicago Journalist." *Journal of the Illinois State Historical Society* 105 (Summer–Fall 2012): 133–166.

Szabó, Éva Eszter. "The Migration Factor in the American Civil War: The Impact of Voluntary Population Movements on the War Effort." *Americana* (e-Journal of American Studies in Hungary) 12 (Spring 2016), https://americanaejournal.hu /vol12no1/szabo (consulted January 18, 2022).

Taylor, Steven. "Progressive Nativism: The Know-Nothing Party in Massachusetts." *Journal of Massachusetts History* 28 (Summer 2000): 167–184.

Temple, Wayne C. "The Linguistic Lincolns: A New Lincoln Letter." *Lincoln Herald* 94 (1994): 108–114.

Trautmann, Frederic. "New York Through German Eyes: The Travels of Ludwig Gall, 1819." *New York History* 61 (October 1981): 439–461.

Uminski, Sigmund H. "Two Polish Confederates." *Polish American Studies* 23 (July–December 1966): 65–81.

Villard, Henry. "Recollections of Lincoln." *Atlantic Monthly* 93 (February 1904): 165–174.

Vocke, William. "The Germans and the German Press." *Transactions of the McLean County Historical Society* 3 (1900): 48–58.

Vorenberg, Michael. "Abraham Lincoln and the Politics of Black Colonization." *Journal of the Abraham Lincoln Association* 14 (Summer 1993): 22–45.

Wagner, Maria. "Mathilde Anneke's Stories of Slavery in the German-American Press." *MELUS* (Journal of the Society for the Study of the Multi-Ethnic Literature of the United States) 6 (1979): 9–16.

Winkle, Kenneth J. "The Second Party System in Lincoln's Springfield." *Civil War History* 44 (December 1998): 267–284.

Witkiewicz, Kate. "'Damned Dutch': St. Louis Germans in the Civil War Era." *Journal of Undergraduate Research* (University of Florida) 10 (Summer 2010): 1–15.

Wittke, Carl F. "Friedrich Hassaurek: Cincinnati's Leading Forty-Eighter." *Ohio Historical Quarterly* 68 (January 1959): 1–17.

———. "The German Forty-Eighters. A Centennial Appraisal." *American Historical Review* 53 (1948): 711–725.

Wong, Celia. "Two Polish Women in the Confederacy." *Polish American Studies* 23 (July–December 1960): 97–101.

Woods, Michael E. "Charleston, City of Mourners: Anticipations of Civil War in the Cradle of Secession." *Civil War History* 67 (March 2021): 7–28.

Zucker, A. F. "Dr. Theodore Canisius, Friend of Lincoln." *American-German Review* 16 (February 1950): 13–40.

Dissertations

Bielski, Mark Francis. "Divided Poles in a Divided Nation: Poles in the Union and Confederacy in the American Civil War." Ph.D. thesis, University of Birmingham College of Arts and Law, May 2014.

Bodger, John Charles, Jr. "The Immigrant and the Union Army." Ph.D. dissertation, Columbia University, 1951.

Brumfield, Eric R. "A Nativist Upsurge: Kentucky Know Nothing Party of the 1850s." M.A. thesis, University of Louisville, 2016.

Carriere, Marius Michael, Jr. "The Know-Nothing Movement in Louisiana." Ph.D. dissertation, Louisiana State University, 1977.

French, John. "Irish-American Identity, Memory, and Americanism During the Eras of the Civil War and World War I." Ph.D. dissertation, Marquette University, 2012.

Koch, Flora M. "German Immigration to Southern Illinois, 1820–1860." B.A. thesis, University of Illinois, June 1, 1911.

Lohne, Raymond. "Founded at the Bier of Lincoln: A History of the Germania Club of Chicago, 1856–1986." Ph.D. dissertation, University of Illinois at Chicago, 2007.

Meyer, Mary D. "The Germans in Wisconsin and the Civil War: Their Attitude Toward the Union, the Republicans, Slavery, and Lincoln." M.A. thesis, Catholic University of America, 1937.

Scisco, Louis Dow. "Political Nativism in New York State." Ph.D. dissertation, Columbia University, 1901. www.columbia.edu/cu/lweb/digital/collections/cul/texts/ldpd_6316631_000/.

Wallace, Christopher Elliott. "The Opportunity to Grow: Springfield, Illinois During the 1850s." Ph.D. dissertation, Purdue University, 1983.

Monographs and Conference Papers

Carlson, A. Cheree. "The Rhetoric of the Know-Nothing Party: Nativism as a Response to the Rhetorical Situation." Paper presented at the annual meeting of the Eastern Communication Association, Baltimore, April 1988.

Current, Richard N. *What Is an American: Abraham Lincoln and "Multiculturalism"* (Frank L. Klement Lecture). Milwaukee: Marquette University Press, 1993.

NOTES

★ Introduction ★

1. Annual Message to Congress, December 6, 1864, in Roy P. Basler, ed., *The Collected Works of Abraham Lincoln*, 8 vols. (New Brunswick, NJ: Rutgers University Press, 1953–1955), 8:141 (hereinafter cited as *CW*).

2. "From Washington. Special Dispatches [. . .] Personal," *New York Times*, December 11, 1862.

3. Democrats had picked up twenty-three seats in the House the previous November, but according to reigning tradition, the new members did not take office for some thirteen months, until December 1863—just in time to hear the President's annual message.

4. Noah Brooks, *Washington in Lincoln's Time*, orig. pub. 1888 (New York: Century Co., 1895), 285–286.

5. Annual Message to Congress, December 8, 1863, *CW*, 7:49, 51.

6. Annual Message to Congress, December 8, 1863, *CW*, 7:40. Lincoln likely used the construct "I again submit for your consideration" because Congress had already considered, but failed earlier that year to act on, a bill establishing the federal Bureau of Immigration. See *Congressional Globe*, 37th Congress, 3rd Session, 1029.

7. Annual Message to Congress, December 8, 1863, *CW*, 7:44.

8. George Washington to Joshua Holmes, December 2, 1793, Founders Online, National Archives, https://founders.archives.gov/documents/Washington/99-01-02-12127?.

9. George Washington to John Adams, November 15, 1794, Founders Online, https://founders.archives.gov/documents/Washington/05-17-02-0112.

10. Quoted in Edward C. Carter II, "A 'Wild Irishman' Under Every Federalist's Bed: Naturalization in Philadelphia, 1789–1806," *Proceedings of the American Philosophical Society* 133 (June 1989): 334.

11. See Terri Diane Halperin, *The Alien and Sedition Acts of 1798: Testing the Constitution* (Baltimore: Johns Hopkins University Press, 2017).

12. For an expert analysis of the debate over citizenship in the early republic, see James H. Kettner, "The Development of American Citizenship in the Revolutionary Era: The Idea of Volitional Allegiance," *American Journal of Legal History* 18 (1974): 208–242.

13. Annual Message, December 8, 1863, *CW*, 7:53.

14. *New York Tribune*, December 10, 1864; *Richmond Examiner*, quoted in Herbert Mitgang, ed., *Lincoln as They Saw Him* (New York: Rinehart, 1956), 364.

15. Special Message to Congress, July 4, 1861, *CW*, 4:438.

16. *Chicago Tribune*, December 15, 1863.

17. Helen Nicolay, *Lincoln's Secretary: A Biography of John G. Nicolay* (New York: Longmans, Green, 1949), vii.

18. Noah Brooks, *Mr. Lincoln's Washington: Selections from the Writings of Noah Brooks, Civil War Correspondent*, ed. P. J. Staudenraus (South Brunswick, NJ: Thomas Yoseloff, 1967), 254.

19. Veteran Lincoln scholar Wayne C. Temple, longtime chief deputy director of the Illinois State Archives, discovered the remarkable fact that Nicolay did not become an American citizen until 1871, after he had served not only as White House chief of staff but as American consul in Paris. See Temple, *Lincoln's Springfield/Pittsfield Connection: "A Tale of Two Cities"* (Mahomet, IL: Mayhaven, 2017), 137–139, 144.

20. Nicolay quoted in Mario M. Cuomo and Harold Holzer, eds., *Lincoln on Democracy: His Own Words, with Essays by America's Foremost Historians* (New York: HarperCollins, 1990), 309.

21. Lincoln used this phrase many times. For an early example, see his Fragment for a Speech, ca. December 28, 1857, *CW,* 2:453.

22. "Altar of Freedom" from Lincoln's letter to Lydia Bixby, November 21, 1864, *CW,* 8:117; "nation might live" from the Gettysburg Address, November 19, 1863, *CW,* 7:23.

23. Richard Nelson Current, *Speaking of Abraham Lincoln: The Man and His Meaning for Our Times* (Urbana: University of Illinois Press, 1983), 49. Current's observations were based on his lecture at the Library of Congress, February 11, 1960.

Chapter One ★ A World in Miniature

1. Waldo Lincoln, *History of the Lincoln Family: An Account of the Descendants of Samuel Lincoln of Hingham Massachusetts, 1637–1920* (Worcester, MA: Commonwealth Press, 1923), 1–2.

2. See, for example, Rabbi Jeffrey A. Kahn, "Was Lincoln a Member of the Tribe?" (February 11, 2016), www.reformjudaism.org/blog/was-abraham-lincoln-member-tribe; and an August 24, 2017, post on https://www.barbrastreisand.com/news/abe-lincoln-jewish/. Another unsubstantiated theory held that Lincoln's ancestors were German. See "Lincoln's Blood German? Allegations Made by a German Historian Living in Baltimore," *New York Times*, May 29, 1910.

3. Isaac M. Wise, "Lincoln Funeral Address at the Lodge Street Temple, Cincinnati, April 19, 1865," in Emanuel Hertz, *Abraham Lincoln: The Tribute of the Synagogue* (New York: Bloch, 1927), 98, 169.

4. Lincoln, *History of the Lincoln Family*, 4–6; see also J. Henry Lea and J. R. Hutchinson, *The Ancestry of Abraham Lincoln* (Boston: Houghton Mifflin, 1909), 4–6; and Edward Steers Jr., *The Lincoln Tree: 300 Years of the Lincoln Ancestry, 1500 to 1837* (privately printed, 2021), 29–30.

5. Autobiographical sketch prepared for Jesse W. Fell, December 20, 1859, in Roy P. Basler, ed., *The Collected Works of Abraham Lincoln*, 8 vols. (New Brunswick, NJ: Rutgers University Press, 1953–1955), 3:511 (hereinafter cited as *CW*).

6. Second autobiographical sketch, June 1860, *CW,* 4:60–61; Lincoln to Solomon Lincoln, March 6, 1848, *CW,* 1:456.

7. Lincoln to Jesse Lincoln, April 1, 1854, *CW,* 2:217.

8. Lincoln to Solomon Lincoln, *CW,* 1:456.

9. William H. Herndon and Jesse William Weik, *Herndon's Lincoln: The True Story of a Great Life [. . .]*, 3 vols. (Chicago: Belford & Clark, 1889), 1:3–4.

10. Anthony Gross, ed., *Lincoln's Own Stories* (New York: Harper & Bros., 1912), 12.

11. "Lincoln's Teacher," undated clipping in the Lincoln Financial Corporation collection.

12. Henry Clay Whitney, *Lincoln the Citizen* (New York: Baker & Taylor, 1908), 22.

13. Etienne Mazureau to Alexis de Tocqueville, quoted in Richard Campanella, *Lincoln in New Orleans: The 1828–1831 Flatboat Voyages and Their Place in History* (Lafayette: University of Louisiana at Lafayette Press, 2010), 300; Basil Hall, *Travels in North America in the Years 1827 and 1828* (Edinburgh: Robert Cadell, 1830), 330.

14. John Adems Paxton, *The New-Orleans directory and register: containing the names, professions, & residences, of all the heads of families, and persons in the business of the city [. . .]* (New Orleans: Benjamin F. Levy, 1822), quoted in George Wilson Pierson, *Tocqueville in America* (Baltimore: Johns

Hopkins University Press, 1996), 627–628. Except as noted, all italicized passages are from the original sources.

15. W. D. Howells, *Life of Abraham Lincoln* (Columbus, OH: Follett, Foster & Co., 1860), 25.

16. Notes from William H. Herndon interview with John Hanks, ca. 1865, in Douglas L. Wilson and Rodney O. Davis., eds., *Herndon's Informants: Letters, Interviews, and Statements About Abraham Lincoln* (Urbana: University of Illinois Press, 1998), 457.

17. Recollections of Mrs. S. A. Ware (William Florville's great-great-granddaughter), in John E. Washington, *They Knew Lincoln* (New York: E. P. Dutton, 1942), 187.

18. "William Florville the Barber" to Lincoln, December 27, 1863, Abraham Lincoln Papers, Library of Congress; see Harold Holzer, ed., *Dear Mr. Lincoln: Letters to the President* (New York: Addison-Wesley, 1993), 321. By this time, Florville knew that Willie Lincoln had died the previous year.

19. The standard source is still Benjamin P. Thomas, *Lincoln's New Salem* (1934; Chicago: Lincoln's New Salem Enterprises, 1973), 38–40.

20. James H. Matheny interview with William H. Herndon, November 1866, in Wilson and Davis, *Herndon's Informants*, 432.

21. Communication to the People of Sangamo County, March 9, 1832, *CW*, 1:5.

22. Autobiographical sketch, June 1860, *CW*, 4:64.

23. Speech in the House of Representatives on the Presidential Campaign, July 27, 1848, *CW*, 1:510.

24. "Winked out," from Autobiographical sketch, June 1860, *CW*, 4:65.

25. Clark E. Carr, *My Day and Generation* (Chicago: A. C. McClurg, 1907), 107.

26. Joseph H. Gillespie quoted in Wilson and Davis, *Herndon's Informants*, 182.

27. Jane Martin Johns, "A Momentous Incident in Illinois History," *Journal of the Illinois State Historical Society* 10 (January 1918): 551.

28. For the best analysis of the sub-treasury issue, see G. [Gabor] S. Boritt, *Lincoln and the Economics of the American Dream* (Memphis, TN: Memphis State University Press, 1978), 65–71.

29. Address on the Sub-Treasury issue, Springfield, December 26 [?], 1839, *CW*, 1:177.

30. Address on the Sub-Treasury issue, *CW*, 1:177–178.

31. P. M. Zall, *Abe Lincoln Laughing: Humorous Anecdotes from Original Sources by and About Abraham Lincoln* (Berkeley: University of California Press, 1982), 13–14. In this very serious study of Lincoln's humor, Zall lists the story as number 1 of 225.

32. *Sangamo Journal*, February 25, 1842.

33. Address to the Washington Temperance Society of Springfield, February 22, 1842, *CW*, 1:272, 274, 276.

34. *CW*, 1:276.

35. William Herndon to Jesse W. Weik, November 17, 1885, in William H. Herndon, *Herndon on Lincoln: Letters*, ed. Douglas L. Wilson and Rodney O. Davis (Urbana: University of Illinois Press, 2016), 166.

36. Zall, *Abe Lincoln Laughing*, 1.

37. *New York Tribune*, November 11, 1844.

38. Paul Angle, ed., *Herndon's Life of Lincoln* (1930; Cleveland: World Publishing Co., 1949), 183.

39. What follows is a new version of the story related in Holzer, *Lincoln and the Power of the Press* (New York: Simon & Schuster, 2014), 47–50.

40. Dr. Anson G. Henry quoted in Francis B. Carpenter, *Six Months at the White House with Abraham Lincoln. The Story of a Picture* (New York: Hurd & Houghton, 1866), 303.

41. "Letter from the Lost Townships," *Sangamo Journal*, August 27, 1842, in *CW*, 1:295.

42. "Letter from the Lost Townships," *Sangamo Journal*, in *CW*, 1:295–296.

43. Shields described in J. G. Holland, *The Life of Abraham Lincoln* (Springfield, MA: Gurdon Bill, 1866), 88.

44. *Sangamo Journal*, September 16, 1842, quoted in Richard Lawrence Miller, *Lincoln and His World: Prairie Politician, 1834–1842* (Mechanicsburg, PA: Stackpole Books, 2008), 519. Mary's coauthor was likely Julia Jayne.

45. Mary Lincoln to Francis B. Carpenter, December 8, 1865, in Justin G. Turner and Linda Levitt Turner, eds., *Mary Todd Lincoln: Her Life and Letters* (New York: Alfred A. Knopf, 1972), 298–299.

46. *Sangamo Journal*, October 14, 1842.

47. Shields to Lincoln, and Lincoln to Shields, both September 17, 1842, *CW*, 1:299–300.

48. Memorandum to Elias H. Merryman, September 19, 1842, *CW*, 1:301.

49. Memorandum to Elias H. Merryman, September 19, 1842; Henry quoted in Carpenter, *Six Months at the White House*, 304.

50. Ward Hill Lamon, *The Life of Abraham Lincoln, from His Birth to His Inauguration as President* (Boston: James R. Osgood, 1872), 263. For a quite different account, sympathetic to Shields, see William H. Condon, *Life of Major-General James Shields, Hero of Three Wars and Senator from Three States* (Chicago: Blakely Printing Co., 1900), 43–50.

51. Lincoln to Joshua Fry Speed, October 4, 1842, *CW*, 1:302.

52. Herndon and Weik, *Herndon's Lincoln*, 2:231.

53. Mary Lincoln to Mary Jane Welles, December 6, 1865, and to Josiah G. Holland, December 4, 1865, in Turner and Turner, *Mary Todd Lincoln*, 292–293, 296. J. G. Holland had recently retold the Shields duel story in his biography of the late president.

54. Henry in Carpenter, *Six Months at the White House*, 305; Mary Lincoln to Francis B. Carpenter, December 8, 1865, in Turner and Turner, *Mary Todd Lincoln*, 299.

55. Turner and Turner, *Mary Todd Lincoln*, 299.

Chapter Two ★ So Much Savage Feeling

1. Benjamin Franklin, *Observations Concerning the Increase of Mankind, Peopling of Countries, &c.* (Boston: S. Kneeland, 1755), 10. See also Franklin, *Information to Those Who Would Remove to America, and Remarks Concerning the Savages of North America* (London: John Stockdale, 1784). Thirty years after first raising objections to immigration, Franklin, by then a revered Founder, dismissed as "wild imaginations" proposals "not only to pay the expence of personal transportation" for European emigrants but "giving lands gratis to strangers" (see pp. 4–5)—proposals Lincoln would embrace four score years later.

2. Benjamin Franklin to Peter Collinson, May 9, 1753, *The Papers of Benjamin Franklin*, vol. 4, *July 1, 1750, Through June 30, 1753*, ed. Leonard W. Larabee (New Haven, CT: Yale University Press, 1961), 477–486; also available at Founders Online, National Archives, https://founders .archives.gov/documents/Franklin/01-04-02-0173.

3. The August 1834 "Flying Horses" race riot was so named because it began near the site of a Philadelphia carousel. For details, see Kerri K. Greenidge, *The Grimkes: The Legacy of Slavery in an American Family* (New York: Liveright, 2023), 8–10.

4. Hector Orr, *The Native American: A Gift for the People* (Philadelphia: Hector Orr, 1845), 154.

5. Samuel F. B. Morse wrote a series of anti-Catholic articles for the *New York Observer* under the pseudonym "Brutus," then pseudonymously published a book-length version from which these quotes are extracted. See "Brutus" [Morse], *Foreign Conspiracy Against the Liberties of the United States* (New York: Leavitt, Lord & Co., 1835), 45.

6. *New York Observer*, June 12, 1841.

7. Quoted in David Montgomery, "The Shuttle and the Cross: Weavers and Artisans in the Kensington Riots of 1844," *Journal of Social History* 5 (Summer 1972): 431.

8. Anonymous letter to the editor signed "A Catholic," *New York Tribune*, May 10, 1844.

9. [A Protestant and a Philadelphian], *The Full Particulars of the Late Riots, With a View of the burning of the Catholic Churches, St. Michaels and St. Augustines* (Philadelphia: n.p., 1844), 32.

10. Quoted in Margaret E. Fitzgerald, "The Philadelphia Nativist Riots" (1992), Irish Cultural Society web archive, Consulted October 1, 2021.

11. *The Full Particulars of the Late Riots*, 4.

12. *Sangamo Journal*, May 23, 1844.

13. Kenneth J. Winkle, *The Young Eagle: The Rise of Abraham Lincoln* (Dallas: Taylor Trade, 2001), 201.

14. Michael Burlingame, *An American Marriage: The Untold Story of Abraham Lincoln and Mary Todd* (New York: Pegasus Books, 2021), 62–65. Burlingame stresses Mary's violent streak—suggesting it approached the level of domestic abuse—whereas biographers like Jean H. Baker and Catherine Clinton offer a more nuanced view of Mary's volatile temperament. Evidence exists that the Lincolns also hired a live-in boy named Peter Dinkel, the son of German-born neighbors. See Wayne C. Temple, *The Dinkels and the Lincolns* (Springfield, IL: Abraham Lincoln Association, 2020).

15. *Sangamo Journal*, June 20, 1844; Roy P. Basler, ed., *The Collected Works of Abraham Lincoln*, 8 vols. (New Brunswick, NJ: Rutgers University Press, 1953–1955): 1:337 (hereinafter cited as *CW*).

16. *New York Tribune*, May 16, 1844. The *Tribune* devoted several days of coverage to the riots, heaping "much censure" on the Irishmen who upended the nativist meeting. But the paper also questioned the wisdom of staging an anti-Catholic rally "in a ward of which a large majority" were hostile, "and declining to palliate the crime of firing the churches" (*Tribune*, May 16, 1844). Editor Horace Greeley also condemned both nativist and Democratic newspapers, noting, "The object of some writers would seem to be rather to provoke similar atrocities than to prevent them" (May 17, 1844).

17. *New York Tribune*, May 17, 1844.

18. Proceedings of Public Meeting at Springfield regarding Philadelphia Riots, June 12, 1841, Papers of Abraham Lincoln, Springfield, Illinois.

19. Resolutions of the June 12, 1844, Springfield Meeting, *CW*, 1:337–338.

20. Resolutions of the June 12, 1844, Springfield Meeting, *CW*, 1:338.

21. *Illinois State Register* June 21, 1844.

22. *Illinois State Register* June 21, 1844.

23. *A Full Account of the Late Awful Riots in Philadelphia* (Philadelphia: John B. Perry, 1844), 2, 13; *Full Particulars of the Late Riots*, 20.

24. George Templeton Strong, *The Diary of George Templeton Strong*, ed. Allan Nevins and Milton Halsey Thomas, 4 vols. (New York: Macmillan, 1952), 1:228, 240.

25. Address to the Young Men's Lyceum of Springfield, January 27, 1838, *CW*, 1:111.

26. Democratic Party Platform, May 27, 1844, from the American Presidency Project, https://www.presidency.ucsb.edu/documents/1844-democratic-party-platform; Whig Party Platform, May 1, 1844, https://www.presidency.ucsb.edu/documents/whig-party-platform-1844.

27. "Beau ideal" from the first Lincoln–Douglas debate, Ottawa, Illinois, August 21, 1858, *CW*, 3:29; Don E. Fehrenbacher and Virginia Fehrenbacher, eds., *Recollected Words of Abraham Lincoln* (Stanford, CA: Stanford University Press, 1996), 99. (Lincoln reportedly said this upon meeting ex-congressman James Brown Clay of Kentucky, the late statesman's son.)

28. See Resolutions Adopted at a Whig Convention in Peoria, June 19, 1844, *CW*, 1: 338–340.

29. James C. Klotter, *Henry Clay: The Man Who Would Be President* (New York: Oxford University Press, 2018), 314–315.

30. Henry Clay to James Watson Webb, October 25, 1844, quoted in David S. Heidler and Jeanne T. Heidler, *Henry Clay: The Essential American* (New York: Random House, 2010), 380.

31. For Whig Party successes in Springfield between 1836 and 1848, see Kenneth J. Winkle, "The Second Party System in Lincoln's Springfield," *Civil War History* 44 (December 1998): 267–284, esp. 273. Winkle's research also confirmed the Democrats' grip on foreign-born Catholic as well as Lutheran voters.

32. V. Bouligny to Henry Clay, December 4, 1844, in Michael F. Holt, *The Rise and Fall of the American Whig Party: Jacksonian Politics and the Onset of the Civil War* (New York: Oxford University Press, 1999), 204.

33. Sheldon H. Harris, "John Louis O'Sullivan and the Election of 1844 in New York," *New York History* 41 (July 1960): 294; *New York Tribune*, May 17, 1844; *New York Tribune*, November 11, 1854.

34. Clay comment, December 1844, quoted in Holt, *American Whig Party*, 212.

35. G. Melville to Samuel Medary, November 4, 1844, quoted in Holt, *American Whig Party*, 291. Medary was at the time editor of the *Ohio Statesman* and a former state legislator who backed Polk at the 1844 Democratic National Convention. During the Civil War, his Copperhead newspaper *The Crisis* would be shut down, and Medary arrested, for criticizing the Union.

36. Strong, *Diary of George Templeton Strong*, 1:94, 249.

37. "Our Defeat in New York" and "Native Americanism," *New York Tribune*, November 11, 1844.

38. Thomas R. Whitney, *A Defence of the American Policy, as Opposed to the Encroachments of Foreign Influence, and Especially to the Interference of the Papacy [. . .]* (New York: De Witt & Davenport, 1856), 67, 70.

39. For statistics, see Raymond L. Cohn, "Mortality on Immigrant Voyages to New York, 1836–1853," *Journal of Economic History* 44 (June 1984): 289–300. The alarming migrant death rate was chronicled in a series of exposés in the *New York Tribune*, November 19, 22, 26, and December 3, 1853.

40. Roger Daniels, *Coming to America: A History of Immigration and Ethnicity in American Life*, 2nd ed. (1991; New York: Harper Perennial, 2002), 133.

41. *Report of the Select Committee to Whom Was Referred the Subject of the Practicability of Preventing the Induction of Foreign Paupers into the State*, Boston, 1835, quoted in Kunal M. Parker, "State, Citizenship, and Territory: The Legal Construction of Immigrants in Antebellum Massachusetts," *Law and History Review* 19 (Autumn 2001): 594.

42. Francis Wyse, *America: Its Realities and Resources; Comprising Important Details Connected with the Present Social, Political, Agricultural, Commercial, and Financial State of the Country [. . .]*, 3 vols. (London: T. C. Newby, 1846), 3:33, 36–37.

43. John Thornton, *Diary of a Tour Through the Northern States of the Union, and Canada [. . .]* (London: F. Barker, 1850), 87.

44. "God and Our Native Land," advertisement in the *Baltimore Clipper*, quoted in Mary St. Patrick McConville, *Political Nativism in the State of Maryland, 1830–1860* (Washington, DC: Catholic University of America, 1928), 29.

45. Kevin Kenny, "Abraham Lincoln and the American Irish," *American Journal of Irish Studies* 10 (2013): 42. The reference to "urban pioneers" is on p. 41.

46. Edward Laxton, *The Famine Ships: The Irish Exodus to America* (New York: Henry Holt, 1997), 10.

47. *The Seventh Census. Report of the Superintendent of the Census for December 1, 1852* (Washington, DC: Robert Armstrong), 14, 18. For a good analysis, see Edward J. O'Day, "The 'Second Colonization of New England' Revisited: Irish Immigration Before the Famine," in Charles Fanning, ed., *New Perspectives on the Irish Diaspora* (Carbondale: Southern Illinois University Press, 2000), esp. 93–94.

48. Principles adopted by the American Protestant Union, *New York Observer*, June 12, 1841, quoted in Louis Dow Scisco, *Political Nativism in New York State* (New York: Columbia University Press, 1901), 34.

49. Its editor was clergyman William Brownlee—an immigrant from Scotland—who in 1836 cofounded the anti-Catholic American Society to Promote the Principles of the Protestant Reformation. See Thomas J. Curran, "Assimilation and Nativism," *International Migration Digest* 3 (Spring 1966): 21.

50. Records of the American Brotherhood, December 1844, in Scisco, *Political Nativism in New York*, 64.

51. Lincoln's "Spot" Resolutions, U.S. House of Representatives, December 22, 1847, *CW*, 1:420–421.

52. Speech in the House of Representatives on Internal Improvements, June 20, 1848, *CW*, 1:487.

53. Marshall Brown, *Bulls and Blunders* (Chicago: M. C. Griggs & Co., 1894), iii, 9, 12, 38, 309; L[ucius]. E. Chittenden, *Recollections of President Lincoln and His Administration* (New York: Harper & Bros., 1891), 38.

54. Lincoln to William H. Herndon, June 12, 1848, *CW,* 1:476–477.

55. Tyler V. Johnson, "Punishing the Lies on the Rio Grande: Catholic and Immigrant Volunteers in Zachary Taylor's Army and the Fight Against Nativism," *Journal of the Early Republic* 30 (Spring 2010): 63–66.

56. "Spread of Slavery" and "German Whig Rally," *New York Tribune,* November 1, 1848. For an excellent account of the paper's outreach to immigrant voters in 1848, see Gregory A. Borchard, "Revolutions Incomplete: Horace Greeley and the Forty-Eighters at Home and Abroad," *American Journalism* 27 (Winter 2010): 7–35.

Chapter Three ★ No Objection to Fuse with Any Body

1. "Abraham Lincoln. A Talk with the Late President's Law Partner," *New York Tribune,* February 15, 1867 (conversation on January 25), reprinted in George Alfred Townsend, *The Real Life of Abraham Lincoln: A Talk with Mr. Herndon, His Late Law Partner* (New York: Bible House, 1867), 9.

2. Townsend, *The Real Life of Abraham Lincoln,* 8–9.

3. Thomas R. Whitney, *A Defence of the American Policy, as Opposed to the Encroachments of Foreign Influence, and Especially to the Interference of the Papacy in the Political Interests and Affairs of the United States* (New York: De Witt & Davenport, 1856), 236.

4. William H. Herndon to Jesse W. Weik, February 11, 1887, in William H. Herndon, *Herndon on Lincoln: Letters,* ed. Douglas L. Wilson and Rodney O. Davis (Urbana: University of Illinois Press, 2016), 234.

5. William H. Herndon and Jesse W. Weik, *Herndon's Lincoln: The True Story of a Great Life,* 3 vols. (Chicago: Belford, Clarke & Co., 1889), 3:625.

6. Bonnie E. Paull and Richard E. Hart, *Lincoln's Springfield Neighborhood* (Charleston, SC: History Press, 2015), 74, 77.

7. James H. Matheny, "History of Springfield," *Springfield City Directory for 1857–'58* (Springfield, IL: S. H. Jameson & Co., 1857), 17.

8. *Rock Island Republican,* December 17, 1851, quoted in Nels Hokanson, *Swedish Immigrants in Lincoln's Time* (New York: Harper & Bros., 1942), 43. Hokanson's is still the best book on Swedish immigration to the American West.

9. Hokanson, *Swedish Immigrants,* 54. For Robert Lincoln and Illinois State University, see Jason Emerson, *Giant in the Shadows: The Life of Robert Todd Lincoln* (Carbondale: Southern Illinois University Press, 2012), 35–36.

10. *Sangamo Journal,* October 30 and November 10, 13, 14, 1849; see also George Rawlings Poage, "The Coming of the Portuguese," *Journal of the Illinois State Historical Society* 18 (April 1925): 130–132.

11. Carl Schurz, speech at Faneuil Hall, Boston, April 19, 1859, in Frederic Bancroft, ed., *Speeches, Correspondence and Political Papers of Carl Schurz,* 6 vols. (New York: G. P. Putnam's Sons, 1913), 1:49–50.

12. See Bruce Levine, *The Spirit of 1848: German Immigrants, Labor Conflict, and the Coming of the Civil War* (Urbana: University of Illinois Press, 1992).

13. Jacob Mueller, *Memories of a Forty-Eighter* (1896), quoted in Alison Clark Efford, *German Immigrants, Race, and Citizenship in the Civil War Era* (New York: Cambridge University Press, 2013), 17.

14. Carl Wittke, "The German Forty-Eighters in America: A Centennial Appraisal," *American Historical Review* 53 (July 1948): 714–715; "*Et Afskedsquad til Emigranter til Emigrater paa Reusen till Amerika* (A Farewell Ode to Emigrants on Their Journey to America)" (Boston: n.p., 1853), original in the Gilder Lehrman Collection, GLC 04059, translation by the Gilder Lehrman Institute of American History.

15. Peter H. Olden, "Anton C. Hesing: The Rise of a Chicago Boss," *Journal of the Illinois State Historical Society* 35 (September 1942): 267–268.

16. For an introduction to the Turner ethos, see Frank Baron, *Abraham Lincoln and the German Immigrants: Turners and Forty-Eighters* (Lexington: University of Kentucky Press, 2012), esp. 1–11.

17. Raymond Lohne, "Team of Friends: A New Lincoln Theory and Legacy," *Journal of the Illinois State Historical Society* 101 (Fall–Winter 2008): 290.

18. *Memoirs of Gustave Koerner, 1809–1896: Life-Sketches Written at the Suggestion of His Children*, ed. Thomas J. McCormack, 2 vols. (Cedar Rapids, IA: Torch Press, 1909), 1:443–444.

19. *Memoirs of Gustave Koerner*, 1:479.

20. Resolutions of Sympathy with the Cause of Hungarian Freedom, September 6, 1859, in Roy P. Basler, ed., *The Collected Works of Abraham Lincoln*, 8 vols. (New Brunswick, NJ: Rutgers University Press, 1953–1955), 2:62 (hereinafter cited as *CW*).

21. "The Welcome to Kossuth," *New York Times*, December 8, 1851.

22. Julian Kune [Kuné], *Reminiscences of an Octogenarian Hungarian Exile* (Chicago: published by the author, 1911), 9.

23. Springfield Resolutions in Support of Kossuth and Hungarian Freedom, January 9, 1852, *CW*, 2:115–116.

24. *CW*, 2:115–116.

25. Call for a Kossuth Meeting, January 26, 1852, *CW*, 2:118.

26. Whitney, *A Defence of the American Policy*, 192; Ben: Perley Poore, *Perley's Reminiscences of Sixty Years in the National Metropolis [. . .]*, 2 vols. (Philadelphia: Hubbard Brothers, 1886), 1:405.

27. Earl Schenck Miers, ed., *Lincoln Day by Day: A Chronology, 1809–1865*, 3 vols. (Washington, DC: Lincoln Sesquicentennial Commission, 1960), 1:300.

28. Eulogy for Henry Clay, July 6, 1852, *CW*, 2:132. The literature on Lincoln's long flirtation with voluntary Black colonization—which lasted until at least December 1863—is substantial. See, for example, G. [Gabor] S. Boritt, "A Voyage to the Colony of Lincolnia," *The Historian* 37 (August 1975): 619–632; Michel Vorenberg, "Abraham Lincoln and the Politics of Black Colonization," *Journal of the Abraham Lincoln Association* 14 (Summer 1993): 22–45; and Philip Shaw Paludan, "Lincoln and Colonization: Policy or Propaganda?," *Journal of the Abraham Lincoln Association* 25 (Winter 2005): 23–37.

29. Winfield Scott to the Whig committee notifying him of his nomination, in *Life of General Winfield Scott, Commander of the United States Army [. . .]* (New York: A. S. Barnes, 1852), 195–196. The campaign biography was adapted from an 1846 book by Edward D. Mansfield.

30. "A True History of How Winfield Scott Got Nominated and Tried to Be President" [1852], original broadside in the Rare Book and Special Collections Division, Library of Congress.

31. *Letter of Hon. James Shields [. . . to Messrs. H. B. McGinnis, Matthew Plumstead, John J. Craw-ford, and others in Galena, Illinois]*, August 5, 1852, published as a Pierce campaign pamphlet, Washington, 1852.

32. *Boston Pilot*, August 14, 1852; *Voice of the Catholics of New Hampshire, Letter of James Shields* (pamphlet, n.p., n.d.).

33. Speech to the Springfield Scott Club, August 14 or 26, 1852, *CW*, 2:136.

34. Speech to the Springfield Scott Club, *CW*, 2:143; see also "Hon. A. Lincoln's Address Before the Springfield Scott Club, in Reply to Judge Douglas' Richmond Speech," *Illinois Weekly Journal*, September 22, 1852. For the courthouse locale, see *Illinois Daily Journal*, August 7, 1852, original in the Abraham Lincoln Presidential Library and Museum, Springfield, Illinois.

35. Speech to the Springfield Scott Club, *CW*, 2:143.

36. Speech to the Springfield Scott Club, *CW*, 2:143.

37. Speech to the Springfield Scott Club, *CW*, 2:145–146.

38. Speech to the Springfield Scott Club, *CW*, 2:145, 149.

39. S. W. Jackman, ed., *Acton in America: The American Journal of Sir John Acton 1853* (Shepherdstown, WV: Patmos Press, 1979), 676.

40. Stephen A. Douglas, Statement to the St. Joseph Convention, December 17, 1853, in *The Letters of Stephen A. Douglas*, ed. Robert W. Johannsen (Urbana: University of Illinois Press, 1961), 270; see also James C. Malin, "The Motives of Stephen A. Douglas in the Organization of the

Nebraska Territory: A Letter Dated December 17, 1853," *Kansas Historical Quarterly* 19 (November 1951): 352.

41. Extrapolated from autobiographical sketches of December 10, 1859, and June 1860, *CW*, 3:512, 4:67.

42. Fragment on Slavery, ca. June 1854, *CW*, 2:222.

43. James R. Thompson letter, August 14, 1855, quoted in William Gienapp, *Origins of the Republican Party* (New York: Oxford University Press, 1987), 287.

44. Poore, *Reminiscences*, 1:406. Richard Hofstadter called the phenomenon "Know-Nothing mania." See Hofstadter, *The American Political Tradition and the Men Who Made It* (New York: Alfred A. Knopf, 1948), 110.

45. Horace Greeley, *Recollections of a Busy Life; Including Reminiscences of American Politics and Politicians, from the Opening of the Missouri Contest to the Downfall of Slavery [. . .]* (New York: J. B. Ford, 1868), 290.

46. Whitney, *A Defence of the American Policy*, 283–284.

47. Based on what was then Matthew Pinsker's unpublished essay, "If You Know Nothing: Abraham Lincoln and Political Nativism," David Herbert Donald used this story in his *Lincoln* (New York: Simon & Schuster, 1995), 170.

48. Matthew Pinsker rediscovered the reminiscence. See Pinsker, "Not Always Such a Whig: Abraham Lincoln's Partisan Realignment in the 1850s," *Journal of the Abraham Lincoln Association* 29 (Summer 2008): 37–38. The original is in Noah Levering, "Recollections of Abraham Lincoln," *Iowa Historical Record* 12 (July 1896): 495–497.

49. Speech at Springfield, September 9, 1854, *CW*, 2:229; *Illinois State Register*, September 11, 1854.

50. Address at Bloomington, September 26, 1854, *CW*, 2:234. The best book on the Peoria speech is Lewis E. Lehrman, *Lincoln at Peoria: The Turning Point* (Mechanicsburg, PA: Stackpole Books, 2008).

51. Address at Peoria, October 16, 1854, *CW*, 2:263, 275.

52. For an excellent study of this subject, see Kate Masur, *Until Justice Be Done: America's First Civil Rights Movement, from the Revolution to Reconstruction* (New York: W. W. Norton, 2021).

53. Paul Selby, "George Schneider," in *Transactions of the Illinois State Historical Society 1906* (Springfield: Illinois State Journal, 1906), 329–331; Frank Baron, *Abraham Lincoln and the German Immigrants*.

54. Kune, *Reminiscences*, 73.

55. "A Talk with Lincoln's Friend [Joseph Medill]: Becoming the First Republican President," *Saturday Evening Post*, August 5, 1899, reprinted in *Chicago Tribune*, Sunday supplement, February 5, 1944.

56. For Douglas's speech in Philadelphia, July 4, 1854, and the *Tribune*'s comment, see Robert W. Johannsen, *Stephen A. Douglas* (New York: Oxford University Press, 1973), 446, 454.

57. For the von Schneidau image, see Charles Hamilton and Lloyd Ostendorf, *Lincoln in Photographs: An Album of Every Known Pose* (1963; Dayton, OH: Morningside, 1985), 19–20. Joining the duo on their walk in Chicago was politician Isaac N. Arnold, who probably invited George Schneider to join them. Based on testimony by von Schneidau's daughter, historian Matthew Pinsker has suggested that the picture might have been taken as early as August 9, 1854. See Pinsker, "Not Always Such a Whig," 44.

58. See descriptions of this phenomenon in Raymond L. Cohn, "Nativism and the End of the Mass Migration of the 1840s and 1850s," *Journal of Economic History* 60 (June 2000): 374; and Michael F. Holt, *The Rise and Fall of the American Whig Party: Jacksonian Politics and the Onset of Civil War* (New York: Oxford University Press, 1999), 606.

59. Lincoln to Richard Yates, October 30, 1854, *CW*, 2:284. The entry includes Yates's 1869 recollections about the matter to Isaac N. Arnold.

60. Lincoln to Yates, November 1, 1854, *CW*, 2:284.

61. William H. Randolph to Lincoln, December 38, 1854, Abraham Lincoln Papers, Library of Congress.

62. Lincoln to Hugh Lemaster, November 29, 1854, *CW*, 2:289.

63. Douglas to Charles H. Lanphier, editor of the *Illinois State Register*, December 18, 1854, and to James W. Sheahan, editor of the *Chicago Times*, September 14, 1854, in *Letters of Stephen A. Douglas*, 330–331.

64. Article III, Section 7, of the 1848 Illinois State Constitution, cited in Sunderine Temple and Wayne C. Temple, *Abraham Lincoln and Illinois' Fifth Capitol*, 2nd ed. (Mahomet, IL: Mayhaven, 2006), 201.

65. Charles H. Ray to Congressman Elihu B. Washburne, December 29, 1854, E. B. Washburne Papers, Library of Congress. For the *Chicago Tribune*'s temporary embrace of Know-Nothingism, see Thomas M. Keefe, "Chicago's Flirtation with Political Nativism, 1854–1856," *Records of the American Catholic Historical Society of Philadelphia* 82 (1971): 131–158; and Keefe, "The Catholic Issue in the *Chicago Tribune*," *Mid-America* 57 (1975): 227–245.

66. *Chicago Free West*, and dis-endorsement by J. L. D. Morrison, cited in Donald, *Lincoln*, 181–183.

67. Opinion Concerning John Fitzgerald, December 18, 1854, *CW*, 2:294–295.

68. *Memoirs of Gustave Koerner*, 1:626.

69. Lincoln to Elihu B. Washburne, February 9, 1855, *CW*, 2:306.

70. Lincoln to Joshua Fry Speed, August 24, 1855, *CW*, 2:323.

71. Lincoln to Owen Lovejoy, August 11, 1855, *CW*, 2:316.

72. Lincoln to Owen Lovejoy, August 11, 1855, *CW*, 2:316.

73. Lincoln to Owen Lovejoy, August 11, 1855, *CW*, 2:316–317.

74. "One of 'Em," ed., *The Wide-Awake Gift: Know-Nothing Token for 1855* (New York: J. C. Derby, 1855), 55.

Chapter Four ★ Our Equals in All Things

1. Otto R. Kyle, "Lincoln Steps Out: The Anti-Nebraska Editor's Convention," *Abraham Lincoln Quarterly* 5 (March 1948): 33. See also Kyle, *Abraham Lincoln in Decatur* (New York: Vantage Press, 1957), 62–63, 69–74.

2. Paul Selby, "The Editorial Convention of 1856," *Journal of the Illinois State Historical Society* 5 (October 1912): 346. Selby, who attended the conference in his role as editor of the antislavery *Morgan* (County) *Journal*, first wrote a version of this recollection for the *Chicago Tribune* (February 22, 1906) to mark the fiftieth anniversary of the meeting. See also Frank Baron, *Abraham Lincoln and the German Immigrants: Turners and Forty-Eighters*, Yearbook of German-American Studies, Supplemental Issue, vol. 4 (Topeka: Society for German-American Studies, University of Kansas, 2012), 85.

3. Kyle, *Lincoln in Decatur*, 141; Barron, *Abraham Lincoln and the German Immigrants*, 85.

4. *Illinois State Register*, February 25, 1856.

5. No manuscript of the speech survives. According to legend, reporters on the scene were so transfixed that they failed to transcribe it. The problem with this myth is that stenography was not yet in widespread use in 1856. The only book on the subject is Elwell Crissey, *Lincoln's Lost Speech: The Pivot of His Career* (New York: Hawthorn Books, 1967).

6. *The Diary of Orville Hickman Browning*, ed. Theodore Calvin Pease, 2 vols. (Springfield: Illinois State Historical Library, 1925), 1:237.

7. For more, see Thomas M. Keefe, "Chicago's Flirtation with Political Nativism, 1854–1856," *Records of the American Catholic Historical Society of Philadelphia* 82 (September 1971): 139–140.

8. *Illinois State Register*, June 15, 1854.

9. *Basis* [sic] *Principles of the American Party of Virginia*, 1856 broadside, Duke University Libraries, https://dp.la/exhibitions/outsiders-president-elections/anti-outsider-platforms/know-nothing -party-1856.

10. W. S. Tisdale, ed., *Know Nothing Almanac and True Americans' Manual for 1856* (New York: De Witt & Davenport, 1855), 19; Thomas R. Whitney, *A Defence of the American Policy, as Opposed to the Encroachments of Foreign Influence, and Especially to the Interference of the Papacy in the Political Affairs of the United States* (New York: De Witt & Davenport, 1856), 294–296.

11. William H. Bailhache had recently purchased the paper in partnership with Edward L. Baker. For Bailhache's sympathy for Fillmore, expressed in a letter to his father, see Ian Iverson, "Conservative to the Last Degree: The Emerging Illinois Republican Party and the Election of 1856," *Civil War History* 68 (December 2022): 358, 370. Bailhache ultimately endorsed Republican nominee John C. Frémont.

12. *Memoirs of Gustave Koerner, 1809–1896: Life-Sketches Written at the Suggestion of His Children*, ed. Thomas J. McCormick, 2 vols. (Cedar Rapids, IA: Torch Press, 1909), 2:21.

13. Paul M. Angle, *"Here I Have Lived": A History of Lincoln's Springfield* (1935; Chicago: Abraham Lincoln Book Shop, 1971), 221.

14. Keefe, "Chicago's Flirtation with Political Nativism," 133.

15. Mary Lincoln to Emilie Todd Helm, November 23, 1856, in Justin G. Turner and Linda Levitt Turner, eds., *Mary Todd Lincoln: Her Life and Letters* (New York: Alfred A. Knopf, 1972), 46. Emilie would marry Ben Hardin Helm, later a Confederate general.

16. These were among the "Great Anti-Catholic Works" advertised in the endpapers of Whitney, *A Defence of the American Policy*, after p. 370.

17. Whitney, *A Defence of the American Republic*, 329–330.

18. Tisdale, *Know Nothing Almanac and True Americans' Manual*, 16.

19. John Hancock Lee, *The Origin and Progress of the American Party in Politics: Embracing a Complete History of the Philadelphia Riots in May and July, 1844, With a Full Description of the Great American Procession of July Fourth, and a Refutation of the Arguments Founded on the Charges of Religious Proscription and Secret Combinations* (Philadelphia: Elliott & Gihon, 1855).

20. Anna Ella Carroll, *The Great American Battle; or the Contest Between Christianity and Political Romanism* (New York: Miller, Orton & Mulligan, 1856), 30.

21. Louis Schade, *The Immigration into the United States of America, from a Statistical and National-Economical Point of View* (Washington, DC: Daily Union, 1856), 4, 14.

22. See *Fremont's Romanism Established. Acknowledged by Archbishop Hughes. How Fremont's Nomination was Brought About. Hughes, Seward, Fremont, and the Foreigners—a Most Foul Coalition* (anonymous American Party campaign pamphlet, 1856).

23. Thurlow Weed to Edwin D. Morgan, August 9, 1856, quoted in William E. Gienapp, *The Origins of the Republican Party, 1852–1856* (New York: Oxford University Press, 1987), 369.

24. William H. Herndon to Jesse W. Weik, February 11, 1887, and to Ward Hill Lamon, March 1, 1870, in William H. Herndon, *Herndon on Lincoln: Letters*, ed. Douglas L. Wilson and Rodney O. Davis (Urbana: University of Illinois Press, 2016), 235, 92.

25. Lincoln to Lyman Trumbull, August 11, 1856, in Roy P. Basler, ed., *The Collected Works of Abraham Lincoln*, 8 vols. (New Brunswick, NJ: Rutgers University Press, 1953–1955), 2:360 (hereinafter cited as *CW*).

26. "Dear Sir" letter to Fillmore Men, September 8, 1856, *CW*, 2:374.

27. Angle, *"Here I Have Lived,"* 221.

28. Wayne C. Temple, "The Linguistic Lincolns: A New Lincoln Letter," *Lincoln Herald* 94 (1994): 108–114. See also Sabine Freitag, *Friedrich Hecker: Two Lives for Liberty*, trans. Steven Rowan (1955; St. Louis: St. Louis Mercantile Library, 2006), 174–176. For Lincoln [to Charles H. Ray], September 8, 1856, see the online catalog for the Christie's auction *Fine Printed Books and Manuscripts Including Americana*, June 12, 2008, www.christies.com/en/lot/lot-5085827.

29. Some historians have credited Lincoln for refusing to panic over the rise of Know-Nothingism. See, for example, Stephen L. Hansen and Paul G. Nygard, "Abraham Lincoln and the Know Nothing Question, 1854–1859," *Lincoln Herald* 94 (Summer 1992): esp. 69–70.

30. Charles W. Johnson, ed., *Proceedings of the First Three Republican National Conventions of 1856, 1860 and 1864, Including Proceedings of the Antecedent National Convention Held at Pittsburg in*

February, 1856, as Reported by Horace Greeley (Minneapolis: Harrison & Smith, 1893), 226. For the final 1856 Republican platform, see https://www.presidency.ucsb.edu/documents/republican -party-platform-1856.

31. Salmon P. Chase to Edward Hamlin, February 9, 1855, in Walter Stahr, *Salmon P. Chase: Lincoln's Vital Rival* (New York: Simon & Schuster, 2021), 213.

32. Lincoln to James Berdan, July 10, 1856, *CW*, 2:347.

33. William H. Herndon to Jesse W. Weik, February 11, 1887, in Herndon, *Herndon on Lincoln*, 235.

34. "What's in the Wind?," unsigned editorial on the right of foreigners to vote, originally published in the *Galena* (IL) *Daily Advertiser*, July 23, 1856, *CW*, 2:355–356. The words are generally accepted as Lincoln's because editor H. H. Houghton kept a copy of the weekly edition of his paper with its front page marked by hand in pencil: "The editorial ... was written by Abraham Lincoln."

35. Douglas's July 4, 1856, speech reprinted in James W. Sheahan, *The Life of Stephen A. Douglas* (New York: Harper & Bros., 1860), 269.

36. Remarks at Belleville, October 18, 1856, *CW*, 3:379–380; *Belleville Advocate*, October 22, 1856; Donald Allendorf, *"Your Friend, as Ever, A. Lincoln": How the Unlikely Friendship of Gustav Koerner and Abraham Lincoln Changed America* (Gretna, LA: Pelican Publishing, 2014), 9; Mark E. Steiner, *Lincoln and Citizenship* (Carbondale: Southern Illinois University Press, 2021), 41.

37. Lincoln to Friedrich Hecker, September 14, 1856, *CW*, 2:376.

38. Gustave Koerner to Lincoln, July 17, 1858, Abraham Lincoln Papers, Library of Congress (hereinafter cited as ALPLC).

39. Speech at Jacksonville, Illinois, September 7, 1856, *CW*, 2:373.

40. William H. Herndon to Ward Hill Lamon, March 1, 1870, in Herndon, *Herndon on Lincoln*, 92.

41. Speech to a Republican banquet, December 10, 1856, *CW*, 2:485. The quotes come from a report published in the *Illinois State Journal* on December 16, 1856, reportedly from Lincoln's subsequently lost manuscript.

42. William J. Cooper Jr., *Jefferson Davis, American* (New York: Random House, 2000), 294.

43. "Rioting and Lawlessness," *Chicago Tribune*, March 5, 1857; "Scene in the Bloody Seventh," *Chicago Tribune*, March 7, 1857.

44. Lincoln to Elihu B. Washburne, May 15, 1858, *CW*, 2:447.

45. Speech at Chicago, July 10, 1858, *CW*, 2:496.

46. "First and only" and recollections of the Illinois Republican state convention in *Memoirs of Gustave Koerner*, 2:58.

47. "House Divided" address, June 16, 1858, *CW*, 2:461.

48. Anton Hesing to Lincoln, June 29, 1858, ALPLC. Hesing hoped Lincoln would participate in the unfurling of an antislavery banner at the German Seventh Ward Club.

49. Lincoln to Anton C. Hesing, Henry Wendt, Alexander Fisher, and others, June 30, 1858, *CW*, 2:475.

50. "The German Festival in Wright's Grove," *Chicago Tribune*, July 7, 1858.

51. *Chicago Press and Tribune*, July 12, 1858. Douglas would die at the Tremont House three years later, in 1861, and Mary Lincoln would stay there temporarily in 1865 after her husband's assassination.

52. For Hesing's presence on July 10, see Raymond Lohne, "'Five Times as Enthusiastic': Abraham Lincoln and the Bloody Seventh of Chicago," *Yearbook of German-American Studies* 50 (2015): 115.

53. Speech at Chicago, July 10, 1858, *CW*, 2:499–500.

54. Lincoln to Joseph Gillespie, July 16, 1858, *CW*, 2:503.

55. Joseph Gillespie to Lincoln, July 18, 1858, ALPLC.

56. Lincoln to Joseph Gillespie, July 25, 1858, *CW*, 2:523.

57. Lincoln to Gustave Koerner, July 25, 1858, *CW*, 2:254.

58. Lincoln to Stephen A. Douglas, July 24, 1858, *CW*, 2:522.

59. Lincoln to Gustave Koerner, July 15, 1858, *CW*, 2:502–503.

60. The author's version of the debate transcripts—the unedited texts printed by the opposition newspapers in 1858—appear in Holzer, ed., *The Lincoln–Douglas Debates: The First Complete, Unexpurgated Text* (New York: HarperCollins, 1993).

61. *New York Evening Post*, September 21, 1858.

62. *Philadelphia Press*, August 26, 1858; *New York Evening Post*, August 3, 1858. See also Edwin Erle Sparks, *The Lincoln–Douglas Debates of 1858* (Springfield: Illinois State Historical Library, 1908), 125, 129.

63. *Chicago Press and Tribune*, October 15, 1858; Sparks, *Lincoln–Douglas Debates*, 436.

64. *Freeport* (IL) *Weekly Bulletin*, quoted in Richard D. Schwartz, *The Prairies on Fire: Lincoln Debates Douglas, 1858* (Charleston, SC: privately printed, 2010), 178.

65. Third Lincoln–Douglas debate at Jonesboro, September 15, 1858, *CW*, 3:108–109; fourth debate at Charleston, September 18, 1858, *CW*, 3:173. The "phonographic reporter" born overseas was Henry Binmore, who hailed from England. That Douglas quoted a speech by Lincoln's old friend James H. Matheny no doubt added to his discomfort.

66. "Development of the Campaign," *New-Yorker Staats Zeitung*, September 16, 1858, in Allen C. Guelzo, *Lincoln and Douglas: The Debates That Defined America* (New York: Simon & Schuster, 2008), 89–90.

67. Henry "Villardt" to Stephen A. Douglas, August 24, 1858—three days after the first Lincoln–Douglas debate in Ottawa, Illinois—in Henry Villard, *Sixteenth President-in-Waiting: Abraham Lincoln and the Springfield Dispatches of Henry Villard, 1860–1861*, ed. Michael Burlingame (Carbondale: Southern Illinois University Press, 2018), 3.

68. *Memoirs of Henry Villard, Journalist and Financier, 1835–1900*, 2 vols. (Boston: Houghton Mifflin, 1904), 1:96–97.

69. Villard, *Sixteenth President-in-Waiting*, 4; *Memoirs of Henry Villard*, 1:93–94.

70. *Memoirs of Gustave Koerner*, 2:61.

71. Carl Schurz, *The Reminiscences of Carl Schurz*, 3 vols. (New York: McClure Co., 1907), 2:90–94.

72. Holzer, ed., *Lincoln–Douglas Debates*, 267.

73. *Political Debates Between Hon. Abraham Lincoln and Hon. Stephen A. Douglas, in the Celebrated Campaign of 1858, [. . .]* (Columbus, OH: Follett, Foster & Co., 1860), 37. Lincoln, who arranged for this edition to be published, made sure it included Douglas's Bloomington address, which preceded the debates. See also speech at Carlinville, IL, August 31, 1858, *CW*, 3:79–80.

74. *Memoirs of Gustave Koerner*, 2:67–68. See also Allendorf, *"Your Friend, as Ever, A. Lincoln,"* 208–210.

75. Reply at the seventh Lincoln–Douglas debate at Alton, October 15, 1858, *CW*, 3:315.

76. Speech at the Charleston debate, September 18, 1858, *CW*, 3:145. Lincoln's unpleasant remarks at Charleston are still cited as evidence that he was racist.

77. Speech at Meredosia, Illinois, October 18, 1858, *CW*, 3:328–329.

78. Speech at Meredosia, Illinois, October 18, 1858, *CW*, 3:329.

79. Lincoln to Edward Lusk, October 30, 1858, *CW*, 3:333.

80. Lincoln to Norman Judd, October 20, 1858, *CW*, 3:329–330.

81. The Davis and *Missouri Democrat* warnings are quoted in Michael Burlingame, *Abraham Lincoln: A Life*, 2 vols. (Baltimore: Johns Hopkins University Press, 2008), 1:546.

82. *Chicago Press and Tribune*, October 23 and 15, 1858. For a full discussion of the 1858 fraud warnings, see Guelzo, *Lincoln and Douglas*, 206–215.

83. Quoted in Burlingame, *Lincoln: A Life*, 1:546.

84. "War on the Irish," *Illinois State Register*, September 2, 1858.

85. William A. Grimshaw to Lincoln, November 11, 1858, online at House Divided, Dickinson College, https://hd.housedivided.dickinson.edu/node/27478.

86. Lincoln to Henry Asbury, November 19, 1858, and to Anson Miller, November 19, 1858, *CW*, 3:339, 340.

87. William H. Herndon to Theodore Parker, November 8, 1858, quoted in David Herbert Donald, *Lincoln* (New York: Simon & Schuster, 1995), 228.

88. "Young Men's Republican Association," notice of a public meeting, *Illinois State Journal*, May 14, 1859.

89. Citing the "danger" of "unassimilating" immigrants, Governor Gardner had initially proposed a twenty-one-year wait for citizenship. See *Address of His Excellency Henry J, Gardner to the Two Branches of the Legislature of Massachusetts, January 9, 1855* (Boston: William White, 1855), 4, 6, 16–17.

90. *New York Tribune*, April 25, 1859.

91. Carl Schurz, "True Americanism," address at Faneuil Hall, Boston, April 18, 1859, in Frederic Bancroft, ed., *Speeches, Correspondence and Political Papers of Carl Schurz*, 6 vols. (New York: G. P. Putnam's Sons, 1913), 1:71.

92. Gustave Koerner to Lincoln, April 4, 1859, ALPLC.

93. "Massachusetts Citizenship—Speech of Wm. H. Herndon," *Illinois State Journal*, May 17, 1859.

94. See F. I. Herriott, *The Premise and Significance of Abraham Lincoln's Letter to Theodore Canisius* (reprinted from *Deutsch-Amerikanische Geschichtsblätter Jahrbuch der Deutsch-Amerikanischen Historischen Gesellschaft von Illinois—Jahrgang 1915 [vol. 15]*: 37–45).

95. Lincoln to Theodore Canisius, May 17, 1859, *CW*, 3:380.

96. *Dubuque Daily Express and Herald*, May 25, 1859, quoted in Herriott, *Lincoln's Letter to Theodore Canisius*, 2.

97. *Illinois State Journal*, May 18, 1859. Canisius ordered a second round of reprints after noting that initial translations were inaccurate. See report in *Illinois State Journal*, June 20, 1859. The *Chicago Tribune* published Lincoln's letter on May 21, 1859.

98. See Henry J. Carman and Reinhard H. Luthin, "Some Aspects of the Know-Nothing Movement Reconsidered," *South Atlantic Quarterly* 29 (1940): 232.

99. Lincoln to Schuyler Colfax, July 6, 1859, *CW*, 2:390–391.

100. The previous month, Lincoln had sent a public letter to organizers of a Republican rally in Boston marking Thomas Jefferson's birthday ("Those who deny freedom to others, deserve it not for themselves"). It was printed in many Republican papers. See Lincoln to Henry L. Pierce and Others, April 6, 1859, *CW*, 3:374–376. Coincidentally—or perhaps not—Pierce's brother, Edward, had denounced the Massachusetts amendment back in 1857, presciently warning: "*Pass those amendments, and at once every Douglas demagogue and newspaper will repeat week after week and day after day, 'Germans who voted for Fremont, look here, see what the Legislature of a State, which is almost unanimously Republican . . . has just done! It has declared that you are not fit to vote or hold office.'"* See *Letter of Edward L. Pierce, Esq., of Chicago, Containing Important Statistics in Regard to the Foreign Vote at the Presidential Election* (Boston: Commercial Printing House, 1857), 4.

101. Theodore Canisius to Lyman Trumbull, January 15, 1858, Lyman Trumbull Papers, Library of Congress.

102. Dr. Amos Willard French quoted in *Chicago Times Herald*, August 25, 1895; Barron, *Abraham Lincoln and the German Immigrants*, 146–147. See also Wayne C. Temple, "A. W. French: Lincoln Family Dentist," *Lincoln Herald* 63 (1961): 151–154.

103. Norman Judd to Lincoln, May 13, 1859, ALPLC. The date of this letter—likely a reply from a lost Lincoln letter to Judd—suggests that negotiations to save Canisius's paper coincided with those to lure Lincoln to the anti-Massachusetts meeting.

104. Carl Sandburg, *Abraham Lincoln: The Prairie Years*, 2 vols. (New York: Harcourt, Brace & Co., 1926), 2:35–36. The story of Lincoln's alleged appropriation of his law firm's fee was never told by Herndon in any of his own writings.

105. For the disappearance of all known copies of the *Staats-Anzeiger*, see James Cornelius, *From out of the Top Hat: A Blog from the Abraham Lincoln Presidential Library and Museum*, August 30, 2011, which noted: "Lincoln's ownership of the paper—profits going to Canisius, for his efforts—was secret. Unfortunately, its contents have remained secret, too, since *not a single copy* of it exists today to the knowledge of anyone in the Lincoln field." See http://www.alplm.org/blog/tag/theodore-canisius/, consulted August 14, 2022.

106. Raymond Lohne, "Team of Friends: A New Lincoln Theory and Legacy," *Journal of the Illinois State Historical Society* 101 (Fall–Winter 2008): 298–300.

107. Contract with Canisius, May [?] 1859, *CW*, 3:383.

108. In fact, the Republican National Convention had yet to meet; it would gather in June and nominate John C. Frémont as its candidate for president.

109. Contract with Canisius, *CW*, 3:383.

110. "German Campaign Paper for Central Illinois [. . .]," *Illinois State Journal*, June 21, 1860.

111. Lincoln to Frederick W. Koehle July 11, 1859, *CW*, 3:391. Koehle was assistant circuit clerk in the first town named in Lincoln's honor: Lincoln, Illinois.

112. *Davenport Daily Gazette*, August 6, 1859, quoted in Edward Achorn, *The Lincoln Miracle: Inside the Republican Convention That Changed History* (New York: Atlantic Monthly Press, 2023), 195.

113. "Adopted Citizens and Slavery," *Douglass' Monthly*, August 1859.

114. Lecture on Discoveries and Inventions, Jacksonville, Illinois, February 11, 1859, *CW*, 3:358, 363.

115. Lincoln had delivered speeches at Council Bluffs, Columbus, Cincinnati, Dayton, Indianapolis, Milwaukee, Beloit, and Janesville.

116. Mark A. Delahay to Lincoln, June 15, 1859, ALPLC.

117. Lincoln to Lyman Trumbull, April 29, 1860, *CW*, 4:45.

118. Speech at Clinton, Illinois, October 14, 1859, *CW*, 3:487–488.

119. James A. Briggs to Lincoln, October 12, 1859, ALPLC.

Chapter Five ★ A Vital Part of Freedom

1. Edward Dicey, *Spectator of America*, ed. Herbert Mitgang (Chicago: Quadrangle Books, 1971), 10.

2. "James A. M'Master Dead," *New York Times*, December 30, 1886.

3. *New York Herald*, May 14, 1840.

4. See, for example, Edwin William Clay, *Race Between Bennett and Greeley for the Post Office Stakes*, a lithographed cartoon published in New York ca. 1843, reproduced in Bernard F. Reilly Jr., *American Political Prints 1766–1876: A Catalog of the Collections in the Library of Congress* (Boston: G. K. Hall, 1991), 196. For "His Satanic Majesty," see, for example, Joseph Medill to Lincoln, June 19, 1860, Abraham Lincoln Papers, Library of Congress (hereinafter cited as ALPLC).

5. Printmakers like Currier & Ives were nonpartisan—that is, they produced images not because they supported or opposed candidates or political organizations, but for commercial reasons, in response to public demand. In 1860, they would produce flattering lithographic portraits of both Lincoln and Stephen Douglas, as well as cartoons critical of each.

6. H. Wilson, *Trow's New York City Directory for the Year Ending May 1, 1860* (New York: John F. Trow, 1860), 99. The *New York Times* announced Brady's move to Bleecker Street on August 23, 1859. See also George Gilbert, "The Brady Photograph Which Introduced Lincoln to the American Public," *Photographica* 20 (October 1991): 4.

7. Brady's true origin story was most recently confirmed by Jeff L. Rosenheim, in *Photography and the American Civil War* (New York: Metropolitan Museum of Art, 2013), 18. I am grateful to Rosenheim, chairman of photography, for sharing a copy of the 1860 census page on which Brady indicated he had been born in Ireland.

8. Charles Hamilton and Lloyd Ostendorf, *Lincoln in Photographs: An Album of Every Known Pose* (1963; Dayton, OH: Morningside Books, 1985), 10–11; Henry C. Whitney, *Life on the Circuit with Lincoln* (Boston: Estes & Lauriat, 1892), 50.

9. See John Stauffer, Zoe Trodd, and Celeste-Marie Bernier, *Picturing Frederick Douglass: An Illustrated Biography of the Nineteenth Century's Most Photographed American* (New York: Liveright, 2015).

10. Brady Scrap Book, quoted in Roy Meredith, *Mr. Lincoln's Camera Man* (New York: Charles Scribner's Sons, 1946), 59.

11. Lincoln to Harvey G. Eastman, April 7, 1860, in Roy P. Basler, ed., *The Collected Works of Abraham Lincoln*, 8 vols. (New Brunswick, NJ: Rutgers University Press, 1953–1955), 4:39–40 (hereinafter cited as *CW*).

12. "Still Taking Pictures: Brady, the Grand Old Man of American Photography, Hard at Work at Sixty-Seven," *New York World*, April 12, 1891, in Mary Panzer, *Mathew Brady and the Image of History* (Washington, DC: Smithsonian Institution Press, 1997), 224.

13. For examples, see Jay Monaghan, ed., *Lincoln Bibliography 1839–1939*, 2 vols. (Springfield: Illinois State Historical Library, 1943), 1:14–15, 18.

14. Quoted in Donald Allendorf, *"Your Friend, as Ever, A. Lincoln": How the Unlikely Friendship of Gustav Koerner and Abraham Lincoln Changed America* (Gretna, LA: Pelican Publishing, 2014), 241.

15. Lincoln to Mary Lincoln, March 4, 1860, Roy P. Basler, ed., *The Collected Works of Abraham Lincoln: Supplement, 1832–1865* (Westport, CT: Greenwood Press, 1974), 49. One can dismiss as a tired husband's sympathy-inducing lament to his wife Lincoln's assertion that, had he foreseen the "toil" he faced on his trip, "I would not have come East at all."

16. *New York Times*, February 22, 1860.

17. Charles Dickens, *American Notes for General Circulation* (New York: Harper & Bros., 1842), 35.

18. J. H. Bartlett, *The Life and Public Services of Hon. Abraham Lincoln [. . .]* (Cincinnati: Moore, Wilstach & Keys, 1860), 189.

19. Samuel B. Halliday, *The Lost and Found; or Life Among the Poor* (New York: Phinney, Blakeman & Mason, 1860), 187.

20. Francis Fisher Browne, *The Every-day Life of Abraham Lincoln* (New York: N. D. Thompson, 1886), 323. For Mary's December 31, 1860, letter to Samuel Bryam Halliday, a future pastor of the Plymouth Church, see Justin G. Turner and Linda Levitt Turner, *Mary Todd Lincoln: Her Life and Letters* (New York: Alfred A. Knopf, 1972), 67–68.

21. Earl Schenck Miers, ed., *Lincoln Day by Day: A Chronology, 1809–1865*, 3 vols. (Washington, DC: Lincoln Sesquicentennial Commission, 1960), 2:276.

22. William Gross journal, March 17, 1860, Abraham Lincoln Presidential Library and Museum, quoted in Tara McClellan McAndrew, "The History of the Irish in Springfield," NPR Illinois, March 16, 2017, https://www.nprillinois.org/illinois/2017-03-16/the-history-of-the-irish-in -springfield.

23. Carl Schurz, *The Reminiscences of Carl Schurz*, 3 vols. (New York: McClure Co., 1907), 2:176.

24. R. M. Corwine to Lincoln, May 28, 1860, ALPLC.

25. *Memoirs of Henry Villard: Journalist and Financier, 1835–1900*, 2 vols. (Boston: Houghton Mifflin, 1904), 1:137–138.

26. Reprinted under the title "The Turn-Zeitung out for Abraham Lincoln" in the *Illinois State Journal*, April 30, 1860, and as "Mr. Lincoln and the Germans" in the *Chicago Tribune*, May 2, 1860.

27. *Memoirs of Gustave Koerner, 1809–1896: Life-Sketches Written at the Suggestion of His Children*, ed. Thomas J. McCormack, 2 vols. (Cedar Rapids, IA: Torch Press, 1909), 2:85.

28. Reinhard H. Luthin, *The First Lincoln Campaign* (Gloucester, MA: Peter Smith, 1964), 59–60; *Indianapolis Daily Journal*, February 21, 1860, quoted in Edward Achorn, *The Lincoln Miracle: Inside the Republican Convention That Changed History* (New York: Atlantic Monthly Press, 2023), 199.

29. *Memoirs of Gustave Koerner*, 2:84–85.

30. Edward C. Wallace to Lincoln, October 17, 1859, ALPLC.

31. M. W. Delahay to Lincoln, April 13, 1860, ALPLC; Lincoln to Delahay, May 12, 1860, *CW,* 4:49.

32. Emanuel Hertz, "The Conference of German-Republicans in the Deutsches Haus, Chicago, May 14–15, 1860," reprinted from *Transactions of the Illinois State Historical Society* 35 (1928): 60–61.

33. Hertz "The Conference of German-Republicans in the Deutsches Haus," 63–95.

34. The other German Americans on the Platform Committee were John P. Hatterscheidt of Kansas and John A. Kasson of Iowa. In total, four of the seventeen committee members were German.

35. *Memoirs of Gustave Koerner,* 2:87.

36. Republican Party Platform of 1860, American Presidency Project, https://www.presidency.ucsb.edu/documents/republican-party-platform-1860.

37. Lewis D. Campbell (a former Ohio congressman), quoted in *Cincinnati Daily Commercial,* August 14, 1860, reprinted in Tyler Abinder, *Nativism and Slavery: The Northern Know Nothings and the Politics of the 1850s* (New York: Oxford University Press, 1992), 92.

38. *Republikanische Platform und Candidaten [. . .]* (n.p., ca. 1860), original broadside in author's collection.

39. *Memoirs of Gustave Koerner,* 2:88–89.

40. *Anzeiger des Westens* ("Gazette of the West") quoted in Kay Witkiewicz, "'Damned Dutch': St. Louis Germans in the Civil War Era," *Journal of Undergraduate Research* (University of Florida) 10 (Summer 2010): 9.

41. Schurz, *Reminiscences,* 1:186.

42. *Memoirs of Gustave Koerner,* 2:91; Carl Schurz, *Abraham Lincoln: A Biographical Essay, with an Essay on the Portraits of Lincoln by Truman H. Bartlett* (Boston: Houghton Mifflin, 1907), 87.

43. *Memoirs of Gustave Koerner,* 2:91, 92.

44. *Memoirs of Gustave Koerner,* 2:94.

45. *Memoirs of Gustave Koerner,* 2:93–94.

46. Schurz, *Reminiscences,* 2:187–188; Lincoln's reply to the Committee, May 19, 1860, is in *CW,* 4:51.

47. Carl Schurz to Lincoln, May 22, 1860, ALPLC.

48. Lincoln to Schurz, June 18, 1860, *CW,* 4:78.

49. Hans L. Trefousse, *Carl Schurz: A Biography* (Knoxville: University of Tennessee Press, 1982), 90.

50. Donnal V. Smith, "The Influence of the Foreign-Born of the Northwest in the Election of 1860," *Mississippi Valley Historical Review* 19 (September 1932): 200.

51. Carl Schurz to John P. Sanderson, December 22, 1860, Carl Schurz Papers, Library of Congress; Luthin, *The First Lincoln Campaign,* 198.

52. Schurz, *Reminiscences,* 2:196.

53. Trefousse, *Carl Schurz,* 89.

54. Schurz, *Reminiscences,* 2:197–199.

55. Excerpted from two letters from Carl Schurz to Margarethe Schurz, July 19 and July 20, 1860, in *Intimate Letters of Carl Schurz, 1841–1869,* ed. Joseph Schafer (Madison: State Historical Society of Wisconsin, 1929), 214.

56. Carl Schurz to Lincoln, August 22, 1860, ALPLC; Schurz, *Reminiscences,* 3:106.

57. James Peckham to Schurz, June 25, 1860, H. L. McKee to "Karl" Schurz, August 11, 1860, Carl Schurz Papers, Library of Congress.

58. Carl Schurz to Charles Sumner, June 8, 1860, Carl Schurz Papers, Library of Congress.

59. *Memoirs of Gustave Koerner,* 2:101.

60. *Memoirs of Gustave Koerner,* 2:89.

61. Albert Bernhardt Faust, *The German Element in the United States,* 2 vols. (Boston: Houghton Mifflin 1909), 2:132–133n.3.

62. Abram J. Dittenhoefer, *How We Elected Lincoln: Personal Recollections of Lincoln and Men of His Time* (New York: Harper & Bros., 1916), 36.

63. Quoted in Frank Baron, *Abraham Lincoln and the German Immigrants: Turners and Forty-Eighters* (Topeka: Society for German-American Studies, University of Kansas, 2012), 142.

64. *Charleston Mercury*, triweekly edition, March 17, 1860.

65. Lincoln, Imaginary Dialogue Between Douglas and Breckinridge, September 29, 1860, *CW*, 4:124.

66. August Belmont to Stephen A. Douglas, May 18, 1860, in David Black, *The King of Fifth Avenue: The Fortunes of August Belmont* (New York: Dial Press, 1981), 189.

67. August Belmont to Stephen A. Douglas, July 28, 1860, in Luthin, *The First Lincoln Campaign*, 213.

68. For examples, see Stephen A. Douglas to George Washington Sheehan, April 11, 15, 1859, in *The Letters of Stephen A. Douglas*, ed. Robert W. Johannsen (Urbana: University of Illinois Press, 1961), 443–445.

69. James W. Sheahan, *The Life of Stephen A. Douglas* (New York: Harper & Bros., 1860), 265.

70. Luthin, ed., *The First Lincoln Campaign*, 186.

71. A. Morton Braley to Lincoln, August 2, 1860, ALPLC.

72. Ellen Sherman to William T. Sherman, July 3, 1860, Sherman Family Papers, University of Notre Dame, https://archives.nd.edu/Sherman/png/04-0732.htm.

73. The definitive book on this subject is Thomas A. Horrocks, *Lincoln's Campaign Biographies* (Carbondale: Southern Illinois University Press, 2014).

74. Allen Carden and Thomas L. Ebert, *John George Nicolay: The Man in Lincoln's Shadow* (Knoxville: University of Tennessee Press, 2019), 69–73.

75. Henry Clay Whitney to William H. Herndon, July 18, 1887, in Douglas L. Wilson and Rodney O. Davis, eds., *Herndon's Informants: Letters, Interviews, and Statements About Abraham Lincoln* (Urbana: University of Illinois Press, 1998), 622.

76. The German translations were published by (Howard) Follett, Foster & Company, and (Vose) by Friedrich Gerhard, both in 1860. The author is grateful to Thomas Horrocks, author of *Lincoln's Campaign Biographies*, for sharing this information.

77. *Das Leben von Abraham Lincoln* (New York: New-Yorker Demokrat, 1860), 16. A surviving original of this scarce publication is in the Lincoln Financial Foundation Collection, Fort Wayne, Indiana. For a detailed listing of eleven of the principal German-language Lincoln titles issued in 1860, see Monaghan, *Lincoln Bibliography* 2:405–407, Nos. 3733–3743. R. Gerald McMurtry, director of the Lincoln National Life Foundation, unearthed a total of eighty-two publications about Lincoln in German as of 1962—more than in any other language. No such study has been undertaken since. See McMurtry, "Lincoln Publications in Foreign Languages," *Lincoln Lore* no. 1498 (December 1962): 2.

78. Carl Frederick Wittke, *The German-Language Press in America* (Lexington: University of Kentucky Press, 1957), 146.

79. Harold Holzer, Gabor S. Boritt, and Mark E. Neely Jr., *The Lincoln Image: Abraham Lincoln and the Popular Print* (New York: Charles Scribner's Sons, 1984), 30–34. Lincoln's June 8, 1860, letter (written by Nicolay and signed by the candidate) to Mendel was published in the *Tazewell County Republican* (Pekin, IL), July 13, 1860. For Mendel's prominence in Chicago, see I. D. Guyer, *History of Chicago; Its Commercial and Manufacturing Interests and Industry [. . .]* (Chicago: Church, Goodman & Cushing, 1862), 99–100. For the discovery of the original Lincoln letter to Mendel, see Harold Holzer, "An Apology to Edward Mendel: The Original of Lincoln's Letter Found in Chicago," *Chicago History* 8 (Summer 1979): 78–79.

80. Thomas Hicks essay, in Allen Thorndike Rice, ed., *Reminiscences of Abraham Lincoln by Distinguished Men of His Time* (New York: North American Review, 1886), 594. For Hesler image see Hamilton & Ostendorf, *Lincoln in Photographs*, 46.

81. Donn Piatt, *Memories of the Men Who Saved the Union* (Chicago: Belford, Clarke & Co., 1887), 29–30.

82. Lincoln to Samuel Haycraft, June 4, 1860, *CW,* 4:70.

83. Abraham Jonas to Lincoln, July 20, 1860, ALPLC.

84. Lincoln to Abraham Jonas, July 21, 1860, *CW,* 4:85–86.

85. Lincoln to Abraham Jonas, July 21, 1860, *CW,* 4:86.

86. "How Would You Like It?," *Chicago Tribune,* November 6, 1860.

87. *Chicago Tribune,* November 2, 1860.

88. For charts that demonstrate Lincoln's strength with German voters in the Northwest, see Allison Clark Efford, *German Immigrants, Race, and Citizenship in the Civil War Era* (New York: Cambridge University Press, 2013), 237–239. See also Jay Monaghan, "Did Abraham Lincoln Receive the Illinois German Vote?," *Journal of the Illinois State Historical Society* 41 (June 1942): 133–139. See also Efford, "Abraham Lincoln, German-Born Republicans, and American Citizenship," *Marquette Law Review* 93 (Summer 2010): 1375–1381. The best book on the subject is Frederick C. Luebke, ed., *Ethnic Voters and the Election of Lincoln* (Lincoln: University of Nebraska Press, 1971).

89. Nels Hokanson, *Swedish Immigrants in Lincoln's Time* (New York: Harper & Bros., 1942), 60, 65.

90. "The Swedish Republicans of Chicago," *Chicago Tribune,* November 2, 1860.

91. Bruce Levine, *The Spirit of 1848: German Immigration, Labor Conflict, and the Coming of the Civil War* (Urbana: University of Illinois Press, 1992), 251–252.

92. *New York Herald,* December 9, 1860.

93. Quoted in Trefousse, *Carl Schurz,* 94; see also Smith, "The Influence of the Foreign-Born." In Smith's assessment, "without the vote of the foreign-born, Lincoln could not have carried the Northwest, and without the Northwest . . . he would have been defeated" (p. 204). Historians still debate the impact of the German vote on the 1860 election.

94. Correspondence of Otto Albrecht, November 11, 1860, in Walter D. Kamphoefner and Wolfgang Helbich, eds., *Germans in the Civil War: The Letters They Wrote Home,* trans. Susan Carter Vogel (Chapel Hill: University of North Carolina Press, 2006), 38.

Chapter Six ★ Teutonic Expectants

1. For further analysis of the impact of the 1860 German vote—still a matter of historical debate—see the essays in Frederick C. Luebke, ed., *Ethnic Voters and the Election of Lincoln* (Lincoln: University of Nebraska Press, 1971), esp. Donnal V. Smith, "The Influence of the Foreign-Born of the Northwest in the Election of 1860," pp. 1–15; Charles Wilson Emery, "The Iowa Germans in the Election of 1860," pp. 16–45; and Joseph Schafer, "Who Elected Lincoln?," pp. 46–61.

2. Carl Schurz to Margarethe Schurz, October 2, 1860, September 24, 1860, in *Intimate Letters of Carl Schurz, 1841–1869,* ed. Joseph Schafer (Madison: State Historical Society of Wisconsin, 1929), 224, 226.

3. Carl Schurz, speech in Milwaukee [November 17, 1860], *Milwaukee Daily Sentinel,* November 18, 1860.

4. Former Republican state legislator Caspar Butz of Cook County, an original Forty-Eighter, had urged Lincoln to meet Schurz in Chicago; Lincoln replied that he was leaving for home the next morning: "I therefore regret to say I can not see Mr. Schurz here to-morrow." As it turned out, the President-elect remained in Chicago an additional two days but still did not add a Schurz meeting to his schedule. See Caspar Butz to Lincoln, November 23, 1860, Abraham Lincoln Papers, Library of Congress (hereinafter cited as ALPLC), and Lincoln endorsement on Butz's letter, November 24, 1860, in Roy P. Basler, ed., *The Collected Works of Abraham Lincoln,* 8 vols. (New Brunswick, NJ: Rutgers University Press, 1953–1955), 4:144 (hereinafter cited as *CW*).

5. *New York Herald,* November 24, 1860; *Illinois State Journal,* November 17, 1860.

6. For the Alschuler image, see Charles Hamilton and Lloyd Ostendorf, *Lincoln in Photographs: An Album of Every Known Pose* (1963; Dayton, OH: Morningside Books, 1985), 67. As it depicted Lincoln half bearded and half clean-shaven, the photograph never achieved wide

circulation. It came into the possession of Lincoln's lawyer friend Henry Clay Whitney, who had accompanied the President-elect to Alschuler's studio for the sitting.

7. *Illinois State Journal*, November 10, 1860.

8. Lincoln Testimonial for Theodore Canisius, August 14, 1860, *CW*, 4:44–45.

9. See Theodor Canisius, *Abraham Lincoln. Historisches Characterbild* (Vienna: Christoph Reiser, 1867).

10. Original contract (Canisius copy) at the John Hay Library, Brown University, Providence, Rhode Island.

11. Lincoln testimonial for Theodore Canisius, August 14, 1860, *CW*, 4:44–45.

12. *New York Herald*, December 9, 1860.

13. Quoted in Albert Bernhardt Faust, *The German Element in the United States*, 2 vols. (Boston: Houghton Mifflin, 1909), 2:132n. Hassaurek later wrote a memoir of his years in South America but never mentioned how he had obtained the diplomatic appointment there. See Friedrich Hassaurek, *Four Years Among the Ecuadorians*, ed. C. Harvey Gardiner (1868; Carbondale: Southern Illinois Press, 1967). Swiss authorities proved hostile to Bernays because he was Jewish.

14. Lincoln to William H. Seward (on Hassaurek), March 14, 1861, *CW*, 4:283; Gustave Koerner to Lincoln, June 13, 1861, ALPLC. Further testifying to the almost obsessive secrecy surrounding Lincoln's investment in the *Staats-Anzeiger*, Koerner never mentioned Canisius's name in his two-volume, 1,500-page memoir, though he surely knew of his newspaper deal with Lincoln.

15. Lincoln to William H. Seward, June 29, 1861, *CW*, 5:418. In truth, the Vienna position paid a higher salary than Lincoln acknowledged or knew: $1,500 per year.

16. For Hoffmann, see J. H. A. Lacher, "Francis A. Hoffmann of Illinois and Hans Buschbauer of Wisconsin," *Wisconsin Magazine of History* 13 (June 1930): 327–355.

17. *New York Herald*, January 1, 1861; *Memoirs of Gustave Koerner, 1809–1895: Life-Sketches Written at the Suggestion of His Children*, ed. Thomas J. McCormack, 2 vols. (Cedar Rapids, IA: Torch Press, 1909), 2:104, 114, 116.

18. Koerner ascribed no date to this meeting, so it is possible he met Lincoln in a private office only because the President-elect had been compelled to abandon his borrowed governor's suite at the state capitol in January once Governor Richard Yates took office and the legislative session began.

19. *New York Herald*, January 1, 1861.

20. *Memoirs of Gustave Koerner*, 2:114–115; Koerner to Lincoln, October 8, 1861, ALPLC.

21. Gustave Koerner to Lincoln, October 8, 1861, ALPLC.

22. *Memoirs of Gustave Koerner*, 2:114–115.

23. *Memoirs of Gustave Koerner*, 2:118.

24. Ward Hill Lamon, *The Life of Abraham Lincoln, from His Birth to His Inauguration as President* (Boston: James R. Osgood, 1872), 482.

25. C. Goepp to Lincoln, November 10, 1860, ALPLC.

26. Daniel Ullmann to Lincoln, January 25, 1861, ALPLC; Lincoln to Ullmann, February 1, 1861, *CW*, 4:183–184.

27. *New York Herald*, November 20, 1860, in Henry Villard, *Lincoln on the Eve of '61: A Journalist's Story by Henry Villard*, ed. Harold G. Villard and Oswald Garrison Villard (New York: Alfred A. Knopf, 1954), 17. Villard's comments echoed an editorial Theodor Hielscher had published months earlier. See "Candidates for the Presidency," *Indianapolis Daily Journal*, February 21, 1860, quoted in Frank Baron, *Abraham Lincoln and the German Immigrants: Turners and Forty-Eighters* (Topeka: Society for German-American Studies, University of Kansas, 2012), 111. By mid-December, Villard conceded, "there are dormant qualities in 'Old Abe' which occasion will draw forth, develop and remind people to a certain degree of 'Old Hickory,'" *Lincoln on the Eve of '61*, 36.

28. Villard's dispatches also appeared regularly in the *Cincinnati Commercial* and *San Francisco Bulletin*.

29. John Hay diary entry, November 8, 1864, in John Hay, *Inside Lincoln's White House: The Complete Civil War Diary of John Hay*, ed. Michael Burlingame and John R. Turner Ettlinger (Carbondale: Southern Illinois University Press, 1999), 245.

30. *New York Herald*, November 24, 1860.

31. *New York Herald*, November 20, 1860.

32. Dispatch for the *San Francisco Bulletin*, December 22, 1864 (Report of November 24), in Henry Villard, *Sixteenth President-in-Waiting: Abraham Lincoln and the Springfield Dispatches of Henry Villard, 1860–1861*, ed. Michael Burlingame (Carbondale: Southern Illinois University Press, 2018), 48; *New York Herald*, December 17, 1860, in Villard, *Sixteenth President-in-Waiting*, 107.

33. *Cincinnati Commercial*, November 21, 1860, in Villard, *Sixteenth President-in-Waiting*, 33.

34. *Memoirs of Henry Villard: Journalist and Financier, 1835–1900*, 2 vols. (Boston: Houghton Mifflin, 1904), 1:143.

35. *Memoirs of Henry Villard*, 1:147.

36. *Memoirs of Henry Villard*, 1:143–144.

37. Villard, *Lincoln on the Eve of '61*, 23.

38. Remarks on Making Concessions to Secessionists, ca. January 19–21, 1861, *CW*, 4:175–176.

39. Carl Schurz to Margarethe Schurz, January 29, 1861, *Intimate Letters of Carl Schurz*, 240. Lincoln's statement was also published in the *Chicago Tribune* and *New York Tribune*.

40. For Schurz's visit, see Michael Burlingame, ed., *Lincoln's Journalist: John Hay's Anonymous Writings for the Press, 1860–1864* (Carbondale: Southern Illinois University Press, 1998), 24. See also Jason H. Silverman, *Lincoln and the Immigrant* (Carbondale: Southern Illinois University Press, 2015), 87.

41. Although he had shown no previous sympathy for Mexicans, Lincoln did meet in Springfield with Matías Romero, an emissary sent by Mexican revolutionary Benito Juárez, and forged a cordial relationship that would continue in Washington. See William Moss Wilson, "Lincoln's Mexican Visitor," *New York Times Opinionator*, January 17, 2011, https://archive.nytimes.com /opinionator.blogs.nytimes.com/2011/01/17/lincolns-mexican-visitor/.

42. Geza Mihalotzy to Lincoln, February 4, 1861, original in the Chicago Historical Society; reprinted, along with Lincoln's endorsement, in Harold Holzer, ed., *Dear Mr. Lincoln: Letters to the President* (New York: Addison-Wesley, 1993), 199–200.

43. Henry Adams, *The Great Secession Winter of 1860–61 and Other Essays*, ed. George Hochfield (New York: Sagamore Press, 1958), 1. Adams wrote the original essay for *Atlantic Magazine*.

44. Harry J. Carman and Reinhard H. Luthin, *Lincoln and the Patronage* (New York: Columbia University Press, 1943), 62; Villard, *Lincoln on the Eve of '61*, 70 (here representing the views of Villard's sons, not the journalist himself).

45. William H. Herndon to Jesse W. Weik, February 5, 1891, in William H. Herndon, *Herndon on Lincoln: Letters*, ed. Douglas L. Wilson and Rodney O. Davis (Urbana: University of Illinois Press, 2016), 335.

46. *Memoirs of Henry Villard*, 1:147–148. For a good account of this story, along with a full list of sources, see John Hay, *At Lincoln's Side: John Hay's Civil War Correspondence and Selected Writings*, ed. Michael Burlingame (Carbondale: Southern Illinois University Press, 2000), 189, 272n18.

47. Jonathan D. Sarna and Benjamin Shapell, *Lincoln and the Jews: A History* (New York: St. Martin's Press, 2015), 72–73.

48. Farewell Address, February 11, 1861, *CW*, 4:190. Lincoln did not make this specific point in his original, extemporaneous speech, according to the transcription of his remarks by a local journalist.

49. John Hay to Abraham S. Cohen, November 18, 1860, in Gary P. Zola, *They Called Him Rabbi Abraham: Lincoln and American Jewry* (Carbondale: Southern Illinois University Press, 2014), 36.

50. Allen Carden and Thomas J. Ebert, *John George Nicolay: The Man in Lincoln's Shadow* (Knoxville: University of Tennessee Press, 2019), 59.

51. *Cleveland Plain Dealer*, February 13, 1861.

52. Ward Hill Lamon, *Recollections of Abraham Lincoln, 1847–1865*, ed. Dorothy Lamon Teillard (Washington, DC: Dorothy Lamon Teillard, 1911), 33–34.

53. Remarks to Germans in Cincinnati, Ohio, February 12, 1861, *CW*, 4:201.

54. *New York Times*, February 18, 1861.

55. "The German Visitors," *Cincinnati Commercial*, February 13, 1861; "Great Reception of Mr. Lincoln at Cincinnati," *Cleveland Leader*, February 14, 1862.

56. *Cincinnati Commercial*, February 13, 1861.

57. *Cincinnati Commercial*, February 13, 1861.

58. *Cincinnati Commercial*, February 13, 1861. See also *Cincinnati Deutsche Republikaner* [ca. February 13, 1861], undated clipping in the Lincoln Collection of Allen County Library, Fort Wayne, Indiana. See also R. Gerald McMurtry, "Lincoln Visited by a Delegation of Workingmen in Cincinnati, Ohio, February 12, 1861," *Lincoln Lore* no. 1575 (May 1969): 1–3.

59. "Cincinnati and the President Elect," *Sandusky Daily Commercial Register*, February 14, 1861.

60. Speech in Cincinnati, February 12, 1861, *CW*, 4:201–203.

61. "Hair Lippers Rebuked," *Cleveland Plain Dealer*, February 20, 1861.

62. Zola, *They Called Him Rabbi Abraham*, 200–201.

63. "No Life Without Humbug," *The Israelite* (Cincinnati), February 15, 1861.

64. See Arnold Schrier, "A Russian Observer's Visit to 'Porkopolis,' 1857," *Cincinnati Historical Society Bulletin* 29 (Spring 1971); 43, cited in Ted Widmer, *Lincoln on the Verge: Thirteen Days to Washington*, Chapter 5, "Porkopolis" (New York: Simon & Schuster, 2020), 143–169, 514n.

65. Burlingame, *Lincoln's Journalist*, 64.

66. "Arrival and Reception in New-York," *New York Times*, February 21, 1861; Walt Whitman, *Specimen Days in America* (1882), in *Walt Whitman's Memoranda During the War, Written on the Spot in 1863–'65*, ed. Peter Coviello (New York: Oxford University Press, 2004), 39–40; reply to New York City mayor Fernando Wood, city hall, February 20, 1861, *CW*, 4:232.

67. *New York Times*, February 25, 1861.

68. Allan Pinkerton, *The Spy of the Rebellion* (Philadelphia: H. W. Kelley, 1883), 54–55.

69. Michael J. Kline, *The Baltimore Plot: The First Conspiracy to Assassinate Abraham Lincoln* (Yardley, PA: Westholme Publishing, 2008), 60.

70. Allan Pinkerton to William H. Herndon, August 23, 1866, in Douglas L. Wilson and Rodney O. Davis, eds., *Herndon's Informants: Letters, Interviews, and Statements About Abraham Lincoln* (Urbana: University of Illinois Press, 1998), 321.

71. A. K. McClure, *Abraham Lincoln and Men of War-Times: Some Personal Recollections of War and Politics During the Lincoln Administration*, 2nd ed. (Philadelphia: Times Publishing, 1892), 45.

72. George W. Hazzard to Lincoln, ca. January 1861, ALPLC.

73. Lamon, *The Life of Abraham Lincoln*, 523; Lincoln quoted in Benson J. Lossing, *Pictorial History of the Civil War in the United States of America*, 2 vols. (Philadelphia: George W. Childs, 1866–1868), 1:280.

74. *The Flight of Abraham (as Reported by a Modern Daily Paper)*, *Harper's Weekly*, March 9, 1861. See also *The MacLincoln Harrisburg Highland Fling*, *Vanity Fair*, March 9, 1861.

75. George McCullough Anderson, *The Work of Adalbert Johann Volck, 1828–1912 [. . .]* (Baltimore: George McCullough Anderson, 1970), 84–85.

76. For more on Volck's life, art, and influence, see Mark E. Neely Jr., Harold Holzer, and Gabor S. Boritt, "'Confederate' War Sketches," chapter 4 in *The Confederate Image: Prints of the Lost Cause* (Chapel Hill: University of North Carolina Press, 1987), 44–54.

77. McClure, *Lincoln and Men of War-Times*, 48.

78. *Washington Evening Star*, February 27, 1861.

79. *Memoirs of Henry Villard*, 1:156.

80. *New York Herald*, December 9, 1861.

81. *New York Herald*, December 9, 1861.

82. Carl Frederick Wittke, *The German-Language Press in America* (Lexington: University of Kentucky Press, 1957), 147.

83. Adam Gurowski, *Diary, from March 4, 1861, to November 12, 1862* (Boston: Lee & Shepard, 1862), 13, 16–17.

84. Carman and Luthin, *Lincoln and the Patronage*, 102–103. The authors ranked most German appointees as "highly qualified" for their diplomatic posts because of their "knowledge of the Teutonic tongue and university training" (106). See also Reinhard H. Luthin, "Lincoln Appeals to German Voters," *German-American Review* 25 (June–July 1959): 4–6.

85. Carman and Luthin, *Lincoln and the Patronage*, 101; *New York Tribune*, March 29, 1861.

86. Sarna and Shapell, *Lincoln and the Jews*, 170–174.

87. William O. Stoddard, *Inside the White House in War Times* (New York: Charles L. Webster, 1890), 166 (hereinafter cited as Stoddard, *Inside the White House* [1890]). See also James B. Conroy, *Lincoln's White House: The People's House in Wartime* (New York: Rowman & Littlefield, 2017), 25–26.

88. Stoddard, *Inside the White House* [1890], 10. Stoddard repeated a slightly altered version of the story in the memoir he later prepared for his children. See Harold Holzer, ed., *Lincoln's White House Secretary: The Adventurous Life of William O. Stoddard* (Carbondale: Southern Illinois University Press, 2007), 220.

89. Helen Nicolay, *Lincoln's Secretary: A Biography of John G. Nicolay* (New York: Longmans, Green, 1949), 121; William O. Stoddard, *Abraham Lincoln: The True Story of a Great Life*, rev. ed. (New York: Fords, Howard & Hulbert, 1884), 343–344.

90. Stoddard, *Inside the White House* [1890], 10.

91. William O. Stoddard, White House Sketch No. 2, *New York Citizen*, August 25, 1866, in Stoddard, *Inside the White House in War Times: Memoirs and Reports of Lincoln's Secretary*, ed. Michael Burlingame (Lincoln: University of Nebraska Press, 2000), 152.

92. Stoddard, *Inside the White House* [1890], 46–47.

93. Stoddard, *Inside the White House* [1890], 10; William O. Stoddard Jr., ed., *Lincoln's Third Secretary: The Memoirs of William O. Stoddard* (New York Exposition Press, 1955), 74.

94. Stoddard, *Inside the White House* [1890], 47; Noah Brooks, "Personal Recollections of Abraham Lincoln," *Harper's New Monthly Magazine* 31 (July 1865): 229; Stoddard, *Memoirs*, 74.

95. Noah Brooks, *Lincoln Observed: Civil War Dispatches of Noah Brooks*, ed. Michael Burlingame (Baltimore: Johns Hopkins University Press, 1998), 49.

96. Brooks, *Lincoln Observed*, 49; Brooks, "Personal Recollections of Abraham Lincoln," 229.

97. Dispatch of March 12, 1865, in Brooks, *Lincoln Observed*, 172–173.

98. Mary Lincoln to Abram Wakeman, January 30, February 18, 1865, in Justin G. Turner and Linda Levitt Turner, eds., *Mary Todd Lincoln: Her Life and Letters* (New York: Alfred A. Knopf, 1972), 200–201.

99. Lincoln to "Whom it may concern," March 4, 1862, *CW*, 5:143. *Collected Works* editor Roy P. Basler, like many Lincoln scholars before and after, confused Burke with McManus—reflecting the historical challenge of understanding a domestic staff dominated by men named "Edward." For John Hay comments, see Hay to Charles G. Halpine, November 22, 1863, in Hay, *At Lincoln's Side*, 68.

100. Allen C. Clark, "Abraham Lincoln in the National Capital," *Records of the Columbia Historical Society* 27 (1925): 37–38; *Washington Post*, August 3, 1924. For Lincoln, astronomy, and the new telescope, see David J. Kent, *Lincoln: The Fire of Genius: How Abraham Lincoln's Commitment to Science and Technology Helped Modernize America* (Essex, CT: Lyons Press, 2022), 224.

101. Thomas F. Pendel, *Thirty-Six Years in the White House: Lincoln to Roosevelt* (Washington, DC: Neale Publishing, 1902), 32–33.

102. Noah Brooks, *Mr. Lincoln's Washington: Selections from the Writings of Noah Brooks, Civil War Correspondent*, ed. P. J. Staudenraus (South Brunswick, NJ: Thomas Yoseloff, 1967), 178.

103. John E. Washington, *They Knew Lincoln* (New York: E. P. Dutton, 1942), 128.

104. Washington, *They Knew Lincoln*, 129; Lincoln to "Whom it may concern," March 7, 1861, *CW*, 4:277; Lincoln to Gideon Welles, March 16, 1861, 4:288; Lincoln to Edwin M. Stanton, November 29, 1861, 5:33. See also Jonathan W. White, *A House Built by Slaves: African American Visitors to the Lincoln White House* (New York: Rowman & Littlefield, 2022), 172–174.

105. Stoddard, White House Sketch No. 2 in *Inside the White House in War Times*, 151; Hay to Halpine, Hay, *At Lincoln's Side*, 68.

106. Gustav Gumpert, "Tad Lincoln and Gus Gumpert," *Journal of the Illinois State Historical Society* 48 (Spring 1955): 43–44; Mary Lincoln to George Harrington[?], December 20, 1864, in Turner and Turner, *Mary Todd Lincoln*, 195–196. For "fiery furnace," see Mary Lincoln to Hannah Shearer, November 20, 1864, in Turner and Turner, *Mary Todd Lincoln*, 189.

107. *New York Herald*, March 13, 1861.

108. Carl Schurz, *Reminiscences*, 3 vols. (New York: McClure Co., 1907), 2:219–220.

109. *New York Herald*, March 13, 1861.

110. Schurz, *Reminiscences*, 2:220.

111. Hans L. Trefousse, *Carl Schurz: A Biography* (Knoxville: University of Tennessee Press, 1982), 89.

112. Barbara Donner, "Carl Schurz as Office Seeker," *Wisconsin Magazine of History* 20 (December 1936): 130–131.

113. William H. Seward to Thurlow Weed, March 15, 1860, in *Memoir of Thurlow Weed*, ed. Thurlow Weed Barnes (Boston: Houghton, Mifflin & Co., 1884), 261.

114. Schurz, *Reminiscences*, 2:222.

115. *New York Tribune*, March 11, 1861.

116. Schurz, *Reminiscences*, 2:221–222. See also Donner, "Carl Schurz as Office Seeker," 127–142.

117. "Charleston Under Arms," *Atlantic Monthly* 7 (April 1861): 496. For more on that city's mood after secession, see Michael E. Woods, "Charleston, City of Mourners: Anticipations of Civil War in the Cradle of Secession," *Civil War History* 67 (March 2021): esp. 7–8.

118. *New York Herald*, March 19, 1861.

119. Montgomery Blair to Cassius M. Clay, March 26, March 27, 1861, in Clay, *The Life of Cassius Marcellus Clay. Memoirs, Writings, and Speeches [. . .]*, 2 vols. (Cincinnati: J. Fletcher Brennan & Co., 1886), 1:278.

120. Schurz, *Reminiscences*, 2:221; Carl Schurz to Margarethe Schurz, March 28, 1861, in *Intimate Letters of Carl Schurz*, 252–253.

121. Proclamation calling the militia and convening Congress, April 15, 1861, *CW*, 4:331–332.

Chapter Seven ★ I Fights Mit Sigel

1. *Milwaukee Daily News*, reprinted in the *Milwaukee Sentinel*, April 1, 1861, quoted in Barbara Donner, "Carl Schurz as Office Seeker," *Wisconsin Magazine of History* 20 (December 1936): 139. Some national publications joined in criticizing Schurz. The humor magazine *Vanity Fair* lectured him about his ambitions: "To be sure, 'twould be a great crow for you . . . to sail back in glory whence you run like a good fellow—but 'twould be death for us." See "Can't Have a Foreign Mission," *Vanity Fair*, March 28, 1861.

2. Carl Schurz, *The Reminiscences of Carl Schurz*, 3 vols. (New York: McClure Co., 1907), 2:224.

3. Schurz, *Reminiscences*, 2:223–224.

4. Ignatz Koch quoted in "The Union Forever! Immense Demonstration in This City. The Entire Population in the Streets," *New York Times*, April 21, 1861.

5. Schurz, *Reminiscences*, 2:239.

6. Schurz, *Reminiscences*, 2:239–240.

7. Schurz, *Reminiscences*, 2:228–229.

8. Schurz, *Reminiscences*, 2:229.

9. John Hay diary entry for April 26, 1861, in John Hay, *Inside Lincoln's White House: The Complete Civil War Diary of John Hay*, ed. Michael Burlingame and John R. Turner Ettlinger (Carbondale: Southern Illinois University Press, 1999), 12.

10. Diary entry for May 11, 1861, Hay, *Inside Lincoln's White House*, 13, 23. See also Hans L. Trefousse, *Carl Schurz: A Biography* (Knoxville: University of Tennessee Press, 1982), 105. According to Trefousse, Schurz lulled Lincoln to sleep with his impromptu piano concert.

11. Schurz, *Reminiscences*, 2:230.

12. For Schurz's recruitment efforts and Cameron's authorization, see William H. Beach, *The First (Lincoln) Cavalry from April 19, 1861, to July 7, 1865* (New York: Lincoln Cavalry Association, 1902), 12–14; Schurz to Lincoln, May 19, 1861, Abraham Lincoln Papers, Library of Congress (hereinafter cited as ALPLC).

13. Carl Schurz to Lincoln, May 19, 1861, ALPLC.

14. Schurz, *Reminiscences*, 2:239–240.

15. Lincoln to Simon Cameron, May 13, 1861, in Roy P. Basler, ed., *The Collected Works of Abraham Lincoln*, 8 vols. (New Brunswick, NJ: Rutgers University Press, 1953–1955), 4:367 (hereinafter cited as *CW*).

16. Gustave Koerner to Lincoln, April 5, 1861, ALPLC.

17. Gustave Koerner to Lincoln, April 5, 1861, ALPLC.

18. "How to Win the War," *Douglass' Monthly*, May 1861. In Douglass's words: *"Let the slaves and free colored people be called into service, and formed into a liberating army*, to march into the South and raise the banner of Emancipation among the slaves."

19. Frederick Kitt quoted in "The Union Forever!," *New York Times*, April 21, 1861.

20. The best book on this subject is David Work, *Lincoln's Political Generals* (Urbana: University of Illinois Press, 2009). See esp. chapter 2, "Hunting for Generals," 6–25. A defining new Butler biography is Elizabeth D. Leonard, *Benjamin Franklin Butler: A Noisy, Fearless Life* (Chapel Hill: University of North Carolina Press, 2022).

21. *Memoirs of Gustave Koerner, 1809–1896: Life-Sketches Written at the Request of His Children*, ed. Thomas J. McCormick, 2 vols. (Cedar Rapids, IA: Torch Press, 1909), 2:205–206.

22. Ella Lonn, *Foreigners in the Union Army and Navy* (Baton Rouge: Louisiana State University Press, 1951), 41–48.

23. Lincoln to Simon Cameron, July 22, 1861, *CW*, 4:374.

24. Julian Allen to Lincoln, May 31, 1861, ALPLC.

25. *Revised Regulations for the Army of the United States* (Philadelphia: J. G. L. Brown, 1861), 496 (Article LII, Rule 1642).

26. Lonn, *Foreigners in the Union Army and Navy*, 162–163.

27. Thurlow Weed to William H. Seward, July 5, 1861, quoted in Work, *Lincoln's Political Generals*, 21.

28. See Christopher Phillips, *Missouri's Confederate: Claiborne Fox Jackson and the Creation of Southern Identity in the Border West* (Columbia: University of Missouri Press, 2000).

29. Still one of the best overviews of the political situation in Missouri is William E. Parrish, *Turbulent Partnership: Missouri and the Union, 1861–1865* (Columbia: University of Missouri Press, 1963).

30. Stephen D. Engle, *Yankee Dutchman: The Life of Franz Sigel* (Fayetteville: University of Arkansas Press, 1993), 58–60, 85.

31. Henry Boernstein, *Memoirs of a Nobody: The Missouri Years of an Austrian Radical, 1849–1866*, trans. Steven Rowan (1881; St. Louis: Missouri Historical Society Press, 1997), 340.

32. Engle, *Yankee Dutchman*, 65.

33. Report by Major S. D. Sturgis, August 20, 1861, *OR*, ser. 1, vol. 3, p. 71; Franz Sigel, "The Flanking Column at Wilson's Creek," in Robert Underwood Johnson and Clarence Clough Buell, eds., *Battles and Leaders of the Civil War [. . .]*, 4 vols. (New York: Century Co., 1887–1888), 1:305–306.

34. General John Schofield to General Henry W. Halleck, February 12, 1862 (*OR*, vol. 3, p. 95), quoted in Work, *Lincoln's Political Generals*, 39; *Anzeiger des Westens*, August 28, 1861, quoted in Engle, *Yankee Dutchman*, 85.

35. John S. Carville to Salmon Chase, August 18, 1861, with an endorsement from Chase to Lincoln, ALPLC.

36. Grant P. Robinson, "I Fights Mit Sigel," in Frank Moore, ed., *Songs of the Soldiers* (New York: George P. Putnam, 1864), 156–158; "I'm Going to Fight Mit Sigel," published by H. de Marsan, New York, ca. 1861, Rare Books and Special Collections Division, Library of Congress, https://www.loc.gov/resource/amss.sb20220b/?st=text. Poole also composed the song "No Irish Need Apply." See also John F. Poole Collection, Music Division, Library of Congress. For other Sigel poems and songs, see Engle, *Yankee Dutchman*, 83–84.

37. For a sampling of Franz Sigel images, see Mark E. Neely Jr. and Harold Holzer, *The Union Image: Popular Prints of the Civil War North* (Chapel Hill: University of North Carolina Press, 2000), 32–35, 240n21. For the Volck etching, see George McCullough Anderson, *The Work of Adalbert Johann Volck, 1818–1912 [. . .]* (Baltimore: George McCullough Anderson, 1970), 38–39.

38. *Anzeiger des Westens*, December 8, 1861.

39. P. A. Ladue to Francis P. Blair Jr. (forwarded to Lincoln), January 6, 1861, ALPLC.

40. Franz Sigel to Henry Halleck, January 14, 1862, and Sigel to Gustave P. Koerner, January 25, 1862, both in ALPLC.

41. P. A. Ladue to Francis Preston Blair Jr., January 6, 1861, ALPLC.

42. *Memoirs of Gustave Koerner*, 2:197–198, 201; Lincoln to John C. Frémont, September 2, September 11, 1861, *CW*, 4:506, 517–518, and to Samuel R. Curtis, October 24, 1861, *CW*, 4:562–563. For a good recent analysis of Missouri antislavery sentiment, see Kristen Layne Anderson, *Abolitionizing Missouri: German Immigrants and Racial Ideology in Nineteenth-Century America* (Baton Rouge: Louisiana State University Press, 2016), esp., apropos of the Frémont affair, p. 99.

43. R. A. Witthaus to Lincoln (with resolutions), January 21, 1862, ALPLC.

44. Lincoln seemed unsure how Koerner had achieved his rank, noting, "He was appointed from civil life, but from here, and not by Gen. Fremont, as I remember." According to a recent biography of Koerner, Halleck believed that "Germans constitute a very dangerous element in society as well as the army." See Donald Allendorf, *Your Friend, as Ever, A. Lincoln": How the Unlikely Friendship of Gustav Koerner and Abraham Lincoln Changed America* (Gretna, LA: Pelican Publishing, 2014), 322. Lincoln to George B. McClellan, November 29, 1861, Roy P. Basler, ed., *The Collected Works of Abraham Lincoln: Supplement, 1832–1865* (Westport, CT: Greenwood Press, 1974), 112.

45. *Memoirs of Gustave Koerner*, 2:167. For "one of the greatest perplexities," see Special Message to Congress, July 4, 1861, *CW*, 4:432.

46. *Memoirs of Gustave Koerner*, 2:155–156; Lincoln to Gustave Koerner, *CW*, 4:479.

47. *Memoirs of Gustave Koerner*, 2:169; Gustave Koerner to Lincoln, October 8, 1861, ALPLC.

48. *Memoirs of Gustave Koerner*, 2:191; Lincoln to George B. McClellan, November 29, 1861, in Roy P. Basler, ed., *The Collected Works of Abraham Lincoln: Supplement, 1832–1865* (Westport, CT: Greenwood Press, 1974), 112.

49. Lincoln to Henry W. Halleck, January 15, 1862, *CW*, 5:100.

50. For examples, see John F. Marszalek, *Commander of All Lincoln's Armies: A Life of General Henry W. Halleck* (Cambridge, MA: Harvard University Press, 2004), 122.

51. Henry W. Halleck to Lincoln, January 21, 1862, ALPLC.

52. Gustave Koerner to Lincoln, January 26, 1862, ALPLC.

53. Gustave Koerner to Lincoln, January 26, 1862, ALPLC. Koerner signed this letter "Gustavus Koerner."

54. Gustave Koerner to Lincoln, February 7, 1862, ALPLC.

55. J. Kurkardier to Lincoln, May 17, 1862, ALPLC.

56. Reinhold Solger, Address at the Boston Music Hall, April 28, 1861, reprinted in the *Boston Daily Atlas*, clipping enclosed in J. Kurkardier's May 17, 1862, letter to Lincoln, ALPLC.

57. Account by James B. Fry in Allen Thorndike Rice, ed., *Reminiscences of Abraham Lincoln by Distinguished Men of His Time* (New York: North American Review, 1886), 391–392. Fry spelled the general's name "Schemmilfinnig." Schimmelfennig was named a brigadier general in November 1862.

58. Sabine Freitag, *Friedrich Hecker: Two Lives for Liberty*, trans. Steven Rowan (1955; St. Louis: St. Louis Mercantile Academy, 2006), 226–233.

59. Herman Salomon, "The Civil War Diary of Herman Salomon," *Wisconsin Magazine of History* 10 (December 1926): 205.

60. Jean Powers Soman and Frank L. Byrne, eds., *A Jewish Colonel in the Civil War: Marcus M. Spiegel of the Ohio Volunteers* (1985; Lincoln: University of Nebraska Press, 1994), 10–19, 116.

61. Soman and Byrne, *A Jewish Colonel in the Civil War*, 315–316. See also Jean Powers Soman, "Remembering Colonel Marcus M. Spiegel, a Jewish Civil War Colonel," *American Jewish Archives Journal* 65 (2013): 40.

62. Simon Wolf, *The American Jew as Patriot, Soldier and Citizen* (Philadelphia: Levytype Co., 1895), 109. For statistics on immigrant enlistees, see Adam D. Mendelsohn, *Jewish Soldiers in the Civil War: The Union Army* (New York: New York University Press, 2022), 51.

63. For soldier life under Osterhaus, see Earl J. Hess, ed., *A German in the Yankee Fatherland: The Civil War Letters of Henry A. Kircher* (Kent, OH: Kent State University Press, 1983).

64. David T. Dixon, *Radical Warrior: August Willich's Journey from German Revolutionary to Union General* (Knoxville: University of Tennessee Press, 2020), 132–133.

65. John Strausbaugh, *City of Sedition: The History of New York City During the Civil War* (New York: Twelve, 2016), 175.

66. August Belmont and Louis Blenker quoted in "The German Rifle Regiment. Three Flags in the Park [. . .]," *New York Times*, May 18, 1861.

67. *New York Tribune*, July 6, 1861.

68. *Illinois Staats-Zeitung*, June 13, 1861, quoted in Lonn, *Foreigners in the Union Army and Navy*, 95.

69. Gustave Koerner to Lincoln, January 26, 1861, ALPLC.

70. Boernstein, *Memoirs of a Nobody*, 306.

71. Gustave Koerner to Lincoln, January 26, 1862, ALPLC.

72. Original in the New-York Historical Society, reprinted in Don H. Doyle, *The Cause of All Nations: An International History of the American Civil War* (New York: Basic Books, 2015), 161.

73. Kay Witkiewicz, "'Damned Dutch': St. Louis Germans in the Civil War Era," *Journal of Undergraduate Research* (University of Florida) 109 (Summer 2010): 10–11.

74. Anthony Trollope, *North America*, 2 vols. (Philadelphia: J. B. Lippincott & Co., 1862), 2:129.

75. See (especially regarding Texas Germans) Walter D. Kamphoefner and Wolfgang Helbich, eds., *Germans in the Civil War: The Letters They Wrote Home*, trans. Susan Carter Vogel (Chapel Hill: University of North Carolina Press, 2006), 13–19.

76. Letters to his parents from Alexander Dupré (a German despite his French-sounding name), July 14, August 15, 1861, in Kamphoefner and Helbich, *Germans in the Civil War*, 46–47.

77. Kamphoefner and Helbich, *Germans in the Civil War*, 6–7.

78. Christian B. Keller, "Pennsylvania and Virginia Germans During the Civil War: A Brief History and Comparative Analysis," *Virginia Magazine of History and Biography* 109 (2001): 50.

79. Stephen D. Engle, "German Americans," in David S. Heidler and Jeanne T. Heidler, *Encyclopedia of the American Civil War: A Political, Social and Military History* (New York: W. W. Norton,

2000), 822–824; Megan L. Bever, *At War with King Alcohol: Debating Drinking and Masculinity in the Civil War* (Chapel Hill: University of North Carolina Press, 2022), 47.

80. James McPherson, *Battle Cry of Freedom: The Civil War Era* (New York: Oxford University Press, 1988), 606. According to McPherson, "Immigrants were proportionally under-represented in the Union's armed services." For a contrary argument—that the North's foreign-born amounted to 18 percent of a 21.5 million population, but produced 22 percent of new recruits—see Éva Eszter Szabó, "The Migration Factor in the American Civil War: The Impact of Voluntary Population Movements on the War Effort," *Americana* (e-Journal of American Studies in Hungary) 12 (Spring 2016): 3, www.americanaejournal.hu/vol12no1/szabo.

81. Message to a Special Session of Congress, July 4, 1861, *CW,* 4:438.

82. The only biography is James S. Pula, *For Liberty and Justice: A Biography of Brigadier General Włodzimierz B. Krzyżanowski, 1824–1887* (Utica, NY: Ethnic Heritage Studies Center, 2008). See also Mark Francis Bielski, "Divided Poles in a Divided Nation: Poles in the Union and Confederacy in the American Civil War" (Ph.D. thesis, College of Arts and Law, University of Birmingham, May 2014), 164–177. For his failed promotion, see Schurz, *Reminiscences,* 2:407.

83. Joseph L. Kostecki, "Polish Medics in the Civil War," *Polish American Studies* 27 (Spring–Autumn 1970): 111. For the wartime experience of Southern Poles, see Sigmund H. Uminski, "Two Polish Confederates," *Polish American Studies* 23 (July–December 1966): 65–81.

84. *Cleveland Morning Leader,* July 17, 1862, quoted in Bielski, "Divided Poles in a Divided Nation," 52.

85. The unit was named for noted marksman Hiram Berdan, who later clashed bitterly with Trepp. The two exchanged charges of cowardice, and both faced courts-martial, though they were each acquitted. Trepp was killed by a sniper at the Battle of Mine Run on November 30, 1863. Trepp's papers are at the New-York Historical Society. Biographical information is at https://dlib.nyu.edu/findingaids/html/nyhs/ms670_25_caspar_trepp/bioghist.html.

86. Lonn, *Foreigners in the Union Army and Navy,* 390–391; for more on Swiss units, see pp. 79, 149.

87. Original broadside in the New-York Historical Society; see Doyle, *Cause of All Nations,* 160–161. The Garibaldi Guard originally asked for only 250 volunteers. See also Villard, *Memoirs,* 1:71.

88. Strausbaugh, *City of Sedition,* 173.

89. Mendelsohn, *Jewish Soldiers in the Civil War,* 85–86, 88.

90. H. Nelson Gay, "Lincoln's Offer of a Command to Garibaldi: Light on a Disputed Point of History," *Century Illustrated Monthly Magazine* 75 (November 1907): 66, 69. The year after Gay published his explosive article, Charles Francis Adams Jr., son of the wartime U.S. minister to Great Britain, made it a point to clarify that his father had played no role in this intrigue. For this, and the appraisal of Antwerp consul James W. Quiggle as "cunning," see Adams, "Lincoln's Offer to Garibaldi," *The Magazine of History* 7 (January–June 1907): esp. 160.

91. "Spirit of the Norsemen," *Chicago Tribune,* April 24, 1861.

92. Eric Young, "To the Scandinavians in America," December 2, 1862, from the exhibition *Swedes and the Civil War in America,* Swenson Center, Augustana College, Rock Island, IL, https://digitalcommons.augustana.edu/swensonexhibits_civilwar/.

93. Amanda Foreman, *A World on Fire: Britain's Crucial Role in the American Civil War* (New York: Random House, 2010), 116–119.

94. For the Brady photo, see Ronald S. Coddington, "Full Highlander," *Civil War Monitor,* Fall 2022, 14; James Todd to Governor William Dennison, April 16, 1861, in Lonn, *Foreigners in the Union Army and Navy,* 67. For more on Scottish American enlistments, see Diana L. Dretske, *The Bonds of War: A Story of Immigrants and Esprit de Corps in Company C, 96th Illinois Volunteer Infantry* (Carbondale: Southern Illinois University Press, 2021).

95. Tyler Wentzell, "Mercenaries and Adventurers: Canada and the Foreign Enlistment Act in the Nineteenth Century," *Canadian Military History* 23 (2014): 7–8.

96. Charles P. Cullop, "An Unequal Duel: Union Recruiting in Ireland, 1863–1864," *Civil War History* 13 (June 1967): 164.

97. William F. Fox., *Regimental Losses in the American Civil War, 1861–1865 [. . .]* (Albany, NY: Albany Publishing, 1889), 62.

98. For a roster of prominent Hungarian veterans of the Union cause, see Edmund Vasvary, *Lincoln's Hungarian Heroes: The Participation of Hungarians in the Civil War, 1861–1865* (Washington, DC: Hungarian Reformed Federation of America, 1939).

99. "The President and Mrs. Lincoln," *Washington Star,* June 26, 1861.

100. Julian Kune [Kuné], *Reminiscences of an Octogenarian Hungarian Exile* (Chicago: published by the author, 1911), 94–95, 97–98; a slightly different version, also attributed to Kuné, is in "Notes and Letters," *Hungarian Quarterly* 7 (Spring 1941): 168–169.

101. For more on Kuhne, alias George Kuhna and G. Wolk, see the Shapell Roster of Jewish Service in the American Civil War, www.shapell.org/civil-war-soldier-database/soldier/550. For the condemned men's appeal to Lincoln, General Meade's comments, and Lincoln's decision to deny the men a pardon and commutation, see Kuhne and others to Lincoln, August 26, 1863; Meade to Lincoln, August 27, 1863, ALPLC; and Lincoln to Meade, August 27, 1863, *CW,* 6:414. Kuhne was consoled in his final hours by Hungarian immigrant Rabbi Benjamin Szold of Baltimore.

102. George B. McClellan, *McClellan's Own Story: The Fight for the Union [. . .]* (New York: Charles L. Webster & Co., 1887), 143.

103. *Report of the Joint Special [Congressional] Committee to Investigate Chinese Immigration* (Washington, DC: Government Printing Office, 1877). For a period refutation, see Samuel E. W. Becker, *Humors of a Congressional Investigating Committee. A Review of the Report of the Joint Special Committees to Investigate Chinese Immigration* (Washington, DC: privately printed, 1877). In 2008, the U.S. House of Representatives passed a resolution honoring Edward Day Cahota, Joseph L. Pierce, and other AAPI "veterans of Asian and Pacific Islander descent who fought in the United States Civil War." See https://www.congress.gov/bill/110th-congress/house-resolution/415.

104. William C. Davis, *Lincoln's Men: How President Lincoln Became a Father to an Army and a Nation* (New York: Free Press, 1999), 51; for Mexican troops, see Lincoln to Simon Cameron, September 12, 1861, *CW,* 4:519.

105. Fox, *Regimental Losses,* 60–61.

Chapter Eight ★ God Bless the Irish Flag

1. Abundant numbers of Irishmen fought for the Confederacy, too. See, for example, Phillip Thomas Tucker, *Irish Confederates: The Civil War's Forgotten Soldiers* (Abilene, TX: McWhiney Foundation, 2006); and Ella Lonn, *Foreigners in the Confederacy* (Chapel Hill: University of North Carolina Press, 1940).

2. O'Gorman speech in Frank Moore, ed., *The Rebellion Record [. . .],* 11 vols. (New York: G. P. Putnam, 1861–1868), 1:102; see also "Richard O'Gorman Dead," *New York Times,* March 2, 1895.

3. W. S. Wilkinson, "Abraham Lincoln. A Statesman's Tact. Reminiscences by W. S. Wilkinson," *New York Tribune,* July 12, 1885. Famous for arguing the first-ever successful insanity defense in the murder trial of future Civil War general Daniel Sickles, W. T. Brady later served pro bono as a defense attorney for Jefferson Davis.

4. Quoted in Ryan W. Keating, *Shades of Green: Irish Regiments, American Soldiers, and Local Communities in the Civil War Era* (New York: Fordham University Press, 2017), 25.

5. Thomas F. Meagher, *Memoirs of Gen. Thomas Francis Meagher, Comprising the Leading Events of His Career [. . .],* ed. Michael Cavanagh (Worcester, MA: Messenger Press, 1892), 373. The Sixty-Ninth was formed in 1851 in an effort to coalesce existing units of predominately Irish state militia into a single regiment of the New York State Militia.

6. W. F. Lyons, *Brigadier-General Thomas Francis Meagher: His Political and Military Career; with Selections from His Speeches and Writings* (New York: D. & J. Sadlier & Co., 1870), 76.

7. "Our Irish Soldiers," *Harper's Weekly,* October 20, 1860.

8. "Our Irish Soldiers," *Harper's Weekly.*

9. Lincoln Memorandum on James Shields, ca. July 1861, in Roy P. Basler, ed., *The Collected Works of Abraham Lincoln,* 8 vols. (New Brunswick, NJ: Rutgers University Press, 1953–1955), 4:418

(hereinafter cited as *CW*). The date attributed to this (undated) memo in the *Collected Works* is undoubtedly wrong. Lincoln must have written it no later than May.

10. Quoted in Harold Holzer, *The Civil War in 50 Objects* (New York: Viking, 2013), 95.

11. Quoted in Susannah J. Ural, "'Ye Sons of Green Erin Assemble': Northern Irish American Catholics and the Union War Effort, 1861–1865," in Ural, ed., *Civil War Citizens: Race, Ethnicity, and Identity in America's Bloodiest Conflict* (New York: New York University Press, 2010), 106.

12. "The President and Mrs. Lincoln," *Washington Star*, June 26, 1861; Frederick Phisterer, *New York in the War of the Rebellion, 1861 to 1865*, 2nd ed. (Albany, NY: Weed, Parsons & Co., 1890), 400–401.

13. D. G. Crotty, *Four Years Campaigning in the Army of the Potomac* (Grand Rapids, MI: Dygert Bros. & Co., 1874), 18–19. Crotty's recollection is plausible though flawed. Lincoln reviewed a brigade of New Jersey troops from the White House on July 3, not July 4, 1861, following a cabinet meeting. But Crotty recalled seeing not only Lincoln, Seward, and Scott on the grandstand but also Edwin M. Stanton—who did not become secretary of war until 1862. See Earl Schenck Miers, ed., *Lincoln Day by Day: A Chronology, 1809–1865*, 3 vols. (Washington, DC: Lincoln Sesquicentennial Commission, 1960), 3:51.

14. See, for example, Christian G. Samito, *Becoming American Under Fire: Irish Americans, African Americans, and the Politics of Citizenship During the Civil War Era* (Ithaca, NY: Cornell University Press, 2009), esp. 108–109.

15. For some reason, Shields later claimed he had been in *New* Mexico, not "Old Mexico," when Sumter fell. See the *Irish World*, quoted in William H. Condon, *Life of Major-General James Shields: Hero of Three Wars and Senator from Three States* (Chicago: Blakely Printing Co., 1900), 283.

16. Lincoln Memorandum on Corcoran and Shields, July 1[?], 1861.

17. Lincoln Memorandum on Corcoran and Shields; and Henry A. Castle, "General James Shields: Soldier, Orator, Statesman," *Collections of the Minnesota Historical Society* 15 (May 1915): 722. For Koerner's comments on "My friend Shields," see *Memoirs of Gustave Koerner, 1809–1876: Life-Sketches Written at the Suggestion of His Children*, ed. Thomas J. McCormack, 2 vols. (Cedar Rapids, IA: Torch Press, 1909), 2:221.

18. F. B. Murdock to Lincoln, December 10, 1861, Abraham Lincoln Papers, Library of Congress (hereinafter cited as ALPLC).

19. Ira P. Rankin to Simon Cameron, December 10, 1861, ALPLC.

20. Miers, *Lincoln Day by Day*, 3:88. For the Lincoln–Seward–Shields meeting, see David Work, *Lincoln's Political Generals* (Urbana: University of Illinois Press, 2009), 23.

21. Castle, "General James Shields," 722–723; and Condon, *Life of Shields*, 241.

22. *The Irish Brigade.—To the Public*, pamphlet enclosed in John T. Doyle (Secretary of the Committee) to Postmaster General Montgomery Blair, November 13, 1861, forwarded to Lincoln, in ALPLC.

23. *Memoirs of Gustave Koerner*, 2:221.

24. Condon, *Life of Shields*, 260, 266.

25. Castle, "General James Shields," 724.

26. "Sketch of General Meagher," in William McCarter, *My Life in the Irish Brigade: The Civil War Memoirs of Private William McCarter, 116th Pennsylvania Infantry*, ed. Kevin E. O'Brien (1896; Cambridge, MA: Da Capo Press, 2003), 15.

27. The most engaging modern biography is Timothy Egan, *The Immortal Irishman: The Irish Revolutionary Who Became an American Hero* (Boston: Houghton Mifflin, 2016). For Meagher's background, see pp. 3–127. For his arrival in New York, see pp. 137–139.

28. *Memoirs of Gen. Thomas Francis Meagher*, 369.

29. *Memoirs of Gen. Thomas Francis Meagher*, 372.

30. Martin Crawford, ed., *William Howard Russell's Civil War: Private Diary and Letters, 1861–1862* (Athens: University of Georgia Press, 1993), 98. Russell admitted that he had heard this account from *New York Tribune* correspondent Edward House.

31. George Templeton Strong, *The Diary of George Templeton Strong*, ed. Allan Nevins and Milton Halsey Thomas, 4 vols. (New York: Macmillan, 1952), entry for *"BLACK MONDAY,"* July 22, 1861, 3:169.

32. Joseph G. Bilby, *The Irish Brigade in the Civil War: The 69th New York and Other Irish Regiments of the Army of the Potomac* (1995; Cambridge, MA: Da Capo Press, 1997), 17.

33. Holzer, *Civil War in 50 Objects*, 98.

34. Lincoln to Simon Cameron, August 19, 1861, *CW*, 4:492. Owing to a series of bureaucratic errors, Corcoran's promotion was not forwarded to the Senate until December 23, 1862, and not confirmed until March 11, 1863—but at least was made retroactive to July 22, 1861—the day after the Battle of Bull Run.

35. *New York Herald*, July 24, 1861, quoted in *CW*, 4:458.

36. *Memoirs of Gen. Thomas Francis Meagher*, 381.

37. *Fine Arts*, quoted in Holzer, *Civil War in 50 Objects*, 99.

38. See Currier & Ives, *Col. Michael Corcoran at the Battle of Bull Run, VA. July 21, 1861 [. . .]*, copy in the Old Print Shop, New York.

39. *Frank Leslie's Illustrated Newspaper*, July 5, 1862. See also John Adler, *America's Most Influential Journalist: The Life, Times and Legacy of Thomas Nast* (Sarasota, FL: HarpWeek, 2022), 106.

40. The original oil painting, *Return of the 69th (Irish) Regiment, N.Y.S.M. from the Seat of War*, is in the collection of the New-York Historical Society, donated in 1886 by its artist, Louis Lang (1814–1893).

41. *Memoirs of Gen. Thomas Francis Meagher*, 415.

42. The first regimental history was D. P. Coyningham, *The Irish Brigade and Its Campaigns [. . .]* (New York: William McSorley & Co., 1867).

43. John T. Doyle to Lincoln, November 13, 1861, ALPLC.

44. John R. G. Hassard, *Life of the Most Reverend John Hughes, D. D., First Archbishop of New York [. . .]* (New York: D. Appleton, 1866), 449, 463–468, 470–475. For an overview of both official and unofficial efforts to maintain European neutrality, see Lynn M. Case and Warren F. Spencer, *The United States and France: Civil War Diplomacy* (Philadelphia: University of Pennsylvania Press, 1970). For Hughes's assurances, published in *Le Monde* on December 17, 18, and 21, 1861, see Serge Gavronsky, *The French Liberal Opposition to the American Civil War* (New York: Humanities Press, 1968), 102–103, 106–107.

45. Thomas F. Meagher to Lincoln, July 30, 1862, ALPLC.

46. *Memoirs of Gen. Thomas Francis Meagher*, 431.

47. Quoted in Work, *Lincoln's Political Generals*, 23.

48. Thomas Francis Meagher to Lincoln, December 5, 1861, ALPLC.

49. *Memoirs of Gen. Thomas Francis Meagher*, 434.

50. Testimony of L. D. O'Grady, *New York Herald*, February 2, 1917, quoted in Bilby, *The Irish Brigade*, 49.

51. McCarter, *My Life in the Irish Brigade*, 13.

52. St. Clair A. Mulholland, *The Story of the 116th Regiment Pennsylvania Volunteers in the War of the Rebellion: The Record of a Gallant Command* (Philadelphia: F. McManus, Jr., 1903), 97.

53. "Noble object" quoted in Richard Wheeler, *Witness to Gettysburg: Inside the Battle That Changed the Course of the Civil War* (1994; Mechanicsburg, PA: Stackpole Books, 2006), 201; Meagher's drinking mentioned in William Corby, *Memoirs of Chaplain Life* (Chicago: La Monte, O'Donnell & Co., 1893), 28–29.

54. McCarter, *My Life in the Irish Brigade*, 15.

55. J. J. McDaniel, *Diary of Battles, Marches and Incidents of the Seventh S.C. Regiment* (privately printed, ca. 1862), 18–19. For other reports of drinking among Irishmen in the ranks, see Megan L. Bever, *At War with Alcohol: Debating Drinking and Masculinity in the Civil War* (Chapel Hill: University of North Carolina Press, 2022), 46–47.

56. Lincoln's dinner invitation to Edwin M. Stanton, Henry W. Halleck, and George A. McCall, August 18, 1862, *CW,* 5:380–381.

57. Thomas F. Meagher to Lincoln, June 16, 1863, ALPLC; Lincoln to Meagher, June 16, 1863, *CW,* 6:283.

58. Thomas F. Meagher, speech at the Boston Music Hall, June 23, 1863, in W. F. Lyons, *Brigadier-General Thomas Francis Meagher: His Political and Military Career; with Selections from His Speeches and Writings* (New York: D. & J. Sadlier & Co., 1870), 118.

59. Lyons, *Brigadier-General Thomas Francis Meagher,* 91.

60. *Irish People,* December 16, 1863, quoted in Ryan W. Keating, "Immigration in the Union Army," Essential Civil War Curriculum, https://www.essentialcivilwarcurriculum.com/immigrants-in -the-union-army.html.

61. Carl Schurz, *The Reminiscences of Carl Schurz,* 3 vols. (New York: McClure Co., 1907), 2:247–248, 329.

62. Hans L. Trefousse, *Carl Schurz: A Biography* (Knoxville: University of Tennessee Press, 1982), 114.

63. Lincoln to Horace Greeley (a public letter anticipating the Emancipation Proclamation), August 22, 1862, *CW,* 5:388; Schurz, *Reminiscences,* 2:314.

64. Schurz, *Reminiscences,* 2:330.

65. Carl Schurz, *Abraham Lincoln: An Essay* (Boston: Houghton Mifflin, 1891), 73. Schurz made this comment in describing Seward's 1861 bid to gain more influence in the administration, which Lincoln deftly outmaneuvered.

66. Schurz, *Reminiscences,* 2:338–339.

67. Schurz, *Reminiscences,* 2:339–340.

68. *Memoirs of Gustave Koerner,* 2:224–227.

69. Allan Pinkerton, *The Spy of the Rebellion* (New York: H. W. Kelley, 1886), 153, 155, 467.

70. For the Antietam photograph by Alexander Gardner, see Charles Hamilton and Lloyd Ostendorf, *Lincoln in Photographs: An Album of Every Known Pose* (1963; Dayton: Morningside Books, 1985), 108–109. Lincoln also posed that day with General McClellan and other officers. Lincoln soon dismissed McClellan, who later challenged Lincoln for the presidency. Pinkerton, who had known and admired the deposed commander since their days working for the railroads, always maintained that "no General in the history of the Nation was ever so shamefully treated by his government" (p. 571).

71. Quoted in John Fabian Witt, *Lincoln's Code: The Laws of War in American History* (New York: Free Press, 2012), 180.

72. Francis Lieber, *An Address on Secession. Delivered in South Carolina in the Year 1851* (New York: Loyal Publication Society, 1865).

73. The definitive study is still Frank Friedel, "The Loyal Publication Society: A Pro-Union Propaganda Agency," *Mississippi Valley Historical Review* 26 (December 1939): 359–376.

74. See Francis Lieber, *Instructions for the Government of Armies of the United States in the Field* (General Orders No. 100), Washington: U. S. Government Printing Office, 1898.

75. Lieber to Charles Sumner, December 14, December 19, 1861, in Francis Lieber, *The Life and Letters of Francis Lieber,* ed. Thomas Sergeant Perry (Boston: James R. Osgood, 1882), 321–322; *New York Tribune,* June 27, 1861.

76. Lieber to Henry W. Halleck, May 20, 1863, September 1, 1864, in *The Life and Letters of Francis Lieber,* 334, 350.

77. J. [John] Ericsson to Lincoln, August 29, 1861, in Ruth Morris White, *Yankee from Sweden: The Dream and the Reality in the Days of John Ericsson* (New York: Henry Holt, 1960), 125, 189–191.

78. Frederick Bushnell, "Negotiations for the Building of the 'Monitor,'" in Robert Underwood Johnson and Clarence Clough Buell, eds., *Battles and Leaders of the Civil War [. . .],* 4 vols. (New York: Century Co., 1887–1888), 1:748.

79. Assistant Secretary of the Navy G. [Gustava] V. Fox to General George B. McClellan, March 9, 1862, in Robert Means Thompson and Richard Wainwright, eds., *Confidential Correspondence of Gustavus Vasa Fox*, 2 vols. (New York: De Vinne Press for the Naval Historical Society, 1918), 1:435.

80. Frederick Keller, quoted in Craig L. Symonds, *Lincoln and His Admirals* (New York: Oxford University Press, 2008), 150. This book has the best account of the development and deployment of the *Monitor* and of Lincoln's involvement in encouraging Ericsson and his backers.

81. For Lincoln's visit, see Chester D. Bradley, "President Lincoln's Campaign Against the Mer-rimac," *Journal of the Illinois State Historical Society* 51 (Spring 1957): 78–80; and Nathaniel Hawthorne [A Peaceable Man], "Chiefly About War-Matters," *Atlantic Monthly* 10 (July 1862): 57–58. For Lincoln's patent for a "new and improved manner of combining adjustable buoyant air chambers with a steamboat or other vessel," see Jason Emerson, *Lincoln the Inventor* (Carbondale: Southern Illinois University Press, 2009); and David J. Kent, *Lincoln: The Fire of Genius: How Abraham Lincoln's Commitment to Science and Technology Helped Modernize America* (Essex, CT: Lyons Press, 2022), 69–82.

82. Gideon Welles, *Diary of Gideon Welles*, ed. John T. Morse, 3 vols. (Boston: Houghton Mifflin, 1911), 1:62–63.

83. Miers, *Lincoln Day by Day* (April 2, 1862), 3:104. Lincoln actually met Ericsson before he toured the *Monitor*.

84. Noah Brooks, "Personal Recollections of Lincoln," *Scribner's Monthly* 15 (March 1878): 678; Noah Brooks, "Personal Recollections of Abraham Lincoln," *Harper's New Monthly Magazine* 31 (July 1865): 224; Kent, *Lincoln: Fire of Genius*, 179–180.

85. *New York Herald*, October 3, 1862.

86. Testimonial to Dr. Issachar Zacharie, September 20, 1862, original in the Shapell Manuscript Collection.

87. Testimonial for Dr. Zacharie, September 22, 1862, *CW*, 5:436.

88. Testimonial for Dr. Zacharie, September 23, 1862, Shapell Manuscript Collection.

89. *New York Herald*, October 3, 1862.

90. I. Zacharie, *Surgical and Practical Observations on the Diseases of the Human Foot, With Instructions for their Treatment* (New York: Charles B. Norton, 1860), and title page for the 1876 edition published in London.

91. Quoted in Adam D. Mendelsohn, *Jewish Soldiers in the Civil War: The Union Army* (New York: New York University Press, 2022), 116.

92. George S. Denison to Salmon P. Chase, February 1, 1863, in Charles M. Segal, "Isachar Zach-arie: Lincoln's Chiropodist," *Publications of the American Jewish Historical Society* 43 (December 1953): 90–91. Dr. Zacharie alternatively spelled his first name "Isachar," and occasionally listed his family name as "Zachariah."

93. Issachar Zacharie to Lincoln, March 27, 1863, November 3, 1864, ALPLC. For Zacharie's mysterious 1863 visit to Richmond, see Fred Harvey Harrington, "A Peace Mission of 1863," *American Historical Review* 46 (October 1940): 76–86; for the claim he met Jefferson Davis, see Zacharie to General Nathaniel Banks, October 9, 1863, in Segal, "Isachar Zacharie," 107.

94. Issachar Zacharie to Lincoln, February 13, May 13, 1864, ALPLC.

95. Lincoln to Issachar Zacharie, September 19, 1864, *CW*, 8:12.

96. Lincoln to Edwin M. Stanton, January 25, 1865, *CW*, 8:238.

97. *OR*, ser. 3, vol. 1, sect. 9, pp. 380–382.

98. Compelling new research by Adam D. Mendelsohn puts the lie to the long-accepted story that Colonel Friedman defiantly engineered Allen's appointment as a test case. See Mendelsohn, *Jewish Soldiers in the Civil War*, 13–15.

99. Mendelsohn, *Jewish Soldiers in the Civil War*, 106–107.

100. Lincoln to Arnold Fischel, December 14, 1861, *CW*, 5:69.

101. Jonathan D. Sarna and Benjamin Shapell, *Lincoln and the Jews: A History* (New York: St. Martin's Press, 2015), 100–106.

102. General Orders No. 11, signed by Assistant Adjutant General John A. Rawlins, December 17, 1862, *OR*, ser. 1, vol. 17 (part 2), p. 424; see also, and for context, Ulysses S. Grant, *The Papers of Ulysses S. Grant*, ed. John Y. Simon and John F. Marszalek, 32 vols. (Carbondale: Southern Illinois University Press, 1967–2012), 7:50. Simon's source notes are invaluable.

103. Jonathan D. Sarna, *When General Grant Expelled the Jews* (New York: Nextbook/Shocken, 2012), 4–6.

104. D. Wolf & Bros., Cesar J. Kaskel, and J. W. Kaskel, telegram to Lincoln, December 29, 1862, in *OR*, ser. 1, xvii (part 2), p. 506; Grant, *Grant Papers*, 54n.

105. See, for example, *Cincinnati Enquirer*, January 5, 6, 1863; *Washington Star*, January 7, 1863; and *Washington Chronicle*, January 8, 1863.

106. *New York Times*, January 18, 1863.

107. Bertram Korn, *American Jewry and the Civil War* (Philadelphia: Jewish Publication Society of America, 1951), 125.

108. Henry W. Halleck to Ulysses S. Grant, January 21, 1863, *OR*, ser. 1, vol. 24 (part 1), p. 9.

109. Grant to Brigadier General Isaac F. Quinby, Grant, *Papers of Ulysses S. Grant*, 5:238. For Sherman's complaints about "swarms of Jews," see Michael Fellman, *Citizen Sherman: A Life of William Tecumseh Sherman* (New York: Random House, 1995), 153–154.

110. "Shoddy Patriotism," *Phunny Fellow*, November 1861, in Gary L. Bunker and John Appel, "'Shoddy,' Anti-Semitism and the Civil War," *American Jewish History* 82 (1994): 47–48.

111. Rabbi Isaac M. Wise to "Edward" Stanton, December 30, 1862, from the Isaac Mayer Wise Digital Archive at the American Jewish Archives, https://sites.americanjewisharchives.org /collections/wise/view.php?id=2630.

112. *The Israelite* (Cincinnati), January 16, 1863, in Sarna, *When General Grant Expelled the Jews*, 23. See also Stephen V. Ash, "Civil War Exodus: The Jews and Grant's General Orders No. 11," *The Historian* 44 (August 1982): 510–523.

113. Declaring himself "fortunately or unfortunately born of Jewish parents," Captain Philip Trounstine of the Fifth Ohio Cavalry sent in his "immediate and unconditional resignation"—surely an intentional reference to Grant's nickname "Unconditional Surrender"—on March 3, 1863; see Grant, *Papers of Ulysses S. Grant*, 7:53n. According to newspaperman Sylvanus Cadwallader, Trounstine, who enlisted early, was "the only cavalry officer in the service that was of Hebraic extraction." See Benjamin P. Thomas, ed., *Three Years with Grant as Recalled by War Correspondent Sylvanus Cadwallader* (New York: Alfred A. Knopf, 1955), 40.

114. "The German Loyalty," *New York Times*, March 16, 1862.

115. Mark E. Neely Jr., "'Unbeknownst' to Lincoln: A Note on Radical Pacification in Missouri During the Civil War," *Civil War History* 44 (September 1998): 214. Neely discovered this then-unknown letter in the Hiram Birney Collection at the Huntington Library in San Marino, California.

116. See P. M. Zall, *Abe Lincoln Laughing: Humorous Anecdotes from Original Sources by and About Abraham Lincoln* (Berkeley: University of California Press, 1982), 51.

117. Interview with Artemus Ward (Charles Farrar Browne), *Lockport* (NY) *Journal*, May 21, 1893, quoted in Wayne Whipple, *The Story-Life of Lincoln* (Philadelphia: John C. Winston Co., 1908), 481–482 118. George B. McClellan to Frederica M. English, May 3, 1846, in Thomas W. Cutrer, ed., *The Mexican War Diary and Correspondence of George B. McClellan* (Baton Rouge: Louisiana State University Press, 2009), 16–17.

118. George B. McClellan to Frederica M. English, May 3, 1846, in Thomas W. Cutrer, ed., *The Mexican War Diary and Correspondence of George B. McClellan* (Baton Rouge: Louisiana State University Press, 2009), 16–17.

Chapter Nine ★ More of the Quarrel

1. Carl Frederick Wittke, *The German-Language Press in America* (Lexington: University Press of Kentucky, 1957), 150, 152.

2. Carl Schurz to Lincoln, June 12, 1862, Abraham Lincoln Papers, Library of Congress (hereinafter cited as ALPLC).

3. Lincoln to Carl Schurz, June 16, 1862, Roy P. Basler, ed., *The Collected Works of Abraham Lincoln*, 8 vols. (Rutgers, NJ: Rutgers University Press, 1953–1955), 5:274 (hereinafter cited as *CW*). The same day as Lincoln wrote to Schurz, he penned a harsh letter to Frémont reminding him that he had accomplished little since requesting, and receiving, reinforcements, *CW*, 5:273–274.

4. Technically, Bohlen died in one of the pre-battle skirmishes that preceded Bull Run. Ezra J. Warner, *Generals in Blue: Lives of the Union Commanders* (1964; Baton Rouge: Louisiana State University Press, 1992), 39.

5. Lincoln to John C. Frémont, June 16, 1862, *CW*, 5:273. It is possible Lincoln confused—or at least rhymed—"Blecker" with his old friend General Friedrich Hecker.

6. Dispatch of December 6, 1862, forwarded to Abraham Lincoln, ALPLC.

7. Resolutions Adopted at a Sigel Mass Meeting, Philadelphia, September 30, 1862, and forwarded to Lincoln, ALPLC.

8. Franz Sigel to Lincoln, September 26, 1862, ALPLC.

9. Ben Field to Lincoln, October 20, 1862, ALPLC; Lincoln to Field, October 23, 1862, *CW*, 5:472.

10. Carl Schurz, *Reminiscences of Carl Schurz*, 3 vols. (New York: McClure Co., 1907), 2:377, 378.

11. Schurz, *Reminiscences*, 2:381.

12. Historian James McPherson has persuasively argued that Antietam was the war's most consequential battle because it liberated Lincoln to proclaim emancipation. See McPherson, *Crossroads of Freedom: Antietam, the Battle That Changed the Course of the Civil War* (New York: Oxford University Press, 2002).

13. When the new Congress met, Republicans would be required to forge a coalition with border state Unionists.

14. District lines had changed a bit over the previous fifteen years, but the House seat had remained anchored in Illinois's state capital, Lincoln's hometown of Springfield. Although Stuart had once defeated Democrat Stephen A. Douglas to serve as a Whig congressman, Lincoln's old friend now opposed the administration. In the House, he would later vote against the Thirteenth Amendment.

15. Postmaster General Montgomery Blair had earlier "deprecated" the Emancipation policy "on the ground that it would cost the administration the fall elections." Lincoln recalled this warning, adding that he had "already fully anticipated" that likelihood and "settled it in my own mind." See Francis B. Carpenter, *Six Months at the White House with Abraham Lincoln. The Story of a Picture* (New York: Hurd & Houghton, 1866), 21. For a comparison linking hometown battlefield casualties and Republican election losses, see Jamie L. Carson, Jeffrey A. Jenkins, David W. Rhode, and Mark A. Souva, "The Impact of National Tides and District-Level Effects on Electoral Outcomes: The U.S. Congressional Elections of 1862–63," *American Journal of Political Science* 45 (October 2001): 892.

16. Carl Schurz to Lincoln, November 8, 1862, ALPLC.

17. Carl Schurz to Lincoln, November 8, 1862, ALPLC.

18. Schurz, *Reminiscences*, 2:393–394.

19. Lincoln to Carl Schurz, November 10, 1862, *CW*, 5:494–495.

20. Carl Schurz to Lincoln, November 20, 1862, ALPLC.

21. Lincoln to Carl Schurz, November 24, 1862, *CW*, 5:509.

22. Lincoln to Carl Schurz, November 24, 1862, *CW*, 5:509.

23. Schurz, *Reminiscences*, 2:395–396.

24. Schurz, *Reminiscences*, 2:395–396. For further discussion of this episode, see Hans L. Trefousse, *Carl Schurz: A Biography* (Knoxville: University of Tennessee Press, 1982), 126–127.

25. Schurz, *Reminiscences*, 2:402.

26. Both letters appeared in the *Irish-American*. See Captain William J. Nagle to his father, December 14, 1862, published on December 27; and Private William McClelland's letter to the editor,

published January 10, 1863, both in William McCarter, *My Life in the Irish Brigade: The Civil War Memoirs of Private William McCarter, 116th Pennsylvania Infantry*, ed. Kevin E. O'Brien (1896; Cambridge, MA: Da Capo Press, 2003), 226–229.

27. Annual Message to Congress, December 1, 1862, *CW*, 5:525.

28. Annual Message to Congress, December 1, 1862, *CW*, 5:526.

29. Louis Hensel, *My Life in America Before, During, and After the Civil War: Includes Meeting President Abraham Lincoln*, trans. Sigrid Wilshinsky (New York: Jo-An Books, 2009), 131–133. The White House gathering included leaders of the Cheyenne, Kiowa, Arapaho, Comanche, Apache, and Caddo tribes. Hensel wrote his recollection thirty-seven years after the fact, in May 1900, but the facts were substantiated by accounts published in Lincoln's own time. For Lincoln's remarks to the delegation, March 27, 1863, see *CW*, 6:151–152.

30. Kevin Kenny, "Mobility and Sovereignty: The Nineteenth-Century Origins of Immigrant Restriction," *Journal of American History* 109 (September 2022): 284–285. See also An Act to Prohibit the "Coolie Trade" by American Citizens in American Vessels, ch. 27, 132, Stat. 340 (February 19, 1862). For translation of "coolie," see Mary Roberts Coolidge, *Chinese Immigration* (New York: Henry Holt, 1909), 42.

31. Lincoln to the House of Representatives, December 23, 1861, *CW*, 5:79. See also *Asiatic Coolie Trade. Message from the President of the United States*, Report to the House of Representatives, 37th Congress, 2nd Session, Executive Document No. 16. The report featured thirty-seven pages of testimony by ships' officers and mates on the shipment of Chinese workers to the United States. For Nicolay's warning against "Colie [*sic*] slavery," see Nicolay notebook, 1856–1858, John G. Nicolay Papers, Library of Congress.

32. Governor John McDougal quoted in Coolidge, *Chinese Immigration*, 22.

33. Moon-Ho Jung, "Outlawing 'Coolies': Race, Nation, and Empire in the Age of Emancipation," *American Quarterly* 57 (September 2005): 696. For background, see Mark Kanazawa, "Immigration, Exclusion and Taxation: Anti-Chinese Legislation in Gold Rush California," *Journal of Economic History* 65 (September 2005): 780.

34. Carl Schurz to Lincoln, February 14, 1863, ALPLC. Technically, Schurz actually wrote this letter *after* Lincoln had sent his name to Congress for a promotion, only to see the nomination stalled.

35. Lincoln to Edwin M. Stanton, January 12, 1863, *CW*, 6:55.

36. Franz Sigel to Lincoln, January 23, 1863, ALPLC; Lincoln to Sigel, January 26, 1863, *CW*, 6:79–80.

37. Lincoln to Franz Sigel, February 5, 1863, *CW*, 6:93; telegram printed in *OR*, ser. 1, vol. 25, 2:71. For his requests to promote Colonels Robert Nugent and Patrick Kelly of the Irish Brigade, see Lincoln to Henry W. Halleck, February 12, 1863, *CW*, 6:101.

38. Schurz, *Reminiscences*, 2:349–350, 404.

39. Carl Schurz to Lincoln, April 6, 1863; Adolph von Steinwehr to O. O. Howard, April 5, 1863, ALPLC; Lincoln to Schurz, April 11, 1863, *CW*, 6:168.

40. Carl Schurz to Lincoln, March 11, 1863, ALPLC; Noah Brooks, "Personal Reminiscences of Lincoln," *Scribner's Monthly Magazine* 15 (1877–1878): 674; Earl Schenck Miers, ed., *Lincoln Day by Day: A Chronology*, 3 vols. (Washington, DC: Lincoln Sesquicentennial Commission, 1960), 3:178–179.

41. Schurz, *Reminiscences*, 2:407.

42. "From the Army of the Potomac; [. . .] Terrible Battles Fought on Saturday and Sunday at Chancellorsville," and "The Great Battle on Sunday," *New York Times*, May 5, 1863. "Perfidy" cited in the Pittsburgh *Freiheits Freund*, May 9, 1863, quoted in Christian B. Keller, "New Perspectives in Civil War Ethnic History and Their Implications for Twenty-First-Century Scholarship," in Andrew L. Slap and Michael Thomas Smith, eds., *This Distracted and Anarchical People: New Answers for Old Questions About the Civil War–Era North* (New York: Fordham University Press, 2013).

43. "The Situation," *New York Herald*, May 6, 1863.

44. *New York Tribune*, May 6, 1863. For an excellent account of the press coverage of the battle, and an expert analysis of its impact on German American reputation and morale, see Christian B.

Keller, *Chancellorsville and the Germans: Nativism, Ethnicity, and Civil War Memory* (New York: Fordham University Press, 2007), esp. 87–91.

45. *Report of the Joint Committee on the Conduct of the War* (Washington, DC: Government Printing Office, 1865), xlix; Carl Schurz, "Reminiscences of a Long Life," *McClure's Magazine* (June 1907): 175; Keller, *Chancellorsville and the Germans*, 1–2.

46. Quoted in Trefousse, *Carl Schurz*, 135.

47. *New York Times*, May 11, 1863.

48. Keller, *Chancellorsville and the Germans*, 104.

49. *Philadelphia Freie Presse*, quoted in Keller, "Pennsylvania and Virginia Germans During the Civil War: A Brief History and Comparative Analysis," *Virginia Magazine of History and Biography* 109 (2001): 56.

50. Schurz, *Reminiscences*, 2:430; *Report of the Joint Committee on the Conduct of the War*, xlix.

51. *Highland* (IL) *Bote* ("Messenger"), May 8, 1863, quoted in Keller, *Chancellorsville and the Germans*, 109; second quote from Keller, "New Perspectives in Civil War Ethnic History," 137.

52. *Freiheits Freund und Pittsburger Courier*, June 17, 1863, quoted in Keller, *Chancellorsville and the Germans*, 96.

53. Corporal Friedrich Kappelman quoted in Keller, *Chancellorsville and the Germans*, 110.

54. William Cullen Bryant to Lincoln, May 11, 1863, ALPLC.

55. Lincoln to Bryant, May 14, 1863, *CW*, 6:216.

56. Kristen Layne Anderson, *Abolitionizing Missouri: German Immigrants and Racial Ideology in Nineteenth-Century America* (Baton Rouge: Louisiana State University Press, 2016), 130–132. In a mark of the diminished stature of the Germans, and perhaps a revival in nativism, one Democratic paper attacked rally organizers for scheduling the meeting on a Sunday, "contrary to all American ideas of the proper observance of the Sabbath." See *Missouri Republican*, May 7, 1863.

57. Emil Preetorius et al. to James Taussig, May 16, 1863, forwarded to Lincoln, ALPLC. When the meeting was delayed, Taussig turned to Lincoln's German-born private secretary to gain admittance. See Taussig to John G. Nicolay, May 30, 1863, John G. Nicolay Papers, Library of Congress.

58. "Views of President Lincoln's Missouri Affairs," *Daily Missouri Democrat*, June 9, 1863.

59. "Views of President Lincoln's Missouri Affairs," *Daily Missouri Democrat*.

60. This was not the first time Lincoln deployed the "excrescence" metaphor to defend his preference for gradual over immediate emancipation. He had made the same point to Kentucky politician Cassius Marcellus Clay aboard a train near New Haven shortly after the 1860 Cooper Union address. See Clay's recollections in Allen Thorndike Rice, ed., *Reminiscences of Abraham Lincoln by Distinguished Men of His Time* (New York: North American Publishing Co., 1886), 297.

61. John Hay, *Inside Lincoln's White House: The Complete Civil War Diary of John Hay*, ed. Michael Burlingame and John R. Turner Ettlinger (Carbondale: Southern Illinois University Press, 1997), 101 (diary entry for October 28, 1863).

62. "Views of President Lincoln's Missouri Affairs." Taussig's published account stirred debate in newspapers from New York to Illinois, with some articles denouncing the attorney for presuming to dictate policy to Lincoln. See, for example, "Rejoicing Over Ill-Treatment of Loyal Men," *Alton Telegraph*, June 1, 1863, reprinted in *Missouri Democrat*, June 13, 1863; "A 'Talk' with the President," *New York Evening Post*, n.d., reprinted in *Missouri Democrat*, June 17, 1863; and "The Great 'Ego,'" *Missouri Democrat*, June 27, 1863.

63. Friedrich Kapp, Sigismund Kaufmann, and Charles Kressman to Lincoln, June 13, 1863, ALPLC; Lincoln to "Kapp & others," June 16, 1863, *CW*, 6:282.

64. Schurz, *Reminiscences*, 3:36–37.

65. For details on the Irish Confederates who fought at Gettysburg, see Phillip Thomas Tucker, *The Irish at Gettysburg* (Charleston, SC: History Press, 2018).

66. Thomas F. Meagher, *Memoirs of Gen. Thomas Francis Meagher, Comprising the Leading Events of His Career [. . .]*, ed. Michael Cavanagh (Worcester, MA: Messenger Press, 1892), 477–478.

67. Colonel St. Clair Mulholland quoted in William Corby, *Memoirs of Chaplain Life* (Chicago: La Monte, O'Donnell & Co., 1893), 181–184. Corby is not forgotten: a statue of the priest giving his blessing still stands on the campus of football-mad Notre Dame University, where its perennially upraised arm has earned it the nickname of "First-Down Father."

68. Stephen W. Sears, *Gettysburg* (Boston: Houghton Mifflin, 2003), 288–291.

69. Sears, *Gettysburg*, 187–189.

70. St. Clair A. Mulholland, *The Story of the 116th Regiment Pennsylvania Volunteers in the War of the Rebellion: The Record of a Gallant Command* (Philadelphia: F. McManus Jr. & Co., 1903), 154.

71. John W. Busey and David G. Martin, *Regimental Strengths and Losses at Gettysburg*, 4th ed. (East Windsor, NJ: Longstreet House, 2005), 128; John W. Busey, *These Honored Dead: Union Casualties at Gettysburg* (1958; East Windsor, NJ: Longstreet House, 1996), 251. For Rorty, see Joseph G. Bilby, *The Irish Brigade in the Civil War: The 69th New York and Other Irish Regiments of the Army of the Potomac* (1995; Cambridge, MA: Da Capo Press, 1997), 91–92.

72. The letter reflected the sentiment of many New York Irishmen but actually originated in Chicago. See "An Adopted Citizen" to the editors of the *Chicago Tribune*, March 4, 1863, and forwarded to Lincoln, ALPLC.

73. Conscription provoked violent outbreaks in several Northern cities, including Boston and Charleston, Illinois (scene of a Lincoln–Douglas debate five years earlier), but, as usual, press coverage focused on New York City, the town with the largest number of people and newspapers.

74. For Germans, see *New York World*, July 14, 1863.

75. *New York Herald*, July 13, 1863. For a statistics-driven analysis of the protestors as draft resisters, see Peter Levine, "Draft Evasion in the North During the Civil War, 1863–1865," *Journal of American History* 67 (March 1981): 816–834.

76. D. [Dennis] A. Mahony, *The Prisoner of State* (New York: Carleton, 1863), 29–31.

77. *New York World*, July 13, 1863; *New York Daily News*, July 11, 1863. See also Barnet Schecter, *The Devil's Own Work: The New York City Draft Riots and the Fight to Reconstruct America* (New York: Walker, 2005), 26–27. There were exceptions: "At last we are to have war in earnest," cheered the *Philadelphia Catholic Herald* when Lincoln first proposed the draft. See Joseph George Jr., "Philadelphia's *Catholic Herald* Evaluates President Lincoln," *Lincoln Herald* 82 (Fall 1980): 449.

78. *New York Daily News*, July 13, 1863.

79. *New York Daily News*, July 10, 1863. Spring would later publish the retrograde book *The Negro at Home: An Inquiry After His Capacity for Self-Government and the Government of Whites [. . .]* (New York: Lindley Spring, 1868).

80. "Onslaught on Negro Dwellings," *New York Times*, July 15, 1863; "Negroes Assaulted," *New York World*, July 14, 1863; "In Thirty-Second Street," *New York World*, July 16, 1863.

81. John Adams Dix, *Memoirs of John Adams Dix Compiled by His Son Morgan Dix*, 2 vols. (New York: Harper & Bros., 1883), 2:74.

82. *New York Times* report, quoted in "The Riots in New York," *Harper's Weekly*, August 1, 1863.

83. George Templeton Strong, *The Diary of George Templeton Strong*, ed. Allan Nevins and Milton Halsey Thomas, 4 vols. (New York: Macmillan, 1952), 3:335, 337–338.

84. *New York Times*, July 14, 1863; Iver Bernstein, *The New York City Draft Riots: Their Significance for American Society and Politics in the Age of the Civil War* (New York: Oxford University Press, 1990), 23.

85. "The Riot in Second Avenue," *New York Times*, July 15, 1863; "The Body of Colonel O'Brien," *New York Times*, July 16, 1863. For the search for the colonel's killers, see "Another Arrest in the Colonel O'Brien Murder Case," *New York World*, August 1, 1863.

86. James R. Gilmore, *Personal Recollections of Abraham Lincoln and the Civil War* (Boston: L. C. Page & Co., 1898), 170.

87. "The N——rhead and Copperhead Organs," *New York Herald*, July 16, 1863.

88. "Aid and Comfort to the Enemy," *New York World*, July 16, 1863.

89. *New York Times*, July 16, 1863.

90. Sir Edward M. Archibald to Lord Palmerston, July 18, 1863, in Amanda Foreman, *A World on Fire: Britain's Crucial Role in the American Civil War* (New York: Random House, 2010), 507.

91. Strong, *Diary of George Templeton Strong*, 3:341. Strong added that "Albany, Troy, Yonkers, Hartford, Boston, and other cities" endured similar outbreaks.

92. Strong, *Diary of George Templeton Strong*, 3:345. Schecter, *The Devil's Own Work*, 237.

93. *Irish-American*, July 5, 1863.

94. Peter Welsh, *Irish Green and Blue: The Civil War Letters of Peter Welsh, Color Sergeant, 28th Regiment Massachusetts Volunteers*, ed. Lawrence Frederick Kohl with Margaret Cossé Richard (New York: Fordham University Press, 1986), 110, 115.

95. Quoted in William Hayes Ward, *Abraham Lincoln: Tributes from His Associates—Reminiscences of Soldiers, Statesmen and Citizens* (New York: T. Y. Crowell, 1895), 220. For more on this obscure commander, see James Moore, *Kilpatrick of Our Cavalry* (New York: W. J. Widdleton, 1965).

96. "Archbishop Hughes' Address," *New York World*, July 18, 1863.

97. Historian Frank L. Klement argued that "the story of Civil War Copperheads is incomplete without giving a role to American Catholics." See Klement, "Catholics as Copperheads During the Civil War," *Catholic Historical Review* 80 (January 1994): 57. For a modern analysis, see William B. Kurtz, *Excommunicated from the Union: How the Civil War Created a Separate Catholic America* (New York: Fordham University Press, 2016), 111–116.

98. "The Draft," *Harper's Weekly*, July 25, 1863.

99. "The Riots at New York," *Harper's Weekly*, August 1, 1863.

100. Seymour at one point addressed the mob as "My friends," a salutation his political enemies never let him forget, especially when he ran unsuccessfully for president in 1876.

101. Gilmore, *Personal Recollections*, 199.

102. Patrick McCarty and others to Lincoln, November 16, 1863, ALPC; for the full text, see Harold Holzer, ed., *The Lincoln Mailbag: America Writes to the President, 1861–1865* (Carbondale: Southern Illinois University Press, 1998), 107.

103. Dean B. Mahin, *The Blessed Place of Freedom: Europeans in Civil War America* (Washington, DC: Brassey's, 2002), 187; Lincoln's conversation with Preetorius excerpted in Don E. Fehrenbacher and Virginia Fehrenbacher, eds., *Recollected Words of Abraham Lincoln* (Stanford, CA: Stanford University Press, 1996), 370.

104. Charles G. Halpine, *The Life and Adventures, Songs, Services, and Speeches of Private Miles O'Reilly* (New York: Carleton, 1864), 55, 57.

105. Quoted in William Hanchett, *Irish: Charles G. Halpine in Civil War America* (Syracuse, NY: Syracuse University Press, 1970), 83–84.

106. Noah Brooks, "Personal Recollections of Abraham Lincoln," *Harper's New Monthly Magazine* 31 (July 1865): 229.

107. [Charles G. Halpine], *The Poetical Works of Charles G. Halpine (Miles O'Reilly) [. . .]*, ed. Robert B. Roosevelt (New York: Harper & Bros., 1869), viii, x.

108. [Charles G. Halpine], "A Great Day for Ireland. Miles O'Reilly at the White House. Mr. Lincoln, the Cabinet and the Foreign Diplomatic Body [. . .] Mr. Lincoln Tells His Best Story [. . .]," *New York Herald*, November 28, 1863.

109. Halpine, "A Great Day for Ireland."

110. Halpine, "A Great Day for Ireland." The "talk foolishly" line was a not-so-subtle reference to Lincoln's own impromptu remarks at Gettysburg on November 18, 1863, the day before he delivered his formal address at the Soldiers' National Cemetery. Appearing outside the home of his host, he eschewed greeting a crowd of well-wishers by declaring, "In my position it is somewhat important that I should not say any foolish things." The remark appeared two days later in the *New York Tribune*. (See *CW*, 7:17.)

111. Halpine, "A Great Day for Ireland."

112. John Hay to Charles G. Halpine, ca. December 1863, quoted in Hanchett, *Irish*, 93.

113. John Hay to Charles G. Halpine, November 22, 1863, in John Hay, *At Lincoln's Side: John Hay's Civil War Correspondence and Selected Writings*, ed. Michael Burlingame (Carbondale: Southern Illinois University Press, 2000), 68–69.

114. Hanchett, *Irish*, 77–78; [Halpine], *Poetical Works of Halpine*, xi–xii. See also Eugene C. Murdock, "New York's Civil War Bounty Brokers," *Journal of American History* 52 (September 1966): 259–278.

115. Halpine, *Life and Adventures of Private Miles O'Reilly*, 61.

Chapter Ten ★ This Noble Effort

1. Proclamation Concerning Aliens, May 8, 1863, in Roy P. Basler, ed., *The Collected Works of Abraham Lincoln*, 8 vols. (New Brunswick, NJ: Rutgers University Press, 1953–1955), 6:203–204 (hereinafter cited as *CW*). Longtime noncitizen residents were eligible to vote in some local contests—a right enshrined in several state constitutions and previously supported by Lincoln.

2. Annual Message to Congress, December 8, 1863, *CW*, 7:38–39; Special Message to Congress, July 4, 1861, *CW*, 4:203.

3. Annual Message to Congress, December 8, 1863, *CW*, 7:40.

4. Annual Message to Congress, December 1, 1862, *CW*, 5:530, 534, 537.

5. *Gold Hill* (NV) *Daily News*, December 10, 1863.

6. Frederick W. Seward, ed., *Seward at Washington, as Senator and Secretary of State [. . .]* (New York: Derby & Miller, 1891), 202.

7. *Hardware Reporter*, December 1863, quoted in Jason H. Silverman, *When America Welcomed Immigrants: The Short and Tortured History of Abraham Lincoln's Act to Encourage Immigration* (Charleston, SC: Palmetto Publishing, 2020), 41–42. Silverman unearthed and made expert use of this long-neglected source, and cleverly called the 1864 bill "Lincoln's Dream Act." Williams had moved his pro-immigration newspaper from Long Island to New York City in December 1863. See "Hardware Reporter," *New York Times*, December 24, 1863.

8. Annual Message to Congress, December 8, 1863, *CW*, 7:38 and 11n.

9. Quoted in Silverman, *When America Welcomed Immigrants*, 33.

10. Voorhees floor speech, March 5, 1864, *Appendix to the Congressional Globe*, 38th Congress, 1st Session, House of Representatives, 77.

11. Elihu Washburne to Lincoln, January 6, 1863, Abraham Lincoln Papers, Library of Congress (hereinafter cited as ALPLC); *Report on Foreign Emigration*, House of Representatives, Report No. 56, 38th Congress, 1st Session, 1–2.

12. Senate Committee on Agriculture, Report No. 15, 38th Congress, 1st Session, February 18, 1864, 8; Silverman, *When America Welcomed Immigrants*, 30–31.

13. Gideon Welles, *Diary of Gideon Welles*, ed. John T. Morse, 3 vols. (Boston: Houghton Mifflin, 1911), 1:543.

14. An earlier proposal from the House Agriculture Committee had suggested placing "an Emigrant Bureau" within the Interior Department. House Committee on Agriculture, Report No. 42, 37th Congress, 3d Session, 1.

15. William L. Dayton (American minister to France) to William H. Seward, September 9, 1862; Seward to the New-York Chamber of Commerce, September 24, 1862, in *Fifth Annual Report of the Chamber of Commerce of the State of New-York, for the Year 1862–'63* (New York: John W. Amerman, 1863), 47.

16. William H. Seward to Elihu B. Washburne, March 30, 1864, in *Report on Foreign Emigration*, 4–5.

17. "The New Bill to Promote Emigration," *New York Times*, April 18, 1864.

18. "The New Bill to Promote Emigration," *New York Times*.

19. An Act to Encourage Immigration, https://memory.loc.gov.

20. An Act to Encourage Immigration, *New York Times*, August 3, 1864.

21. "Immigration," *Semi-Weekly Tribune* (a national edition of the New York daily), June 20, 1864.

22. "Foreign Enlistments," *New York Tribune*, June 30, 1864. Between 1862 and 1863, however, more than a thousand foreign-born U.S. residents claimed they had been illegally drafted. See Michael Douma, Anders Bo Rasmussen, and Robert Faith, "The Impressment of Foreign-Born Soldiers in the Union Army," *Journal of American Ethnic History* 38 (Spring 2019): 76.

23. *Congressional Globe*, July 2, 1864, 38th Congress, 1st Session, 1019.

24. Lincoln to William P. Fessenden, August 9, 1864, *CW*, 7:489.

25. Charlotte Erickson, *American Industry and the European Immigrant, 1860–1885* (Cambridge, MA: Harvard University Press, 1957), 9, 11, 12. Erickson argued that the 1864 act proved little more than a federally sanctioned system of indenture.

26. Erickson, *American Industry and the European Immigrant*, 42–43.

27. *Irish-American*, July 23, 1864.

28. Francis Lieber to Charles Sumner, August 31, 1864, quoted in Michael Burlingame, *Abraham Lincoln: A Life*, 2 vols. (Baltimore: Johns Hopkins University Press, 2008), 2:646.

29. "Old Abe's Prophecy About the Next Presidency," *Nick Nax*, April 1864, quoted in Gary L. Bunker, *From Rail-Splitter to Icon: Lincoln's Image in Illustrated Periodicals, 1860–1865* (Kent, OH: Kent State University Press, 2001), 261.

30. Francis B. Carpenter, *Six Months at the White House with Abraham Lincoln. The Story of a Picture* (New York: Hurd & Houghton, 1866), 155.

31. *Neue Zeit*, reprinted in "Spirit of the German Press," *Missouri Republican* (a pro-Democratic paper), December 10, 1863.

32. Joseph Medill to Lincoln, February 17, 1864, ALPLC.

33. For a succinct, authoritative account of Chase's failed bid to supplant Lincoln, see Walter Stahr, *Salmon P. Chase: Lincoln's Vital Rival* (New York: Simon & Schuster, 2021), 481–492.

34. Headquarters, Department of the Missouri, General Order No. 65, April 29, 1864, www.civil warmo.org/educators/resources/info-sheets/1864-labor-unrest-and-general-order-no-65.

35. Charles L. Bernays to Lincoln, May 2, 1864, ALPLC. There is evidence that Bernays did not speak for all St. Louis Germans. A year earlier, a group of Lincoln's old Illinois friends had forwarded to the President a petition, "signed by nearly every leading German in St. Louis," demanding Bernays's ouster as an army paymaster. See Lincoln's reply to Montgomery Blair (enclosing the petition), February 13, 1863, in Roy P. Basler, *The Collected Works of Abraham Lincoln: Supplement 1832–1865* (Westport, CT: Greenwood Press, 1974), 177. Bernays remained in his post through the war and beyond.

36. "Great Radical Meeting in Chicago[: . . .] The Germans in Earnest Against Old Abe," *Chicago Times*, March 28, 1864, reprinted in the *Wisconsin Daily Patriot*, March 29, 1864.

37. *Wisconsin Daily Patriot*, March 29, 1864; "weakest and worst" quoted in Carl Frederick Wittke, *Refugees of Revolution: The German Forty-Eighters in America* (Philadelphia: University of Pennsylvania Press, 1970), 246.

38. *New York Herald*, March 11, 1864.

39. "The German Movement for Fremont and Against Lincoln," *Cincinnati Daily Enquirer*, May 14, 1864.

40. John Hay, *Inside Lincoln's White House: The Complete Civil War Diary of John Hay*, ed. Michael Burlingame and John R. Turner Ettlinger (Carbondale: Southern Illinois University Press, 1997), 198 (entry for May 24, 1864).

41. Stephen D. Engle, *Yankee Dutchman: The Life of Franz Sigel* (Fayetteville: University of Arkansas Press, 1993), 194.

42. David E. Long, *The Jewel of Liberty: Abraham Lincoln's Re-election and the End of Slavery* (Mechanicsburg, PA: Stackpole Books, 1994), 180. Major figures expected at the Cleveland convention— including Horace Greeley, Frederick Douglass, and abolitionist Wendell Phillips—failed to materialize there.

43. Missouri delegates cast—and then withdrew—a symbolic protest vote for Ulysses S. Grant.

44. Republican (National Union) Party Platform, June 7, 1864, American Presidency Project, https://www.presidency.ucsb.edu/documents/republican-party-platform-1864.

45. Republican (National Union) Party Platform, June 7, 1864, Plank No. 8.

46. Quoted in the *Cincinnati Daily Enquirer*, June 15, 1864.

47. "The German Feeling for Fremont," *Cleveland Daily Plain Dealer*, June 15, 1864.

48. *Memoirs of Gustave Koerner, 1809–1896: Life-Sketches Written at the Suggestion of His Children*, ed. Thomas J. McCormack, 2 vols. (Cedar Rapids, IA: Torch Press, 1909), 2:409–410. Koerner left his post in Spain on July 20, 1864.

49. *Boston Pioneer*, quoted in the *Augusta Daily Constitutionalist*, August 18, 1864.

50. See Henry J. Raymond to Lincoln, August 22, 1862, ALPLC ("The tide is setting strongly against us"); Lincoln's memorandum signed, sight unseen, by the cabinet, August 23, 1864, *CW*, 7:514.

51. Carl Schurz, *The Reminiscences of Carl Schurz*, 3 vols. (New York: McClure Co., 1908), 3:98–99.

52. "Mr. Lincoln is already beaten," Greeley declared as the convention got underway. "He cannot be elected. And we must have another ticket to save us from utter overthrow." Quoted in Harlan Hoyt Horner, *Lincoln and Greeley* (Urbana: University of Illinois Press, 1953), 351.

53. Carl Schurz to Lincoln, February 29, March 8, 1864, ALPLC.

54. Lincoln to Carl Schurz, March 13, 1864, *CW*, 7:243–244. See *Argument of Maj.-Gen. Carl Schurz. Delivered February 12th, 1864. Court of Inquiry on Maj. Genl. Hooker's Report of the Night Engagement at Wauhachtie*. Washington, 1864. Original Miscellaneous Pamphlet File, Library of Congress.

55. *Metropolitan Record and New York Vindicator*, February 13, 1864, quoted in Jason H. Silverman, *Lincoln and the Immigrant* (Carbondale: Southern Illinois University Press, 2015), 98.

56. Carl Schurz to Lincoln, March 19, 1864, ALPLC; for "played out," Captain Rudolph Mueller to Colonel Friedrich Hecker, May 30, 1864, quoting the *Wheeling Intelligence[r]*, in Eric Benjaminson, "A Regiment of Immigrants: The 82nd Illinois Volunteer Infantry and the Letters of Captain Rudolph Mueller," *Journal of the Illinois Historical Society* 94 (Summer 2001): 164.

57. Carl Schurz to Lincoln, March 21, 1864, ALPLC; Lincoln to Schurz, March 23, 1864, *CW*, 7:262.

58. Schurz, *Reminiscences*, 3:107.

59. Schurz, *Reminiscences*, 3:103–104.

60. Schurz, *Reminiscences*, 3:104.

61. Schurz, *Reminiscences*, 3:104–105.

62. Carl Schurz to Lincoln, October 19, 1864, ALPLC. Fearing the War Department might "call on me" to return to active service, Schurz actually asked Lincoln "to drop a hint to those concerned."

63. Hans L. Trefousse, *Carl Schurz: A Biography* (Knoxville: University of Tennessee Press, 1982), 146–147.

64. Frederic Bancroft, ed., *Speeches, Correspondence and Political Papers of Carl Schurz*, 6 vols. (New York: G. P. Putnam's Sons, 1913), 1:232, 236.

65. See *Miscegenation: The Theory of the Blending of the Races, Applied to the American White Man and Negro* (New York: Croly & Wakeman, 1864). Authors/publishers David G. Croly and George Wakeman were *New York World* employees. See also Elise Lemire, *"Miscegenation": Making Race in America* (Philadelphia: University of Pennsylvania Press, 2002), esp. chapter 5. For background on this hoax pamphlet—which trumpeted genetic race-mixing, and was sent to Lincoln in the hope of securing an endorsement that would prove he favored integration—see Mark E. Neely Jr., *Lincoln and the Democrats: The Politics of Opposition in the Civil War* (New York: Cambridge University Press, 2017), 108–109.

66. J. H. Howard, *I Knew Him, Horatio [. . .] Hamlet, Act IV, Scene 1*, 1864 lithograph, in Harold Holzer, Gabor S. Boritt, and Mark E. Neely Jr., *The Lincoln Image: Abraham Lincoln and the Popular Print* (New York: Charles Scribner's Sons, 1984), 133. Democratic New York governor Horatio Seymour was aptly depicted as Shakespeare's Horatio.

67. Currier & Ives, *The Chicago Platform and Candidate*, 1864 lithograph, in Bernard F. Reilly Jr., *American Political Prints 1766–1876: A Catalog of the Collections of the Library of Congress* (Boston: G. K. Hall, 1991), 528.

68. William O. Bartlett to James Gordon Bennett, November 4, 1864, in Oliver Carlson, *The Man Who Made News: James Gordon Bennett* (New York: Duell, Sloan & Pearce, 1942), 370; John J. Turner Jr. and Michael D'Innocenzo, "The President and the Press: Lincoln, James Gordon Bennett and the Election of 1864," *Lincoln Herald* 76 (Summer 1974): 66.

69. Quoted in the *Sandusky Commercial Register*, August 23, 1864.

70. Sheridan vaguely reported that he was born "the year after" his parents' "arrival in this country," but never specified precisely when his Irish mother and father arrived. Two of his siblings had been born in Ireland. See Philip H. Sheridan, *Personal Reminiscences of P. H. Sheridan. General United States Army*, 2 vols. (New York: Charles L. Webster & Co., 1888), 1–2.

71. Annie Wittenmyer, "How President Lincoln Received the News of Sheridan's Victory," in *Under the Guns: A Woman's Reminiscences of the Civil War* (Boston: Brown & Co., 1897), 240. Wittenmyer, a Civil War nurse, heard Lincoln make this comment in the White House after he received a telegram reporting Sheridan's 1864 defeat of General Jubal Early in the Shenandoah Valley. Not all Irish officers fought for the Union, of course. Rebel general Patrick Cleburne, born in County Cork, earned considerable fame and popularity in the South, dying in action at the 1864 Battle of Franklin. The "Stonewall of the West" is remembered today as the first Confederate military leader to propose arming enslaved Blacks and promising them freedom in return for fighting in the ranks. See Craig L. Symonds, *Stonewall of the West: Patrick Cleburne and the Civil War* (Lawrence: University Press of Kansas, 1997).

72. Francis Lieber to Henry W. Halleck, September 1, 1864, in Francis Lieber, *The Life and Letters of Francis Lieber*, ed. Thomas Sergeant Perry (Boston: James R. Osgood, 1882), 350–351.

73. Joseph P. Thompson, "A Talk with President Lincoln," *Congregationalist and Boston Recorder*, March 30, 1866 (based on a September 1864 interview), in Don E. Fehrenbacher and Virginia Fehrenbacher, eds., *Recollected Words of Abraham Lincoln* (Stanford, CA: Stanford University Press, 1996), 445.

74. Max Langenschwartz to George B. McClellan, September 26, 1864, George B. McClellan Papers, Library of Congress; Isaac N. Arnold to Lincoln, August 23, 1864, ALPLC; *Memoirs of Gustave Koerner*, 2:434–436.

75. G. Henry Voessler to Lincoln, September 3, 1864, ALPLC.

76. See, for example, John Peyer to Lincoln, September 2, 1864, ALPLC, reporting, "In St. Louis there exists at present no German Newspaper, that advocated the Democratic ticket"; and Bartow A. Ulrich to Lincoln, October 28, 1864, ALPLC. Ulrich, who had met Lincoln as a boy of seven (Obituary, *New York Times*, May 19, 1930), later wrote a book on Lincoln and constitutional democracy.

77. Gustave Koerner to Lincoln, September 22, 1864, ALPLC.

78. *Republican Farmer*, October 14, 1864.

79. Montgomery Blair to Mary Elizabeth Blair, September 23, 1864, in William Ernest Smith, *The Francis Preston Blair Family in Politics*, 2 vols. (1933; New York: Da Capo Press, 1969), 2:288.

80. Francis Lieber, Lincoln or McClellan: *An Appeal to the Germans in America* (New York: Loyal Publication Society, 1864), 2.

81. Carl Schurz to Theodore Petrasch, October 12, 1864, in Bancroft, *Speeches, Correspondence and Political Papers of Carl Schurz*, 1:250.

82. Bancroft, *Speeches, Correspondence and Political Papers of Carl Schurz*, 1:251. A somewhat different version of the Petrasch letter can be found in a later compendium. *Intimate Letters of Carl Schurz, 1841–1869*, ed. Joseph Schafer (Madison: State Historical Society of Wisconsin, 1929), 309.

83. Diana L. Dretske, *The Bonds of War: A Story of Immigrants and Esprit de Corps in Company C, 96th Illinois Volunteer Infantry* (Carbondale: Southern Illinois University Press, 2021), 3, 137. For more on soldier voting patterns, see Jonathan W. White, *Emancipation, the Union Army, and the Reelection of Abraham Lincoln* (Baton Rouge: Louisiana State University Press, 2014).

84. *Boston Pilot*, September 17, 1864; "Mr. Donohoe's Life," obituary, *Boston Herald*, March 18, 1901. A good discussion of this issue (together with the *Pilot* quote) can be found in Susannah J. Ural, "'Ye Sons of Green Erin Assemble': Northern Irish American Catholics and the Union War Effort, 1861–1865," in Ural, ed., *Civil War Citizens: Race, Ethnicity, and Identity in America's Bloodiest Conflict* (New York: New York University Press, 2010), 125–127.

85. "The Presidential Contest," *Irish-American* (New York), November 5, 1864.

86. Christian G. Samito, *Becoming American Under Fire: Irish Americans, African Americans, and the Politics of Citizenship During the Civil War Era* (Ithaca, NY: Cornell University Press, 2009), 131–132.

87. Susannah Ural Bruce, *The Harp and the Eagle: Irish-American Volunteers and the Union Army, 1861–1865* (New York: New York University Press, 2006), 226–232; George Templeton Strong, *The Diary of George Templeton Strong*, ed. Allan Nevins and Milton Halsey Thomas, 4 vols. (New York: Macmillan, 1952), 3:510–511.

88. *New York Tribune*, November 9, 10, 1864.

89. *Irish-American*, November 19, 1864.

90. Dean B. Mahin, *The Blessed Place of Freedom: Europeans in Civil War America* (Washington, DC: Brassey's, 2002), 204.

91. Response to a Serenade, November 10, 1864, *CW*, 8:101.

92. Thanksgiving Proclamation, October 20, 1864, *CW*, 8:55.

93. "President's Message," *Hartford Daily Courant*, December 7, 1864. Although the phrase "state of the union" was not yet used to describe the annual messages, several papers referred to the 1864 version as a "state of the nation" report.

94. Annual Message to Congress, December 6, 1864, *CW*, 8:141.

95. *Congressional Globe*, January 19, 1865, 38th Congress, 2nd Session, 326.

96. Annual Message to Congress, December 6, 1864, *CW*, 8:141.

97. Meditation on the Divine Will, ca. September 2, 1862, *CW*, 5:403–404.

98. "The President's Message," *New London Daily Chronicle*, December 8, 1864.

99. *Daily Eastern Argus* (Portland, ME), December 9, 1864.

100. HR 746, An Act to Amend the Act Entitled "An Act to Encourage Immigration," House of Representatives, February 24, 1864, 38th Congress, 2nd Session.

101. Jason H. Silverman, *Lincoln and the Immigrant* (Carbondale, IL: Southern Illinois University Press, 2015), 116.

102. William T. Sherman, *Memoirs of William T. Sherman by Himself,* 2 vols. (New York: D. Appleton, 1875), 2:326–328. Lincoln apparently used the very same story at his last cabinet meeting. See David Homer Bates, *Lincoln Stories Told by Him in the Military Office in the War Department During the Civil War* (New York: William Edwin Rudge, 1926), 10.

103. Schurz, *Reminiscences*, 3:108–110.

104. Schurz, *Reminiscences*, 3:108–110.

105. There are various versions of this story. Under terms of the Emancipation Proclamation, Richmond's enslaved were freed the moment Union troops occupied the Confederate capital. For Lincoln's reception by African Americans see, for example, Margarita Spalding Gerry, ed., *Through Five Administrations: Reminiscences of Colonel William H. Crook, Body-Guard to President Lincoln* (New York: Harper & Row, 1910), 52.

106. *OR*, ser. 1, vol. 51, pp. 1201–1202. Weitzel actually issued this communication on February 20, 1865, to spur his troops toward Petersburg.

107. Quoted in G. William Quatman, *A Young General and the Fall of Richmond: The Life and Career of Godfrey Weitzel* (Athens: Ohio University Press, 2015), 258.

108. Lincoln to John A. Campbell [April 5, 1865], *CW*, 8:386.

109. Lincoln to Godfrey Weitzel, April 6, 1865, *CW*, 8:389. Lincoln wrote two more letters to the general on April 12. See *CW*, 8:405–407.

110. Charles Chiniquy (1809–1899), a Quebec-born ex–Catholic priest (and anti-Catholic crusader) once exiled from Canada, claimed he met Lincoln three times in the White House. Later, he insisted that the President's assassination was planned by Jesuits who recruited Booth because he had become a "pervert to Romanism." Chiniquy, a former legal client of Lincoln's, also claimed that the newly inaugurated President had confided to him during an August 1861 visit that he was

waging war "not against the Americans of the South, alone," but also "against the Pope of Rome, his perfidious Jesuits and their blind and blood-thirsty slaves." Allegedly the President also prophesied that "Rome will add to all her other iniquities, the murder of Abraham Lincoln." These so-called recollections undoubtedly reflect Chiniquy's anti-Catholic biases, not Lincoln's, yet they have been repeatedly quoted and analyzed. See Charles Chiniquy, *Fifty Years in the Church of Rome* (Chicago: Adam Craig, 1888), 695–697, 723; Paul Laverdure, "Creating an Anti-Catholic Crusader, Charles Chiniquy," *Journal of Religious History* 15 (June 1988): 94–108.

111. Jonathan D. Sarna and Benjamin Shapell, *Lincoln and the Jews* (New York: St. Martin's Press, 2015), 211–214. Liebermann, a professor of surgery at Georgetown Medical College, had earlier been compelled to free an enslaved person in his household under the terms of the DC Emancipation Act signed by Lincoln in 1862. See "Compensation Claim of Dr. Charles H. Liebermann, June 28, 1862," Georgetown Slavery Archive, https://slaveryarchive.georgetown.edu/items/show/251. For more on the ophthalmologist, see Samuel H. Holland, "Charles H. Liebermann, M.D.: An Early Russian-Born Physician of Washington, D.C.," *Medical Annals of the District of Columbia* 38 (1969): 499–504.

112. *New York Times*, April 14, April 15, 1865.

113. Carl Schurz to Lincoln, December 1, 1864, ALPLC.

114. Bancroft, *Speeches, Correspondence and Political Papers of Carl Schurz*, 1:252–253.

115. Margarethe Schurz to Carl Schurz, April 21, 1865, *Intimate Letters of Carl Schurz*, 334.

116. Carl Schurz to Frederick Alschaus, June 25, 1865, *Intimate Letters of Carl Schurz*, 340.

117. *Memoirs of Gustave Koerner*, 2:440–441.

118. *New York Herald*, April 16, 1865.

119. *Irish-American*, April 22, 1865.

120. Quoted in Nels Hokanson, *Swedish Immigrants in Lincoln's Time* (New York: Harper & Bros., 1942), 166.

121. Martha Hodes, *Mourning Lincoln* (New Haven, CT: Yale University Press, 2015), 84, 163.

122. "The Right to Mourn," *New York Times*, April 27, 1865.

123. *The Last Moments of Abraham Lincoln / President of the United States. April 15th 1865*, in Holzer, Boritt, and Neely, *The Lincoln Image*, 154.

124. Funeral Address by Rabbi Isaac M. Wise, Cincinnati, April 19, 1861, in Emanuel Hertz, ed., *Abraham Lincoln: The Tribute of the Synagogue* (New York: Bloch, 1927), 92, 98.

125. Technically, Democrat Grover Cleveland counts as two presidents, the twenty-second and twenty-fourth, having been elected for nonconsecutive terms in 1884 and 1892.

126. W. E. B. Du Bois, "Again, Lincoln" and "Abraham Lincoln," *The Crisis*, September 1922 and May 1922, in Harold Holzer, ed., *The Lincoln Anthology: Great Writers on His Life and Legacy from 1860 to Now* (New York: Library of America, 2009), 435, 438.

127. "The Remains in New York," *New York Times*, April 25, 1865.

128. Augustus Saint-Gaudens, *The Reminiscences of Augustus Saint-Gaudens*, ed. Homer Saint-Gaudens, 2 vols. (New York: Century Co., 1913), 1–52. Saint-Gaudens had also caught brief sight of Lincoln four years earlier when the President-elect paraded through Manhattan. The sculptor's statue *Abraham Lincoln: The Man*, unveiled in Chicago in 1887, is widely considered among the greatest sculpted portraits of Lincoln, and one of the greatest of all American sculptures.

129. Lincoln's First Inaugural Address, March 4, 1861, *CW*, 4:271; Barack Obama's victory speech, November 5, 2008, online at https://www.npr.org/2008/11/05/96624326/transcript-of-barack-obamas-victory-speech.

★ Epilogue ★

1. These included the Chinese Exclusion Act of 1882 and the 1921 and 1924 laws establishing quotas designed to limit the number of immigrants from eastern and southern Europe. On the

other hand, the Fourteenth Amendment to the U.S. Constitution, ratified in 1868, guaranteed American citizenship—known today as "birthright" citizenship—to "all persons born or naturalized in the United States."

2. Jay Bellamy, "Fireworks, Hoopskirts—and Death: Explosion at a Union Ammunition Plant Proved Fatal for 21 Women," *Prologue Magazine* 44 (Spring 2012), www.archives.gov/publications/prologue/2012/sping/arsenal.

3. See Harold Holzer and Edward Steers Jr., eds., *The Lincoln Assassination Conspirators: Their Confinement and Execution, as Recorded in the Letterbook of John Frederick Hartranft* (Baton Rouge: Louisiana State University Press, 2009), 3; A. M. Gambone, *Major-General John Frederick Hartranft: Citizen Soldier and Pennsylvania Statesman* (Baltimore: Butternut & Blue, 1995), 94.

4. D. Mark Katz, *Witness to an Era: The Life and Photography of Alexander Gardner—The Civil War, Lincoln, and the West* (New York: Viking, 1991), 107–109, 128–129, 177–192.

5. The full quote is: "My country, right or wrong; if right, to be kept right; and if wrong, to be set right." See *Congressional Globe*, 42nd Congress, 2nd session, February 29, 1872, pp. 1286–1287.

6. Gustave Koerner, *Memoirs of Gustave Koerner, 1809–1896: Life-Sketches Written at the Suggestion of His Children*, ed. Thomas J. McCormack, 2 vols. (Cedar Rapids, IA: Torch Press, 1909), 2:443–444.

7. "Richard O'Gorman Dead," *New York Times*, March 2, 1895.

8. See Kathryn Allamong Jacob, *Testament to Union: Civil War Monuments in Washington, D.C.* (Baltimore: Johns Hopkins University Press, 1968), 23, 68–71; "Lot Flannery, 86, Sculptor, Is Dead," *Washington Evening Star*, December 19, 1922.

9. John G. Nicolay to Therena Bates [his fiancée], April 17, 1865, John G. Nicolay Papers, Library of Congress.

10. *Chicago Herald*, December 4, 1887, quoted in Don E. Fehrenbacher and Virginia Fehrenbacher, eds., *Recollected Words of Abraham Lincoln* (Stanford, CA: Stanford University Press, 1996), 349.

11. According to some sources, he remained alive—and at large—until perishing in an 1894 fire.

ILLUSTRATION CREDITS

17   W. Ridgeway after J. Wells, Birds-eye view of New Orleans around the time
of Lincoln's visit. Lithograph, New York, ca. 1830, from Charles Mackay and
B. B. Woodward, *History of the United States of America*, vol. 2 (Library of
Congress)

28   Lincoln letter to James Shields, as printed and published in the *Sangamo
Journal*. (Abraham Lincoln Presidential Library and Museum)

30   The Lincoln-Shields "duel." Illustration from Alexander K. McClure, *"Abe"
Lincoln's Yarns and Stories*, 1901, p. 67. (Abraham Lincoln Presidential Library
and Museum, Springfield, IL)

35   James Baillie, after H. Bucholzer, Riot in *Philadelphia, June [sic] 7TH*, 1844.
Lithograph, Philadelphia, 1844. (Library of Congress)

43   Currier & Ives, *The Most Rev. John Hughes, D.D., First Archbishop of New York*.
Lithograph, New York, ca. 1856. (Library of Congress)

46   Artist unknown, Irish immigrants on board a ship bound for the United States.
Engraving, n.d. (Quinnipiac University Library, Ireland Great Hunger
Institute)

50   Lincoln, daguerreotype by N. H. Shepherd, Springfield, IL, ca. 1846. (Library
of Congress)

59   Abraham Jonas. (Quincy, Illinois, Public Library)

73   Lincoln, photograph by Polycarpus von Schneidau, Chicago, October 27, 1854. (Library of Congress)

78   Joshua Fry Speed. (Filson Historical Society, Louisville, KY)

80   Page from Lincoln's letter to Speed, August 24, 1855. (Massachusetts Historical Society)

86   Currier & Ives, *The Right Man for the Right Place: Frémont, Fillmore, and Buchanan.* Lithograph, New York, 1856. (Library of Congress)

91   Banner advocating "21 Years Naturalization," 1856. (Rhode Island School of Design Museum, Providence, RI)

93   Artist unknown, *Irish Whiskey vs. Lager Bier* Woodcut engraving, ca. 1856. (New York Public Library)

100   Robert Marshall Root, *Lincoln and Douglas Debate*, Charleston, IL, September 18, 1858. Oil on canvas, 1918. (Lincoln Financial Foundation Collection)

103   Carl and Margarethe Schurz. (Jewish Women's Archive)

113   Theodore Canisius. (Author's collection)

120   Lincoln, photograph by Mathew B. Brady, New York, February 27, 1860. (Library of Congress)

123   Artist unknown, Lincoln speaking at Cooper Union, February 27, 1860. Period drawing. (Cooper Union Collection)

126   Artist unknown, *Five Points' House of Industry, No. 155 Worth Street.* Woodcut engraving, New York, ca. 1860. (The Miriam and Ira D. Wallach Division of Art, Prints and Photographs: Picture Collection, New York Public Library)

131   Artist unknown, *Prominent Candidates for the Republican Presidential Nomination at Chicago.* Woodcut engraving for *Harper's Weekly*, New York, May 12, 1860. (Lincoln Financial Foundation Collection)

139   John G. Nicolay, ca. 1860–1861. (Library of Congress)

141 Artist unknown, cover of German-language Lincoln campaign biography *Das Leben von Abraham Lincoln*. New York: Young Men's Republican Union, 1860. (Lincoln Financial Foundation Collection)

148 Lincoln, photograph by Samuel Alschuler, Chicago, November 25, 1860. (Library of Congress)

152 Gustave Koerner. (St. Clair County Historical Society, Belleville, IL)

156 Henry Villard, date unknown. (Author's collection)

161 Adolph Forbriger, *Burnet House . . . Hôtel Burnet, Cincinnati, Ohio*. Lithograph, Cincinnati, published by Onken's Lithography, ca. 1859. (Library of Congress)

164 Rabbi Isaac Mayer Wise. (Jacob Rader Marcus Center, American Jewish Archives, Hebrew Union College, Cincinnati)

168 V. Blada (Adalbert Johann Volck), *Passage Through Baltimore* (Lincoln cowering in a freight car). Etching, Baltimore, ca. 1861. (Metropolitan Museum of Art)

169 Dr. Adalbert Volck. (Maryland Center for History and Culture, Baltimore)

189 Feodor Fuchs, *Major General Franz Sigel, United States Army, as Colonel on the Battlefield of Carthage, July 5th, 1861*. Lithograph, Philadelphia, 1862. (Library of Congress)

194 General John C. Frémont. (Library of Congress)

200 Two German-born Union generals: Louis Blenker (left) and Prince Felix Salm-Salm. (Library of Congress)

206 Baker & Godwin, Garibaldi Guard recruitment poster. Lithograph, New York, 1861. (New-York Historical Society)

212 Frank Vizetelly, "Review of Federal Troops on The 4th of July by President Lincoln and General Scott; The Garibaldi Guard filing past." *Illustrated London News*, August 3, 1861. (Library of Congress)

216 Colonel Michael Corcoran, ca. 1862. (Library of Congress)

285 Penfield-Bross, "O'Reilly in the Presence Chamber" (Lincoln and the fictional Miles O'Reilly). Woodcut engraving in Charles G. Halpine, *The Life and Adventures, Songs, Services, and Speeches of Private Miles O'Reilly*. New York: Carleton, 1864. (Author's collection)

290 President Lincoln with his two White House secretaries, John Nicolay and John Hay, Washington, November 8, 1863. Photograph by Alexander Gardner. (Lincoln Financial Foundation Collection)

296 "Enlisting Irish and German Emigrants on The Battery at New York," engraving. *London Illustrated News*, September 17, 1864. (Author's collection)

304 Currier & Ives, *Grand Banner of the Radical Democracy for 1864*, with images of breakaway presidential candidate John C. Frémont and running mate John Cochrane. (Library of Congress)

310 *"Germans Arouse!"*: broadside leaflet advertising an 1864 campaign appearance by Carl Schurtz [*sic*] and others. Origin unknown. (Lincoln Financial Foundation Collection)

311 J. H. Howard, *"I Knew Him, Horatio; a Fellow of Infinite Jest . . . Where be Your Jibes Now—?," Hamlet*, Act IV, Scene 1. Lithograph, New York, 1864. (Lincoln Financial Foundation Collection)

314 Thomas Buchanan Read, *Sheridan's Ride*. Oil on canvas, ca. 1869. (Original in the Union League of Philadelphia; photo courtesy LOC)

319 Thomas Nast, "Citizens Voting," detail from illustration "Election Day/8th November." Woodcut engraving from *Harper's Weekly*, New York, November 12, 1864. (Lincoln Financial Foundation Collection)

324 General Godfrey Weitzel and staff, Richmond, after April 1865. (Library of Congress)

325 Dennis Malone Carter, *Lincoln's Drive Through Richmond*, April 4, 1865. Oil on canvas, 1866. Original in the Chicago Historical Society. (Photo courtesy of Library of Congress)

328 *Lincoln's letzte Stunde. Lincoln's last hour. La dernière heure de Lincoln.* Lithograph, printmaker unknown, 1865. (Library of Congress)

330   New York city hall draped in black for Lincoln's funeral, April 25, 1865.
       (National Archives and Records Administration)

332   German chorus sings at city hall, New York, April 25, 1865, as Lincoln's body
       lies in state at top of stairway. Woodcut, artist unknown, New York. (Author's
       collection)

INDEX

Note: Italicized page numbers indicate material in tables or illustrations.

ABOUT THE AUTHOR

Harold Holzer is a leading authority on Abraham Lincoln and the political culture of the Civil War era. Educated at the City University of New York, he served as a political press secretary for Congresswoman Bella S. Abzug and Governor Mario M. Cuomo, and was a longtime senior vice president at the Metropolitan Museum of Art. A prolific writer and lecturer, Holzer also cochaired the U.S. Abraham Lincoln Bicentennial Commission, appointed by President Clinton. President Bush awarded Holzer the National Humanities Medal in 2008, and in 2015, Holzer earned the Gilder Lehrman Lincoln Prize. He now serves as director of Hunter College's Roosevelt House Public Policy Institute and as chairman of the Lincoln Forum.